ECONOMICS OF
PUBLIC FINANCE

ECONOMICS OF PUBLIC FINANCE

by

EDWARD D. ALLEN

*Department of Economics
Iowa State College*

and

O. H. BROWNLEE

*Department of Economics
Carnegie Institute of Technology*

New York
PRENTICE-HALL, INC.
1947

To

H.E.A.
L.M.B.

PREFACE

This book represents an attempt to approach the problems of public finance largely through welfare economics. Public finance, like any other class of governmental activities, can be directed toward achieving particular objectives of economic policy. The objective which has been held uppermost in most treatments of public finance is that of securing tax revenue adequate to balance the budget of the governmental unit being considered. The functions which should call forth government expenditure have not been too clearly defined. Nor can the important effects of various tax policies be viewed in perspective when analyzed within this restricted definition of adequate tax revenues.

Part I of this book describes the nature of the public economy and outlines the objectives of economic policy which appear to be widely accepted within the United States. A description of the principal ways in which the patterns of taxation, public expenditure, public debt, and intergovernmental fiscal relations have changed in the United States during the past fifty years is also contained in Part I.

For more than a decade, the relationships between fiscal policy and the level of employment have been receiving increasing attention. Full employment appears to be one of the objectives of economic policy to which nearly every citizen subscribes. The relationships between fiscal policies and the level of employment are discussed in Part II of this book. In addition to full employment, equity in the distribution of income and optimum resource allocation appear to be important objectives of economic policy. The definition of an equitable distribution of income which is acceptable to all has not yet been formulated, however. The relationships between fiscal policies, achievement of optimum resource allocation, and various income distributions are treated in Part III.

vii

Part IV evaluates various kinds of taxation in terms of their effects upon resource allocation, income distribution, and the level of employment. This section also contains analysis of the effects of public borrowing and of some of the problems of debt management. Intergovernmental fiscal relationships are described and evaluated in terms of their contributions to welfare objectives in Part V.

The ideas underlying this approach obviously do not originate with us. Our method of looking at the problems has been strongly influenced by our contacts with the works of Abba P. Lerner, Alvin H. Hansen, and others. The concept of the "public economy" used in the book is one extensively employed by Bowman and Bach in their *Economic Analysis and Public Policy*. Also, discussions with our colleagues, particularly Kenneth Boulding, Gerhard Tintner, and Leonid Hurwicz, have decidedly influenced our approach.

Professor Albert G. Hart of Columbia University read the manuscript at various stages and has made many suggestions for improving both the rigor and clarity of the exposition. Chapter IX is an outgrowth of his insistence that some economic criteria can be evolved for guiding political decisions about government expenditure.

Our colleagues at Iowa State College have been of assistance in reading various parts of the manuscript and offering their comments. We are particularly indebted to Lester Blum, Elisabeth Curtiss, Donald Kaldor, W. G. Murray, Gerhard Tintner, and Wallace Wright. We also acknowledge indebtedness to Donald C. Horton of the Bureau of Agricultural Economics who read the first twelve chapters of the book critically. John A. Nordin has given us both his time and his assistance. Finally, we express our appreciation to W. G. Murray, head of the Department of Economics and Sociology, for making it possible for the writers to devote a portion of their time to this piece of work.

E. D. A.
O. H. B.

CONTENTS

PART ONE

AN OVER-ALL VIEW OF THE PUBLIC ECONOMY

PART TWO

PUBLIC FINANCE AND FULL EMPLOYMENT

PART FIVE

INTERGOVERNMENTAL FISCAL COORDINATION

DIAGRAMS

TABLES

PART ONE

AN OVER-ALL VIEW OF
THE PUBLIC ECONOMY

CHAPTER I

NATURE OF THE PUBLIC ECONOMY

THE study of public finance has assumed increasing importance as a field of economic analysis in recent decades.
Several factors have contributed to this trend, one of which has
been the continued growth of government (see Table 1). Of
greater importance has been a growing recognition that the
money expenditures and money receipts of government may affect not only the pattern of production and the distribution of the
total product among the various income receivers, but also the
level of production and employment within the economy.

Virtually any meaningful measure which can be applied to the
available data indicates almost continuous growth in government
in the United States during the past half century.[1] Of course,
there has been an increase in the population of the United States.
Between 1890 and 1940 the population of continental United
States approximately doubled: in 1890 it was 63 million, while in
1940, it was nearly 132 million. During this same period, the
number of Federal employees (excluding military personnel) increased about sixfold. State and local governments also are
employing many more people than they did a half century ago.
There has been an expansion in total dollar expenditures; there
also has been an upward trend in *per capita* money expenditures
(adjusted for changes in the value of money); and the ratio of
public expenditures to national income has increased. The last
two measures are of particular importance. They indicate an
expansion in the role played by government in providing income
(money payments and services) to the average individual and
also that the *relative* share of national income being channeled
through government has been rising. (Refer to Table 1.)

The continued growth of government together with the

---

[1] Chapter II describes in greater detail (as part of a discussion of the changing
pattern of government finance) the changes that have taken place in the size and
scope of government.

3

changes in governmental fiscal activities initiated during the thirties have brought about important changes in the study of public finance. Since about 1930 (the beginning of the major interwar depression) the various aspects of government finance have been studied increasingly with reference to their effects on the economy as a whole as well as their impacts upon the treasury.

Relatively greater attention has been given to the effects of governmental fiscal operations upon the levels of production and employment in the economy. Increased emphasis is being placed upon interrelationships between governmental receipts and expenditures. Less emphasis is being accorded the separate treatment typically given to governmental expenditures, revenues, and borrowing in earlier public-finance studies. Public finance is fast becoming a study of the public economy.

The Public Economy

Governmental activities are both numerous and varied. Governments are charged with the responsibility for formulating and enforcing the rules which will permit our social organization to function smoothly. These rules govern relations between people; some are designed to discourage one person from damaging the body or property of another. Antimonopoly laws supposedly limit inequalities in the relative bargaining powers of the parties in an exchange. Other laws specify the terms of trade. Laws discouraging fraud or misrepresentation are numerous. Even the institution of the family is protected by these rules—witness our laws governing divorce, desertion, and the like.

In our society the rule-making process is largely a legislative one.[3] Most of our laws are enacted by legislative bodies elected from our citizenry. These laws are administered by various governmental agencies whose function it is to see that the various aspects of the "game" are conducted in accordance with the legislatively established rules.[4]

[3] Although administrative agencies may, in interpreting rules, act as "rule-makers," the basic rule-making process is legislative.

[4] This division between "rule-making" and "rule-enforcing" is accepted by many political scientists and economists. See, for example, F. J. Goodnow, *Principles of the Administrative Law of the United States*, New York: G. P. Putnam's Sons, 1905, and Henry C. Simons, "A Positive Program for Laissez Faire," *Public Policy Pamphlet No. 15*, University of Chicago Press, 1934.

TABLE 1[2]

Governmental Expenditures in Relation to National Income and Product, Selected Years, 1890-1943

Year	Total (in millions)		Per Capita		National Income (in millions)	Ratio Expenditures to National Income	National Product (Adjusted) (in millions)	Government Expenditures (Adjusted)	Ratio Expenditures to National Product
	Current Dollars	1939 Dollars	Current Dollars	1939 Dollars					
1890	$ 893	$ 1,600	$ 14.16	$ 25.37	$ 10,700	8.3%			
1903	1,636	2,727	20.20	33.67	19,600	9.0			
1913	2,839	4,157	29.41	43.06	31,400				
1919	22,125	18,530	210.51	176.31	67,600				
1926	9,932	8,049	85.25	69.08	76,800				
1929	11,355	9,582	96.22	81.20	83,300	13.6	$100,100	$11,700	11.7%
1933	12,053	13,604	95.96	108.31	42,300		56,200	10,500	18.7
1936	16,363	16,445	127.81	128.45	64,900		84,600	15,500	18.3
1940	18,608	18,424	141.01	139.61	77,600	24.0	99,700	19,300	19.4
1943	88,214	73,512	646.32	538.60	149,400		191,000	98,000	51.3

[2] For an explanation of the sources of data and procedures used in compiling this table, see Appendix A.

Governments as economic units. Governments, however, do more than make rules and see that they are enforced. Governmental units provide our citizens with many kinds of services other than those of law enforcement. For example, the Federal government organizes and operates the agencies which defend our nation against aggressors, determines and carries out national policy in the conservation of natural resources, cares for war veterans, operates such enterprises as the postal system and the Panama Canal, and makes loans to farmers and business enterprises. State governments construct and maintain a huge network of intercity highways; bear much of the costs of higher education; sell or lease the services of such productive agents as toll bridges, toll highways, warehouses, airports, and port facilities; and in some instances are the sole legal sellers of liquor within the state boundaries. Local governments continue to provide the bulk of street and rural highway service and play the most important governmental role in providing for health, hospitals, and sanitation. City governments frequently operate utility enterprises and sell water, gas, electricity, and transit services. Most of our primary and secondary schools are operated by governmental units (school districts) which have been created solely for this purpose.

In addition to this kind of service-producing activity, our governmental units (especially those of the Federal government) have found themselves increasingly concerned with fiscal activities which involve direct money payments to relatively large groups within the economy. These payments are not made in exchange for goods and services and are frequently called "transfer payments." Examples are found in payments of interest on public debt, bonus payments to war veterans, benefit payments under the social security system, and direct relief payments. Many of these types of payments have involved joint participation by units of government at all levels. A summary of governmental activities at Federal, state, and local levels, as of the fiscal year[5] 1941—the eve of our participation in World War II—is presented in Table 2. (See also Figure 1.)

This is not a complete picture of governmental activities.

[5] The term "fiscal" year refers to the accounting year. For the Federal government and most state governments, the fiscal year begins on July 1, and ends on June 30. Thus, the fiscal year 1940 began on July 1, 1939, and ended on June 30, 1940. Unless otherwise noted, all references are to fiscal years.

However, it does serve to indicate that governmental units are economic units similar in many respects to private businesses. In purchasing productive services or in making payments to individuals or businesses for any reason, a government pays out money just as does a business. In taxing, or in selling water, gas, or any other service, a government takes money out of the stream of expenditure as does a grocer when he sells food or as does a dentist when he collects for extracting a tooth. Governments may issue and sell securities just as a corporation may use this method for obtaining funds to carry on its operations. Like a business, a government may build up its holdings of money—by collecting currently in revenues more than it pays out—or may incur a current deficit by collecting currently less than it expends.

Relative importance of governmental units as economic units. As economic units various governmental units differ greatly in size. In the five fiscal years, 1936-1940, the Federal government expended annually an average of nearly 8.4 billion dollars.[6] This

TABLE 2[7]

Functional Classification of the Net Expenditures of
U.S. Government Units: Fiscal Year, 1940-41

Function	Total Expenditure (in millions of dollars)	Percentage of Total Expenditure
1. Protection of Life and Property...	$7,462	28.04
2. Public Assistance and Welfare....	5,677	21.33
3. Cost Payments of Government Enterprises and Corporations.....	4,100	15.41
4. Education.....................	2,636	9.91
5. Transportation.................	2,023	7.60
6. Interest on Public Debt..........	1,610	6.05
7. Natural Resources..............	1,442	5.42
8. General Administrative, Legislative and Judicial...................	1,236	4.65
9. Miscellaneous and unspecified fiscal aid.........................	423	1.59
10. Total, exclusive of debt retirement	$26,609	100.00
11. Debt retirement...............	1,843	
12. Total, inclusive of debt retirement	$28,452	

[6] Exclusive of budgetary provision for debt retirement. Source: *Annual Reports* of Secretary of the Treasury.

[7] Most of these data were derived from *Financing Federal, State, and Local Governments, 1941*, Department of Commerce, Bureau of the Census, 1942. For detail, see Appendix B.

rate of expenditure is equivalent to nearly three times the combined sales receipts of General Motors and United States Steel for 1940.[8]   The Federal government in 1940 spent approximately as much as the combined expenditures of all of our states and local governments for that year.[9]   During the peak year of Fed-

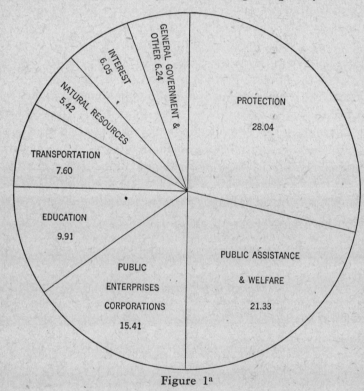

Figure 1[a]

Classification of the Net Expenditures of All Government Units in the United States by Purposes: Fiscal year, 1940-41

eral expenditures, 1944, nearly one-half of the total expenditures for the nation as a whole consisted of the spending of the Federal government for goods and services.[10]

[8] See *Moody's Industrials*, 1941, published by John Moody and Sons, New York, for data on the sales receipts of General Motors and United States Steel.

[9] See Table 3 below.   Further information on the relative importance of government units is given in Chapter II.

[10] In 1944, the gross national product was estimated at 198.7 billion dollars, of which Federal expenditures for goods and services were 91.9 billion dollars, or about 46.2 per cent.   Refer to Department of Commerce, Washington, D. C., *The Survey of Current Business*, February, 1945, page 5.

[a] For more complete information on the content of this Chart, see Table II and the explanation in Appendix B.

The expenditures of some of our states and municipalities also bulk large even when they are compared with those of many of our so-called giant corporations. In 1942, the city of New York spent more than 800 million dollars—nearly as much as the sales receipts of Chrysler Corporation for their prewar peak of 1941, and more than was spent by any single state government. The state of New York spent approximately three-quarters of a billion dollars in 1942. The combined expenditures of the states of California and Pennsylvania totaled more than a billion dollars during this same year. The combined expenditure of the 9 cities with populations between 500,000 and 1,000,000 added up to more than 400 million dollars in 1942—more than the combined expenditure of the 15 smallest state governments in the same period.[11] A picture of the over-all distribution of public expenditures by Federal, state, and local units since 1890 is given in Table 3.

TABLE 3[12]

Distribution of Governmental Expenditure Among Federal, State and Local Governments, Selected Fiscal Years, 1890-1943.

Fiscal Year	Total Expenditure[a] (in millions of dollars)	Percentage of Total Expenditures Made by			Total
		Federal Government	State Governments	Local Governments	
1890	$ 893	35.6%	9.9%	54.5%	100.0
1903	1,636	31.6	12.7	55.7	100.0
1913	2,839	24.6	12.6	62.8	100.0
1919	22,125	83.4	2.8	13.8	100.0
1923	8,540	35.8	14.0	50.2	100.0
1929	11,355	26.1	17.0	56.9	100.0
1933	12,053	38.3	18.4	43.3	100.0
1936	16,363	55.6	16.0	28.4	100.0
1940	18,608[b]	47.6	22.1	30.3	100.0
1943	88,214[b]	90.4	4.2	5.4	100.0

[a] Exclusive of debt retirement.

[b] Figures include "net social security costs," that is, gross payments by social security trust funds less interest paid by the government to social security funds.

If money expenditures are accepted as a measure of economic importance, the significance of government in the United States looms large. In 1940 the combined expenditure of all units of

[11] See United States Department of Commerce, Bureau of the Census, *Statistical Abstract of the United States, 1943*, Tables 292 and 309.

[12] Derived from *Economic Almanac, 1944-45*, National Industrial Conference Board, page 101.

government equaled about one-fifth of aggregate expenditure in the rest of the economy.[13]   The expenditure of the Federal government alone was equivalent to about 10 per cent of aggregate expenditure in the rest of the economy.

Government's economic operations.   Virtually all of the activities of government affect the way in which resources are allocated, the manner in which the total product of the economy is divided among the various recipients, and perhaps the level of total production and employment in the economy.   For example, a protective tariff may shift resources into producing the protected commodity; liquor prohibition may reduce the incomes of bartenders; and minimum wage legislation may increase or decrease the level of production and employment in the economy. However, it is not the effects of various regulatory activities, but the effects of the money-raising and money-spending activities of governments in which we are primarily interested.   It is this area—that of government as an economic unit—that we shall call the *public economy*.   The effects of law-making and enforcing are thus a part of the public economy only in so far as they involve the collection or expenditure of funds and the use of resources.

It is with the public economy—with the effects of governmental money-spending and money-raising activities upon the allocation of resources, the distribution of incomes, and the general level of economic activity within the economy—that the bulk of our analysis will be concerned.

Differences between government and private economic units. Although governments are economic units similar in many respects to businesses or consuming units, their operations differ in many ways from the operations of other units.   Of these differences, four stand out as most important in explaining how and why governments should not and do not conduct their operations as do private businesses:

1. Governments try to achieve objectives which are different from the objectives sought by most private businesses.

2. The terms under which services are received and contributions are made to the public economy by individuals differ from the terms under which the goods and services of the private economy are exchanged.   Participation in much of the public

[13] See Table 1.

economy is compulsory, while participation in any given sector of the private economy is voluntary.

3. Government is more willing and perhaps more able to undertake long term projects. Governments may have less aversion to risk than do private businesses.

4. The Federal government could, if desired, make payments from direct money issues. It should be noted that the banking system is a creator of the most widely used form of money—bank deposits. In recent years the Federal government has used the banking system as a major source of funds. These funds have been secured through the sale of government securities to banks.

The objective of governmental operations is primarily that of maximizing social welfare, whereas the private business usually tries to maximize the welfare of its operators. Consequently, government must take into consideration benefits and losses which are indirect in character. A business usually recognizes only benefits and losses direct enough to affect its receipts and costs. Although a private business may conduct its operations in a manner that will maximize its size, or its economic power, or its diversity, it is usually necessary for the receipts of a business enterprise to be in excess of its expenditures. This is not necessarily an objective in the conduct of most governmental activities.

The compulsion attached to participation in the public economy makes it easier to conduct governmental operations toward maximizing social welfare. The absence of a market which will register participants' preferences, however, makes it difficult to determine whether the public economy is doing too little or too much.

The fact that the national government can, if desired, make payments from money issue rather than out of its receipts from taxes or the sale of goods, services, or securities, means that the government has at its disposal an additional means for injecting money into the economy. Private businesses cannot pay their bills indefinitely by circulating their own I.O.U.'s. Except for a brief period during the Civil War, this money issuing power has not been utilized as a source of Federal funds.

The Public Economy and Social Policy

Although governmental units produce commodities and services, the decisions as to what to produce, how much to produce,

and how to produce—unlike the decisions of private businesses—
are not made always on the basis of expected market conditions.
There is no market, in the accepted sense of the concept, where
the prices of the bulk of the services offered by a government
may be determined.   Public administrators may be reasonably
expected to utilize "production" techniques which are similar to
those employed by nongovernmental enterprises under comparable conditions.[14]   The continuance in office of an administrator,
however, does not depend solely upon turning out the services at
minimum cost, but also upon the numerous other factors that
enter into the ability of administrators to get reelected or re-
appointed.

Decisions relative to what and how much to produce and the
scope and size of government are made collectively as a result
of public discussion and legislative or administrative action.
These decisions are a part of the process of determining social
policy.   Changes in our concept of desirable social policy are
primarily responsible for changes in the size and scope of government as a whole as well as for the trends in the relative importance of various governmental units.

The proper size and scope of government, as conceived by the
formulators of social policy, is dependent upon many factors.
Some goods and services—the provision of educational facilities,
national defense, police protection, and the like—provide considerable benefits to persons other than the immediate users of
these services.   If regular exchange procedures were followed
in determining how much educational services to provide, the
amounts of these services furnished probably would not be as
great as the amounts currently provided in the United States.
The benefits of such services are so widely diffused that the immediate user cannot be expected to bear all of the costs of providing them.   Therefore, we provide for distribution of some of
these services by government.

Production conditions for some goods and services are such
that one or only a few producers can serve a given market efficiently.   The result may be a smaller production of these goods
and services than is in the public interest.   Government may add
to social welfare by operating in such industries.

[14] This area—minimization of the costs of resources used to accomplish a given
objective—is the only one where the term "governmental efficiency" seems to
make sense.

The factors which we consider to be important in determining the proper scope for governmental use of resources are set forth in greater detail in Chapter IX.   In explaining why government has assumed a given size, however, we can say only that the relative importance attached to these and other factors has been weighed in some way by the formulators of social policy.

The objectives of economic policy.   The concept of social policy usually refers to the governmentally established framework which specifies the objectives of a given phase of social organization and the techniques which are to be used in trying to reach these objectives.   This framework includes the rules of economic and social cooperation, and the provisions made for enforcing these rules as well as the effects of the other activities of government.   In this analysis we are interested in a particular sector of social policy—the sector which might be called *economic policy*.   We will consider economic policy as the sum of the activities of government in determining the economic framework within which economic units function.   A policy may be active, that is, it may attempt to alter the framework from what it would be in the absence of a particular governmental action; or a policy may be a passive one of governmental nonintervention in determining the conditions comprising the framework.

The objectives of economic policy are constantly changing as time passes and are, to a large extent, personal or social judgments.   Acceptable objectives of economic policy prepared by the editors of *The Nation* or *The New Republic* would probably differ considerably from a slate prepared by the editors of the *Chicago Tribune*.   In spite of these differences, there are some observations which we can make on the opinions of the majority of our citizens about the most desirable objectives of economic policy.[15]   The following are some of the most important objectives of economic policy:

(*1.*) *Economic policy and economic efficiency.*   There seems to

[15] Determination of the goals of economic policy is an empirical question, so far as the economist is concerned.   A part of his job, if it is not done by the policy makers, may be to investigate what citizens consider these goals to be.   Economists also must check the goals for consistency.   If there are inconsistencies, it must be pointed out that achieving certain objectives may make difficult or even impossible the attainment of other objectives.   Once inconsistencies are brought to the attention of citizens, it is the job of the citizen to decide how much of one objective he is willing to sacrifice in order to achieve more of another.   In our judgment, however, the economist is concerned with what the goals *should be* only in his capacity as a citizen whose values are registered in political decisions.

be almost unanimous agreement among our citizens that, other things being equal, economic policy should encourage efficiency in the use of productive resources—the men, their skills, and the materials available within the economy. By this we mean that there are few people who do not prefer to see a given amount of resources utilized in a manner which will yield a maximum of product. Since a given collection of resources may be utilized to produce any one of a large number of different combinations of products, the concept "maximum product" must be more clearly defined. The importance of each of the various goods and services which make up the product has to be evaluated. In an economy where consumers are free to allocate their incomes as they see fit, consumers are the ones who make the evaluation. The results of their deliberations are reflected in the relative prices which they are willing to pay for various amounts of these goods and services. If a given product collection contains more watches and fewer radios than consumers prefer, that product collection is not the best one which may be obtained from the available resources. And production of a better collection will be encouraged by the way in which the price of radios will rise relative to the price of watches. The concept maximum product thus implies that resources are allocated in line with consumers' preferences.[16]

(2.) *Full production and employment.* A second objective of economic policy—an objective which has been growing in importance since the depression of the thirties—is maintaining conditions such that our resources, our human resources in particular, are fully employed.[17] There is a growing belief that

[16] In modern societies not all resources are allocated by the price mechanism. For example, some goods and services, particularly those produced by government, have no prices attached to them. Where benefits from the use of particular goods or services accrue partially to persons other than the immediate users, the price mechanism may not adequately allocate resources in line with consumer preferences. For a more complete discussion of this case, refer to Chapter IX.

[17] By "full employment" we mean the condition existing when, at current rates of return to the various resources, enterprisers are willing to hire the services of exactly as much of these resources as resource-owners are willing to sell. As applied to labor, full employment would prevail when, at current wage rates, anybody out of a job could get a job promptly (physical capacity to work assumed). Such a condition does not imply that there would be no people seeking work or unemployed. Even under full employment there might be a sizable number of people ascertaining job opportunities, waiting for better jobs, and the like.

economic policy should be directed toward maintaining conditions which will contribute to full employment. This is true in the economies of other countries as well as in that of the United States.

(3.) *Freedom in resource disposal.* Freedom of the individual to dispose of his resources in the way he wishes, given the pattern of prices for these resources, is a goal of economic policy that has been almost taken for granted. Objections to military conscription, to the drafting of labor even during wartime, and to slavery are evidences of the existence of this objective.

(4.) *Economic progress.* Not only do we consider efficiency in the use of resources as an objective of economic policy, but we expect such efficiency to be constantly increasing with the passage of time. This obtaining of more product per capita is often called "economic progress." Technological progress along with its application to production, and full use of increasing knowledge in the efficient combination of productive resources; both are ways in which such progress may come about. The maintenance of conditions favorable to economic progress is a goal of economic policy that is generally acceptable to most citizens.

(5.) *Equity in the distribution of income.* Another objective of economic policy is that of equity in the distribution of the total product of the economy among its various potential recipients. The concept "equity" is a very nebulous one and has a different meaning for virtually every individual. Nevertheless, there is fairly general agreement that equity does not mean that the rich should be made richer and the poor should be made poorer; equity seems to mean to most people that the dispersion of the income distribution should be narrowed from what it would be if incomes were determined only by the pattern of resource ownership and relative resource prices. How much it should be narrowed, however, is a question to which an answer acceptable to all has not yet been given.

This is not an exhaustive list of the goals of economic policy. But it is sufficient to indicate that it is within the framework of these objectives that the size and nature of governmental operations—regulatory activities as well as those which we call the operations of the public economy—are determined.

Consistency of the objectives. If pursued independently some of these objectives may be inconsistent with other objectives.

For example, the kind of income distribution that we might decide to be most equitable might reduce markedly the total product to be distributed and might not be the one which would encourage maximum economic progress; or maintaining employment at a high level might not contribute to a production pattern most in line with consumers' preferences. In a socialist economy, for example, all resources might be kept employed, but too much of the economy's resources might be used in producing watches and too little in producing suits.[18] The conflicts between the various objectives of social policy are analogous to that posed in the old adage, "you cannot have your cake and eat it too." One must decide how much of the cake he will eat and how much he will have. Consequently, in practice it is a combination of objectives—none being achieved to the fullest extent —which social policy attempts to maximize.[19]

For example, one might conceive an equitable distribution of income to be one in which per capita incomes are equalized. Yet with this kind of income distribution, the total product to be distributed probably would be smaller than the total product achieved with some other distribution. The supplies of the various productive agents, particularly the supply of enterprise, would no doubt be reduced; and there might be encountered serious difficulties in allocating resources. Consequently, the concept "equitable distribution of incomes," in so far as it is an objective of social policy, must be framed to consider both the nature of the income distribution and the total income to be distributed.

If direction of production by a central governmental agency were the only way of attaining full employment, there might be a conflict between full employment and optimum resource allocation and the freedom of consumers' choice and resource disposal which accompanies such an optimum. The freedom of consum-

[18] This statement does not imply that misallocation of resources is necessary in a socialist economy. See, for example, Oscar Lange, *et al.*, *On the Economic Theory of Socialism*, Minneapolis, Minnesota: The University of Minnesota Press, 1938. Furthermore, there is no assurance that resources will be allocated in line with consumer's preferences in a capitalist economy. Many economists, however, have considered that misallocation of resources is more probable in a socialist economy because of the greater opportunity for political interference with the price pattern.

[19] This point has been made by Max Weber. Refer to Talcott Parsons, *The Structure of Social Action*, Chapters XIV-XVII, New York: McGraw-Hill Book Co., Inc., 1937.

ers' choice and resource disposal, which might have to be given up, perhaps would be a greater sacrifice than that resulting from underproduction and underemployment. Consequently, if this technique were the only one which would enable our economy to achieve full production and employment, many citizens would prefer not to achieve fully this objective.[20]

In determining over-all social policy these conflicts—real or imaginary—have to be resolved: this is the function of politics. As economists analyzing the effects of the public economy, we must, however, point out that the size and scope of the public economy is an important determinant of its effects, and the nature of the public economy is largely dependent upon social policy.

Effects of the Public Economy on Resource Allocation, Income Distribution and the General Level of Economic Activity

As we have indicated previously, governments are economic units which perform their functions by employing productive resources and spending and collecting money. These activities may have important effects upon the size and composition of the total economic product and upon the way in which this product is distributed among the various potential recipients.

Effects on resource allocation. Governmental activities have three effects upon resource allocation: (1) Resources may be diverted from private to public uses. (2) The distribution of income is altered by governmental activities, and through this change there occurs a change in resource allocation. (3) The general level of economic activity may be altered. Not only will the size of the total product be changed, but there may also be a different allocation of some peoples' time. More (or less) will be spent in producing marketable goods and services, and less (or more) will be spent on leisure.[21]

The diversion of resources from private to public uses has been accepted as a customary role of government in the past. In the building of a bridge, the construction of a public building, or the

[20] This example should not be misinterpreted as a belief that full production and employment is incompatible with an enterprise economy.

[21] The effects of governmental activities on the distribution of income and the general level of economic activity will be considered in more detail later in this chapter.

enforcement of highway regulations, governmental units employ resources that could have been employed to turn out other goods and services. If the government had not used the manpower, steel, cement, and other building materials in constructing the bridge or the court house, these productive agents could have been used for other purposes—perhaps to build houses, or a power plant, or a new factory. The motorcycle used by the highway policeman, the train facilities occupied by the congressman, and even the pencils and paper with which the school clerk takes his notes are, in a sense, diverted into uses which differ from those which would have prevailed had they not been employed by government.

The differences between the pattern of production in the combined public-private economy and the pattern which would have prevailed had some of the resources been used in ways other than by government, is difficult to estimate. Some of the goods and services provided by government probably could not and should not be provided by other agencies; law-making and law-enforcing are examples. Some of the goods and services produced by government—the services of municipal power plants, for example— are similar to those which would have been produced by non-governmental units. The *amounts* of a service produced by government, however, may differ considerably from the amounts which would be produced by the private economy.

Differences may arise in part because the rules followed by government in determining how much to produce are not the same as the rules followed by private producers. Where monopoly elements are important in a particular sector of the private economy, governmental administration of production in this sector may result in expanded amounts of these services. Governmental regulation of prices—rate-making by the Interstate Commerce Commission or by state public utility commissions—might accomplish the same result. Differences may also grow out of variations in the adequacy of the price mechanism as a guide to production. Where the benefits from the use of a particular service are of importance to persons other than the immediate user, the price mechanism may not adequately reflect the preferences of society. The benefits of public education, for example, are so widely disseminated that "selling" them as one sells beans or men's clothing and using sales to determine how much education to provide might result in a smaller output of educational training than is considered socially desirable.[22]

Broadly, the only generalization we can make in comparing allocation of resources in a combined public-private economy with the allocation which would prevail without a public economy is that the patterns are different. The measuring stick of consumers' preferences often cannot be applied to the product of the public economy. Continuous expansion in the proportion of resources used by the public economy is evidence that, through our political processes, we have appraised the benefits from the services provided as at least equal to the costs (those things that could have been produced with the same resources in the private economy).

Effects on income distribution. In spending and collecting money, governments as economic units affect the distribution of purchasing power among the various individuals in society. As a by-product, effects on resource allocation may also be involved. Some of the activities of government—veterans' bonuses, pensions, or relief payments, for example—transfer purchasing power directly to the beneficiaries of these expenditures without requiring an equivalent transfer of goods or services to government. To the extent that the (real) incomes of some people are reduced in order that the incomes of other people may be increased, the production pattern *within* the private sector of the economy is almost certain to be altered. The demands of those whose incomes are increased will almost certainly differ from the demands of those whose incomes are decreased. But within this particular framework, the resources used for public purposes do not change, except for resources required for administration; with this exception, *diversion* of resources from private to public purposes has not occurred.[23]

---

[22] The case for expenditures on public housing, health, and nutrition programs hinges on this inadequacy of the price mechanism. See Chapter IX for a more detailed discussion of relevant factors in determining the size of public expenditures.

[23] In the past, studies of public finance have emphasized the two types of relationship between public expenditures and resource use which have just been distinguished. See, for example, the distinction made by Arthur C. Pigou between "transfer" and "exhaustive" expenditures in his book *A Study in Public Finance*, London: Macmillan & Co. Ltd., 1928. See also the distinction between "transfer" and "public consumption" expenditures made by W. J. Shultz in *American Public Finance*, Chapter I, 3rd edition, New York: Prentice-Hall, Inc., 1942.

It is likely that some resource-using activities of government will be designed to supplement the (real) incomes of some groups in the economy more than others; expenditures to improve health and nutrition, expand facilities for recreation, and subsidize housing are examples. Moreover, progressive taxation[24] affects income distribution; by reducing the relative spread in the distribution of income, for example, it improves the status of the lower-income groups by making a higher proportion of their incomes freely disposable income after taxes.

In general, the larger the expenditure of government, the greater the income redistribution which the government can effect. If the Federal government were to spend only a million dollars a year, it could alter the income pattern little. An annual Federal expenditure of 25 to 30 billion dollars, however, can change the distribution of real income and purchasing power sharply. Opposition to large Federal expenditures may be based partially on this knowledge.

Governmental activities and the general level of economic activity. It is to be expected that government's use of resources and the redistribution of incomes which governmental activities bring about will affect the level of employment and production. A business operator, viewing governmental construction of a building, a highway, or a power dam, may consider such an activity as reducing his chances for profit. He may view the government as a competitor. Or he may expect increased taxes as a result of these activities. Other businessmen may consider such activities as contributing to successful operation of their own businesses. In either case, the operation of the public economy has by-product effects upon the general level of economic activity.

Indirectly, moreover, activities which redistribute income may be taking potential purchasing power from sources where it is not adding to the flow of expenditure and redirecting these funds into the expenditure stream. Where resources are idle, such action may encourage their employment. Income redistribution, however, may also have adverse effects upon employment and production. This is particularly likely if such action influences adversely the supply of enterprise—if it discourages risk-taking

---

[24] That is, taxation which takes a higher proportion of income (or wealth) from those with large incomes (or wealth) than those with smaller incomes (or wealth).

and business expansion.[25] Here is an illustration of the way in which the public economy's operation has by-product effects upon the general level of economic activity.

In addition to these indirect effects, governmental money-spending and money-collecting may be directed specifically toward influencing the over-all level of economic activity. The fiscal system may be used as a framework for altering the quantity of money, and changes in the quantity of money may have important effects upon aggregate expenditure in the private economy.

Recognition that government may have a place in affecting the general level of production and employment has come quite recently. In the United States, the depression of the thirties and appraisal of the techniques employed to combat it greatly stimulated analysis of the effects of government's money-spending and money-collecting activities upon the general level of economic activity. Our concern today is with the analysis of these activities as they may relate to a higher level of production and employment in the postwar years. Later in this text, there will be a critical appraisal of alternative fiscal policies as they may affect the general level of economic activity. Here it need only be said that some of the money-raising and money-spending activities of government may be designed to stabilize the aggregate level of expenditure in the economy. Wartime taxing and borrowing activities of government have been formulated to siphon funds out of the stream of expenditure and to discourage this stream from rising to a level which would result in unduly high commodity prices. Reversing such activities so that they could add to the stream of expenditure could help to keep production and employment from falling.

Summary

Governments are economic units similar in many respects to businesses or consuming units. Governments may buy resources, sell goods and services, spend money, sell securities, collect money, buy securities, and engage in many activities which, like the activities of private businesses, affect the allocation of re-

---

[25] Refer to Jakob Marschak, "Lack of Confidence," *Social Research*, 8:41-62 (February, 1941), and to Oscar Lange, "The Theory of the Multiplier," *Econometrica*, 11:227-45 (July–October, 1943).

sources, the distribution of incomes, and the general level of economic activity within the economy. As economic units, governments vary greatly in size. The Federal government's average annual expenditures in the thirties exceeded twice the combined 1940 expenditures of our two largest corporations. Wartime Federal expenditures have been equivalent to about one half of total expenditures within the economy. If estimated annual expenditures of the Federal government in postwar years following reconversion are realistic, the Federal government as an economic unit will be more important than it was during the immediate prewar years.

Unlike the operations of private businesses, most governmental activities are not designed to maximize profit. The size and scope of the operations of governmental units—and consequently the kinds of activities in which governments engage—are determined by our collective formulation of desirable social policy. Decisions relative to what and how much government should produce are not determined by market forces, but by the legislative rules governing social policy and the administrative interpretations of these rules.

CHAPTER II

CHANGING PATTERNS IN AMERICAN PUBLIC FINANCE, 1890 TO THE PRESENT[1]

ALONG with a change in ideas about the functions of public finance have come important changes in the pattern of public receipts and expenditures during the last half century. (1) There has been continued growth and a marked change in the character of public expenditures. (2) Tax collections have increased, new sources of tax revenues have been tapped and some old sources have become less important in the tax system. (3) The public debt has moved rather consistently upward, emerging during World War II as the principal type of asset held by the banking system. (4) Intergovernmental fiscal transactions have increased in importance. The larger units of government are collecting funds which are allocated to smaller units for expenditure. For example, the Federal government is allocating funds to state and local governments for such uses as highway construction and old age assistance. And state aids to local schools are increasing in importance.

THE GROWTH OF PUBLIC EXPENDITURES

By 1890, the earliest year for which over-all statistics for all units of government are available, slightly more than 8 per cent of national income was being channeled through government. Between 1890 and 1914 the number and scope of governmental expenditures increased. But the relative amount of total money expenditure of the economy as a whole made up by governmental

---

[1] No attempt is made to cover over-all changes prior to 1890. For the years before this date, information on local and state government finance is very sketchy. Per capita Federal expenditures in 1800 were $2.03 and had risen by 1890 to $5.06, a rise somewhat overstated because prices were probably lower in 1800 than in 1890. Nevertheless, these data suggest that the growth of the public economy in the 1800's was relatively small and gradual. For further information, see Chapter I, Table 1.

expenditure remained about the same in 1914 as in 1890. (See Chapter I, Table 1.)

World War I lifted governmental expenditure to a permanently higher level; Federal expenditure in 1919 was more than 25 times as large as in 1914. During the same period the cost-of-living index had risen by about 75 per cent so that 1919 expenditures, in 1914 dollars, were about 15 times as large as those of 1914. Commitments incurred during the war together with an expansion in the number of functions performed by the Federal government kept Federal expenditures during the five years, 1925-1929, at about four times (about two and one-half times in 1909-1914 dollars) the level of 1909-1914. State and local governments also increased their expenditures in the decade following World War I, the expansion coming largely in spending for education and highways. In 1929 the combined expenditure of all units of government was equivalent to nearly 14 per cent of national income.

The decade of the 1930's was marked by a prolonged (but not highly successful) attempt by the Federal government to retrieve the economy from the trough of depression. In 1940 total governmental expenditures made up 19.4 per cent of the gross national product (or 24 per cent of the national income).[2] However, the national income was only 77.6 billion dollars in 1940 as compared with 83.3 billion dollars in 1929.

World War II increased public expenditures to a point where, in 1944, they exceeded 50 per cent of the gross national product. So high a ratio is not to be expected in our peacetime economy; there is, however, nothing to indicate that the sphere of public fiscal activities will shrink to its prewar size. Between 1940 and 1950 the population of the United States will have increased by about 10 per cent; in addition, a rise of at least 50 per cent in the general level of prices seems a reasonable expectation. These two factors alone would bring about a markedly higher level of dollar expenditures in 1950 than we had in 1940. Add to these the expected increases in spending growing out of the last war. The result is that conservative estimates of Federal expenditures in the early 1950's place them at around 25 billion dollars, an increase of nearly 200 per cent (in 1940 dollars) over the levels

[2] See Table 1, Chapter I, and Appendix A.

of immediate prewar years which were themselves peacetime highs.[3]   (See Table 4.)

The estimates of future Federal expenditures in Table 4 are conservative in that they assume relatively high employment and do not include provision for work-creating Federal programs of the type carried on in the last depression.[4]   If we do not have relatively full employment, we are likely to embark again upon policies which will provide such employment, and some of these policies probably will involve increased Federal expenditure.

State and local spending also is likely to average higher per year during the next decade than it did immediately before the war.   A recent estimate places cash expenditure of the states from state sources of funds at about 1 billion dollars more in 1949 than in 1940, when such expenditures were 3.3 billion dollars. The same estimators expect local cash expenditures made from local fund sources to be about 1 billion dollars more in 1949 than in 1940, when such expenditures were 5.6 billion dollars.[5]   These estimates will prove too low in view of the relatively small increase in the general level of prices assumed by the estimators.

Even though state and local activities undergo no expansion from the 1940 level, combined governmental expenditure during the next decade appears likely to total around 40 to 45 billion dollars a year.

Factors Accounting for the Growth in Public Expenditure

Students of fiscal affairs have offered several explanations for the increase in public expenditures.   For this country at least four factors have been considered very important: (1) an increase in the general level of prices, (2) growth in population and expansion in the physical area which government must serve, (3) what has been called "the increasing needs of a more complex society," and (4) wars.

[3] In the year 1940, on the eve of our defense and war effort, Federal expenditures were 9.12 billion dollars.   This was the peak of the peacetime years of the Roosevelt administration.   Source: *Annual Reports* of the Secretary of the Treasury.

[4] More than 18 billion dollars were expended for direct and work relief between 1933 and 1943.   These include expenditures for the Civilian Conservation Corps of about 3 billion dollars, but do not include public works programs administered by the Public Works Administration.

[5] See Lewis H. Kimmel *et al.*, *Postwar Fiscal Requirements*, Washington, D.C.: Brookings Institution, 1945.

TABLE 4[6]

A Federal Budget for 195x

Kind of Expenditure	Billions of Dollars
Military	13.3
Defense	9.8
Veterans' Benefits	3.5
Economic Development[a]	5.1
Social Welfare[b]	1.6
General Government[c]	0.8
Interest on National Debt	5.0
Miscellaneous[d]	0.8
TOTAL[e]	$ 26.6

[a] Includes expenditure for transportation, commerce and industry, labor, and agriculture.

[b] Includes expenditure for education, public health and assistance, recreation, housing, and social security.

[c] Regulatory, enforcement, and general governmental expenditure.

[d] Includes governmental business enterprises.

[e] Regular public works' expenditures are allocated in the various major categories. No emergency public works' expenditure has been estimated.

The increase in money expenditure accounted for by the increase in the general level of prices (reductions in the value of money) can be roughly determined. If we make adjustments for changes in the value of money and take as our base the year 1939, we find that per capita public expenditures increased from about $25 in 1890 to $140 in 1940, instead of from $14 to $141 in the absence of such adjustments.

Increases in population and expansion of the physical area served by government obviously would raise total public expenditure. This factor need not bring about an increase in per capita expenditures, however.

The growth of per capita public expenditures due to the increasing needs of a more complex society shows up in an expansion in such functions as the provision of a higher level of public education, the growth of a network of public highways, and the provision of increased levels of public welfare and assistance as well as in an expansion in the proportion of the population re-

[6] Except for estimates of interest on the national debt all of these estimates are based upon those made by Kimmel and associates (see Lewis H. Kimmel *et al.*, *Postwar Fiscal Requirements*, Washington, D. C.: Brookings Institution, 1945. Our estimates are 25 per cent higher than those made by Kimmel because of our assumption that the general level of prices will be 25 per cent above the 1943-1944 level. Interest payments are largely independent of the general level of prices.

ceiving such assistance. This latter factor became particularly important as the Federal government attempted to combat depression and to care for victims of depression during the thirties.

Increased urbanization is, in itself, a factor raising public expenditure. It brings an expansion in such expenditures as those for protection of life and property. Some services provided by the household in rural areas can no longer be efficiently provided on that same basis in the cities; for example, each city family cannot provide its own water and adequately arrange for its own sewage disposal.

War has been most important of all in pushing public expenditure upward. The channeling of about one half of our national product into the fighting of World War II is a recent vivid experience. Maintenance of our peacetime military establishment and paying for some of war's consequences—servicing war debts and paying military pensions and medical care, for example—are expected to account for about three fourths of total Federal expenditures during the next five years.

The main directions which public expenditure has taken since the turn of the century are shown in Table 5.

Public Expenditures Before 1930

Up to the depression of 1930, the public economy was concentrating on the provision of a highway network, on the construction and staffing of an expanding educational plant, on meeting costs of protection which were swollen by World War I, on broadening social welfare services within the local level (expansion of Federal expenditures in this area was to come in the following decade), and on expanding public service enterprises—particularly the postal system and local public utilities.

Even in 1929, however, public enterprise represented only about 1.8 per cent of gross national product. Except in scattered cases, there was little concern over the encroachment of state on private enterprise. The general impression left by analysis of the changes which took place between 1900 and 1930 is that of a public economy rather intensively developing two accepted public functions—highways and education—and assuming protection costs made necessary by participation in World War I. Stresses and strains which brought about changes in the expenditure pattern during the thirties had not yet developed.

TABLE 5

Governmental Expenditures for Selected Activities, 1902-1941
(in millions of dollars)

Type of Expenditure	1902[b]	1913[b]	1929[b]	1941[a]
Highways...................	$182	$426	$1,936	$1,693
Education...................	282	565	2,490	2,579
Public Assistance and Welfare.	170	342	1,360	5,677
Protection[c].................	410	628	1,947	7,462
Public Enterprises...........	199	489	1,461	4,100

[a] The series for 1941, plus the Protection series for the entire period, is one which the writers developed. For derivation and content, see Appendix B. It should be noted that in Table 5 the item for public enterprises in 1941 includes all cost payments of government corporations and enterprises, whereas in earlier years, the data are for government enterprises only.

[b] For the years prior to 1941, heavy reliance has been placed on the data given in *Fiscal Policy and Business Cycles*, Table X, page 121, by Alvin H. Hansen by permission of W. W. Norton & Company, Inc., New York. Copyright 1941 by the publishers. Using the same primary sources as given by Dr. Hansen, the writers found the same general trends in expenditures which his table shows. They also found it difficult to secure the exact amounts given for the items in his table, except in a few instances. Since there is reason to believe that Dr. Hansen had more complete access to the agencies which classified the data, and since the trends which his data reveal agree with those found by the writers, it has been decided to use the figures given by Hansen for these earlier years. (Excluding the Protection series, which has been developed independently, as indicated above.)

[c] Protection costs in the entire period covered by the table were derived as follows: (1) 1902: National military establishment, from *Wealth, Public Debt and Taxation*, 1913; military pensions, fiscal 1903, from *Statistical Abstract, 1938*; state and local expenditures, from *Wealth, Debt and Taxation, 1902-1903*, page 976. (2) 1913: National military, *Wealth, Public Debt and Taxation, 1913*, military pensions, *Statistical Abstract, 1938*; state and local expenditures, *Wealth, Public Debt and Taxation, 1913*, also partly estimated (3) 1929; National military, *Combined Statement of Receipts and Expenditures of the U. S. Treasury, 1929*; military pensions, *Statistical Abstract 1938*; state and local, partly from *Financial Statistics of States, 1929*, partly estimated for local governments. (4) 1941: the writers used the figure given in *Financing Federal, State, and Local Governments, 1941*, Table 16. All publications are United States government publications.

In 1929 the relative importance of the Federal government in the public economy was less than in 1890 (See Table 3, Chapter I), Federal expenditure as a percentage of total public expenditure having declined from 36 to 26 per cent.

Public Expenditure After 1930

An entirely different picture is presented by developments between 1929 and 1941. While expenditures for highways and education were not very different in 1941 than in 1929, the other three categories of expenditure—public assistance and welfare, protection, and public enterprises—show tremendous increases. This increase was greatest in the field of protection, for the Federal government had already embarked on the national defense program, followed soon after by war itself. As late as 1940, however, the two classes of expenditure that had jumped most since 1929 were public assistance and welfare and public enterprises.

Federal government and unemployment relief. Expansion in governmental expenditures for public assistance and welfare and for public enterprises represented attempts by government to encourage recovery from the depression and provide greater assistance for the millions suffering from depression. Efforts to encourage recovery and to broaden the base for support of public assistance services soon came to center in the Federal government.

During the decade of the thirties financial responsibility for unemployment relief and assistance was assumed by the Federal government for the first time in United States history. From January 1933 to July 1941 total Federal contributions to various direct and work relief measures were over 18 billion dollars.[7] In 1941 alone, the Federal government provided 2.1 billions of the 3 billion dollars spent for relief and assistance.

Expansion in social security. During the period 1929-1941 the Federal government also embarked on a huge social security program, symbolized by the Social Security Act of 1935. This act set up special payroll taxes and expenditure provisions for old-age retirement and unemployment insurance.[8] At the same time the Federal government inaugurated a system of social welfare grants for old-age assistance, aid to dependent children, and aid to the blind. These represented expansion in transfer payments rather than governmental use of resources (refer to page 32 ff. in this chapter). Such grants were made to the states, conditional upon each state providing funds equal to those provided by the Fed-

[7] Expenditures of state-local governments are not readily available. For the period January, 1933, through June, 1938, a WPA progress report estimates contribution of Federal and of state-local governments to all forms of aid and assistance programs at 11.1 and 4.2 billion dollars, respectively. This would make the state-local share about 27 per cent. A 1942 WPA progress report places state-local contributions at 21.6 per cent of a grand total of 12.6 billion dollars expenditure for WPA work since its beginning in (calendar) 1935.

[8] Separate unemployment insurance systems are actually set up and operated by each state, under the supervision of the Social Security Board. Moreover, railroad contributions for retirement and unemployment insurance are administered by the Federal government under separate acts.

eral government. Other Federal agencies made miscellaneous grants to the states for health and welfare programs. In 1941 total social security payments by the Federal government (including all payments to the states) were 1.09 billion dollars. These payments will tend to rise with the increase in payments of old-age insurance from the relatively modest amount of 186 million dollars in 1941 to an expected level of about 1 billion dollars in the middle 1950's. It is expected that total social security payments will probably increase to about 2 billion dollars, even if the present system of insurance and benefit grants is not expanded.

The rise of the government corporation. One of the devices used by the national government in its economic programs of the thirties was the creation of a large number of government corporations and credit agencies. Important among these were the Reconstruction Finance Corporation, the Home Owners' Loan Corporation, the Federal Farm Mortgage Corporation, the Commodity Credit Corporation, and the Tennessee Valley Authority.

Some of these corporations, such as the RFC, HOLC, and FFMC, were designed primarily to help salvage distressed homeowners, farmers, railroads, banks, and other economic units from the depression. In effect, public credit was being extended at a time when private credit was not readily available. Other corporations, such as the TVA and the Rural Electrification Administration, were designed to accomplish such functions as developing river valleys and extending electricity to farmers.

In World War II the government corporation was widely used as a device for encouraging expansion in the output of some commodities badly needed in the war effort. The Defense Plants Corporation administered the expenditure of many billions of dollars for public construction of war plants when the risks appeared so great to private enterprise that it did not wish to undertake such construction. The Rubber Development Corporation was charged with developing a domestic synthetic-rubber industry.

Experience with government corporations as means for doing specific jobs rapidly and efficiently has been rather favorable. However, before the war, public administrators were urging absorption of these corporations within the major departments of the Federal government in order to coordinate and prevent overlapping of functions.[9]   Public administration experts had not agreed that the government corporation should be continued: its future is still uncertain.

· Expansion of public construction.   During the latter 1920's public construction had been but one-fifth to one-fourth of the total of public and private construction (10 to 11 billion dollars annually).   Total new construction fell to a low of 2.5 billion dollars in 1933 and rose to 7.1 billions in 1939, the last year substantially unaffected by the defense- and war-construction period.   Public construction, which had accounted for only 17.3 per cent of the total of 10.3 billion dollars of new construction in 1929, was 50 per cent of the total of 7.1 billions in 1939. In the early years of the 1930's, however, the most that can be said for public construction is that it did not fall as rapidly as did total new construction.   Total new construction fell 75.7 per cent from 1929 to 1933 while public construction was falling 45.8 per cent in the same period.   Nor did public construction pick up very rapidly in the years from 1933 to 1935, when it was supposed to be a major factor in stimulating recovery.   In 1935 only 1.9 billion dollars were spent for public construction.[10]

Federal funds accounted for only 13 per cent of expenditures for public construction in 1929.   But 74.7 per cent of expenditures for public construction in 1936 was Federal expenditure. Even in 1940 when state and local governments had increased their revenues, Federal spending for construction represented 45.6 per cent of the total of public construction expenditure.[11]

The bulk of the increased Federal spending was in the form of grants to state and local units and in WPA spending.   The latter has not been counted in the above estimates.

Prior to the depression of the thirties, highways, public buildings and schools bulked large in the total of public construction.

[9] Report of the President's Committee on Administrative Management, January, 1937.

[10] The use of increased or decreased public investment as a technique of fiscal policy is discussed in Chapter VI, pages 92-103.   Public construction has been a major type of public investment.

The above data are from The Survey of Current Business, June, 1943.   Data are published currently in the Survey.   The amounts spent for construction under work relief agencies are included in final construction figures.   The figures above include expenditures for work relief construction.

[11] These data are from the Construction Analysis Unit of the Works Project Administration.   They exclude defense construction, WPA spending and Federal loans which must be repaid subsequently from state and local funds.

In the late thirties, construction of facilities for waterpower and irrigation had become of greater importance, and there was some public expenditure for residential construction. Highways and educational plants had declined as an outlet for governmental construction expenditure.

Wartime construction activity for the economy as a whole centered largely in the Federal government. Construction of war plants and facilities by the Federal government from 1941 through 1943 dominated total construction during these years. In this three-year period 32.4 billion dollars were spent on new construction (exclusive of work relief), of which public construction (mostly military and industrial) accounted for 22.7 billion dollars, or about 70 per cent.[12]

Increased importance of transfer payments. Since 1929 transfer payments have become increasingly important items of governmental expenditure. Such payments are not for goods, services, or securities and consequently do not involve a net transfer of resources or funds from the private economy to the public economy.

The growth of transfers has been largely tied to the entrance of the Federal government into the field of relief and social security and to the growth of the Federal debt.[13] The bulk of governmental payments to agriculture can be considered as a transfer.

A little more than 2 billion dollars of governmental expenditure in 1929 can be considered as a transfer. In 1941 nearly 5 billion dollars of Federal expenditure and about 1 billion of state and local expenditure fell into this category. Thus about one fifth of expenditures of government in 1929 and about one third in 1941 consisted of transfer payments.

Changes in state and local expenditures. The relative decline of the importance of state and local expenditure in the total of government expenditure since 1930 has already been mentioned.

---

[12] Source: *The Survey of Current Business,* June, 1943, and April, 1944.

[13] There is not complete agreement as to exactly what constitutes a transfer payment. The Department of Commerce has considered only pensions, relief, food stamps, veterans' bonuses, and social insurance payments as transfers. (See *The Survey of Current Business,* April, 1944, page 9.) Hicks and Hart also include interest on the Federal debt. (See J. R. Hicks and A. G. Hart, *The Social Framework of the American Economy,* pages 180 and 182-185, New York: Oxford University Press, 1945.) We have included government payments to farmers on the grounds that farmers did not surrender any goods, services, or titles to goods and services in return for these payments.

TABLE 6[14]

Transfer Payments by the Federal Government in 1941
(in billions of dollars)

1. "Official" transfer payment series:
    a. Pensions and relief.................................... $1.4
    b. Food stamps and veterans' bonus....................   0.1
    c. Social insurance payments...........................   0.9
                                                            _____
                                                            $2.5[a]
2. Government payments to farmers.............................   0.6
3. Interest on public debt...................................   1.9
                                                            _____
                                                            $5.0

[a] Does not represent an exact total of three preceding items, due to rounding.

With the exception of expansion in expenditures for protection, the greatest expansion in public expenditures from 1900 to 1930 centered in the state and local governments. The expenditures of these units of government made up 68.4 per cent of total government expenditure in 1903 and 73.9 per cent in 1929. State and local governments, particularly during the twenties, were feverishly building highways and increasing expenditures for education.

During the depression, however, expenditures of local governments from their own funds dropped from their peak of 6.5 billion dollars in 1929 to a low of 4.6 billions in 1935 and stood at about 5.6 billion dollars in 1941. Although state governments' expenditures rose rather consistently during the depression, the Federal government was making nearly half of total public expenditure in 1940.

Some of the functions performed by local governments were aided financially by the Federal government or the states. This was particularly true in the field of public assistance and welfare. Federal funds came to local areas largely through work relief or direct relief, although social security payments and Federal and state aids for construction also contributed. The local governments were spending more for welfare in the thirties than in the twenties, but they were spending less for education and for highways. State and Federal funds had come to the aid of local government in these areas.

[14] Sources: "Official" series is that used by the Department of Commerce and published in *The Survey of Current Business*, April, 1944, page 9. Government payments are from the *BAE*, "Farm Income Situation." Interest on public debt is from Bureau of the Census, *Financing Governments 1941*, page 74.

State expenditures showed a surprising relative increase during the thirties: they jumped from 2 billion dollars in 1929 to 4.6 billion dollars in 1941. Part of the increase was in the form of larger transfers of state funds to local governments. These transfers rose from 650 million dollars in 1928 to 1,709 millions in 1941. They were primarily for education, highways, public assistance and welfare. Much of the remaining increase in state expenditure went to launch the state portion of the welfare and social security programs set up in the 1930's and to provide additional state funds for state highways and state-operated educational institutions.

CHANGES IN TAXATION

Since the turn of the century, noticeable changes have taken place in our tax system. (1) The amount of tax revenue collected has increased very markedly. In 1902 about 1.4 billion dollars were collected in taxes by all units of government—Federal, state and local. The wartime tax systems of all governmental units raised more than 50 billion dollars in 1944, and we expect to collect around 40-45 billion dollars annually during the period up to 1950. (2) The kinds of taxes utilized have changed greatly in their relative importance as sources of revenue. In 1902 state and local governments relied primarily upon property taxes while Federal tax revenues came largely from taxes on commodities, particularly imported goods, liquor and tobacco. Although the property tax has remained the pillar of local tax systems, its relative importance in the tax structure has declined greatly. The income tax has become the principal source of Federal tax revenue.

Increases in the Amount of Tax Revenues

Even though the growth in tax collections has not kept pace with the growth in public expenditure, particularly during the last two wars and the depression of the thirties, the trend in tax revenues has followed rather closely the trend in public spending.

Tax revenues, for all units of government, rose from 1.4 billion dollars in 1902 to more than 9 billion dollars in 1920. The level of tax collections during the twenties averaged about three and one-half times the level during the decade prior to our entry into World War I. Although tax revenues fell off slightly in the early part of the depression, by 1936 they had reached a new high, and during World War II total annual tax collections passed the 50 billion dollar mark.

Taxes have increased rather steadily at all levels of government. Local governments collected during the thirties about 2 and one-half times as much in tax revenues as they collected during the second decade of this century. State tax collections rose fivefold between these same periods. Federal tax collections have shown the most variability, rising markedly during the two war periods and falling off sharply during the forepart of the depression.

Changes in the Character of Taxation

The principal changes which have taken place in the character of taxation are (1) the rise of the progressive personal-income tax, (2) the increase in business taxation, (3) the emergence of special-benefit taxes of fiscal importance for financing highways and more recently for financing unemployment and retirement benefits, (4) the extension of commodity taxation at the state and Federal levels, (5) an expansion in property tax revenues but a fall in the relative importance of the property tax accompanied by a growing resistance to the tax itself and to the methods employed in administering it, (6) increasing acceptance of death and gift taxes, and (7) increasing use of the same sources of tax revenue by more than one unit of government.

The rise of progressive personal-income taxation. Personal income taxation was the most important single source of government tax revenue in 1944, accounting for nearly 19 billion dollars (about two-fifths) of the 50 billions of taxes collected from all sources. Although it was employed by 33 states, the personal income tax was collected principally by the Federal government.

The personal income tax was incorporated into the Federal tax system in 1913 when the 16th Amendment to the Constitution was adopted.[15] From the date when the first Federal law was enacted, Federal taxes on personal incomes have had a progressive rate structure. The rate of taxation has been higher on large incomes than on small ones. Personal exemptions granted by the Federal laws have been relatively high, however. As late as 1940, less than 4,500,000 individuals paid a Federal tax on their

[15] Personal income taxation was used by the Federal government in 1861-1872.

1939 incomes. Changes during the war period, after 1939, converted the Federal tax into a "mass" tax which reached close to 50,000,000 individuals on their 1944 incomes. The changes were a combination of reduction in personal exemptions, increases in rates, and shift toward a current collection basis, all during a period when national income more than doubled.[16]

Although 33 states tax personal incomes, the relative importance of this kind of taxation at the state level is small. In 1945 less than 10 per cent of state tax revenue consisted of personal income taxes.

The personal income tax could play a very important role in fiscal policy designed to combat inequality and unemployment. If personal exemptions are retained and progressive tax rates employed, the personal income tax probably will be the best working approximation to what is called "ability to pay" in taxation. Its more complete shift at the Federal level to current collection[17] would make relatively easy the gearing of tax collections to changes in the flow of income. By appropriate reductions or increases in tax rates, the Federal income tax could be used to fight deflationary or inflationary forces as they arise.

Development of business taxation. Of greatest importance among business taxes is the corporate income tax. The foundation for corporate income taxation was firmly established in

[16] Personal exemptions for a married couple without dependents, for example, dropped from $2,500 on 1939 net income to $1,000 in 1943. A more detailed account of the changes is given in Chapters XIII and XIV.

[17] A lag of slightly more than one month can be involved between payment of most wage and salary income and payment of Federal taxes withheld on such income. For taxes on incomes not withheld at the source—incomes of self-employed businessmen (except farmers, who are given especially favorable treatment) and for nonfarm income from such sources as interest, dividends, rents, and royalties—quarterly estimates of income to be received during the current year are necessary. Taxes due (if any) on the basis of these estimates are payable in quarterly installments. Such estimates may be revised quarterly during the year. Under the existing "current collection" system, farmers are not required to make even an initial estimate of annual net income until January 15, at which time annual taxes due, if any, are subject to payment. All taxpayers have a subsequent opportunity for determination of final tax liability for the year by submitting their annual tax returns by March 15 of the following year. The lags still present are much shorter than under the tax collection system in effect up until 1943. Until that time, no tax return on the income of the preceding year was required until March 15 of the following year, and tax liability, if any, could be discharged by quarterly payments through December 15 of the year following income receipt. A more complete description of changes in the tax collection process will be given in subsequent chapters on Personal Income Taxation.

1909 by the Federal tax of one per cent levied on the net incomes of corporations.

Since the inception of the tax, the tax rate has been gradually increased until in 1942, it reached 40 per cent for corporations with net incomes above $50,000.[18]   During both World Wars, there have been heavy excess-profits taxes in addition to the regular corporate income tax.   In World War II the excess-profits tax rate was 95 per cent, although an over-all ceiling of 80 per cent was established as the most of corporate net income that could be taken by Federal taxes on income and profits.[19] The excess-profits tax was repealed, effective December 31, 1945.

The states followed the Federal government into the field of general corporation-income taxation.   Within ten years after Wisconsin's tax of 1911, seven other states enacted corporate income taxes.   During the thirties the burst of state tax activity expanded the taxation of corporation income until, in 1944, 33 states used the tax.   In 1944, however, the aggregate of all state taxes on corporation income was only slightly in excess of 0.4 billion dollars, as compared with Federal collections of 5.3 billions, and of 14.8 billions if Federal excess-profits taxes are included.

Business taxes, other than taxation of corporate income, are also employed, particularly by the states.   Public utilities, insurance companies, banks, and railroads are among the forms of business upon which the states have levied taxes.   The amounts of revenue obtained from such taxes have been relatively unimportant, however.

Emergence of special-benefit taxation.   Students of finance have long recognized a category of taxes which they have labeled special-benefit taxes.   Special assessments on such public improvements as streets, sidewalks, street lights, sewers, and the like have fallen into this class.   But until the coming of highway and payroll taxes, special-benefit taxes have never been very important in the public economy.   This is to be expected, for taxes are usually defined as "compulsory payments to a government for

[18] For corporations with lower net income, the rate began at 25 per cent and increased toward 40 per cent as the net income increased.   These rates were slightly reduced in the Revenue Act of 1945.

[19] There were a few other Federal taxes on corporations which were in effect in 1945, but quantitatively they were unimportant.

the purpose of promoting the welfare of the public in general," [20] and taxes to pay for special services or benefits approximate prices to cover costs rather than collections to underwrite general welfare.

If one accepts the point of view that such taxes approximate charges for special services, nearly all special state taxes on motor vehicles (particularly motor fuel and vehicle licenses) constitute special-benefit taxes.[21] Their origin was a result of the growing demand for better highways, and they have been used principally to construct, maintain, and police the highway system. State motor vehicle revenues, which were so small in 1915 as not to merit a separate (Census) classification, were 1,452 million dollars in (calendar) 1941[22] and, except in a few states, were distributed almost entirely for highway purposes. In the aggregate, 85 per cent of state highway revenues were used for highway purposes.

Payroll taxes, unused prior to 1934, amounted to 1,902 million dollars in 1941. Ultimately they will be paid back in special unemployment or retirement benefits to workers who have made some contribution in the form of such taxes.

There has been some pressure to put social security payroll deductions outside the tax category and to consider them in the same class as insurance premiums. In view of the fact that such payments are not voluntary and that the benefits could be financed from other sources, it seems reasonable to consider them as taxes (see Chapter III).

Nearly all of state highway and all of payroll taxes are essentially "consumption taxes" in that a large number of individuals pay such taxes, and the bulk of the expenditure of these individuals is for consumption.[23] Consequently, it is reasonable to include these taxes as consumption taxes—as some economists

[20] Bureau of the Census, *State Finances, 1942,* page 92.

[21] Federal taxes on motor vehicles and motor fuels may reasonably be excluded from the special-benefit category. There is no conclusive evidence that their collection has had any direct tie-up with appropriations for Federal aid to state or local highways.

[22] Source: *Public Roads,* Vol. 23, No. 6 (October–December, 1943), page 140.

[23] Of the various payroll taxes contributions for unemployment insurance are set up to be totally paid by the employers. Part of the costs of old-age insurance supposedly is supported by employees. It appears likely, however, that the employers' contributions to payroll taxes ultimately rest in large part on the workers (see Chapter XII).

have done[24]—rather than as special-benefit taxes. Such taxes, however, are also the closest important approximation to special-benefit taxation in our current tax system.

Expansion of taxes on goods and services. State taxes on business and Federal and state taxes on the sale of goods and services have undergone a notable expansion since 1900. At the turn of the century and until 1914, the Federal government relied for almost all its tax revenue on revenues from customs duties and internal excises on the sale of liquor and tobacco. Internal excises jumped during World War I, but tapered off in the twenties. By 1930 tobacco was the chief source of excise revenue: taxes on tobacco brought amounts of revenue to the Federal government from taxation of commodities exceeded only by customs (taxes on imports).

The depression reduced Federal tax revenues very markedly. In the year 1932 they fell below 2 billion dollars for the first year since 1917. In an attempt to boost Federal tax collections, the Revenue Act of 1932 imposed a variety of internal taxes on goods and services. Beginning in 1933, the repeal of the 18th Amendment brought about the restoration and extension of liquor taxes. This burst of tax activity came at a time when it might have been reasonable for the government to reduce taxes instead of increasing them, if the over-all objective was to strengthen markets. Additional Federal taxation of goods and services came with the national defense program of 1940 and our subsequent participation in World War II. Nearly 5 billion dollars of tax revenue was collected by Federal taxes on goods and services in 1944. This was nearly twice the amount collected in 1941 and more than four times the collections in 1930.

Accompanying the depression sales-tax activity of the Federal government was an increase in state sales taxes. Taxes were levied on alcoholic beverages in all 48 states upon repeal of the 18th Amendment. In 1944, 25 states used some form of general

---

[24] Payroll taxes, for workers covered, are levied only on incomes less than $3,000 per year in size. The United States Treasury estimated that only 12 per cent of 1944 income receivers had an income exceeding $3,000. The National Resources Planning Committee study of *Consumer Expenditure in the United States, 1935-36*, page 20, indicates that there was, on the average, no net saving by a family until its income exceeded $1,250 per year, and that only 11.6 per cent of income was saved when income reached $3,000 per year.

sales tax. State revenues from sales taxes in 1944 were nearly twice as great as in 1935.

Developments in the taxation of property. Between 1902 and 1930 revenue from property taxes increased about sevenfold. The depression of the thirties reduced property values, increased property tax delinquency, and resulted in a fall in revenues. In 1944, the year in which total tax revenues were at their peak, property taxes yielded about 4.6 billion dollars as compared with 5 billion dollars in 1930.

Property taxation has never been a source of revenue for the Federal government. Its importance as a source of revenue for state governments fell off markedly during the last forty years with the imposition of motor vehicle taxes and with the growth of sales and income taxes after 1930. It raised less than five per cent of state government revenue in 1946. The property tax remains the almost exclusive tax source for local governments, yielding nearly 92 per cent of their total tax revenues in 1941.[25] As long as local tax sources are used to finance local governmental functions, the property tax probably will continue to be the principal local tax. It is one of the few taxes which can be successfully levied and collected by local units.

The property tax does not remain in the tax system without resistance, however.[26] For example, lack of correspondence between property taxes and ability to pay has created continuous pressure for revising assessment techniques. It is generally considered desirable to make over-all assessments respond more quickly to changes in the general level of production and employment and to reduce variations in assessed values of properties with comparable earning power. Rapid growth in state and Federal aids to local governments, financed largely by other than property taxes,[27] is also evidence of resistance to property taxes.

Increase in death taxes. The idea that taxes should be levied upon the transfer of property at death had been accepted by 27 states as early as 1903. By 1913, 35 states were levying such taxes. After previous experiments, death taxation became a

[25] Derived from U. S. Department of Commerce, *Financing Federal, State, and Local Government, 1941*, Table 5, page 22.

[26] The tendency for the property tax to decline as a source of state government revenue has already been noted.

[27] Brief reference to this development is made later in this chapter. Intergovernmental fiscal relationships are discussed in the last section of the book.

permanent part of the Federal tax system in 1916.   To encourage
all of the states to utilize this form of taxation, the Federal tax act
of 1924 permitted taxpayers to take a 25 per cent credit for death
taxes paid to the state; the credit was increased to 80 per cent (of
1926 rates) two years later.   The result was the extension of
death taxes to all of the states except Nevada.

Progression in the tax rates on taxable estates was accepted by
some states even before 1900.   It was adopted by the Federal
government in 1916 (rates ranged from 1 to 10 per cent).   Current Federal rates range from 3 per cent on the first $5,000 of
taxable estate to a maximum of 77 per cent on that part of a taxable estate in excess of $10,000,000.   All but four states have
progressive inheritance or estate taxes.[28]

Despite the wide use of progressive death taxes, and the apparent acceptance of the idea that it is a function of the state to
limit the accumulation of wealth by inheritance, death taxes have
never been an important source of revenue in the tax system.
Collections of 596 million dollars from death taxes in fiscal 1945 [29]
constituted a little over 1 per cent of the 50 billion dollars in
total taxes collected in that year.   Although tax rates are fairly
high, exemptions are also high and the loopholes for tax avoidance
are many.[30]   The Federal tax carried a specific exemption of
$60,000; state exemptions varied too widely to be summarized in
any detail here.   However, state exemptions frequently vary with
the degree of relationship of the heir to the deceased.   A common exemption for direct heirs (widows and children) is $10,000.
It will be pointed out in Chapter XVII that Federal exemptions
will have to be lowered drastically, and many available loopholes
must be removed before death and gift taxes can become an important source of tax revenue.

Increase in overlapping taxation.   During the present century
various units of government are increasingly tapping the same
sources of tax revenue.   At the beginning of the century, the
Federal government obtained most of its revenue from customs
duties and taxes on liquor and tobacco.   State and local governments both relied heavily on the property tax.   At present,

---

[28] An estate tax is levied upon the full amount of the net taxable estate: an
inheritance tax is levied upon shares received by various beneficiaries after allowance for permitted exemption.

[29] See *Treasury Bulletin*, December, 1946.

[30] "Death and Gift Taxation" will be examined in Chapter XVII.

property taxes are almost exclusively collected by local governments, having been virtually dropped by the states. Personal income taxes, commodity taxes, and payroll taxes have become important sources of revenue for the states as well as for the Federal government.

The states pioneered in effective taxation of personal income, beginning with Wisconsin in 1911. With the 16th Amendment, the Federal government entered the personal income tax field in 1913 and has since dominated it. Taxation of personal incomes is now used by 33 states, however.

The Federal government led the way in taxing corporate income. Corporate income taxes are now levied by 33 states.

Liquor and tobacco taxes have been important sources of Federal revenues during almost all of our history. All the states are now taxing liquor and 30 states tax tobacco products. Until 1932 the taxation of motor fuel was considered to be reserved for the states. Since that year, however, motor fuel taxation has been an important source of Federal tax revenue.

Payroll taxes are collected in 48 states, and death taxes are

TABLE 7[31]

Important Overlapping and Nonoverlapping Taxes
in the 1941 Tax Structure

(in millions of dollars)

Overlapping Taxes by Type	Yield in Millions		Total
	Federal	State-Local	
1. Corporate income	$2,053	$192	$2,244
2. Payroll	993	906	1,899
3. Individual income	1,418	226	1,644
4. Motor fuel	343	920	1,263
5. Alcoholic beverages	820	308	1,128
6. Tobacco products	698	107	805
7. Death and gift	407	118	525
Nonoverlapping Taxes by Type			
1. Property	—	4,492	4,492
2. General sales	—	641	641
3. Motor vehicles licenses	negligible	439	439
4. Insurance taxes	—	98	98
5. Customs	392	—	392

[31] Sources: *Financing Federal, State and Local Governments, 1941,* page 22; "State Revenue in 1941," *Financial Statistics of States: 1941,* Census release of May, 1943.

levied in 47 states: both of these classes of taxes are also employed by the Federal government.

The Federal government is the only unit constitutionally empowered to levy import (customs) duties. It has not invaded the sacred territory of the states and local governments in general property taxation, general sales taxes, motor vehicle licenses, and taxation of such businesses as insurance companies.

Considerable reduction in the administrative costs of collecting these overlapping taxes could be achieved through greater coordination of Federal, state and local tax systems. Such economies could be brought about through one unit collecting a tax, allocating portions of collections to the other units, and all units sharing collection costs. There is considerable merit in separating partially the collection of tax revenues from the spending of funds. The units of government which are best qualified to administer certain governmental functions are not necessarily the units best qualified to collect the funds.

CHANGES IN THE ROLE OF THE PUBLIC DEBT

Since the turn of the century important changes have taken place in our governmental debt structure: (1) There has been an almost continuous increase in the public debt. (2) During the period 1940-1946, Federal debt obligations became the principal asset of the banking system. The result has been a tremendous increase in the money supply, an increase which poses difficult problems for central banking and for fiscal policy in the future.

Growth of the Public Debt

Between 1902—the first year for which rather complete data on public debt are available[32]—and 1916, the public debt rose from 2.8 billion dollars to 5.8 billions. The Federal government borrowed heavily during World War I, and by the end of 1919 the total debt of all units of government had reached a peak of 31 billion dollars of which 25.6 billions were Federal debt.

During the twenties the Federal debt was gradually reduced, standing at 15.4 billion dollars at the end of 1930. State and local governments were increasing their debt, however, primarily to finance roads and schools. The increase in state and local debt

[32] R. B. Bangs, "Public and Private Debt in the United States, 1916-1942," *The Survey of Current Business*, May, 1943, pages 22-25.

virtually offset the reduction in Federal debt, total public debt in 1930 being 30.1 billion dollars—a reduction of less than 1 billion dollars from the 1919 peak.

In the decade of the thirties, the Federal debt rose by about 20 billion dollars, as the Federal government employed borrowing as the technique for filling the gap between its expanded expenditure program and its tax revenues. Meanwhile, the expansion in state and local debt virtually ceased.

World War II has been responsible for the bulk (nearly four-fifths) of the increase in the public debt. From the end of 1940 until the end of 1945, the total public debt rose by about 225 billions. Tax collections at the Federal level during the war were equal to about one-half of Federal expenditure. The deficit was financed entirely by borrowing from individuals and from banks and other businesses.

Public Debt and the Banking System[33]

Of more economic significance than the increase in the debt itself is the relatively large proportion of Federal debt now held by the banking system. From June 30, 1940, to December 31, 1945, the banks (excluding Federal Reserve Banks) increased their aggregate holdings of government securities by 79 billion dollars, total deposits increasing by only 10 billion more than this amount. During the same period, the Federal Reserve Banks' holdings of such securities rose from around 2.5 billion dollars to more than 24.2 billion dollars. At the end of the calendar year 1945, holdings of United States government bonds in commercial and mutual savings banks represented more than 70 per cent of total bank loans and investments. In 1930, holdings of government securities made up only 6.6 per cent of banks' total loans and investments. Although this percentage increased steadily during the depression, the big gain came during the war.

The long-run implications of this increase in bank holdings of public debt and the associated increase in the money supply cannot be forecasted accurately. It appears relatively certain, however, that effective control of inflation will be hampered by these developments. The increased supply of money is probably "semi-permanent"—that is, it is reasonable to expect that no

[33] The term "banking system" refers to the aggregate of United States banks excluding Federal Reserve Banks.

marked reduction in the supply of money will be accomplished in the next 10 years. Since banks hold largely short-term securities and such securities make up a large part (55 per cent) of total bank assets, banks should have little trouble in meeting their commitments to depositors in the event of an increased demand for cash. Unless there is continued willingness to hold this larger money supply, pressures on prices will be tremendous. The heavy bank holdings of Federal debt may make it very difficult to lessen some of this increased money supply. One way of accomplishing such a reduction would be by issuance of securities which are not readily convertible into money and which consequently would bear higher interest rates than the average of 2 per cent now borne by Federal debt. However, the possible depreciation in the value of bank assets which might result from such a procedure seems likely to eliminate it from serious consideration.[34]

INTERGOVERNMENTAL FISCAL RELATIONSHIPS [35]

"Fiscal compartmentalization"—each governmental unit raising funds to finance the services which it renders—has been gradually breaking down during the last half century. There has been increasing recognition that functions performed by one local government or state may markedly affect other local governments or states. The idea that there could be a division of labor between collecting funds and administering services has become more generally accepted. This has meant a trend toward (1) performance of services by those units óf government where performance can be most efficient and (2) collection of revenues by the units which are best suited to collect them efficiently. Although we have a long way to go before this division of labor is complete, some progress has been made since the beginning of the century.

The recognition of interrelationships between functions performed by different units of government has led to a broadening of the base for financing and administering many of these functions. Only 35 years ago the township was the important unit for financing and administering rural roads. Today, highways

[34] See Chapter V and Chapter XXII.
[35] The final section of this book is devoted to a more complete discussion of this subject.

are jointly financed and administered by the Federal, state, and local governments. In many states the township as a unit for highway finance and administration has completely disappeared. A similar development has taken place in public school finance and administration. State aid to local school districts now represents more than one-third of public school costs. The Federal government and the states have assumed joint responsibility in unemployment relief.

Collection of funds is centering more and more in the higher levels of government, particularly in the Federal government. Funds collected by the larger units are being distributed to smaller units. In 1902 the states made available to local governments only 75.8 million dollars; by 1944 this had increased to 1,795 millions. (This sum was made available for specific functions and through the sharing of taxes.) In 1915 Federal grants to the states amounted to only 5.4 million dollars; in 1944, Federal grants to lower units of government (primarily states) totaled 850 millions. In addition, the Federal government expended 10 billions through WPA in the 8 years, 1935-1942. Nearly all of this was for state and local projects.

Two ways of viewing public expenditures. A study made by the Census Bureau for the year 1941,[36] the results of which are summarized for our purposes in Table 8, indicates that governmental expenditures may be viewed in two ways—by looking at the units which collect the funds or at the units which finally spend these funds. The difference for any one level of government, which is the net transfer of government funds,[37] cancels out when all units are considered.

Federal expenditures from Federal sources made up 57 per cent of all government payments in 1941; state expenditures from state sources made up 20 per cent and local expenditures from local sources constituted 22 per cent. After fund transfers are considered, Federal expenditures made up 53 per cent of the

[36] *Financing Federal, State, and Local Governments, 1941.*
[37] The Table reproduces the complete figures on intergovernmental transfer of funds, which are somewhat larger than intergovernmental grants and shared taxes. This is because the complete figures include loans and payments for debt service as well as outright grants of funds. Thus, the transfer of local funds to the state and Federal governments cover funds to repay loans, pay interest and retire debt, or contribute to state pension funds for retirement of public employees, to mention the most important special cases. These transfers are necessary for a complete accounting of funds, but they are not fiscal aid in the usual sense.

TABLE 8[38]

The Intergovernmental Flow of Funds, 1941

(in millions of dollars)

Expenditure Classification	Unit of Government				
	Local	Federal	State	Territorial	Total
I. Expenditure from own sources........	$5,562	$13,878	$4,837	$154	$24,431
II. Intergovernmental Transfer of Funds...					
A. Funds Paid......	100	905	1,751	—	2,757
B. Funds Received..	1,883	36	818	19	2,757
Net Transfer.....	$1,783	$ −869	$−933	$ 19	0
III. Expenditure for own purposes.......	$7,344	$13,009	$3,904	$172	$24,431

total, state expenditures shrank to 16 per cent, while expenditures for local purposes rose to 30 per cent of the national aggregate. Territorial payments were below 1 per cent under either view of expenditure. Despite their rather rapid development, intergovernmental transfers were still only 11.3 per cent of all government expenditure in 1941, and only 15.5 per cent of all civil government expenditures.

Summary

Important among the changes which have taken place in public finance since the turn of the century are the increase in public expenditures and in taxes, the change in the character of both expenditures and taxes, the growth of the public debt and the heavy holdings of this debt by the banking system, and the increasing separation of the collecting of funds and the spending of these funds.

In spite of the seemingly revolutionary character of these changes, they have not kept pace with the ideas relating to the way in which public finance should be conducted. Tax flexibility as a technique for combating inflation has been only partially utilized, and tax increases rather than decreases were attempted during the depression. Many taxes do not conform to the ac-

[38] See Census Study, page 54. Columns do not necessarily add to totals, due to rounding. The total of 24,431 billion dollars above is decreased by 203 million—unspecified fiscal aid from Federal and state to local governments.

cepted ideal of ability to pay and have few other characteristics to recommend them. Increasing public debt paradoxically has been utilized to fight both depression and inflation and has been rather unsuccessful in accomplishing either task. Intergovernmental fiscal relations are still based largely on the theory that government is like business and that there are no checks on the expenditure of a unit of government except the limitations upon taxes which can be collected by that unit.

This lack of conformity between practices and ideas is to be expected. It is the primary reason for our writing this book. Ideas are "models"; their applicability is unproven. But the practices are real; even though these practices are imperfect, people believe that they know what to expect from them. Their expectations about new practices are more uncertain. Part of our job is to reduce this uncertainty.

SELECTED READINGS

1. Bangs, R. B., "Public and Private Debt in the United States, 1916-42," *The Survey of Current Business*, May, 1943.
2. Bowman, Mary Jean and Bach, George Leland, *Economic Analysis and Public Policy*, Chapters 46-49, New York: Prentice-Hall, Inc., 1943.
3. Hansen, Alvin, *Fiscal Policy and Business Cycles*, Chapters VII and VIII, New York: W. W. Norton & Co., Inc., 1941.
4. Hicks, J. R. and Hart, Albert G., *The Social Framework of the American Economy*, Chapters 11-16, New York: The Oxford University Press, 1945.
5. Kimmel, Lewis H., *et al.*, *Postwar Fiscal Requirements*, Washington, D. C.: Brookings Institution, 1945.
6. Lange, Oscar, *et al.*, *On the Economic Theory of Socialism*, Minneapolis: The University of Minnesota Press, 1938.
7. National Industrial Conference Board, *Economic Almanac, 1944-45*, New York: National Industrial Conference Board, 1944.
8. National Resources Planning Committee, *Consumer Expenditure in the United States, 1935-36*, Washington, D. C.: United States Government Printing Office, 1938.

9. Pigou, A. C., *A Study in Public Finance*, London: Macmillan & Co., Ltd., 1928.

10. Shultz, William J. and Caine, M. R., *Financial Development in the United States*, New York: Prentice-Hall, Inc., 1937. (Sections on history of Federal, state, and local finances.)

11. Simons, Henry C., "A Positive Program for Laissez Faire," Chicago: University of Chicago Press, *Public Policy Pamphlet No. 15*, 1935.

12. United States Department of Commerce, Bureau of the Census, *Financial Statistics of States, 1929*, Washington, D. C.: United States Government Printing Office, 1930.

13. United States Department of Commerce, Bureau of the Census, *Financing Federal, State, and Local Expenditures, 1941*, Washington, D. C.: United States Government Printing Office, 1942.

14. United States Department of Commerce, Bureau of the Census, *State Revenue in 1941*, Washington, D. C.: United States Government Printing Office, May, 1943.

15. United States Department of Commerce, Bureau of the Census, *Statistical Abstract of the United States, 1938 and 1943.*

16. United States Department of Commerce, *The Survey of Current Business*, March, 1942, April, 1943, June, 1943, April, 1944, Washington, D. C.: United States Government Printing Office.

17. United States Department of Commerce, Bureau of the Census, *Wealth, Debt and Taxation, 1902-1903* and *Wealth, Public Debt and Taxation, 1913*, Washington, D. C.: United States Government Printing Office.

PART TWO

PUBLIC FINANCE AND
FULL EMPLOYMENT

CHAPTER III

THE MONETARY FRAMEWORK OF
THE PUBLIC ECONOMY

IN THE first chapter of this book we indicated that nearly everyone considers a high level of production and employment to be an important objective of economic policy. We also suggested that the ways in which a government collects and spends money strongly influence the level of production and employment within the economy. In this chapter, we will point out some of the relationships between fiscal activities and employment. Chapters III through VIII of the book will be devoted to a discussion of some of the possibilities and limitations of fiscal policy in encouraging a high level of production and employment and to analysis of alternative fiscal policies.

Markets and Employment

A high level of production and employment is near the top of our list of objectives of economic policy. But most United States citizens are not willing to sacrifice everything else in order to achieve this objective. In particular, we in the United States seem to want full employment provided largely through private enterprises. If it is possible to achieve full employment in this way, we want the area in which government acts as producer and employer restricted to that in which government can produce more effectively than private producers.[1] This restriction prompts us to look to monetary-fiscal activities as techniques for promoting full employment. Such activities can directly affect the amounts of money which people do or do not have available to spend. At the same time they need not greatly alter the role of government as producer and employer.

In an economy where production is organized and conducted largely by private producers, these producers buy resources, use

[1] Refer to Chapter IX which deals with the proper scope for governmental expenditure and use of resources.

them in producing goods and services, and sell these goods and services to other economic units—to consumers or to other producers. The amounts of resources that producers utilize depend partially upon the amounts of goods and services they expect to sell profitably at various prices. Employment depends upon markets, the volume of sales, as well as upon incentives, the rate of profit.[2]

For example, the operator of a shoe factory buys leather, nails, cloth, and other materials used in making shoes. He leases machines to cut the leather and stitch and tack the shoes together; and he employs labor to operate the machines, keep accounts, and help market the product. If he expects to sell 500,000 pairs of shoes at a given price during a given year, he will utilize about twice as much material and employ about twice as much labor (prices of these resources remaining the same) as he would if he expected to sell only 250,000 pairs of shoes. The amounts of resources that he is willing to buy or hire depend upon the amounts of product that he thinks can be sold at various prices— upon the expected demand for his product.

Markets and Spending Power

Markets obviously depend upon the expenditures of buyers. Markets are weak when buyers are spending relatively little, and markets are strong when buyers are spending heavily. In the period 1929-1932, when national income fell from a high of 83 billion dollars to about 44 billion, markets progressively weakened. Buyers spent progressively less. In 1941-1944, when national income rose from about 93 billion dollars to more than 150 billion, markets were becoming stronger. Buyers were trying to buy heavily. Like a strong wind which seemingly plucks withered leaves from a dormant tree, a strong market whisks away goods and services about as rapidly as they are produced.

A strong market for goods and services as a whole does not mean that there will be a "sellers'" market for every commodity.

---

[2] Important determinants of the level of output and the amounts of resources utilized by a given firm are (1) expected demand conditions for products, (2) expected supply conditions for resources, and (3) expected rates of conversions of resources into products. Markets describe only expected product demand conditions. Discussion of markets as a determinant of the volume of output makes sense only if it is assumed that the supply schedules for resources and the rates of conversion are given.

The quantities of various commodities that buyers take from the market at given prices depend upon buyers' preferences for various goods and services as well as upon buyers' spending power and willingness to spend. The market for shoes may weaken because buyers believe that they do not need as many shoes as they have been buying. More of their expenditure may be directed toward other commodities. A problem of unemployment in the shoe industry may arise. It could be solved by moving resources out of shoe production and into production of these other goods and services. In practice, however, solution of this problem may require special measures to help retrain workers and to assist them in moving into other lines of production.

The market for shoes may weaken also because consumers' total spending power or their willingness to spend has declined. Unemployment in the shoe industry cannot then be solved by shifting men and materials into other industries. Other opportunities for using the unemployed resources of the shoe industry are not likely to exist. The market for nearly all goods and services has weakened. This contraction of markets as a whole is the problem of depression. Its opposite is inflation. Depression and inflation are problems which monetary-fiscal policy can help solve through exerting appropriate effects upon spending power.

Determinants of spending power. Spending power—the amounts of money which a buyer has available to spend—depends upon (1) the buyer's current money income and (2) his holdings of money and things that can be converted into money. If his current income is increasing, a buyer can spend more heavily and still not change his cash holdings or be forced to sell his car, his barn, or a bond. If his current income is falling, a buyer can maintain his spending only by digging deeper into his holdings of money or by selling some asset.

Current incomes, however, are determined by current spending. In fact, income and expenditure are merely two different ways of looking at the same thing. Items of your money receipts constitute items of expenditure to some other economic units—to your employer and the renter of your property, for example. Your money expenditures represent money receipts to your butcher, barber, carpenter, and doctor. Other peoples' expenditures determine your income; and your spending helps to determine their incomes.

Thus, a person cannot increase his money receipts unless some other person is willing to increase his money expenditures. If the person whose income has fallen wishes to maintain his spending by selling an asset and is one of a few such persons in the economy, he may be able to get a satisfactory price for this asset. However, an individual seller may find himself in the midst of a mass liquidation, as in 1931-1933. The price which he gets will be relatively low. He may not be able to keep up his spending by selling his assets.

In any closed economic system,[3] the sum of the expenditures of all of the economic units within the system is always exactly equal to the sum of the receipts of all of the economic units within the system. The receipts and expenditures of any economic unit need not be equivalent. But for the economy as a whole, income and expenditure are opposite sides of the same thing; the expenditures of one unit are the incomes of other units. If total expenditure in the economy falls off, total income declines exactly as does expenditure, for the two are always equal.[4]

Many people consider this phenomenon—"spending power is dependent upon spending"—as an illusion. Certainly the individual does not always find that if he spends more he has more to spend. Although other people's receipts will be increased, they may not spend more for his goods or services. Our personal experiences may mislead us when we try to apply them to the economy as a whole. What is true for the individual is not always true for the economic system. For the aggregate of economic units comprising the economic system, the more that is

[3] A *closed economic system* may be defined as an economy in which there are neither outgoing or incoming payments. For purposes of this discussion, however, an economy in which outgoing money payments and incoming money payments are equal is equivalent to a closed economic system. Although the writers recognize that international as well as domestic factors are important in the United States economy, discussion in this book will be confined to domestic economic transactions. The importance for international trade of successful, domestic full-employment policies has recently been stressed by a number of writers, among them, Alvin Hansen, *America's Role in the World Economy*, New York: W. W. Norton & Co., Inc., 1945.

[4] The assertion that income and expenditure are equivalent in no way suggests the factors that are responsible for variations in the level of expenditure (and income). Some of these factors, non-monetary as well as monetary, will be discussed in subsequent chapters, particularly Chapters IV and V.

spent the larger will be current total money income and the more there will be for the aggregate of economic units to spend.

Willingness to spend. Spending power alone, however, is not sufficient to determine the level of expenditure. A change in an economic unit's current income does not mean that there will be an equivalent change in its current expenditure. The volume of spending depends partially upon what is available to spend; but it also depends upon whether that which is available is spent. It depends upon what is done with current income and with holdings of money accumulated during earlier time periods, for willingness to spend is important.

Assume that the total quantity of money in the economy is fixed. Economic units that try to build up their holdings of money will reduce their spending. Money income obviously will decline for the other units whose income is the expenditure of the units which are trying to build up their cash holdings. And, unless these units whose incomes have fallen are willing to spend as much as before, the incomes of other units to whom they make payments will decrease. Money expenditures and money incomes for the economy as a whole will fall off.

Similarly, if economic units try to let their current money expenditures exceed their current money receipts—to reduce their holdings of money—their money expenditures must increase. The other units whose incomes are the expenditures of these units whose expenditures have been increased will find their incomes are increased.

Unless the quantity of money in the economic system is increased, money holdings for the economy as a whole obviously cannot be increased. Some units can hold more money, but others will have to hold less. A general attempt to increase money holdings will result only in reduced money expenditures and money income.

Similarly, the total of money holdings for the economy as a whole cannot be reduced unless there is a reduction in the quantity of money. Some units can hold less money, but others will have to hold more. A general attempt to reduce money holdings will result in an increase in money expenditure rather than a reduction in the total amount of money held.

If the quantity of money is expanded as economic units try to build up their holdings of money, the attempt to build up cash

balances need not result in a reduction in money expenditure.
There will be more money to hold and as much to spend. Or,
if the quantity of money is contracted as people try to reduce
their holdings of money, the attempt to diminish ·cash balances[5]
need not result in an increase in money expenditure.   There will
be less to hold or less to spend.

Variations in the money supply.   Changes in the level of expenditure, however, are accentuated by a monetary system which
tends to reduce the amount of money in the economy when
people wish to build up their holdings of money, and which increases the quantity of money when people wish to spend more
of it.

Bank deposits have been the major element of money in our
economy.   Under our banking system, the banks as a group (not
an individual bank acting "out of step" with the rest of the banks)
may vary the quantity of bank deposits by expanding or contracting bank loans and investments.   The banks are not required to
hold as a reserve against deposits one dollar of currency for each
dollar of deposits.   Nor are the banks required to keep a constant
ratio between reserves and deposits.   The reserve requirements
establish only a minimum ratio.   The smaller the reserve ratio
required, the greater the potential expansion or contraction in
bank deposits.

Expansion in bank credit has almost always accompanied an
increase in the level of expenditure and in the price level, while
contraction has usually accompanied a fall in expenditure and in
the general level of prices.[6]

Money income and real income.   The changes in money income

[5] An alternative way of presenting the concept of changes in the willingness of
economic units to hold money (or to spend money) is by use of the concept
"velocity of circulation."   An increase in willingness to *spend* money is an increase in velocity of circulation; an increase in willingness to *hold* money is a
decrease in velocity of circulation.   See Irving Fisher and H. G. Brown, *The
Purchasing Power of Money,* The Macmillan Co. (new edition), 1911, and A. C.
Pigou, "The Value of Money," *Quarterly Journal of Economics,* 32:38-65
(November, 1917).

[6] On October 4, 1929, the total of bank loans in the United States was about
42.2 billion dollars.   By December 30, 1933, the total of bank loans had fallen
to around 22.0 billion—a decline of nearly 50 per cent.   Deposits fell by about
one-third (16.7 billion) during the same period.

Between December 31, 1941 and December 31, 1945, bank loans increased by
only about 14 per cent (3.8 billion dollars).   Demand deposits, however, rose
from 44.3 billion on December 31, 1941 to 105.9 billion on December 31, 1945.

Banks greatly increased their investments in government securities rather than
their loans to individuals in the latter period.   The importance of the banking
system for monetary-fiscal policy is examined in Chapter V.

(and expenditure) which we have been discussing may not seem very important. It is real income—the stream of goods and services—rather than money income—the flow of money—which is considered significant by most people. A heavenly shower of new money which quadrupled the money holdings of every economic unit would be very unlikely to quadruple the production of goods and services within the economy.

Yet, as we have already suggested, changes in money expenditure may exert an important influence upon the size of real income. If an individual's money income is expanded, he will be able (and may be willing) to spend more money than he would have otherwise spent for goods and services. These increased expenditures are increased receipts to the sellers of goods and services. Their production schedules are less likely to be cut and may be stepped up. If so, there will be fewer workers discharged, and workers' expenditures for goods and services will be larger since their incomes will continue to be forthcoming. A major contraction in the real income of the economy may then be discouraged.

When there is full employment, however, the stream of real income cannot be expanded except by improved technology or by improved use of resources. Unless it is accompanied by such changes, an augmented stream of money expenditure will serve only to increase prices.

Government and Markets

Government, like other economic units, collects money, spends money, stores money, and—unlike other economic units (except for banks and counterfeiters)—issues money. These monetary activities of government affect the money receipts and money disbursements of other economic units. For example, the salaries of government employees, veterans' pensions, interest payments, payments for materials, the repayment of government debt, and the like go to make up the money expenditures of government. But, to other economic units, these represent money receipts. On the other hand, tax collections and the proceeds from the sale of goods and services which it produces, or securities which it issues, represent money receipts to government. To other economic units, these items represent money disbursements.

Although all of these governmental fiscal transactions alter the money receipts and money expenditures of other economic units, some of them affect the *net worth* of businesses and households while others alter only the liquidity position—*the composition of the assets*—held by these units. For example, tax collections diminish the net worth of the taxpayer. The government takes money from him and need not provide anything in return except a tax receipt. Interest payments and social security benefits increase the net worth of the recipients of these payments. The receivers have more money and no less of other things.

Government purchases or sales of securities or goods and services, however, do not change the net worth of the economic units making exchanges with the government. If government purchases a $100 bond from an individual, he will have $100 more in money. But the value of the bonds he holds will fall by $100. Similarly, if an individual purchases a government bond for $100, he will have $100 less cash; but he will have additional securities worth $100. Government purchases of securities from nonbanking economic units, or sales of securities to these units alter the composition of the assets of these units. Their net worth, however, will be unchanged.

We may speak of governmental fiscal transactions which alter the net worth of other economic units as *transactions on income account*. Government fiscal transactions affecting the composition of assets held by other economic units but not affecting net worth we may call *transactions on capital account*.

Both transactions on income account and transactions on capital account are likely to affect money expenditures for goods and services by economic units. Both kinds of transactions affect the amount of money at the disposal of economic units other than government. Transactions on income account leave these units either richer or poorer than they were before. For example, an income tax reduces both the liquidity of the taxpayer and his net worth. It is to be expected that he will be less eager (as well as less able) to spend after the tax was paid than he was before. Transactions on capital account do not change net worth, but affect liquidity.[7] Such transactions may make economic units

[7] The *liquidity* of an asset may be defined in terms of its nearness or ease of conversion (without loss or gain) to money. Thus currency, by definition, is the most liquid of assets; demand deposits approximate currency in liquidity; short-term government bonds are only slightly less liquid than demand deposits; specialized machinery is rather illiquid; and so forth.

feel richer or poorer than they were before.   Although the value of a farmer's assets is not changed when he sells a cow, the farmer is more likely to spend after the sale than before.   Similarly, after the sale of a bond, an individual is likely to spend more for goods and services than he did when he was holding the security.

A given governmental transaction on income account is likely to have a greater effect upon the money expenditure of other economic units than would a transaction of the same size on capital account.   But both kinds of transactions can be used to influence the expenditures of other economic units.   Increased wartime taxation curbed private spending by making individuals and businesses poorer than they otherwise would have been. Government sales of war bonds to individuals could reduce private spending by making private economic units less liquid.

Receipts and expenditures of the public economy.   The influence which governmental fiscal activities exert upon the level of money expenditure within the economy depends upon the *amounts* of money collected and spent by government and upon the *ways* in which government collects and expends this money.

Imagine that the quantity of money in the economy is fixed. If, during a given period of time, the money receipts of government exceed its money expenditures, government will have built up its cash balance.   The aggregate money expenditure of other units, however, must have been greater than the aggregate of their money receipts.   Not every other unit need have spent more than it received.   But the total of the expenditures of other units must have been greater than the total of their receipts. And the amount of the difference will be exactly equal to the amount by which the money receipts of government have exceeded its expenditure.

On the other hand, if the expenditures of government over a given period of time are greater than its receipts, government will have paid out more than it has taken in.   And the aggregate of other units will have taken in more than they have paid out. They will have accumulated additional funds exactly equal to the excess of government payments over government receipts.   The sum of the expenditures of government and other units, always must be identical with the sum of the receipts of government and other units.

The picture of the expenditures and receipts of the public and private economies in the last quarter of 1945 illustrates this identity of expenditure and income for the economy as a whole. The deficit of government was exactly equal to the surplus of the private economy. The sum of expenditures for all economic units—government, consumers, and businesses—was exactly equal to the sum of the receipts for all economic units. These relationships are portrayed in Table 9.

TABLE 9[8]

The Nation's Budget for the Last Quarter of (calendar) 1945

Economic Unit	Annual Gross Income (in billions of dollars)		Annual Gross Expenditure (in billions of dollars)		Income minus Expenditure (in billions of dollars)	
Government........		35		58		−23
Federal..........	25		50		−25	
State and Local...	10		8		+ 2	
Other Units........		151		128		+23
Consumers.......	140		112		+28	
Businesses[a]......	11		16		− 5	
(including for-						
eign income and						
expenditure)						
All Units..........		186		186		0

[a] Business expenditure is for gross capital outlays while business income represents retained earnings and reserves. Hence, the business deficit does not represent an operating loss for business.

(1) *Sources of funds.* Government has but two sources of funds: (1) money already in its coffers (or made available through new money issues) and (2) money held by nongovernmental units.

With respect to the first source, it is the expenditure of funds rather than the obtaining of these funds that influences aggregate money expenditure within the economy. Government already has the money or can issue it. No transactions with other economic units need be made.[9]

[8] Data are from the *Federal Reserve Bulletin*, February, 1946, page 113, and are on the basis of an annual rate.

[9] Direct money issue can be used only by the Federal government. In recent years, the banks have been a major source for public funds, providing these funds through their purchases of government securities. Some aspects of government obtaining funds by having the banks extend credit were discussed in Chapter II and will be treated further in this chapter.

The second source of funds has been tapped by government through the well-established techniques of taxing and borrowing. This source includes (1) private funds which otherwise have been spent for goods and services and (2) private funds which otherwise would not have been expended.

If government taps funds which otherwise would be spent, the result is a decrease in the cash balance of nongovernmental units and in their expenditure for goods and services. But only cash balances are reduced if government takes away funds which otherwise would not have been spent.

However, as we have indicated previously, the way in which a source is tapped, as well as the kind of source, may be important in determining what happens to money expenditure. Draining away a given amount of money by taxing is likely to reduce expenditure by a greater amount than would draining away the same amount by borrowing. As has been indicated earlier in this chapter, taxation affects both the cash balance and the net worth of the taxpayer. Borrowing affects only cash balances. One kind of asset (securities) is substituted for another kind of asset (money) in the individual's balance sheet. Nearly every tax taps both funds which would have been expended as well as funds which would not have been spent. Some taxes, however, draw more heavily than others upon funds which would have been spent. Progressive income and inheritance taxes, for example, are less likely to draw upon funds which would have been spent than are sales taxes. Progressive income and inheritance taxes are likely to affect more the unused cash balances of higher-income groups. Sales taxes are more likely to cut the cash balances of people who will try to reduce their expenditures for goods and services in order to rebuild their cash holdings. This aspect of taxation will be discussed further in Chapter XI.

(2) *Expenditure of funds.* Government expenditure may affect the income position and asset structure of an economic unit receiving the money in two ways: (1) it may add to the cash balance and the net worth of the unit, or (2) it may add to the cash balance and alter only the composition of the assets rather than the net worth of the unit. We have called transactions of the first kind, "transactions on income account," while transactions of the second kind are labeled "transactions on capital account."

When government makes such payments as wages and salaries, veterans' pensions, or unemployment benefits, it is adding to the cash balances of the recipients. They, however, are giving up no asset in return for this money. Their total assets have increased.

When government buys a bond or some commodity from a business or an individual, that economic unit's increased cash balance is offset by a reduction in the amount of bonds or commodities it holds.

Whether government expenditure adds to the total money expenditure of the economic units receiving the money depends upon the reactions of these units to increases in their cash holdings. Some may not increase their spending, while others may spend all of the additional cash. An increased cash balance, if accompanied by no change in other assets, is likely to bring about a greater increase in money expenditure than an equivalent increase offset by a reduction in other assets.

Ways of influencing markets. Without altering its role as producer and employer, government has several ways of influencing markets.[10] Its influence can be exerted by way of government operations which affect the cash balances of the other economic units in the economic system. These operations can be conducted within the framework of the government budget.[11]

If necessary, the government can inject money into the econ-

[10] Total expenditure for goods and services within the economy may be divided among (1) private expenditure for consumption goods, (2) private expenditure for investment goods, (3) government expenditure for consumption goods, and (4) government expenditures for investment goods. Of these four groups, (3) and (4) may be considered as "policy variables," i.e., variables that can be changed directly by government. Changes in them may have indirect effects upon private expenditures for consumption and investment goods. However, other lines of government action can also indirectly influence private expenditure, particularly upon consumption goods. Counter-cyclical action designed primarily to influence private investment is, in our estimate, not practicable. Decisions with respect to private investment are based upon long-run considerations. Modifications in the tax system may encourage private investment in the long run, although such modifications do not assure continuous full employment. Flexible fiscal policy designed to influence markets must be largely short run and thus cannot be expected to act directly upon private expenditures for investment goods. Private investment is likely to be more stable, however, if consumption markets are kept strong.

[11] For purposes of this exposition, the term "government budget" replaces "Federal budget," but it is recognized that only the Federal government, operating over almost the entire United States economy, is in position to adopt policies which consciously look toward modifying the level of expenditure (and income) in the economy as a whole.

omy by letting its current payments to economic units exceed the amount of money which is paid to it by economic units. The difference between government's current money expenditures and its current money collections from other economic units can be accounted for by reductions in the government's holdings of money;[12] or new money can be issued.[13]

This action permits other economic units to build up their holdings of money, for the total of their current money receipts exceeds the total of their current money expenditures exactly by the amount of the government's deficit. Thus, if other economic units are reducing their expenditure for goods and services in attempts to build up their relative holdings of money, the government's action permits them to increase their stocks of money without decreasing their expenditure.

By the reverse procedure—collecting more money from other economic units than it pays to them—the government can drain money out of the economic system.[14] The total of the expenditures of other economic units then exceeds the total of their receipts; and the size of this deficit will exactly equal the excess of government's receipts over government's expenditures.

Monetary-fiscal policy. There are a number of activities of government which involve collecting or spending money and which could be directed toward influencing the aggregate money expenditure of the economy for goods and services. Some of these activities—taxing, expending money for the goods and services used by government, and incurring and repaying debt, for example—are conducted within the framework of the Federal budget. Such funds as those collected by taxing and borrowing are considered as budgetary receipts. Such funds as those expended to pay the salaries of civil servants, to provide pensions for war veterans, or to pay interest on the Federal debt, are considered as budgetary expenditures.

Other money-spending and money-collecting activities take place outside of the budgetary framework. For example, when the government buys gold, the money issued for such a purchase is not counted as a budgetary expenditure; or when the govern-

---

[12] The term "money" includes government deposits with banks.
[13] The additional money could be issued by the government or by the banks through an expansion in deposit credit extended to government.
[14] The assumption made here obviously is that there is no increase in the quantity of money, bank credit, and related items.

ment sells gold, the money received is not counted as a budgetary receipt. The Federal Reserve System, although not strictly a part of government,[15] buys and sells government securities. The receipts and expenditures involved in such activities are not counted as budgetary receipts and expenditures.

Fiscal activities may be defined as those which operate primarily upon the income accounts of private economic units. Taxation, for example, reduces the incomes of the private economic units from whom the taxes are collected. Government expenditures in salaries, pensions, or relief grants increase the incomes of the private units receiving the money from government. The policies which guide fiscal activities may be termed *fiscal policies.*

Monetary activities may be defined as those which operate primarily upon the capital accounts of private economic units. *Monetary policies* are the policies which guide such activities. Transactions within the framework of the government budget are primarily fiscal, but they have monetary aspects. Taxation and most kinds of government expenditure are within the budget and are fiscal transactions. Debt retirement is within the budget, although it may be properly called a monetary transaction. Government transactions outside the budget are primarily monetary. However, most social security transactions covering unemployment are fiscal transactions and are outside the budget.

In this book, we are dealing primarily with transactions within the budgetary framework. Because these cannot all be identified as fiscal, and because fiscal transactions have cumulative monetary effects (they affect liquidity as well as net worth), we shall usually be concerned with *monetary-fiscal activities,* and with *monetary-fiscal policies.*

Expansionary Effects of Government Receipts and Expenditures

It is commonly asserted that a dollar of government expenditure may increase by more than one dollar the total expenditure of the economy for goods and services, or that a dollar of government tax revenue may decrease total expenditure in the economy by more than a dollar. To get at the basis of these assertions

---

[15] Some of the relationships of the Federal Reserve System to the Treasury and to Congress are indicated in Chapter IV.

we need to describe in greater detail the assumptions which are made about the reactions of economic units to changes in their money incomes (or money outflows).

Private receipts and expenditures may have effects comparable to those brought about by government receipts and expenditures. An additional dollar expended by a consumer or a business may also increase total expenditure within the economy by more than a dollar. An additional dollar taken out of the flow of expenditure by a private business and used to build up its cash balance may decrease total expenditure in the economy by more than a dollar.

The total assets of any economic unit, whether it be a business or a consuming unit, consist of the stock of goods and claims to goods (including money) to which that unit has title. From this stock come the goods to be used; into this stock flows the income of the economic unit.

The stock may not only change in size but it may also change in composition. Out of a business's stock of materials comes that which is converted into final products. Out of the stock of final products come products which are exchanged for money. Out of the stock of money come funds to hire labor or to add to the stock of materials. The stock is like a vat filled from many taps and emptied by many drains. The size and composition of the contents of the vat are altered by changes in the rates of the various inflows and outflows.[16] The economic unit has some control over the nature of the vat's contents. If it wishes a relatively higher concentration of money, it may reduce the rate of money outflow or the rate of inflow of other assets. If it wishes a higher proportion of other assets, it may open wider the money drain and the tap carrying other assets which empty into the vat.

Imagine that government pays an additional dollar to an economic unit—a civil servant, a war veteran, a relief worker, or a building contractor. If the recipient chooses to spend a part of this dollar for goods and services, the money inflows of the units from which purchases are made also will be higher than they otherwise would have been. If these units, in turn, spend a part

[16] These analogies are similar to those of Irving Fisher. Refer to Irving Fisher, *Mathematical Investigations in the Theory of Value and Prices*, New Haven, Conn.: Yale University Press (reprint), 1926.

of their increased money incomes, the money incomes of other
units increase. At any stage in the process, the unit receiving
additional money income finds that the composition of its assets
has been altered. It will have in its vat relatively more money
and relatively less other assets. Unless the new mixture in the
vat contains just the preferred amount (or less than the preferred
amount) of money, the economic unit will try to exchange a part
of the money for other assets.[17]

The conclusion that a dollar of government expenditure results in an increase of more than one dollar in the total money expenditure (and income) within the economy is thus based on the
assumption that the recipient of this dollar does not choose to use
all of it to build up his cash balance. The smaller the proportion
of the increased money outflow which is used to build up the
cash holdings of each successive recipient, the greater the increase in expenditure within the economy as a whole. If there
are unemployed resources so that an expansion in the production
of goods and services is physically possible, the real income of the
economy may also be expanded. If no expansion in production
is possible, only money expenditures are enlarged. The goods
and services available will bring higher prices. But there will
be no more goods or services.

Similarly, the conclusion that a dollar of government tax revenue will reduce expenditure in the economy by more than one
dollar is based on the assumption that as money is drained away
from the taxpaying unit, this unit will try to regain money by
purchasing fewer other assets than it otherwise would have. It
may even try to sell other assets. If the taxpayer is satisfied
with the vat's contents after the dollar has been drained out, the
collection of a dollar in taxes does not decrease expenditure for
goods and services.

Government funds obtained by money issue have no net contracting effects, because such funds are not drained away from
other economic units and hence do not decrease their expenditure. Money issued by government but used only to build up

[17] Refer to K. E. Boulding, "A Liquidity Preference Theory of Market Prices,"
Economica (new series), XI, 42:55-63 (May, 1944). The assumption made
in the "Cambridge version" of the quantity theory of money is that a given percentage of income is held in cash. If this percentage was 20, then of each dollar
received from government, 80 cents would be spent. This assumption has been
modified in more recent theories dealing with the demand for money.

the government's cash balance has no expansionary effect because such funds do not get into the hands of other economic units.   If the government can secure its funds from individuals whose expenditures for goods and services do not decline as their cash balances are reduced, total expenditure within the economy is not contracted.   On the other hand, if individuals must contract their expenditure in order to secure funds to meet tax levies, expenditure within the economy is reduced.

CHAPTER IV

NON-MONETARY FACTORS INFLUENCING ECONOMIC STABILITY

Basic Assumptions of Fiscal Policy

THE assertion that governmental fiscal activities can aid in keeping the over-all level of production and employment within the economy at a high level rests upon two fundamental assumptions. First of all, it is assumed that governmental fiscal activities can encourage economic units to alter their total money expenditure for goods and services: to increase it as population grows, capital is accumulated, and technology is improved, or to diminish it if prices are rising too rapidly. Second, it is assumed that by influencing aggregate money expenditure within the economy, production and employment can be kept from falling to low levels, or the general level of prices can be kept from rising more rapidly than is considered desirable.

Influencing over-all money expenditure, however, may not be sufficient to encourage full employment and at the same time avoid inflation. Certain non-monetary factors may be important in bringing about fluctuations in demands for some kinds of goods and services. For example, variations in the rate of accumulation of capital goods may bring recurrent variations in demands for resources. Fiscal action may not be able to counter such variations without at the same time encouraging unemployment on the one hand or a marked increase in the general level of prices on the other.

Fiscal policies are designed to act primarily upon the total money demand for goods and services. They can help to assure that markets as a whole will always be strong. As a result, if the demand for one commodity declines there still can be adequate markets for other goods and services. Unemployment need not result from a deficiency in money demand. But monetary-fiscal action cannot insure that important impediments to the movement of resources will be removed. "Bottlenecks" may be imposed by policies followed by some groups in the economy. There is danger then that supplies (of labor, especially) will become inelastic before full employment is achieved. If this happens, attempts to bring about full employment through fiscal action will result only in inflation.

Long-Run Changes in Consumers' Preferences and in Technology

Of course, changes in consumers' taste and in methods of production bring about variations in demands for particular goods and services. The invention of the automobile reduced considerably the demand for horse-drawn vehicles; the safety-razor diminished the demand for barbers' services; the electric refrigerator outmoded the icebox. New processes are continuously replacing old ones, and new products are being substituted for old ones. Furthermore, the future relative importance of existing products may not always be the same as it is today. For example, per capita consumption of potatoes and cereals in the United States has been diminishing, while consumption of dairy products and fresh fruits and vegetables has been increasing.

These changes all bring about the need for "structural adjustments" [1]—changes in the pattern of production and the use of resources. Some of them may result in what frequently has been called "technological unemployment" in some lines of production. Monetary-fiscal policies cannot (and should not) keep industries from declining in relative importance. It is not desirable to try to stabilize relative prices by monetary-fiscal action. However, by assuring that markets as a whole remain strong, monetary-fiscal policies can ease the movement of resources from one line of production to another.

As long as these changes are not too rapid and there are no significant impediments to resource movement, these changes need not pose problems with which monetary-fiscal policy cannot cope.[2]

[1] See Allan G. B. Fisher, *Economic Progress and Social Security,* London: Macmillan & Co. Ltd., 1945.

[2] Some business cycle theories assume that uncertainties resulting from such factors as "waves" of technological innovations deter needed structural adjustments and full employment. Monetary-fiscal policy could reduce some uncertainties—those related to large movements in the general level of prices. However, this reduction in uncertainty might not be sufficient to prevent rather wide fluctuations in employment. See J. A. Schumpeter, *Business Cycles,* New York: McGraw-Hill Book Co., Inc., 1939.

Distortions in the Age Distribution of Capital [3]

There are some kinds of demand fluctuations, however, which present special problems. One of these grows out of certain peculiarities which may arise in the pattern of capital accumulation.

In building up stocks of goods of any kind, the rate of production of such goods must exceed the rate of consumption. During the periods in which the stockpiles are being built, demands for these goods are equal to current consumption plus additions to stocks. When the stockpiles have been built, however, demands for these goods will be equivalent only to demands for current consumption. Assuming that the size of the stockpile is kept fairly constant and that the rate of consumption is not increased sufficiently to equal the average rate of production which prevailed during the period in which stocks were accumulated, the rate of production must decline.

For example, during the early part of United States participation in World War II (1942 and 1943) production of war materials was at a level sufficient to cover combat losses, wear and tear, and obsolescence of materials, and also to equip the armed forces—to build up the stockpile. However, once the forces had been equipped, production was needed only to cover combat losses, wear and tear, and obsolescence. It was necessary only to keep the stockpile at a given size. After sufficient stockpiles of a number of items had been accumulated, there were "cutbacks" in production even though current drains on the material were not reduced.

Similar cutbacks in the peacetime economy may be experienced as a result of the "goods starvation" of the war period. During the next few years, demands will be high for such items as automobiles, houses, refrigerators, and radios. Consumers will buy to replenish equipment currently wearing out. But, in addition, there will be purchases to replace items which were worn during the war period and which would have been replenished had such goods been available. Once the purchases post-

[3] By the *age distribution of capital* we mean the percentages of a given kind of capital asset in each age group. For example, 20 per cent of the Ford cars on the road in 1950 might be less than one year old, 20 per cent might be between one and two years old, 18 per cent might be from two to three years old, 15 per cent might be from three to four years old, and so forth.

poned by the war have been made, demands for these goods will be primarily for current replacements. It seems likely that production of these items will then be cut back.

Demands fall off once the stockpile has been built. But replacement demands may contain recurrent "bulges" if the rate of accumulation has not been constant. For example, enough new houses might be constructed during the next five years to meet all housing demands. This would mean building the houses that otherwise would have been built during the war and constructing replacements for houses which will pass out of use during the next five years. After all of these houses have been built, however, the housing demand will consist only of replacements for houses currently wearing out, plus whatever new houses are needed to take care of the additional population. If the new houses built during the next five years are approximately alike in their length of service, a bulge in demand can appear when it comes time to replace them. Thus, bunching in outlays for durable goods follows from irregularity in the rate of accumulation of such goods.

Such fluctuations in demand, due primarily to distortions in the age distribution of capital (the stockpile of production agents and consumers' goods) are cataloged by economists under the acceleration principle.[4] The quantitative importance of these exaggerations is difficult to estimate. Some of the evidence available indicates that they are not the most strategic factors.[5] Such fluctuations in demand for some types of goods may be offset by opposing fluctuations in other types. There is considerable variability in the length of life of the individual items in a given pile of assets. For example, if a million homes are built in a single year, it is very unlikely that most of these will be replaced in the same year in the future.

The importance of the acceleration principle, in so far as monetary-fiscal activities are concerned, lies in the fact that if these fluctuations are of importance, they cannot be controlled to any

[4] Other kinds of factors which, like irregularities in the age distribution of capital, cause a bunching in demands for durable goods, are also termed "acceleration factors" in business cycle theory. See J. M. Clark, *Strategic Factors in Business Cycles*, New York: The Macmillan Company, 1934, and R. F. Harrod, *The Trade Cycle*, Oxford: The Clarendon Press, 1936.

[5] Refer to J. Tinbergen, *Business Cycles in the United States of America, 1919-1932*, Geneva, Switzerland: League of Nations, Economic Intelligence Service, 1939.

significant degree by monetary-fiscal policy. Stabilizing the aggregate level of expenditure in the economy would perhaps aid in reducing the variations in the rate of capital accumulation. Consumption expenditure and investment (capital goods) expenditure have been closely correlated in the past. However, actual control of the rates of capital accumulation would probably have to be inaugurated in order to get at the root of the difficulty. Political resistance to the initiation of such control probably would be very great.

Overaccumulation of Capital

A somewhat debated point among economists is the extent to which a reduced level of production and employment may grow out of the declining rate of return on investment as capital is accumulated. It is contended that the stocks of skyscrapers, swimming pools, railroads, houses, and perhaps even such durable consumers' goods as automobiles, radios, clothing, or canned foods may grow to be very large—so large that the rate of return from additional accumulation may be low relative to the rate of interest. Sufficient investment to keep production and employment at high levels cannot be maintained unless the government does the investing, although consumption might be increased to offset this decline.[6]

Many people question the validity of the basic assumption underlying this thesis.[7] They claim, for example, that our "requirements" for housing and other durable consumers' goods are far in excess any amounts we have ever produced. They point to the undeveloped areas of the world where the lack of capital is very apparent and to war-torn areas where much of the capital that was accumulated no longer exists.

These criticisms imply that, if there is to be a "day of judgment," it is very far in the future. Such criticisms appear to be valid, as far as the world as a whole is concerned. Nevertheless, in the United States capital accumulation has been rapid, and the ratio of capital to human resources is relatively large. Returns to

---

[6] See, for example, J. M. Keynes, *The General Theory of Employment, Interest and Money*, New York: Harcourt Brace & Co., 1936; K. E. Boulding, *The Economics of Peace*, New York: Prentice-Hall, Inc., 1945; and Alvin Hansen, *Fiscal Policy and Business Cycles*, New York: W. W. Norton & Co., Inc., 1942.

[7] Note George Terborgh, *The Bogey of Economic Maturity*, Chicago: Machinery and Allied Products Institute, 1945.

additional capital in this country cannot be expected to approximate those in a country where the ratio of human resources to capital resources is larger than in the United States.

An alternative to reduced production and employment, due to a declining rate of return on internal investment, is to decrease the rate of capital accumulation through increasing consumption. A number of techniques might be employed to achieve a higher level of consumption. One is to encourage increased consumption at all levels of income. Many of the techniques which have been suggested as practicable policies, however, rely largely upon expanding consumption in the lower-income brackets. Monetary-fiscal activities which tend to redistribute purchasing power, taking it from the higher-income groups and giving it to the lower ones, probably would help to raise the aggregate level of consumption for the economy as a whole. However, the idea that it is a good thing to redistribute income because of the favorable effects of redistribution upon employment may be a very difficult one to sell. Wherever possible, the issues of income distribution and full employment should be separated; each issue should be appraised on its own merits.

Another technique for encouraging full production and employment which has been advocated by some economists is to offset variations in private investment by public investment.[8] The advocates of this procedure contend that consumption expenditures cannot be increased sufficiently to take up the slack in production and employment resulting from declining private investment. They claim that such redistribution of income as is politically acceptable will not increase consumption enough to encourage full production and employment. They also argue that consumption patterns at given levels of income are slowly changed. Inducing individuals to consume a larger proportion of their incomes may be accomplished only with great difficulty and perhaps only by measures incompatible with some of our other social objectives.

It may be noted here that using governmental investment as an offset to private investment, even though such a technique may bring full employment, has several disadvantages. The area in which the government may make additional investment

[8] See, for example, Alvin Hansen, *Fiscal Policy and Business Cycles*, Chapter 11, and other writings by Hansen.

is one which is politically determined. Private businesses may consider some governmental investment as "unfair" competition. Policy makers have often insisted and may continue to insist that government investment be noncompetitive—that the government confine its investment activities to spheres where private businesses would not normally operate.[9]

Moreover, decisions with respect to governmental investment involve considerations other than the employment effects of these investments. The resources used by government to construct public works often might be used to produce goods and services generally considered more desirable than the public works—if we could get these resources employed. We should first look for ways to encourage employment of resources for producing these other commodities. If we do not, we may be resigning ourselves to a poorer allocation of resources in order to get full employment. If there are other ways of encouraging full employment, governmental investment as an offset to private investment should receive less emphasis as a major tool of fiscal policy.[10]

Monopoly Elements

It is almost universally recognized that monopoly elements tend to bring about a pattern of resource allocation inferior to that which would probably prevail under more competitive conditions. This is an important consideration, since one of the goals of social policy is to achieve maximum output from the available resources.

In addition, however, monopoly elements have been attacked in recent years because they do not reduce prices at times when

[9] This may not be a valid restriction to public investment, however. Refer to Chapter IX.

[10] An alternative to increased consumption or to a public investment policy taking up slack in private investment, is to encourage a higher and more stable level of private investment. Strengthening markets should help to encourage private investment. Such additional factors as tax considerations and low interest rates may also be of help. But, decisions with respect to the level of private investment are long-run decisions, while measures to counter *a particular* depression must be short run. Refer to Chapter III.

Relatively little consideration has been given to interest rates during recent years. Interest rates have been low, and empirical investigations indicate that changes in interest rates have been unimportant in affecting investment decisions. (See J. E. Meade and P. W. S. Andrews, "Summary of Replies to Questions on Effects of Interest Rates," *Oxford Economic Papers*, October, 1938; and T. F. Ebersole, "The Influence of Interest Rates," *Harvard Business Review*, Vol. 17.

it is believed that price reductions would help to increase employment. Some industrial monopolies, labor unions, and agricultural marketing organizations have, when demands for their goods or services were reduced, maintained prices. Some people have concluded that these producers and labor unions have not tried to maintain sales of their products or resources. It is frequently contended that total production in the economy would fall considerably less if prices could be reduced as easily as they can be increased.[11]

Price reductions not sufficient to assure recovery. As has been indicated by Lord Keynes[12] and more recently by Professors Lange,[13] Hicks,[14] and Boulding,[15] a price reduction may not always assure sales maintenance, and a reduction in money wages is not always the cure for unemployment. The demand for the commodity or service may be further reduced as a result of the price cut.

For example, if money wages are reduced, and the money income of employed workers falls,[16] it is very likely that the workers' money expenditures for goods and services will be reduced. Since the workers' money expenditures are the businessmen's money receipts, these receipts too, will fall. Employers may be no better off than they were before, and there may be no incentive for them to hire additional workers.

Reduction of wages can be expected to increase the equilibrium level of employment only if the willingness to spend money (and the money to spend) contracts proportionately less than the fall in money wages—in other words, if the demand schedule for labor shifts downward proportionately less than does the supply schedule. Reduction of prices can be expected to increase sales only if the total expenditure on the commodity diminishes pro-

---

[11] There are a number of proponents of this argument. A recent version of this contention is found in E. G. Nourse, *Price Making in a Democracy*, Washington, D. C.: The Brookings Institution, 1944.

[12] J. M. Keynes, *The General Theory of Employment, Interest and Money*, New York: Harcourt, Brace & Co., 1936.

[13] Oscar Lange, *Price Flexibility and Employment*, Bloomington, Indiana: Principia Press, 1945.

[14] J. R. Hicks, *Value and Capital*, London: Oxford University Press, 1939.

[15] K. E. Boulding, *The Economics of Peace*, New York: Prentice-Hall, Inc., 1945.

[16] The assumption made here is that there is no shift in the demand for labor until there is an anticipated increase in sales receipts.

portionately less than the decrease in prices.[17]   In other words, if people are willing to hold smaller cash balances as prices and their incomes are reduced, and if the monetary supply does not contract, an expansion in employment may result from a reduction in wages.   The same end might be achieved, however, if wages were not reduced and money was injected into the system so that money demands for goods and services were increased.

Monopoly elements probably have been overrated as factors responsible for drastic reductions in production and employment. There is little evidence that price or wage reductions would have helped very much in increasing employment during most depressions in the United States.   This is largely because the money supply was sharply reduced, and the uncertainty about future prices discouraged spending.   In fact, one might argue that much of what appears to be restrictionist activity may stem from attempts to take out insurance against depression.

Monopoly elements may encourage inflation.   This discussion should not be interpreted as a claim that monopoly does not interfere with full employment.   Monopoly elements may present important blocks to achieving full employment without marked price rises.   There is danger that, if there are important monopoly elements in the economy, the strong market situation which can be stimulated by monetary-fiscal policy may bring inflation instead of full employment.

Imagine that there are in the United States 6 million unemployed workers who are eager to work at existing money wages and have skills comparable to employed workers, but who cannot find employment.   The government begins injecting money into the economy in an effort to strengthen markets.   As a result of the government's action, people spend more money for goods and services.   Goods disappear more rapidly from the market.   Employment starts to pick up.

With this increase in the strength of markets, sellers have a choice.   They may sell about the same amounts as before, but at higher prices, or they may sell larger amounts at about the same prices.   If they choose the latter alternative, it is likely that

---

[17] Even though reducing money wages does not shift downward the real demand curve for the product, there may be no increase in employment in cases where the demand curve is "kinked."   This "kinked" demand schedule is one possible oligopolistic behavior pattern.   Refer to Oscar Lange, *Price Flexibility and Employment.*

fairly full employment can be reached without a marked increase in prices. However, if prices and wages are advanced about as much as markets are strengthened, the increase in employment may be choked before it matures into full employment. Then the government's action will bring only higher prices.

As we indicated in Chapter III, it is assumed that maintaining total money expenditure for the economy as a whole—at an amount which would purchase all of the goods and services produced under conditions of full production—will keep unemployment relatively low. The level of money expenditure needed to purchase the full-employment production depends, obviously, upon the level of prices. If prices increase, either the level of money expenditure must be increased or there must be unemployment.

The danger of getting full employment only if inflation accompanies it or of getting inflation instead of full employment must be met largely by techniques other than monetary-fiscal policy. Fiscal measures might include large excess-profits taxes to discourage price increases,[18] but excess-profits taxes may have undesirable effects upon private investment.[19] Other measures might include governmentally established rules for price and wage increases,[20] or perhaps even the establishment of price and wage ceilings by government. It may be necessary to utilize techniques which disperse economic power and thereby introduce a greater degree of competition into the economic system. Such measures as redefinition and vigorous prosecution of antitrust regulations, and legislation establishing more open membership in labor unions would be steps in this direction.

Techniques to assure that monetary-fiscal action will not bring inflation instead of full employment are of major importance. Much study needs to be devoted to them. All that has been attempted here is to present the problem—not to propose a solution to it.

[18] See, for example, Benjamin Higgins, "Postwar Tax Policy," *Canadian Journal of Economics and Political Science*, Vol. 9, No. 3 (August, 1943), pages 408-28.
[19] Refer to Chapter XV.
[20] See, for example, A. G. Hart's essay in *The Winning Plans in the Pabst Postwar Employment Awards*.

CHAPTER V

EXTRA-BUDGETARY POLICIES IN RELATION TO BUDGETARY POLICY

WE HAVE already pointed out that the Federal government could conduct its money-spending and money-collecting activities to encourage a high-total money expenditure upon the goods and services of the economy as a whole. Continued strong markets for goods and services constitute one of the conditions needed for full employment—unless government is to expand its role as employer through counter-depression measures. Government collection and expenditure of money also could be conducted in a way which would discourage inflation. However, monetary-fiscal measures cannot effectively fight inflation and unemployment at the same time. If inflation and unemployment threaten simultaneously, other measures—price fixing or direct government employment, for example—may have to supplement monetary-fiscal policy.

Most of the government's money-collecting and spending is conducted within the framework of the government budget. But other money-collecting and spending activities of government are carried on outside of the budget. In this book, we are primarily interested in actions which take place inside the budget. Nevertheless, it is advisable to examine further the activities outside the budget. Such activities—purchases and sales of some government securities through the Federal Reserve Banks, purchases and sales of commodities and management of the supply of bank credit through management of the banking system—also may have important effects upon total money expenditures for goods and services.

Until recent years, these operations outside of the budget generally have been looked upon as the proper way for the government to influence the quantity of money directly or through the central bank. (The Federal Reserve System acts as an approxi-

80

mation to a central bank in the United States.) The purchase and sale of a commodity—gold—has been employed to increase or diminish the quantity of money in countries with monetary structures erected on the gold standard. Sale of government securities to individuals and businesses was employed in many countries to help combat inflation during the last war. Many central banks, including our own, have utilized the buying and selling of securities to encourage expansion or contraction in bank loans and deposits.

In trying to achieve the objective of full production and employment or in trying to combat inflation, it may be that the government should rely upon extra-budgetary policies—that additions of money to the economic system or withdrawals of money from the system should be accomplished by activities outside the budget. In this chapter we will analyze the potential effectiveness of extra-budgetary activities as the principal means for encouraging full employment.

Open-Market Operations in Securities

When the government purchases securities from other economic units, it exchanges money for these securities. If the money used by the government to pay for these securities is taken from governmental cash balances otherwise unused, or if it is newly created money, the total money available for other economic units is increased. The purchase of securities is one way for the government to inject money into the economic system. Sales of securities by the government provide a way for the government to drain money out of the economic system.

As long as there is a considerable volume of outstanding debt held by individuals—and there is reason to believe that there will be for some time—purchases of Federal securities could be employed as an antideflationary device. Sales of new securities could be used as an anti-inflationary technique. Relative prices for commodities would be affected by security purchases and sales only to the extent that alterations in the rate of interest exert an impact upon these prices.

Limitations of open-market operations in securities. The limitations of this technique are partially limitations of any procedure which tries to stimulate or retard aggregate money expenditure by acting upon the composition of the assets held by economic units. Increasing or decreasing an economic unit's cash balance by a given amount does not mean that the expenditure of that unit for goods and services will be increased—particularly since the change in cash balances will be offset by an opposite change in securities holdings. Many of the economic units—banks, insurance companies, and some industrial corporations—which would purchase or sell the bulk of the securities are units which are likely to merely substitute securities for money (or *vice versa*) in their portfolios of assets. Their expenditures for goods and services might remain unchanged. The impacts upon production and employment or upon prices in the rest of the economy might be negligible.

A further limitation in using purchases and sales of government securities as a technique for injecting or withdrawing money may arise from the effects which such activities have upon interest rates. When the government sold securities, the prices of these securities probably would fall and the interest rate would rise. When the government purchased securities, the prices of these securities probably would rise and the interest rate would fall.

The function which the interest rate performs in the economy is not clearly understood. In periods of relatively high employment it may be an important determinant of that portion of the total product of the economy currently consumed. In other periods it may determine only the degree of substitution of securities for money. Interest rates may vary considerably without markedly influencing businessmen's decisions to expand or contract their enterprises.[1]

Although interest rates may not be important to businessmen, they may be rather important to banks. Increased interest rates would tend to restrict bank credit expansion. But increases in interest rates would also tend to reduce the value of fixed-interest securities. The value of fixed-interest securities is important to banks because a large proportion (nearly three-fourths) of total bank loans and investments consists of government securities. In a period during which government issuance and sale of securities might help curb inflation, rates of interest on these securities probably would have to be increased in order to get individuals and businesses to part with some of their money and

[1] Note the references in Chapter IV, page 76, footnote 10.

to hold more securities. Given the relatively large bank holdings of government securities, increasing interest rates might be a rather unpopular move.[2]

Fiscal operations may affect interest rates. With any given amount of securities available for economic units to hold, increasing or reducing the money supply by techniques other than government purchase or sale of securities would also influence securities prices. Increasing the money supply tends to increase the price of securities and reduce interest rates. Draining money away from the economy tends to reduce the prices of securities and increase interest rates. When the money supply is changed through government operations in securities, the effect upon the interest rate is double-edged. Government sales of securities increase interest rates by adding to the supplies of securities and subtracting from stocks of money. Government purchases of securities reduce interest rates by adding to stocks of money and diminishing stocks of securities.[3]

If government purchases of securities were to be used to stimulate a sizable increase in private spending for goods and services, the scale of these purchases might have to be very large. The resulting reduction in interest rates might be greater than is generally considered desirable. Or, government sales of securities on a scale sufficient to withdraw enough money to prevent in-

[2] The extent to which banks are made worse off as a result of increases in interest rates depends primarily upon the maturity dates of the securities they hold. If these securities are of short term, as are the securities held by most banks, increases in interest rates would permit banks to reinvest soon the proceeds of maturing issues and get higher returns. The reduction in prices of securities currently held would be small. For example, increasing the interest rate from 2 to 4 per cent would reduce by only 2 per cent the sale value of a security maturing in one year. Refer to Paul A. Samuelson, "The Effect of Interest Rate Increases on the Banking System," *American Economic Review*, XXXV, I:16-27 (March, 1945).

[3] If operations with commercial banks are included (as they really must be in a situation where these institutions hold about half the national debt), then the above statements are inadequate. For instance, if there is government sale of new securities to the banking system as well as to other purchasers, there will be an addition to the money supply by banks as well as a reduction in the supply due to purchases by nonbanking units. Government sale of *existing* securities held by some Federal agency, such as the Federal Reserve Banks, will indeed "mop up" claims to money held both by bank and nonbank groups. Conversely, government purchase of securities outstanding will increase claims to money (typically, bank deposits) of nonbanking groups and will improve the reserve position of the banks themselves. Effects of open market operations in outstanding securities by central banks on the liquid position of bank depositors and banks are a familiar part of modern banking theory.

flation might at the same time raise interest rates above the levels desired by policy makers.   In fact, while government is incurring a budget deficit or adding to the money supply by other techniques, it may be desirable for government agencies to sell securities to keep the interest rate from falling below a given level.   Or, while government agencies are reducing the money supply by other techniques, it might also buy securities in order to keep the interest rate from rising too much.

Banking Policy

During the first quarter of this century, many economists thought that by controlling the expansion and contraction of bank deposit credit through the operations of central banks it would be possible to control, within fairly narrow limits, either inflationary or deflationary movements.   Central bank policy was the center of discussion in monetary circles.

It is not difficult to see reasons for the concern with banking policy.   Demand deposits subject to check are the largest single element of what we call "money" in our economy.   On June 30, 1940 adjusted demand deposits of all United States banks totaled about 32 billion dollars, while the total amount of currency (coins and folding money) outside of the banks was approximately 7 billion.   On June 30, 1946 adjusted-demand deposits of all United States banks aggregated nearly 83 billion dollars, while currency outside of the banks totaled about 27 billion.[4]

Our banking system operates on a fractional reserve basis. Since there are no requirements that banks lend up to the point where they always have no excess reserves, the controls that the Federal Reserve System has had over the banking system have been primarily limitations upon the *expansion* of bank deposits. While the Federal Reserve System could—through open-market operations, changes in reserve requirements, rediscount rates, and other powers familiar to all students of money and banking —*encourage* banks to lend, it could not *force* them to lend.   The result has been marked expansions and contractions in the quantity of deposit credit extended by banks.   For the most part,

[4] These data are from the *Federal Reserve Bulletin*, February, 1947.   For further data on changes in bank deposits and currency during this period, see Chapter II.

these expansions and contractions have accentuated inflation and depression.[5]

The experience of the United States and of many European countries during the late twenties and the thirties has led most economists to abandon the position that inflationary and deflationary movements can be controlled, to any important extent, by banking policy alone. Suggestions have been made for strengthening controls over the banking system—the 100 per cent reserve proposal, for example. Requiring banks to hold one dollar of reserves for each dollar of deposits reduces the extent to which banks can expand and contract the money supply. It will not, however, eliminate, or perhaps even reduce, variations in the willingness to hold money, nor will it provide means for injecting money into, or withdrawing money from, the economic system. Changes in the money supply would have to be brought about outside of the banking system.

Banking policy has not been considered recently as an important tool in fighting depression. Furthermore, as we have suggested previously, banking policy may have been rendered ineffective in checking inflation in the United States because of the heavy bank holdings of government securities.

Operations in the Commodities Market

Government operations in the commodities market (principally gold) have not been used frequently in recent years compared to open-market operations in securities and banking policy as a means for altering the quantity of money. Nevertheless, government purchases and sales of commodities (in general) could be employed to inject money into, or withdraw money from, the economic system.

In the unrestricted gold standard which characterized the monetary systems of many countries prior to 1914, the purchase and sale of one commodity—gold—was widely used. When individuals sold gold to the treasury, the quantity of money was expanded; when individuals bought gold from the treasury, the quantity of money was contracted. The degree of expansion or contraction in the money supply depended upon the extent to which other elements of money were pyramided upon gold.

[5] Earlier reference to the tendency of bank money to expand and contract in periods of inflation and deflation was made in Chapter III.

The monetary effects of operations in a single commodity are not unlike those of operations in many commodities. When the government buys any good or service from other economic units, it exchanges money for this good or service. If the money used by the government to pay for goods and services reduces the government's cash balance or is newly created money, there is a net addition to the total money available for other economic units. Similarly, when the government sells goods or services to other economic units, it exchanges these goods or services for money. If it uses this money to build up its holdings of cash, there is a net decrease in the money available for other economic units.

Advantages of commodity sales and purchases. As a technique for altering the money supply, government purchase and sale of commodities has several advantages.

First of all, such operations minimize the area of foresight and administrative discretion. The rules guiding buying and selling operations can be relatively simple. These rules consist only of the prices established by government for the commodities and the stipulation that the government must buy or sell at these prices. No administrative decisions as to when to buy or sell or how much to buy or sell need be made. The initiative for buying or for selling rests with economic units other than government. So far as government is concerned, these operations can be almost wholly automatic. Under the automatic gold standard the government specified a price at which it would buy or sell gold and stood ready to buy or sell upon the initiative of other economic units.

Second, the technique can be double-edged. It can operate upon money supplies and upon commodity supplies. If the government buys goods, more money will be made available for other economic units. At the same time, however, commodities will be taken off the market. Sellers have an additional demand for their goods. If the government sells goods, money can be drained out of the economy. At the same time more goods are made available for other economic units. Buyers have an additional source of supply.

Disadvantages of commodity purchases and sales. Reduction in the area of foresight and administrative discretion together with the double-edged effect upon both the supply of money and the supply of goods provided by government operations in commodities, makes this tool appear useful in combating either inflation or depression.   However, there may be important limitations to the effectiveness of a government policy of purchasing and selling commodities to encourage full employment or discourage inflation.

Operations in the commodities market affect the composition of the assets rather than the net worth of the individuals or businesses from whom commodities are bought or to whom commodities are sold.   The liquidity position of these units is altered. The individuals or businesses have more or less money and less or more commodities.   Such operations can have the same effects upon cash balances as transactions on income account, but the resulting changes in private expenditures for goods and services are likely to be smaller per unit of change in cash balances.   For example, the increase in total expenditure brought about by the addition of a billion dollars to the money supply, through fiscal means, might be achieved only by a 5 billion dollar expenditure on commodities.

Furthermore, it may be difficult to inaugurate such a program and to continue it in periods of substantial inflationary pressure. A government cannot sell commodities in an attempt to avoid inflation unless it has commodities to sell.   Just as a country may be forced to abandon the gold standard if its treasury runs out of gold, a country cannot maintain the commodity standard unless its government has a stock of commodities.   Unless there are strong deflationary tendencies at work in the economy, a government would have difficulty in inaugurating the commodity standard without bringing about an undesirably large increase in the general level of prices.

One of the costs of using commodity purchases and sales to alter the money supply is the additional resources needed to store any increased commodity stocks required for such operations. Commodity stocks held by the government might include stocks which otherwise would be held by other economic units.   Some of the government's stocks, however, would be an addition to stocks otherwise required.   The cost of storing these additional stocks must be charged to the government's buying and selling operations.

Another important potential danger of employing government

purchases and sales to alter the money supply lies in the opportunity for commodity interest groups to use the program to improve their relative incomes. There is danger that the program may be used to stabilize relative prices—to stabilize for example, the price of wheat or the price of steel. The resulting effects upon resource allocation are likely to be unfavorable. This danger can be minimized, however, by stabilizing the price of a *commodity aggregate* rather than the prices of individual commodities.

The commodity reserve proposal. An attempt to incorporate into governmental policy the advantages of buying and selling operations in commodities and, at the same time, to minimize the disadvantages of such operations is exemplified in the commodity reserve proposal.[6] Under this scheme, the government would stand ready to buy and sell a "bundle" of commodities at a fixed price for this aggregate of commodities. Only the price of the bundle would be stabilized. Relative prices of commodities making up the bundle would be free to vary. Stocks of commodities would form a currency reserve—the currency actually would be convertible into "bundles" of commodities.[7] The government's buying and selling operations would be continuous and automatic; the initiative to buy or sell would rest with economic units other than government.

This proposal has the advantage of acting upon both money supplies and supplies of goods. Furthermore, it lacks the disadvantages of stabilizing relative prices. It has, however, the other disadvantages of government buying and selling operations in commodities; the difficulty of inaugurating selling operations, and the costs of storage. In addition, there is likely to be discrimination between the treatments accorded to domestic and foreign traders. There is no assurance that imported units of

[6] Probably the best known version of this proposal is that expounded by Benjamin Graham. See Benjamin Graham, *World Commodities and World Currency*, New York: McGraw-Hill Book Co., Inc., 1945, and *Storage and Stability*, New York: McGraw-Hill Book Co., Inc., 1937. See also Frank Graham, "Achilles' Heel in Monetary Standards," *American Economic Review*, 30:1 (Part I) (March, 1940), pages 16-32; "Primary Functions of Money and Their Consummation in Monetary Policy," *American Economic Review*, 30:1 (Part II) (March, 1940), pages 1-17; and "Reserve Money and the 100 Per Cent Proposal," *American Economic Review*, 26:3, pages 428-40.

[7] The government could purchase and sell warehouse receipts. A "bundle" might be a 1,000 dollar unit made up of storage receipts of designated commodities. Refer to Benjamin Graham, *Storage and Stability*.

goods included in the bundle would be bought by government or that sales of goods would be permitted for export.

Monetary Policy Alone Not Sufficient

Although it might be possible for the Federal government to alter the money supply by means of its purchases and sales of commodities and government securities, there are a number of rather serious shortcomings to such operations as the major techniques for controlling inflation or deflation. The most serious limitations of operations in either commodities or securities lie in the fact that such operations alter only the composition of assets held by the economic units making exchanges with the government. Changing the liquidity position of an individual or a business without changing the net worth of that economic unit may have only small impacts upon its expenditure for goods and services.

In the future, control of inflation by open-market operations in securities or commodities may be impossible to achieve. Government has no sizable commodity stocks to sell. And the money supply probably could not be reduced by selling securities unless the rate of interest could be increased. A rise in interest rates might prove politically unacceptable.[8]

Added to these difficulties are the costs of commodity operations and the danger that a commodity program might be captured by special interest groups. The result would be a greater misallocation of resources than need occur if other techniques were used.

These limitations appear to be important enough to make it improbable that governmental operations in the securities and commodities markets could, in themselves, maintain stability in the aggregate money expenditure of the economy. This does not mean that such techniques should not be used. But it does indicate the desirability for examining further the budgetary activities of the Federal government as a means for encouraging greater stability in aggregate money expenditure.

[8] Considerable rigidity in interest rates has been assumed to be a political necessity because of the large bank holdings of government securities. The creation of special issues for banks together with the establishment of requirements for minimum holdings of these securities could divorce the value of these issues from movements in interest rates on the securities. Refer to Chapter XXII.

The Need for Coordinating Budgetary and Extra-Budgetary Policies

Although we are not certain about their strength, it appears unlikely that policies outside the budget could adequately counter inflationary or deflationary movements in the economy alone. Nevertheless, it is desirable that budgetary and extra-budgetary activities be coordinated so that they are at least pulling in the same direction, if public policies related to governmental collection and spending of money are to make their maximum contribution toward controlling inflation and minimizing depression. Both kinds of activities affect the total money expenditure within the economy.

If, for example, it is Federal policy to accumulate a budgetary surplus in order to drain off spending power and prevent inflation, but banks are expanding deposit credit, the two kinds of activities are working against each other. If it is Federal policy to check deflation through injecting money by means of a budgetary deficit, this activity may be relatively unsuccessful if the banks are contracting their loans and deposits.

Separated budgetary and extra-budgetary powers. Under our Constitution many of the powers which relate to the raising and spending of money and the issuance and retirement of money rest ultimately with the Federal government. Some of these powers have been placed by Congress in the hands of agencies which are, in a sense, outside of the government. Government departments, particularly the Treasury, administer the money-raising and money-spending activities of the Federal government. But the Federal Reserve System exercises the powers, feeble though they may be, that are available to control the banking system.

All control over the money supply is not in the hands of the banking system. The Federal government has retained, and exercised from time to time, control over money. In 1934 it increased the price of gold and stimulated a vast inflow of this commodity from abroad. In the same year, it expanded its purchases of silver and the issuance of silver certificates. The operations of the Federal Reserve System are, within limits, not entirely independent of the Federal government. The laws authorizing the System are Federal laws; upper and lower limits of reserve requirements for member banks of the Federal Reserve System are stipulated by Congress in the Banking Act of 1936, though the Board of Governors may alter requirements within these limits.

Coordination needed among monetary and fiscal authorities. Various activities which influence the money supply need to be coordinated, if monetary-fiscal policies are to make their maximum contribution toward maintenance of full employment. Consistency in the policies of the various agencies would give greater assurance that our monetary-fiscal policies in the future would be administered toward the same objective.[9]

Suppose, for example, that activities directed toward checking deflationary forces were in order. It might be desirable simultaneously to lower banks' reserve requirements, purchase securities in the open market, and let government expenditures exceed government receipts. The resulting budgetary deficit might be financed through currency issues which would soon filter back to the banks and add to bank reserves. Increased banks' reserve requirements might be in order. If "monetization" of some of the government debt held by the banks was desirable in order to reduce interest charges, it could be accompanied by higher bank reserve requirements.

Coordination of monetary-fiscal tools may involve greater centralization of power over monetary-fiscal matters *within* the Federal government. Additional powers could be granted to the Board of Governors of the Federal Reserve System or to the Treasury. Of these choices, granting additional powers to the Treasury appears to be most feasible; with the Treasury rest the ultimate powers, delegated by the Constitution, over our monetary system. The Federal Reserve System could retain important administrative functions such as supervision of the clearing systems; it could be made the sole national agency responsible for bank examination. Its monetary and banking policies would, however, be determined by the Treasury. Such a change, of course, could be made only with the consent of Congress.

[9] An increased amount of coordination between Federal, state and local fiscal policies is also desirable. Means for achieving such coordination will be discussed in the final section of this book.

CHAPTER VI

ALTERNATIVE. FISCAL POLICIES
AND FULL EMPLOYMENT

IN PREVIOUS chapters we have pointed out that governmental fiscal activities could be directed toward strengthening markets for goods and services or toward combating inflation. It has also been indicated that monetary activities outside the budget might be utilized to help reduce fluctuations in money expenditure for goods and services. However, the conditions likely to prevail during the next decade or longer may make monetary policy inadequate as the sole instrument for encouraging high production and employment or for discouraging inflation.

Governmental fiscal activities may stimulate or retard aggregate money expenditure for goods and services by (1) altering the total amount of disposable income in the private economy or (2) redistributing income among the various economic units. Increasing the total amount of disposable income as a means for strengthening markets can be accomplished by the government incurring a budgetary deficit and financing it from new money which it has issued or which has been created by, and borrowed from, the banks. Siphoning money out of the economic system in order to diminish aggregate money expenditure for goods and services, can be accomplished by the government accumulating a budgetary surplus.[1] Redistribution of income occurs when government taxes some economic units and transfers this spending power to other units. Such transfers may alter the proportion of total disposable income which is spent on goods and services.

Thus, there are a number of methods which government may

[1] Money can also be siphoned out of the system by government sale of securities to nonbanking buyers. It has been recognized earlier that government may also be able to affect the supply of money *indirectly* through the effects of the operations of the central bank (Federal Reserve Banks) in the securities market. This, however, may be classed as a monetary rather than fiscal device. Refer to Chapter V.

employ to stimulate or retard markets. It may keep its budget balanced, increasing or reducing both its expenditures and its tax receipts. It may incur budget deficits or accumulate budget surpluses. However, there are also alternative ways of bringing about these deficits or surpluses: Expenditures may be held relatively constant while tax collections are diminished to counter depression or increased to discourage inflation; or tax collections may be kept relatively constant while expenditures are increased to discourage depression or decreased to choke off inflation.

Fiscal Action Within a Balanced Budget

This method has received considerable professional attention during recent years, but it receives little professional support. Most of those who believe in a balanced budget do not favor fiscal action to counter unemployment, and most of those who favor fiscal action to counter unemployment do not favor a balanced budget. Consequently, this discussion should not be considered as one dealing with a serious policy proposal but rather a description of a technique which could be employed.

Some people prefer to have the Federal budget always balanced. This preference appears to be largely the result of drawing an erroneous analogy between the budget of an individual and the budget of the Federal government. As we have indicated before, the Federal government has means for securing money which are not available to private units. Government can always obtain money by printing it or by having the banks issue deposit credit and lend it to government. In fact, securing funds by taxation is desirable primarily to prevent inflation.[2] Perhaps fear of abuse of the money-issuing privilege and the consequent inflation is responsible for some of the preferences for a balanced Federal budget.

Fiscal policies restricted by a balanced budget are not likely to be very effective in combating strong inflationary or deflationary tendencies. On the one hand, if government hires the unem-

[2] It is recognized that "taxes for revenue" will continue to dominate state-local tax policies and that the approximately 155,000 state-local taxing units can scarcely be expected to mold their fiscal policies on a national pattern. Probably the most that can be expected is that they do not adopt policies to obstruct national policy. Obstructionist policies could modify, but scarcely cancel out, the effects of a national fiscal policy under the existing pattern of total public expenditures, where Federal expenditures are two to three times the total state-local spending. A more detailed discussion of this problem is given in Chapter XI.

ployed rather than devote full effort to encouraging employment in the private economy, misallocation of resources may result. In the past, important restrictions have been placed upon the areas in which government could produce, since government competition with private enterprise was considered undesirable. Too few resources may be employed in the restricted areas. On the other hand, the extent to which transfers can be made is (and should be) limited by considerations other than the encouragement of full production and employment or discouragement of inflation. For example, the kind of income distribution sanctioned by social policy or the socially desired scale of operations involving government as producer and employer will restrict the kinds and sizes of transfers.

We believe that these limitations are serious and that the restriction of a balanced budget does not offer great possibilities for promoting full employment without unduly interfering with the achievement of other objectives, particularly optimum resource allocation. Nevertheless, the writers will analyze briefly the effects of operations within the framework of a balanced budget.

A balanced budget: government hires the unemployed.[3] Imagine that there is in the economy a considerable number of unemployed workers—people who are willing to work at current wages, but for whom jobs are not available. Assume further that every consumer, regardless of the size of his income, spends the same percentage of his additional income for goods and services. The government's budget is balanced and Congress will authorize no expenditure that is not financed from current tax receipts.

A tax is levied upon current incomes. The proceeds of this tax are used to hire the unemployed workers. Since the disposable incomes (incomes after taxes) of those taxed have fallen, their expenditures for goods and services will fall. But this decline will be exactly counterbalanced by an increase in the expenditures of those formerly unemployed. Their incomes have been increased. Total expenditures on consumption goods are unchanged, so there is no reason to expect a fall in employment

[3] See Trygve Haavelmo, "Multiplier Effects of a Balanced Budget," *Econometrica*, 13:4 (October, 1945), pages 311-318, and the comments and replies in *Econometrica*, 14:1 (April, 1946).

in the industries producing these goods.[4]   But, the gross national product has been augmented from the goods and services produced by the workers hired by government.   If the payments made to these workers represent the value of the goods and services they have produced, the national product is increased by an amount equal to the tax, and some of the unemployed workers have been put to work.

The principal objection to this procedure is the large size of the budget which would be required if there were substantial deflationary tendencies to combat.   This would increase the importance of the role played by government as producer and employer.   Such a procedure would also require considerable flexibility in government expenditure.

For example, in order to raise the gross national product by 30 billion dollars, under the assumptions made in the previous example, a 30-billion-dollar increase in government revenues and expenditures would be required.   Government would be making serious inroads upon private enterprise, or might be relegated to producing goods and services low on the scale of consumer preference.   Uncertainty about the extent of public fiscal activities—the level of taxes as well as potential government competition with business—might discourage employment in the private economy.   However, this does not mean that some standards for determining various kinds of government expenditure could not be maintained.   Some of the difficulties of large variations in public expenditures are discussed later in this chapter.

A balanced budget: government redistributes income.   Empirical studies indicate that the percentage of income spent by a consuming unit for consumption goods decreases as that unit's income increases.[5]   Thus, total money expenditure for goods and services might be increased by shifting income from high-income receivers to low-income receivers.   The decrease in the expenditure of the high-income earner would be more than offset by the increase in expenditure of the low-income receiver.   Or, total money expenditure for goods and services might be decreased if

---

[4] It is assumed that factor supplies will not be altered as a result of the increased taxation.

[5] See, for example, *Family Expenditures in the U. S., 1935-36, Statistical Tables and Appendixes,* National Resources Planning Board.

income were shifted from low-income earners to high-income earners. Within the framework of a balanced budget, expenditures for goods and services could be augmented or diminished by such transfers of income, and government's role as producer and employer would be unchanged.

An important objection to this procedure is the way in which it ties income distribution to employment policy. The nature of the distribution of personal incomes is made dependent upon whether the government is fighting inflation or depression. In periods of inflation, a more unequal distribution than is desired on other grounds could easily result. In periods of depression, a more equal distribution of income than is generally considered desirable might be the outcome.

As we have indicated, encouraging or deterring markets can be accomplished within a wide variety of *relative* income distributions. The kind of income distribution resulting from various social policies conceptually need not be influenced by the potential effects of various distributions upon employment. Income distribution and full employment can be treated as separate objectives of economic policy.

Fiscal Action With Budget Deficits and Surpluses

If the government is not restricted to fiscal action within a balanced budget, it need not vary its role as producer and employer in order to combat depression or inflation. Also, income distribution need not be dependent upon employment policy. However, many of the fiscal measures suggested as antidotes to depression combine changes in the money supply with alterations in the scale of governmental employment and with income redistribution.

For example, increasing government expenditures and expanding government employment can be financed by incurring a budget deficit and expanding the money supply.[6] Or diminishing government expenditure and reducing government employment can result in the accumulation of a budget surplus and a reduction in the money supply.

---

[6] The expansion in the money supply would occur if the government filled the gap from money which it printed or which was issued by the banks and loaned to government.

Varying Public Expenditure as a Fiscal Technique

Maintaining a given tax structure with specified rates of taxation and exemptions automatically brings reduced tax collections in periods of deflation and increased tax receipts in periods of inflation. If rates and exemptions are unchanged and national income (and expenditure) declines, tax collections also fall. If national income (and expenditure) rises, tax collections also rise. These increases and decreases, however, are apparently not sufficient to check inflation or deflation. They do not encourage people to spend proportionately more, particularly through drawing upon their accumulated liquid holdings, in periods of deflation, nor do they sufficiently discourage expenditure in periods of inflation. Something more must be done. In periods of deflation either public expenditures must be increased or there must be further deliberate cuts in tax collections. When inflation threatens, taxes must be increased or government expenditures cut. Sometimes, such direct controls as price ceilings and rationing must be utilized as well. (Refer to Chapter VII.)

Assuming that a given tax structure is maintained, and consequently that tax collections vary with inflationary and deflationary tendencies, let us examine the effects of altering Federal expenditures to encourage additional money expenditure for goods and services or to discourage excess money expenditure for goods and services.

Flexible and inflexible Federal expenditures. As is indicated in Chapter II, the Federal government spends money for a variety of purposes. The items for which government makes expenditure have been shifting rather continuously with the passage of time. During the years 1942-1947, a large percentage of Federal expenditures were for prosecuting and "liquidating" the war. During the depression of the thirties, expenditures for welfare—relief, public works, and so forth—were at a relatively high level. It is estimated that after the period of reconversion from war to peace, assuming full production and employment, the Federal government will spend at least 25 billion dollars annually. The distribution of this estimated expenditure among the various governmental functions is indicated in Table 4, Chapter II.

Of these expenditures some might lend themselves to expansion and contraction from year to year, as offsets to inflation or deflation, while others would not.   For example, of the total estimated expenditures of the Federal government, about one-half is for military purposes, about one-fifth is for interest on the national debt, and approximately one-fourth for the ordinary expenses of government (including legislative, administrative, and judicial expenses, pensions, farm benefits, and regular public works).

Interest payments, general administrative, legislative, and judicial expenses, and military expenses are commitments that probably should not be reduced as offsets to inflation.   Increasing them as an offset to deflation also appears undesirable.   For example, the scale of military expenditure is determined by estimated military needs.   Although the estimates made may not be appropriate for years in the future, in general, military needs are largely independent of internal inflation or depression.   Interest payments are dependent upon outstanding Federal debt although the debt itself may be expanded or contracted.   Administrative, legislative, and judicial expenses should be determined on the basis of what it takes to perform adequately these functions.

This means that of the types of expenditure outlined in the prospective Federal budget, the types that might be expanded or contracted to offset expected inflationary or deflationary movements include: (1) public works expenditures and (2) grants of income, in money or in kind (transfer payments), to individuals. In addition, expenditures for debt repayment could be varied.

Each of these three types of expenditure—public works, net debt repayment, and grants of income—may be suited to expansion or contraction as means of offsetting inflation or deflation. The desirability of using each must be evaluated in terms of economic effects and political acceptability.

Varying public investment as a tool of fiscal policy.   There are many economists who argue that public investment should be expanded or contracted to offset declines in total money expenditure for the goods and services of the private economy or to discourage inflation.[7]   They point to the close relationship between investment and national income and to the relatively greater

---

[7] Few economists would contend that all of the slack in private demand should be countered by public investment.   But many have argued that increased public investment will help to increase private demand as well as take up part of the slack.

stability in consumption expenditure as compared to investment. Furthermore, they consider expansion in some types of public investment as a politically feasible means for trying to check depression.

Some of the people who advocate increasing public investment as a politically feasible means for checking depression may be assigning to investment a greater role in determining the general level of economic activity than it actually plays. A close correlation between high investment and high employment does not mean that the former brings the latter. Nevertheless, some kinds of public investment could be expanded as a stimulus to employment or contracted as a deterrent to inflation.

Expanding public investment may encourage employment in two ways. First, the government increases the scale of its employment or underwrites private contractors who expand the size of their labor force. Second, when public investment is accompanied by monetary expansion, the increase in the incomes of the new employees need not be entirely offset by increased taxes on other income receivers. A strengthening of markets in the private economy may result. There could be assurance of continuous full employment via the public investment approach. This is a distinct advantage—if full employment is the only objective.

Full employment in itself, however, is not the sole objective of economic policy. As we have pointed out in Chapter I, other goals, including reasonably efficient use of the resources employed, are also desired. In the United States one of the politically determined conditions imposed upon the attainment of full production and employment appears to be that it must be achieved within the framework of an enterprise economy. If this condition is recognized, the area in which government may act as producer and employer is limited in both scale and nature.

(1) *Public investment and resource allocation.* Given the other objectives of social policy and the framework within which full employment must be achieved, expanding public investment to take up the slack in employment may not be the most desirable means of attaining this end. The public-investment approach may result in an allocation of resources which brings forth a smaller total product than would be produced if the same resources were fully employed and allocated in accordance with

consumers' preferences.[8] There still are undoubtedly many areas where public investment would yield a product equal to, or in excess of, many private investments which probably will be undertaken.[9] The nation's population might be very willing to divert additional resources to improving highways and public parks further, to constructing hydroelectric plants, airports, and hospitals, and to conserving (investing in) soil resources. However, this area of potential public investment is not unlimited. It is easily conceivable that the point might be reached where there was an excess of investment in soil resources, parks, or highways. The marginal social yields from additions to these capital assets might be considerably below the marginal social yields from investments in additional textile factories, breweries, or soda fountains. *If the resources would otherwise be unused,* a dozen public parks in Paducah or a twelve-lane highway in Nevada is probably preferred to nothing at all. But some other approach may permit both full employment and a more effective resource allocation.

The government could, of course, invest in the textile factories, breweries, and soda fountains which consumers would prefer to the public parks in Paducah or the super highway in Nevada. This kind of investment, however, is considered as (and undoubtedly would be) competitive with private enterprise. It would probably discourage private investment in the fields in which there was government investment and necessitate further public investment to take up the additional slack in employment.[10] Whether private business's fear of government competition is real or imaginary is irrelevant.[11] So long as these fears are translated into action—failure of private enterprise to produce at levels as high as would prevail in the absence of government investment —there is a necessity for consistent expansion in the area in which government acts as producer and employer.

[8] See Chapter I, page 13, footnote 15.
[9] See Chapter IX.
[10] The area in which government can expand its investment without bringing about reduced private investment is difficult to determine and is probably changing through time. For example, TVA probably was expected to reduce private investment in electric-power generating facilities. It appears, however, that TVA has stimulated additional private investment in power facilities as well as in some other fields.
[11] Policy makers must, of course, distinguish between businessmen's words and businessmen's actions. What businessmen do and what they say they will do, in response to particular governmental actions, may be quite different things.

Where governmental operation is more efficient than private operation, and *if there is general agreement that efficiency in this field of production is the major objective,* or that governmental operations in this field would not infringe too much upon accepted personal rights such as freedom of speech and of the press, governmental investment is desirable. Governmental operation may be desirable in some fields such as operation of natural monopolies, to prevent private business from exploiting the aggregate of consumers. But, in such areas, governmental investment should be undertaken because it is in the public interest for government to produce in these fields, not because it is necessary for the government to find more jobs. This area can be blocked out as one in which governmental operation is to be expected. We consider governmental operation of the postal system, most highways, and some public utilities as desirable. Social policy may widen this area to include enterprises now forbidden government. However, in those areas where governmental operation is not considered as more efficient or as otherwise in the public interest, private producers should be given reasonable assurance that as long as they produce efficiently, government will not be one of their competitors. Entrance of the government into a particular sphere of production simply as a means of providing employment does not seem desirable if there are other techniques which will maintain full production and employment.[12]

(2) *Other economic aspects of public investment.* Other factors may make public investment less desirable than other techniques which might be used to promote full production and employment. One of these is that many potential areas of public investment may not lend themselves to the rather abrupt changes in scale which may be necessary if public investment is to take up the slack in employment. At some times, when private employment is increasing, public works projects may have to be abandoned when they are only partially complete in order that labor will be available for private industry. Although many of these projects could be completed at later dates, some of them may tie up a considerable amount of resources from which no services will be provided.[13] A substantial amount of such heavy public

---

[12] Refer to Chapter IX.

[13] This is not an important consideration, of course, if the resources so immobilized would have been involuntarily unemployed.

works seems justified when there are prospects for considerable unemployment for a relatively long period of time in the future. When this condition is not met, governmental investment might be largely confined to construction of housing, investments in soil and forest conservation, and to other kinds of investments which could be completed rapidly, could be completed by private industry, or would yield some returns in their unfinished form.

The importance of flexibility in public investment depends primarily upon the rate at which employment in private industry changes. If this rate is relatively slow, flexibility in public investment is not a major consideration. Total nonagricultural employment in the United States decreased by more than 11 million persons from 1929 to 1933, falling by nearly 3 million in the 6 months from October, 1929 to March, 1930. From March, 1933 to October, 1933 more than 3 million people were re-employed by private industry.[14] Adding 3 million persons to, or subtracting that many from, the labor force employed in public investment would necessitate a very flexible public investment program.

(3) *Tentative appraisal.* Varying public investment expenditure as a fiscal tool has the advantage of acting directly upon the level of employment. If there are unemployed laborers, they can be absorbed by increased public investment.

Public investment as a technique for offsetting deflation and inflation has, however, several disadvantages. First of all, if it competes (or businessmen think it competes) with private investment, employment provided by private businesses may be at a lower level than it would otherwise be. The scope of the government as employer and producer may have to be almost continually expanding. This may be incompatible with the maintenance of an enterprise economy.

Second, if public investment is compatible with the maintenance of an enterprise economy, it may be incompatible with most efficient resource allocation. There are many forms of public investment not competing with private investment, sanctioned by most of our citizens and yielding returns which would justify allocating resources to them. However, if public investment is to be used as the principal means of combating deflation, these

[14] See Federal Reserve Charts on Bank Credit, Money, Interest Rates and Business.

areas may soon be exploited.   Where the alternatives are unused resources or public investment, the choice is obvious.   But where the resources used in public investment could, by other means, be used to produce consumers' goods or private capital assets, public investments probably should be justified on grounds other than that they provide employment.

Debt repayment.   Another form of expenditure which could be increased as a means of combating deflation is repayment of the Federal debt.   The government could, as a means of injecting money into the economy, plan to pay off the debt ahead of its maturity schedule.   Postwar debt management will be discussed in some detail in Chapter XXII.   Here, it will be examined only as an antideflationary factor.   The assumption which will be made is this: If additional money needs to be injected into the economy, more rapid repayment of the debt will be possible.

Since the substitution of money for government securities in bank portfolios would automatically increase bank reserves, monetary-fiscal authorities would find it desirable to increase the reserve requirements of banks, if and when the threat of *deflation* turned into a threat of *inflation*.

In so far as nonbank holdings of government securities are involved, the creation of new money or use of existing surplus funds would be a matter of relative indifference, as far as immediate effects are concerned.   There would occur an alteration in the composition of the assets of nonbank holders of securities, but no alteration in their net worth position.   Given a choice between use of existing surplus funds and issue of new money in a debt retirement program for nonbanking investors, monetary-fiscal authorities might prefer to use accumulated surplus funds for various reasons, among them the still lively suspicion of money issue, based on past experience with its relatively uncontrolled use.[15]

As suggested above, repayment of its debt ahead of schedule by government would alter the composition of sellers' assets, though it would not alter their net worth position.   Businesses and individuals selling the securities have more cash and less securities.   Such transactions on capital account are likely to

---

[15] Proposals for money issue in this book consistently assume its use within a specified framework of rules.

exert less effect on expenditure for the goods and services of the private economy than would transactions of similar scale affecting the incomes of these individuals and businesses.[16]

Furthermore, the bulk of the public marketable Federal debt is held by banks, insurance companies, and government, or quasi-government agencies.[17] Paying off the debt ahead of schedule will principally increase the cash holdings of these economic units. Although it would only increase the cash holdings of other economic units, some increase in expenditure could reasonably be expected, even if their capital position only and not their net worth position is affected. For units such as banks and insurance companies, an improvement in liquidity position is no guarantee of increased lending in a time of threatened (or actual) deflation. The general conclusion is that, as an effective antideflationary device, stepping up the debt repayment schedule is likely to be relatively ineffective.

Grants of income to individuals. It has been proposed that the government enlarge the scope of its grants of income to individuals, expanding them in periods of depression and contracting them in periods of inflation.[18] Under this procedure, the government would not be expanding its role as a producer and hence would not provide increasing competition for private industry. Furthermore, individuals would be free to allocate this income as they wished. The resulting resource allocation could be determined largely by consumers' preferences.[19]

These grants could be made in money without restriction as to the way in which the money should be allocated, or they could be made in kind—in the form of coupons which could be used to purchase certain goods or services such as food, medical care, or

[16] For a more complete discussion of the different effects of expenditures on income account and on capital account, see Chapter V.

[17] On September 30, 1946 about three-fourths (75.3 per cent) of the public marketable Federal debt was held by banks, insurance companies, and United States government agencies, trust funds, and Federal Reserve Banks. See Table 36, Chapter XXII. The nonmarketable public debt consists of United States savings bonds and Treasury tax and savings notes. About 30 per cent of the total Federal debt outstanding on September 30, 1946 was nonmarketable.

[18] See, for example, John H. Q. Pierson, "The Underwriting of Aggregate Consumption Spending as a Pillar of Full-Employment Policy," *The American Economic Review*, 44: (No. I, Part I) 21-55 (March, 1944). For political reasons, reducing the size of grants in periods of inflation probably would be more difficult than increasing the size of grants in periods of deflation.

[19] If the grants were made in kind, or were conditional upon their use in a specified manner, this condition might not be completely fulfilled.

housing. In periods of inflation, total governmental expenditure involved in making these grants would be contracted.

This technique has many economic advantages over the public-investment approach. It does not act directly upon the level of employment—no additional employees are hired by government. But it is very probable that employment would be stimulated (in time of unemployment) if the expenditure involved in such grants was increased.

One of the political objections to such a proposal is very likely to be that it provides, or appears to provide, some people with "something for nothing." If there is an increase in expenditure for goods and services as a result of increased grants and there is no marked increase in the general level of prices, it is very likely that production and employment will be stimulated. Consequently, the bulk of the goods and services provided by such grants is likely to be the equivalent of the product of resources which would have been unemployed, if no steps had been taken to counter deflation. An alternative, however, is public investment. Many groups might prefer public investment to grants of income, even though the resources were allocated less effectively, because the government seems "to be getting something for its money." If policy makers achieve a more complete understanding of the economic system and the way in which it works, this objection to grants of income may not be as widely held.

A further political difficulty may arise in establishing the criteria which would determine who should receive grants. This difficulty arises primarily because we, as a society, have not answered the question "what kind of income distribution should we have?" [20] Once this question is answered, grants of income could be used to help achieve the desired distribution and could be varied to help combat deflation and inflation. Until this question is answered, however, opposition to grants of income will arise partially because of disagreement over virtually any kind of income distribution which this procedure would bring about. Those individuals who believe that the income distribution should be determined by individuals' contributions—that is, should not be modified from that which would prevail if incomes were deter-

[20] This may be partially the result of ignorance about the nature of the income distribution as well as differences in opinions as to what the distribution should be. Refer to the subsequent chapter on income distribution.

mined solely by the given pattern of resource ownership and resource prices—may be expected to oppose grants of income if
such grants tend to bring about any other income pattern.   Other
individuals, particularly those in the low-income groups, may
oppose such grants because they do not consider that they modify
the income distribution sufficiently.

Welfare programs and fiscal policy. It has been proposed
that the Federal government expand the scope of direct assistance provided to individuals.   It is contended that in addition to
the provision of funds or direct services for education, recreation,
transportation, unemployment benefits, old-age assistance, and
the like, the Federal government should assure every citizen that,
regardless of his income, reasonable medical care and adequate
food will be available to him.   A minimum medical or nutritional
standard and the income at which this minimum should be met
without governmental assistance might be defined.   Individuals
receiving less than the minimum income would be given additional purchasing power to be utilized for purchasing food or
medical aid.

This kind of proposal is very likely to be partially evaluated as
public policy upon nonfiscal grounds.   Some persons who believe
that the distribution of income should be more equalitarian may
favor such a program.   Others who oppose further modification
of the income distribution may be against such a program.

Such a proposal, however, has fiscal implications.   If adopted
as part of a food progam it would mean that a floor under expenditure for food would be provided and that the contribution
which government would make to expenditure for food would rise
or fall as personal incomes decreased or increased.   The level
of governmental assistance would be automatically increased as
unemployment increased and incomes fell.   As employment increased and incomes rose, fewer persons would be eligible for
governmental assistance and the amount provided to many of
those eligible for such assistance would tend to decrease.

Adoption of such a proposal may result in a less economic allocation of resources than would be achieved if grants of money
were made to consumers.   For example, there is danger that the
minimum expenditure on food may be set at too high a level relative to expenditure on other items.   Nevertheless, this kind of
program appears to have a greater probability of being accepted

than does a program of unrestricted grants.   It may be that, for political reasons, some fiscal policies will have to hang on to the coat-tails of such welfare programs.

Varying Tax Collections

Another approach by which the Federal government could inject money into or withdraw money from the economic system in order to combat deflation or inflation would be the holding of Federal expenditures relatively constant and varying tax collections. In order to combat threatening inflation, tax collections could be increased.   When deflation needed to be combated, tax collections could be decreased.   Some provisions for tax changes can be "built in," that is, tax revenues will be automatically reduced or increased as employment falls or prices rise.   However, provisions must be made for deliberate changes which can be made as unforeseen economic events are unfolded.   "Built in" and deliberate flexibility are discussed more fully in Chapter VII.

There are a number of economists who consider varying taxes superior to varying Federal expenditures as a means for encouraging stability in the aggregate money expenditure of the economy.[21]   They consider it desirable for the government to map out its expenditure program on grounds other than those of providing employment or stabilizing the money expenditure of the economy.   The pattern of Federal expenditure would be designed to provide the pattern of services which the public defines as desirable for the government to provide.   Taxation at the Federal level would be necessary only to avoid inflation.[22] Otherwise the government could finance its expenditure program from money which it issued (or had the banks issue).

There are a number of advantages to this approach.   It avoids the inefficiency in resource allocation which may occur as a result of using public investment as the balancing item.   It does not expand the role of government as producer and employer in order to combat unemployment.   It minimizes the opportunities for

[21] See, for example, Kenneth E. Boulding, *The Economics of Peace.* New York: Prentice-Hall, Inc., 1945.   This approach is also implicit in Abba P. Lerner, *The Economics of Control,* New York: The Macmillan Company, 1944, and "Functional Finance and the Federal Debt," *Social Research* (Febraury, 1943).

[22] Flexible taxes as a fiscal tool at the state and local levels are probably out of the question.   State and local governments are more inclined to collect enough taxes to cover expenditures.

political allocation of resources—a danger inherent in grants of income to individuals, particularly if such grants are part of a public welfare program.

With an annual Federal budgetary expenditure of around 25 billion dollars—the prospective future expenditure for purposes other than debt repayment—a sizable injection of money could be achieved by cutting taxes and leaving people with more of their own money to spend. Continuation of the trend toward current collection of Federal income taxes at the source of income, would make it practicable for changes in tax rates to be made at quarterly intervals. Not only could a tax reduction for the current quarter be announced, but a part of last quarter's taxes could be canceled and immediately refunded.

Flexible taxes may, however, be rather ineffective in combating depression because tax reductions may leave the money with the wrong people—with those who will be satisfied with increased cash balances and will not spend additional amounts for goods and services. Whether this is true depends both upon the extent of unemployment and the nature of the tax structure. A reduction in a personal income tax with high exemptions would have little effect upon the disposable incomes of low-income groups. If a person pays no Federal tax, increases in his expenditure can hardly be encouraged by reducing his Federal taxes.

Tax cuts which left the unemployed with additional disposable income probably would be more effective in encouraging employment than would reductions in the taxes paid by those whose incomes have not fallen. Many of the unemployed are likely to pay little or no personal income taxes. Consequently, reductions in personal income taxes have little immediate effects on their disposable incomes. Furthermore, it might be considered inequitable to reduce the taxes of those who still have substantial income. "Built-in" flexibility which provides for rebating in the current periods a portion of taxes paid in a previous period would help to strengthen the disposable incomes of those who recently may have become unemployed.

No one knows exactly what the future Federal tax structure will be. Assume, however, that the Federal government is collecting annually about 20 billion dollars from a Federal income tax and that the distribution of this tax bill is as indicated in Table 10. If we know how individuals' expenditures respond to changes in their incomes, we can make some estimates of the stimulus to total expenditure for goods and services which might follow from various patterns of tax reduction. Certain assumptions about changes in expenditure as they are related to changes in income have been made in constructing Table 10. These estimates are only for illustrative purposes and should not be interpreted as a picture of the exact manner by which income is likely to change as revisions are made in tax collections.

Under these assumptions a reduction in tax collections at the rate of 2 billion dollars per year (500 million per quarter), brought about by reducing everyone's tax bill by 10 per cent, would result in increased consumption expenditure of about 3.7 billion dollars per year.[23] Canceling 2 billions of taxes which would have been paid by the lowest-income taxpayers would result in increased consumption expenditure of about 5 billion. Canceling 2 billions of taxes which would have been paid by the highest-income group would increase consumption expenditure by about 2.7 billion. *All of these estimates assume that Federal expenditures remain unchanged.*

Negative Taxation

Reducing Federal income-tax collections from a 20 billion level to a 15 billion level probably would provide considerable stimulus to additional expenditure for goods and services, even if personal exemptions were relatively high and rates in the lowest tax-paying brackets were low. If such a reduction was not sufficient, a larger one could be made.

It may be, however, that sizable reductions in Federal income-tax collections would alter so greatly the *relative* income distribution that some other technique should be used to supplement tax reductions. Although tax reductions could be made so that relative income positions within the taxpaying group were unchanged, tax reductions tend to make taxpayers better off compared to nontaxpayers.

[23] By examining Table 10, it will be noted that an initial increase in disposable income of 2 billion dollars comes about as a result of a 2 billion dollar tax cut. If this tax cut is distributed uniformly among all taxpayers, the initial increase in expenditure for goods and services is 1,107 billion. If this initial increase is in turn spread uniformly among all income receivers, the first subsequent expansion will be about 775 million. From this another 542 million dollars of additional expenditure will be made, and so forth. The total expansion, under the assumption made, will be around 3.7 billion. See footnote *d*, Table 10, for further explanation.

TABLE 10[24]

Estimated Changes in Equilibrium Level of Total Annual Consumption
Expenditure Resulting from Various Patterns of Tax Reduction

Income per family per year (Dollars)	Ratio of increment in consumption expenditure to increment in income[a]	Federal income taxes collected[b] (millions of dollars per year)	Initial Increase in Consumption Expenditure, if:		
			A. Everybody's tax bill is reduced by ten per cent (in millions of dollars)	B. 2 billions of taxes of lowest income groups are canceled (in millions of dollars)	C. 2 billions of taxes of highest income groups are canceled (in millions of dollars)
0-500	0.9	0	0	0	0
500-1,000	0.8	0	0	0	0
1,000-1,500	0.8	300	24	240	0
1,500-2,000	0.8	500	40	400	0
2,000-3,000	0.7	1,500	105	840	0
3,000-5,000	0.7	3,000	210	0	0
5,000-10,000	0.6	5,000	300	0	0
10,000-15,000	0.5	2,000	100	0	0
15,000-20,000	0.5	2,000	100	0	0
20,000 & over	0.4	5,700	228	0	800
All income receivers	0.7[c]	20,000	1,107	1,480	800
Total annual increase in consumption expenditures[d]			3,690	4,933	2,667

[a] The assumption made here is that an individual with an income A who finds his income increased to B, will have the same expenditure pattern as another individual whose income was B.

[b] This tax bill assumes a personal exemption of $1,000. Except for the taxes paid by the low-income groups and by "singles" with exemption of only $500, the tax pattern is similar to that for 1943.

[c] This figure is a weighted marginal propensity to consume, the propensities of each income group being weighted according to the proportion of total income received by each.

[d] It is assumed that the initial expenditure flow is distributed among the various income groups in proportion to the percentage of total income received by each. If the initial increase in consumption expenditure is ΔE, the total expenditure will be $\Delta E + 0.7 \Delta E + (0.7)^2 \Delta E + \ldots$. The sum of this series is $3\frac{1}{3} \Delta E$. This means that after the initial expenditure, the multiplier is assumed to be two and one-third.

If tax reductions cannot sufficiently stimulate expenditures for goods and services, or if it is considered desirable to maintain a given relative income structure, the government might employ

[24] Estimated from data in *Family Expenditures in the U. S. Statistical Tables and Appendixes*, National Resources Planning Board, June, 1941, Table 1, page 1.

negative taxation.[25] Instead of paying taxes, some individuals might receive payments from the government.

This scheme is essentially equivalent to grants of income. Negative taxes could be administered as a negative sales tax or as a negative income tax, payments being made to individuals who would not have paid income taxes. Although negative taxation is a potential fiscal tool, it seems very unlikely (in the opinion of the writers) that it would need to be used so long as steps were taken to stop a depression before it reached depths comparable to those of 1932. The minimum estimates of Federal expenditures for a considerable period in the future put them at a level of about 25 billion dollars annually. Reducing taxes from this level could stem depression, at least in its early stages, without resort to negative taxation. Furthermore, the novelty of negative taxation may make it one of the least acceptable of fiscal techniques.

Summary

Government may encourage expansion in production and employment or discourage inflation and still keep its budget balanced. But, the limits to antidepression or anti-inflation effects which can be obtained within a balanced budget are considerably narrower than those within which fiscal policy can operate if the budget need not be balanced. These limits are determined partially by the degree to which government may act as producer and employer and partially by the extent to which the citizens will permit governmental redistribution of income.

The effects of governmental fiscal activities depend upon the receipts of government and upon the expenditure of government. These effects are influenced by the *quantitative* relationship between receipts and expenditures and also by the *qualitative* relationship—the manner in which the money is secured and the ways in which it is spent.

A comparison of the effects of various fiscal techniques upon the level of money expenditure for goods and services is presented in Table 11. The examples in the table are merely hypothetical constructions intended as illustrations, not as guides to economic policy. Additional empirical research would be required to determine more accurately such factors as the impacts

[25] See, for example, Kenneth E. Boulding, *Economics of Peace*, Chapter 9.

TABLE 11

Hypothetical Changes in Government Money Product, Private Money
Expenditure, and Total Money Product Resulting from Alternative
Fiscal Changes

	Change in Gov't Money Product (in millions of dollars)	Change in Private Money Expenditure (in millions of dollars)	Change in Total Money Product (in millions of dollars)
I. Balanced Budget: a 5-billion-dollar Increase in Government Expenditure			
A. Increase in Gov't Expenditure for Public Works; no change in relative income distribution[a]	+5,000	0	+ 5,000
B. Increase in transfers of income; no increase in public works; incomes of highest one-half of income receivers reduced; incomes of lowest one-half of income receivers increased[b]	0	+ 5,000	+ 5,000
C. Increase in Gov't Expenditure for Public Works; incomes of highest one-half of income receivers taxed; payments made to lowest half of income receivers[b]	+5,000	+ 5,000	+10,000
II. Unbalanced Budget: A 5-billion-dollar Deficit financed from money issue			
A. Increase in Gov't Expenditure for Public Works; no reduction in anybody's income[c]	+5,000	+11,667	+16,667
B. Increase in Grants of Income; all incomes increased by the same absolute amount[c]	0	+11,667	+11,667
C. Increase in Grants of Income; payments made only to lower half of income receivers[b]	0	+15,000	+15,000
D. Increase in Gov't Expenditure for Public Works; only individuals in lower half of income receivers hired by government[b]	+5,000	+15,000	+20,000

TABLE 11 (*Continued*)

	Change in Gov't Money Product (*in millions of dollars*)	Change in Private Money Expenditure (*in millions of dollars*)	Change in Total Money Product (*in millions of dollars*)
E. Equal proportionate reduction in personal taxes paid by all income receivers[c].....	0	+11,667	+11,667
F. Reduction in personal taxes paid by lower half of income receivers[b].................	0	+15,000	+15,000

[a] This is the equivalent of assuming no change in the marginal propensity to consume for the economy as a whole.

[b] Assumes marginal propensity to consume of upper half of income receivers is 2 while marginal propensity to consume of lower half of income receivers is 3.

[c] Assumes marginal propensity to consume for the economy as a whole is $2\frac{1}{3}$.

of increased public works upon the actions of private employers and the additions to expenditure for goods and services resulting from an expansion in deficit-financed government expenditure or a reduction in taxes.

CHAPTER VII

"PRACTICAL" PROBLEMS IN OPERATING FISCAL POLICIES

THROUGHOUT this section of the book we have been discussing various ways to maintain full employment and the conditions within which this goal probably should be reached. Achievement of this objective in the United States appears subject to the maintenance of an enterprise economy—an economy in which government as producer and employer is restricted to that area where it is agreed that government can produce more efficiently than private producers. Furthermore, maintaining full employment should not result in inflation.

We have been attempting to show how full employment might be maintained through proper monetary-fiscal policies. Such policies could strengthen markets for goods and services or could discourage undesirable price increases. The possibility that we may, however, get inflation instead of full employment in the future must be recognized. There is danger that supplies of productive agents will become inelastic before full employment is reached. This danger arises not from the use of monetary-fiscal devices to stimulate markets, but from other factors in the economic system. Wage policy is particularly important and may have to be coordinated with monetary-fiscal policy, if we are to maintain full employment without inflation.

Stimulating or retarding markets through tax flexibility appears, in our judgment, to be one of the most promising fiscal techniques. More flexibility may be "built-in" to the tax structure through automatically providing for greater increases in tax collections as prices rise or larger tax decreases as employment falls. Or powers may be granted to monetary and fiscal agencies to increase or reduce taxes as prices rise or employment falls.

There are many supporters for built-in flexibility. Although the writers favor more built-in flexibility than is now present in the tax structure, we do not consider such built-in flexibility as adequate to maintain full employment. Because of our inability to forecast accurately future economic events, some discretionary flexibility in addition to built-in flexibility is required. Both built-in and discretionary tax flexibility avoid the inefficiency in resource allocation which may result from a variable government expenditure program in which government alters the scope of its activities as buyer or producer and employer in order to take up the slack in the private economy. Flexible taxation also does not have to tie income distribution to employment policy— a condition which might prevail if government expanded or contracted its transfer payments to discourage depression or inflation.

Flexible tax policy may be effective in avoiding serious depression or inflation. It may not, however, be successful in pulling the economy out of a deep depression—a depression comparable to that of the thirties, for example. Consequently, other measures which act directly upon employment may need to be held in reserve. If a serious depression is permitted to develop, a huge public works program planned in advance may be necessary to speed recovery.

Timing Fiscal Action

Regardless of the kind of fiscal techniques which are to be utilized—whether they consist of flexible taxes, flexible transfer payments, or public works—decisions must be made as to when the course of fiscal action should be changed.

It will not be difficult for the monetary-fiscal authority—Congress or whatever agency is responsible for changes in fiscal action—to recognize a bad situation. But it is such situations that we wish to prevent. In so far as possible, action should be taken before the situation becomes bad.

Anticipatory action necessitates forecasting. Taking action to prevent a bad situation from arising involves making estimates of the future. The future, however, is almost completely uncertain. No one knows exactly what tomorrow may bring. Each of us expects certain things to happen in the future. Most of us believe with a high probability that the sun will continue to rise in the east each morning and sink beyond the western horizon each evening. Our expectation about tomorrow's temperature, tomorrow's rainfall, or the headlines of tomorrow's newspaper are less certain.

Forecasts of tomorrow are based largely upon the events of today and preceding days. Some continuities do exist. The average summer day is warmer than the average winter day. Trees leaf in the spring and drop their leaves in the fall. Grain turns from green to brown as it ripens. Comparable continuities in economic events are less frequently observed, however.

Furthermore, our knowledge of important economic events of the past is very sketchy. We do not always have all of the information necessary adequately to test the various hypothesis constructed as explanations of certain events that have already occurred. We do not know where we are going, or exactly where we are, and we are not entirely sure where we have been.

Uncertainty can be met with flexibility. It is not necessary that our knowledge of the present and the past continue to be as incomplete as it has been. We are constantly improving the collection of data relating to such factors as the size and distribution of national income, the size of the labor force, the number of unemployed, the prices for various goods and services, the volume of liquid assets held by various economic units, and the ways in which economic units receive and spend money. It appears very likely that in the future we shall know more (though not all that needs to be known) about where we are and where we have been.

Such information, however, will not permit us to forecast with perfect accuracy. Our estimates of the future can still be wrong. In particular we are unlikely to be able to forecast turning points in general business activity—to determine when general business activity will reach a peak in a period of prosperity or will reach a low point in a period of depression. Nevertheless, the level of taxation needed to make fiscal policy effective could be forecasted fairly accurately for short periods during either prosperity or deflation.

Preparations must be made for the course of action to be altered in case the forecast is in error. Our plan must be flexible. Imagine that economic conditions prompted monetary-fiscal agencies to cut taxes in order to avoid an anticipated weakening of markets. The size of this tax reduction is based upon certain advance estimates of the way markets and employment would have been had taxes remained unchanged. These estimates might turn out to be accurate forecasts and the tax reduction would be sufficient to strengthen markets and not large enough to increase prices. On the other hand, markets may turn out to be weaker than were expected. A further tax reduction is in order. Or markets may be stronger than were expected and prices may rise. An increase in taxes would be needed.

Provision for flexibility is a common means for meeting uncertainty. A person going to a restaurant for a meal may anticipate a steak with French-fried potatoes. But, if an entree which he prefers to steak is unexpectedly on the menu, he is usually prepared to alter his plan and order the unexpected dish. Entrepreneurs are not able to forecast accurately market conditions for their products or the productive agents which they use. They may try to incorporate into their production plans provisions for changing these plans in order to meet unexpectedly favorable or unfavorable conditions.[1]

In a full-employment economy, the road between inflation and depression may be very narrow and winding. The road ahead cannot be clearly seen. A turn too far toward stimulating or retarding markets may result in a sudden collision with the cliff of inflation or a fall into the abyss of depression. We must be prepared always to turn away from the cliff or the precipice. Our steering wheel must not be locked after any particular turn is made.

Automatic features reducing administrative discretion area. It appears almost inescapable that considerable discretion in initiating anti-inflationary or antideflationary action will be necessary to maintain full employment or avoid inflation. As long as we can never be reasonably certain about what is going to happen in the future, we cannot correctly specify in advance what should be done and when it should be done. Furthermore, most nondiscretionary devices—the commodity reserve proposal, for example—can be more effective in stabilizing prices than in stabiliz-

---

[1] Refer to Albert Gailord Hart, "Anticipation, Uncertainty and Dynamic Planning," *Studies in Business Administration*, XI, No. 1, 1940, The School of Business, University of Chicago, 1941; and George J. Stigler, "Production and Distribution in the Short Run," *Journal of Political Economy*, 47:3 (June, 1939), pages 305-27. See also A. G. Hart, "The Problem of 'Full Employment,' Facts, Issues, and Policies," *American Economic Review*, Vol. XXXVI, No. 2 (May, 1946, Supplement), pages 280-303.

ing employment. Although this can avoid inflation, it may not be sufficient to curb depression.

Nevertheless, certain automatic features may be built into the monetary-fiscal system to help reduce the area of administrative discretion. Recent developments toward currency in income tax payments make reductions in employment more rapidly reflected in reduced tax collections. Quick refunds together with provisions for carry-back of unused personal exemptions would make our tax system automatically more flexible in periods of increasing unemployment. The commodity reserve proposal discussed in Chapter V is another automatic device, although the writers do not believe that it is sufficient to maintain full employment. It would act toward stabilizing the price of an aggregate of commodities. The price of the bundle and the relative amounts of the various commodities comprising it would be specified. Government would buy or sell at the discretion of private sellers and buyers. No decision by a government administrator as to when to buy or sell would be necessary.

Unemployment insurance is also automatic. In periods of falling employment, the amount of payments made by government to the unemployed would automatically increase and payments to government would decrease. In periods of rising employment the amount of such payments to individuals would automatically diminish and payments to government would expand. Counter-cyclical effects also could be expected from some other programs, such as public health and nutrition programs, which would supplement personal incomes.

Guides to Monetary-Fiscal Action

Any agency charged with administering monetary-fiscal policies must make decisions as to when to initiate certain kinds of actions —when to change tax rates, to increase or decrease grants of income, or to alter the scale of public works. Changes will supposedly be made to improve conditions if they are bad or, preferably, to keep conditions from becoming bad. What are the indicators to which the monetary-fiscal authority might look for clues which will suggest when to act?

The over-all objectives which the monetary-fiscal authority may have in mind are keeping employment at a high level and at the same time preventing inflation. A sharp fall in the general

level of prices not accompanied by a marked decline in employment seems unlikely. Such a situation has not occurred in the
past, and it seems improbable that the structure of our economy
will be changed sufficiently to bring about such a situation in
the future.

A fall in employment without a decline in the general level
of prices seems more probable. The existence of administered
or customary prices for many items makes prices rather sluggish
in response to shifts in demand. Money wage-rates for much of
organized labor are relatively inflexible downward. Employment might fall off considerably before most prices fell.

The index of industrial employment and the index of wholesale prices started falling at about the same time in 1929 and began recovery at about the same time in 1932. This suggests
that the wholesale-price index would have served as a fairly good
guide to action in this period. In the 1937 recession, price falls
lagged somewhat behind the decline in employment, and recovery in employment preceded the rise in prices. In 1920, employment began falling in March. By July the employment
index had declined 7 points, falling by more than 2 points between April and May and between June and July. The index of
wholesale prices *rose* by more than 8 points between March and
May and did not fall as rapidly as 2 points per month until
August. In 1924, the index of employment fell nearly 8 points
between April and July, falling by more than 2 points each month.
An index of wholesale prices fell only 1.7 points during this 3
months period.

Thus changes in a price index—a wholesale-price index,[2] for
example—would not always have given a monetary authority the
proper signal for antidepression action in the past. It appears
likely that prices, because of their increased inflexibility in the
downward direction, are not going to be as useful in guiding antidepression policy in the future as they would have been in the
past.

[2] A retail-price index is obviously less flexible than an index of wholesale prices.
Some components of the wholesale-price index—agricultural prices, for example—
are more flexible than the index as a whole. However, movements in an agri-
cultural-price index would not serve as an adequate guide to monetary-fiscal action.
A serious drought raising agricultural prices could call for anti-inflationary action
sufficient to reduce employment, and a bumper crop could suggest antidepression
action even though employment is not likely to be reduced by such a crop situation.

Price increases, however, are the factors to be observed in guiding anti-inflationary action. Both the level of prices and the rate at which the level is moving upward can provide signals for action against inflation.

The level of unemployment and the rate of change in unemployment are about the only available indicators for anti-depression action. A decrease in aggregate money expenditure for goods and services may precede an increase in unemployment. But, because of large and somewhat peculiar seasonal movements, changes in aggregate money expenditure are difficult to detect until some time after they have occurred. When it is evident that such changes are taking place, monetary-fiscal agencies should act to check developments which are either inflationary enough to cause general price rises or deflationary enough to bring about general unemployment.

Monetary-Fiscal Rules

We have tried to emphasize the importance of flexibility in the operations of monetary-fiscal agencies. In trying to prevent the occurrence of a bad situation—serious unemployment or inflation —advance estimates will have to be made. The conditions assumed in designing these estimates may not hold. No one can forecast the future perfectly. Consequently, although some automatic features can be incorporated into monetary-fiscal operations, the monetary authority must have some freedom to reverse its line of action or to strengthen it as events unfold.

In order to minimize the unfavorable effects of this flexibility upon the operations of other economic units, the rules—the broad framework—within which the monetary-fiscal authority operates should be clearly set forth. This will permit businesses and consuming units to anticipate the kinds of action which may be undertaken by the monetary-fiscal authority.

These rules can consist of (1) a clear statement of the objectives—the maximum level of unemployment which will be tolerated and perhaps the maximum rate of increase in the general level of prices which will be permitted—to be pursued by the monetary-fiscal authority, and (2) an indication of the order in which the various techniques may be brought into use.

What is "Full Employment"?

Much of the controversy over full-employment policy centers

around a definition of full employment.[3] Some people appear to believe that a relatively large pool of unemployed is desirable so that there will always be labor available without wage increases. Others believe that unemployment in the United States cannot be consistently kept below 5 or 6 million persons without a marked increase in the general level of prices resulting.[4] These people apparently consider inflation as more undesirable than moderate unemployment. Still other people believe that all except "frictional" unemployment can and should be eliminated.[5]

It is possible that an objective of "over employment" could be established. Such an objective probably could be achieved only with rapidly rising prices. As we have already pointed out, even a moderately low level of unemployment may not be attainable without inflation, if wages and prices are pushed up rather than employment, and production expanded as markets are strengthened. Controls on wages and prices may be required.

Nevertheless, the objective of preventing unemployment from exceeding, say, 3 million persons does not appear unreasonable. Although data relating to the size of the labor force are not complete, unemployment probably did not exceed 2.5 million (about 6 per cent of the nonfarm labor force) during most of the twenties. During most of 1946, unemployment was less than 2.5 million. Although there was a marked increase in the general level of prices, many of the factors contributing to this increase— the existence of fairly effective price control during the war and its relaxation after the war, the scarcity of goods during the 4 years preceding 1946, and the large wartime expansion in liquid holdings—are likely to be of less importance in future situations.

If further experience indicates that unemployment cannot be kept below 3 million without inflation, a choice must be made between more direct controls over wages and prices or more unemployment. It appears preferable, to us, to set the tolerable level of unemployment relatively low and to watch for non-monetary factors bringing inflation rather than to establish a relatively high

[3] Refer to previous discussion in Chapter I.
[4] See, for example, William J. Fellner, "The Problem of 'Full Employment'— Discussion," *American Economic Review*, Vol. XXXVI, No. 2 (May, 1946, Supplement), pages 323-26.
[5] Refer to William H. Beveridge, *Full Employment in a Free Society*, New York: W. W. Norton & Co., Inc., 1945; John H. Q. Pierson, "The Problem of 'Full Employment'—Discussion," *American Economic Review*, Vol. XXXVI, No. 2 (May, 1946, Supplement), pages 319-23.

limit to unemployment and to neglect these non-monetary factors.

What is Inflation?

Inflation may be defined as an undesirably rapid rate of increase in the general level of prices. Consequently, what is meant by inflation depends upon what is considered undesirable in the way of price advances. Some people would tolerate a rather rapid rate of increase in prices if this would make the maintenance of full employment less difficult. Others believe that the general level of prices should not be permitted to rise at all.

There is some question as to whether a definite limit to the rise in the general level of prices should be stated as a rule of monetary-fiscal policy—if the minimum level of employment constituting full employment is low and is also stated. Without direct controls, monetary-fiscal policy may not be able to maintain full employment and at the same time keep prices stable. And, if a definite limit to the rate of increase in prices is stated, this may encourage price increases. Instead of some economic units expecting no change in prices, others expecting a rise, and still others a decline, soon all may have the expectation of price increases.

Consequently, if a definite limit to price increases is to be a rule, this limit probably will have to be no increase. But enforcement of such a rule, if full employment is also to be maintained, may have to be accomplished by non-monetary devices—direct controls over prices and wages.

Use of monetary-fiscal techniques. Almost regardless of how full employment and inflation are defined, monetary-fiscal agencies seeking to attain the defined objectives are likely to have some choice of various fiscal techniques. Monetary-fiscal agencies may be able, for example, to alter tax rates, to buy or sell securities, or to change the level of public works. Some of the uncertainty with respect to what these agencies are going to do can be eliminated if the order in which the various techniques are to be used is clearly specified.

The notion of deliberate flexibility in the fiscal structure as a means of combating inflation or depression needs to be incorporated into legislation. Until this is done, however, some means which could be used immediately (but only once) are available. For example, in the years immediately ahead, Federal excise taxes should be reduced and provisions should be made to permit averaging of income over a period of years for tax purposes—with carry-backs of unused exemptions and refunds of overpaid taxes.[6]

Such steps should be taken immediately and made a part of the tax structure, in order to introduce a greater degree of equity. However, at the time of writing (1947), these steps should be countered by increases in personal income tax collections, since without such increases the proposed measures would be inflationary. In the absence of legislative willingness to take such combined action, provision might be made for (1) automatically reducing excises and (2) introducing averaging, when economic conditions warrant antideflationary action.

(1) *Changes in tax collections.* The writers have already indicated preference for varying tax collections as the first line of defense against depression or inflation. If forces develop which work toward depression, an encouragement to markets can be provided by a reduction in taxes. If inflation is expected, it can be combated by tax increases. Tax changes, however, cannot fight both inflation and depression at the same time. If employment is falling while prices are rising, either direct controls upon wages and prices or a program directly affecting employment—public works, for example—will also be needed. This does not mean, however, that monetary-fiscal agencies cannot try first to combat inflation or depression by tax changes.

Using the tax system most effectively to fight inflation or depression will require that changes in tax collections be closely related to changes in current expenditure for goods and services. The personal income tax—independently of its adaptability as a flexible tax—should be the major tax. It has already been geared rather closely to current income. Further changes in personal income taxation to permit greater flexibility in over-all tax collections and at the same time to preserve the equity aspects of this tax are discussed in Chapters XIII and XIV.

(2) *Alterations in the scale of public expenditure and public works.* In the event that planned reductions in tax collections

---

[6] Averaging of corporate losses, with a carry-back for two years and a carry-forward for two years, is already permitted.

are not successful in strengthening markets or that stronger markets are not adequate to maintain or increase employment, direct action upon employment itself may be necessary.

Public works expansion can increase employment, because the government expands its role as producer and employer. An expansion in public works sufficient to employ an additional million workers does not mean, however, that unemployment will be reduced by one million. An increase in the level of public works may discourage as well as encourage private employment.

Because of their potentially adverse effect upon resource allocation—particularly the limitations which are likely to be imposed upon the kinds of goods and services which can be produced by government—public works should, in our estimate, be classed as a reserve in any antidepression scheme. First on the reserve list should come relatively small expenditures on such projects as housing construction, soil and forest conservation, and other kinds of public construction which can be rapidly completed or could be completed by private industry. Such measures might have some effect in countering unemployment centered in the construction industry. Expansion of heavy public works to combat depression should not take place until unemployment has reached a fairly sizable level—say 5 or 6 million.

Varieties of public expenditure other than for public works, however, might be expanded with less adverse effects upon resource allocation. For example, subsidization of mass consumption centering around public housing, family allowances, or the underwriting of a minimum food budget do not increase the government's role as producer and employer. Such programs, however, do direct consumption into particular channels and thus indirectly influence resource use.

These transfers are likely to be made primarily to low-income groups and consequently will bring about a closer tie between income distribution and employment policies than is necessary, but they may prove more effective than tax reductions in strengthening markets. We do not know enough about the relative reactions of people to changes in their disposable incomes to state definitely that tax reductions can do everything that could be done by increased transfer payments. If tax reductions do not sufficiently strengthen markets, expanded transfer payments might be the next tool brought into use. If neither reduced taxes nor increased transfer payments do the job, public works expansion would be in order.

Where Does the Money Come From?

Use of the fiscal system to inject or withdraw money would mean discarding a balanced budget as a goal of fiscal policy. Of course, if conditions warrant a balanced budget—if there is no need either to withdraw money or inject it—such a budget is appropriate. But it would be a coincidence, not an objective. Situations warranting a balanced budget rather than a budgetary deficit or surplus certainly do not appear to have been "most probable" situations during the last 50 years and are unlikely to be most probable in the future.

Deficits need not mean an increase in the Federal debt. It is not too difficult for the uninitiated to see what would happen if government accumulated a surplus each year for a relatively large number of years. The bank account of the government would grow at the expense of the bank accounts of taxpayers, or the vaults of the government would hold a growing pile of money.[7]

The incurrence of deficits without the growth of the public debt, or inflation, or both, is more difficult to visualize, unless, of course, there are the accumulations of previous surpluses upon which to draw. In the United States deficit financing has become particularly associated with a rising public debt, partially as an outgrowth of unbalanced budgets and increased public debt during two wars and a depression.

This association is an unfortunate one. When the Federal government wants money, it does not have to collect taxes in order to secure this money, nor does it have to borrow—at least not in traditional ways. The alternative of creating additional money purchasing power is available. If it desires to be subtle in creating this money, the Federal government could borrow directly from the Federal Reserve Banks by issuing interest-free or low-interest securities and exchanging these for deposits with the Reserve banks.

We are not suggesting that government should resort exclu-

[7] There might be difficulties in keeping the accumulated surplus untouched, *i.e.* in inducing legislators to formulate an expenditure program independent of the size of the surplus. As the surplus grew, it might be difficult to keep expenditures from rising. Conversely, it might be difficult to keep expenditures from being cut as the accumulated surplus dwindled.

sively to the printing press for money to pay its bills. However, decisions to tax, to borrow, or to issue money should be based upon an analysis of the probable effects on prices, employment, and interest rates.[8] If commodity prices do not rise as a result of meeting budget deficits from newly issued money, the value of money in terms of goods and services has not fallen. If interest rates do not fall, the value of money in terms of securities has not been depreciated.

Government borrowing from banks, as we have pointed out previously, has been essentially equivalent to printing money and paying the banks a sizable fee—the interest on the government securities offered to them in exchange for deposit credit —for the printing job. If government must borrow from banks rather than issue the money itself, a special low-interest-bearing security for banks might be employed.

The desirability of taxing hinges upon what will happen to prices and employment. If there will be no increase in prices without taxing, "deficit financing" is the procedure to follow. The decision as to how much of the gap to fill by borrowing depends on the impacts upon interest rates. If the size of the gap is given, filling all of it by borrowing may increase interest rates (reduce the prices of outstanding securities); filling it by issuing money is likely to reduce interest rates (increase the prices of existing securities). By varying the combination of borrowing and issuing money, interest rates can be increased, reduced, or kept stable.[9]

[8] These factors are discussed more fully in Chapter XXI which is devoted to consideration of the role of borrowing.

[9] Refer to Abba P. Lerner, *The Economics of Control,* Chapter 24, New York: The Macmillan Company, 1944. Other writers also urge filling the deficit by money issue or its equivalent. See, for example, M. Polanyi, *Full Employment and Free Trade,* Cambridge: Cambridge University Press, 1945; John Philip Wernette, *Financing Full Employment,* Cambridge, Mass.: Harvard University Press, 1945; and Donald C. Marsh, *Taxes Without Tears,* Lancaster, Pennsylvania: Jaques Cattell Press, 1945.

CHAPTER VIII

FISCAL POLICY AND UNEMPLOYMENT: A SUMMARY

How Fiscal Policy Can Affect Employment

IN RECENT economic analyses, there has been growing recognition that the money expenditures and money receipts of government may affect not only the pattern of production and distribution of total product among income receivers, but also the *level* of production and employment within the economy. We have recognized the objective of full employment as one of the most important objectives of public economic policy.

The primary contribution which fiscal policy may make to the achievement and maintenance of full employment is through its influence upon markets—the aggregate level of money expenditure for goods and services. Government's collecting and spending of money can influence markets in two general ways:[1]

(1) *Through influencing the money supply.* The total stock of money can be increased through a budget deficit. A budget surplus can reduce the money supply. Both deficits and surpluses can be accomplished by holding government expenditures for goods and services unchanged and varying tax collections.

(2) *Through altering the distribution of disposable income.* By altering the composition of government receipts and expenditures, income can be shifted among various economic units. If the expenditures are transfer payments, the net effect upon markets depends upon the relative propensities to spend of those from whom the money is collected and those to whom the money is paid. If the expenditures are for goods and services, the effect upon markets is twofold—markets are strengthened directly as a

---

[1] Refer to Chapters III and VI. It is recognized that if fiscal policy is to focus on maintenance of full employment, action must come largely from the Federal government rather than from the various state and local governments. The dominant role of Federal expenditures in the postwar economy seems to justify the assumption that the policies of the Federal government could provide an important influence even if state and local governments do not arrange their fiscal policies to contribute to the Federal objective of full employment.

result of government purchases and influenced directly as a result of the redistribution of disposable income.

Injecting or withdrawing money as a result of budget surpluses or budget deficits affects the cash holdings and the net worth of many individuals and businesses. When government accumulates a budget surplus, the cash balances of the private economy are reduced. Money is withdrawn from individuals and businesses, and no other assets are added to replace the money. When government incurs a budget deficit and fills the gap by issuing money, this money is added to the private sector of the economy. The cash balances of the aggregate of economic units other than government are increased, and no other assets are withdrawn to offset this increase in money holdings. An increase in the quantity of money in the hands of individuals and businesses will strengthen markets for goods and services—if individuals and businesses are unwilling to hold all of this additional money without first trying to acquire additional goods and services.

Through taxing and spending, government may shift purchasing power from one economic unit to another. The units from which net purchasing power (the difference between taxes paid and government expenditures received) is taken are not likely to have the same incomes and preferences as the units to which net purchasing power is given. Consequently, the level as well as the pattern of expenditure for goods and services may be changed as a result of this redistribution of income. Shifting purchasing power from high-income receivers to low-income receivers is likely to result in an expansion in total money expenditure for goods and services—in a strengthening of markets. If the shifts are from low-income to high-income groups, a contraction in money expenditure—a weakening of markets—is to be expected.

As a buyer of goods and services, government may directly affect markets. Government may expand or contract its role as producer and employer, thereby directly affecting employment.

Relations of Employment Policy, Income Distribution, and Resource Allocation

We believe that the first of the methods mentioned above—if it can be effective—is the most desirable path for government to follow in trying to maintain full employment. Strengthening or weakening markets by injecting or withdrawing money can separate the achievement of full employment from the problems of income distribution and resource allocation.[2] The kind of income distribution which is considered desirable because of considerations other than its impact upon markets, may not be the kind of income distribution to bring full employment. Consequently, an important conflict between employment policy and income distribution policy could arise if redistributing income were used as the major technique to promote full employment. Similarly, public expenditure for, or production of, some goods and services may, through influence upon the use of resources, result in a production pattern considerably out of line with consumers' preferences.

Extra-Budgetary Procedures May Be Ineffective

The government budget does not offer the only framework within which money may be injected into, or withdrawn from, the economic system. Commercial banks have been the principal money source in the United States and in many western European countries. However, effective means have not been developed for assuring that the banks will expand the money supply when it would be desirable to try to stimulate markets. The banks cannot be forced to lend, and people cannot be forced to borrow from banks. Open-market operations in commodities or in securities might also be utilized by government to contract or expand the money supply.[3] Suggestions have been made for influencing the demand for cash balances through measures— taxes or subsidies, for example—affecting the value of bank deposits or currency holdings. While such measures have some merit, they are (in our judgment) unlikely to be considered seriously by policy makers.

Although we are not certain about the strength of these techniques, most of them appear likely to be less effective than some

[2] It is recognized that separating full-employment policy and income distribution policy is more easily accomplished in theory than in practice. For example, a change in tax collections is likely to alter the relative income distribution. Although changes in transfer payments could be made to restore the previous relative distribution, such changes are less likely to be made than the tax changes, in our judgment.

[3] These techniques have been discussed in more detail in Chapter V.

fiscal techniques in influencing markets. They also pose difficulties not presented by some budgetary techniques. First of
all, such transactions affect mostly the composition of assets held
by various potential buyers. For each dollar of money injected
by government, a dollar's worth of other assets—securities or
commodities—is removed. Although markets may be influenced
by buyers' liquidity, the effect of a given change in money holdings is likely to be smaller when only liquidity is affected than
when both liquidity and total assets are changed in the same
direction.

Trading in securities may affect largely the cash balances of
economic units whose expenditures for goods and services are not
likely to be influenced strongly by changes in their cash balances.
Furthermore, purchase and sale of securities by government
might change interest rates more than is desirable. Because of
the relatively large bank holdings of government securities, a
potential increase in interest rates may impose a particularly important limitation upon securities sales in combating inflation.
Government sale of securities could mean a marked increase in
interest rates and a consequent reduction in the prices of existing
government securities.[4]

Considerable merit is recognized in trading in commodities,
particularly the commodity reserve proposal, under which a
specified bundle of commodities would be bought and sold by
the government at some fixed price. But it was recognized that
the costs of holding stocks of commodities might be relatively
large, that it would be difficult to initiate such a program as an
anti-inflation measure if stocks of the various commodities were
not already held, and that if a considerable amount of a commodity had been accumulated, political pressure on the government to prevent its sale might be great.[5]

In view of these considerations, using the fiscal system seems
preferable to using these extra-budgetary devices, as the basic
means for influencing markets.

[4] It was recognized in Chapter V that the effects of trading in securities will be
more complex when government purchase and sale of securities to the banking
system are involved.
[5] This is well illustrated in the experience of the Federal government in accumulating over 9 million bales of cotton through the last dozen years. Open-
market sale of this cotton at "free" prices recently has not been considered
politically feasible.

Influencing Markets May Not Be Sufficient

Throughout the preceding chapters in this book we have tried to emphasize an important limitation to achievement of full employment through influencing the demands for goods and services. Even though monetary-fiscal policies may be successful in influencing demand—in encouraging expansion or contraction of total private expenditure for goods and services—this may not be sufficient to guarantee both full employment and a stable general level of prices. In fact, only rising prices may result. Supplies may become relatively inelastic before full employment is reached.[6]

This possibility of getting inflation instead of full employment is not a straw man. There is evidence that price and wage increases contributed to choking recovery in the United States in 1937, long before full employment was reached. In 1947, it was widely predicted that the postwar boom would end prematurely because of rising costs and prices catching up too rapidly with strong markets.

We need much additional analysis of the factors which may contribute to this substitution of inflation for full employment. A choice may have to be made between full employment and stable prices as an objective of monetary-fiscal policy. If we want both full employment and stable prices and we use monetary-fiscal policy to get *one* of these objectives, other devices must be employed to reach the other. Monetary-fiscal policies can help to maintain full employment if direct controls on prices and wages are applied. But this may be a greater sacrifice of "free" markets than we will want to make. Relatively high excess-profits taxation and a dispersal of the powers of large selling units may be more acceptable but less effective techniques.

Fiscal Policies Must Be Flexible[7]

Because of the desirability of taking fiscal action to prevent the occurrence of a bad situation—a large number of unemployed, for example—present action must be based upon fore-

---

[6] Refer to Chapter IV and VI. See also Martin Bronfenbrenner, "The Dilemma of Liberal Economics," *Journal of Political Economy,* Vol. LIV, No. 4, pages 334-46.

[7] Refer to Chapter VII.

casts of the future. Unfortunately, these forecasts can and frequently will be considerably in error.

This means that the course of fiscal action cannot be completely charted in advance. Enough flexibility must be permitted to enable adjustment to unexpected contingencies. Some automatism may be built into the fiscal system. But personal judgment about when to do what cannot be completely avoided.

However, the area for administrative discretion can, and undoubtedly will, be delimited by legislation enacted by Congress. Although a set of rules cannot be formulated which will specify exactly what monetary-fiscal agencies should do in every situation, such things as limitations upon the size of the budget deficit or surplus, maximum quarterly changes in the tax rates, and limitations upon the variations in the rate of interest can be set forth by Congress. Administration of fiscal and monetary policy within the framework of these rules clearly implies coordination of the fiscal and monetary activities of the Federal government.

Conclusions: Some Implications of Full-Employment Fiscal Policy

It is evident that full-employment fiscal policy would be primarily concerned with the impact of fiscal activities upon such factors as the general level of prices, employment, and interest rates. Consequently, decisions to tax, borrow, or issue money (at the Federal level) would be based on what would happen to prices, employment, and interest rates as a result of various combinations of taxation, borrowing, and money issue.

This clearly means that some of our traditional canons of sound, conservative finance would have to be abandoned. It means that the role of public finance would become more than simply raising money to pay public bills.

But full-employment fiscal policy does not mean that the public will be without control over the formulation and administration of this policy. Monetary-fiscal agencies, operating under rules formulated by Congress, are not free to act without limitations.

As one writer has said, "Full employment means a flexible fiscal policy if we retain the price system . . . and full employment may be essential to the maintenance of 'free enterprise.'" [8] For

---

[8] Donald C. Marsh, *Taxes Without Tears*, pages 92-94, by permission of The Ronald Press Company.

those who (like the writers of this book) would like to see the system of "free enterprise" continued, a full-employment fiscal policy is a small price to pay.

SELECTED READINGS

1. Beveridge, William H., *Full Employment in a Free Society*, New York: W. W. Norton & Co., Inc., 1945.
2. Boulding, Kenneth E., *The Economics of Peace*, Chapter 6, New York: Prentice-Hall, Inc., 1945.
3. Bowman, Mary Jean and Bach, George Leland, *Economic Analysis and Public Policy*, Chapters 45 and 50, New York: Prentice-Hall, Inc., 1943.
4. Bronfenbrenner, Martin, "The Dilemma of Liberal Economics," *Journal of Political Economy*, 54:4 (August, 1946), pages 334-46.
5. Clark, J. M., *Strategic Factors in Business Cycles*, New York: National Bureau of Economic Research, 1934.
6. Federal Reserve Board, *Federal Reserve Bulletin*, February, 1946-1947, Washington, D. C.: United States Government Printing Office.
7. Fisher, Allan G. B., *Economic Progress and Social Security*, London: Macmillan & Co., Ltd., 1945.
8. Haavelmo, Trygve, "Multiplier Effects of a Balanced Budget," *Econometrica*, 13:4 (October, 1945), pages 311-18.
9. Hansen, Alvin H., *America's Role in the World Economy*, New York: W. W. Norton & Co., Inc., 1945.
10. ———, *Economic Policy and Full Employment*, Chapter XVI, New York: McGraw-Hill Book Co., Inc., 1947.
11. Hart, Albert G., "Anticipations, Uncertainty and Dynamic Planning," *Studies in Business Administration*, Chicago: School of Business, University of Chicago, 1940.
12. ———, Allen, Edward D., *et al.*, *Paying for Defense*, Philadelphia: The Blakiston Company, 1941.
13. ———, "The Problem of 'Full Employment,' Facts, Issues and Policies," *American Economic Review*, 36: Supplement. (May, 1946), pages 280-90.
14. Hicks, J. R., *Value and Capital*, Chapters 6-9 and 15-17, Oxford: Clarendon Press, 1939.
15. Keynes, J. M., *The General Theory of Employment, Interest and Money*, New York: Harcourt, Brace & Co., 1936.

16. Klein, Lawrence R., "The Use of Econometric Models as a Guide to Economic Policy," *Econometrica*, 15:2 (April, 1947), pages 111-51.

17. Lange, Oscar, *Price Flexibility and Employment*, Bloomington, Indiana: Principia Press, 1944.

18. Lerner, Abba P., *The Economics of Control*, Chapters 22, 23, and 24, New York: The Macmillan Company, 1944.

19. —— and Graham, Frank D., editors, *Planning and Paying for Full Employment*, Princeton: Princeton University Press, 1946.

20. Marsh, Donald B., *Taxes Without Tears*, Lancaster, Pennsylvania: Jaques Cattell Press, 1945.

21. Modigliani, Franco, "Liquidity Preference and the Theory of Interest and Money," *Econometrica*, 12:1 (January, 1944), pages 45-88.

22. Pierson, John H. Q., "The Underwriting of Aggregate Consumption Spending as a Pillar of Full Employment Policy," *The American Economic Review*, 34:1 (March, 1944), pages 21-55.

23. Polanyi, Michael, *Full Employment and Free Trade*, Cambridge, England: Cambridge University Press, 1945.

24. Samuelson, Paul A., "The Effect of Interest Rate Increases on the Banking System," *American Economic Review*, 35:1 (March, 1945), pages 16-27.

25. Schumpeter, J. A., *Business Cycles*, New York: McGraw-Hill Book Co., Inc., 1939.

26. Six Economists, *Public Finance and Full Employment*, Postwar Economic Study No. 3, Board of Governors of the Federal Reserve System, 1945, Washington, D. C.: United States Government Printing Office.

27. Stigler, George J., "Production and Distribution in the Short Run," *Journal of Political Economy*, 47:3 (June, 1939), pages 305-27.

28. Symposium of Economists, *Financing American Prosperity*, New York: The Twentieth Century Fund, 1945.

29. Treasury Department, *Treasury Bulletin*, November, 1946, Washington, D. C.: United States Government Printing Office.

30. Wernette, John Phillip, *Financing Full Employment*, Cambridge, Massachusetts: Harvard University Press, 1945.

PART THREE

GOVERNMENT EXPENDITURES AND
EFFECTS OF FISCAL POLICIES
UPON INCOME DISTRIBUTION
AND RESOURCE ALLOCATION

CHAPTER IX

THE ROLE OF GOVERNMENT EXPENDITURE

IN THE fiscal year 1940, all units of government in the United States spent about 17.4 billion dollars, exclusive of funds spent for debt retirement. Expenditure may be 20 to 25 billions greater than this in the years ahead, and the relative amounts spent for various purposes will be somewhat different than in 1940. Units of government, however, will continue to spend for about the same things as in 1940.[1]

For purposes of our analysis, government expenditures may be divided into two groups: (1) resource-using and (2) transfer expenditures. About three-fourths of expenditures in 1940 were for the use of resources. In a year (such as 1950) following reconversion, resource-using expenditures are expected to constitute about two-thirds of total government expenditures.[2]

To discuss when government should use resources which otherwise could be used in the private economy is the principal purpose of this chapter. The level of transfer expenditures affects the division of resources between the public and private sectors of the economy only to a minor extent. Consequently, the desirable level of transfer payments is dependent upon the desired income distribution, a subject to be examined in the following chapter. To say that resources could be used in the private economy does not mean that they always will be used. Where there are unemployed resources, there may be a place for in-

---

[1] For a summary of the kinds and amounts of public expenditures made during the fiscal year 1941, see Table 2, Chapter I. For recent estimates on postwar expenditures, see Lewis H. Kimmel, *et al.*, *Postwar Fiscal Requirements, Federal, State and Local,* page 12, Washington, D. C.: Brookings Institution, 1945.

[2] The increase in transfer expenditures is expected to arise mainly from increased interest on Federal debt and increased benefits to veterans. If there is relatively full employment, the relevant distinction between types of expenditures would be *exhaustive* (resource-diverting) and *transfer* (not involving the diversion of resources to public purposes). For earlier reference to this distinction, see Chapter I, page 19. The estimates are based largely on data provided in *Postwar Fiscal Requirements, Federal, State and Local.*

creased use of resources by government. This problem will be briefly considered in the final section of this chapter.

Economic factors are not the only ones which are weighed by policy makers in determining the proper sphere for governmental use of resources in our essentially private economy. Let us assume, however, that this problem is being solved in terms of economic considerations and that the objective in transferring resources from the private economy to the public economy (or *vice versa*) is to maximize the size of the total product.

Criterion for Determining When Total Product Is Maximized

Imagine that our entire economy is a private economy—that is, that government uses no resources—and that the economy is divided into two sectors, A and B. Both sectors use the same resources, and units of this resource are homogeneous and freely transferable from one sector to the other. Sector A produces only pork while sector B produces only beans. If consumers exercise free choice in their purchases of pork and beans, the total product is maximized when a small amount of the resource used in B adds to the total product an amount of beans worth exactly as much as the amount of pork this resource would produce if it were used in A. This equality of the values of the marginal products of a resource in each of its alternative uses is the guiding principle for the "best" allocation[3] of the resource.

If government were to take over sector B and to continue to produce beans, this same criterion for allocating the resource would still be valid. Unless there was a change in the relative prices or the efficiency with which government produced was greater or less than the level of efficiency which had prevailed before government took over sector B, the size of the total product could not be increased by any shift of resources out of one sector and into the other.

Criterion neglects differences between the public and private economies. In order to apply this criterion to comparisons between two sectors of the economy, the different goods which are produced must have prices attached to them. Otherwise total product cannot be measured in any convenient manner.

[3] Refer for example, to Oscar Lange, "The Foundations of Welfare Economics," *Econometrica*, 10:215-28 (July–October, 1942).

Since many of the services produced by government are not sold in the usual sense, the relative weights which are attached to these services are not determined in the market.   The formulation and administration of our laws is a service which we could hardly afford to sell, and, although the kind of services provided by public schools and public roads could be sold, such services are not distributed among our citizens in the same manner as pork, beans, autos, and the like.

Consequently, the relative weights attached to most of the services provided by the public economy are determined politically. The values of these various services as compared with the values of the services which could be produced in the private economy are determined rather crudely by legislators when they decide what level of government services to provide.

This criterion is not always valuable.   Equality of the values of the marginal products of a resource in each of its various uses is a valid guide to resource allocation, if relative prices are an accurate measure of relative social benefits and if the best technology is being utilized in each line of production.   If these conditions are not present, an increase in the total product may be achieved by shifting resources from one use to another even though there is equality in the values of the marginal products in the various uses.

Thus, in determining whether to shift resources from the private to the public economy or *vice versa,* two important factors which should guide our decision are: (1) the relative efficiencies of public and private production of a given product and (2) the degree to which relative prices are an adequate index of relative social benefits.

Relative prices may not accurately indicate relative social benefits if (1) the prices which people are willing to pay for given amounts of a product are less than the marginal benefits provided by these products to society as a whole, and (2) the prices at which supplies of a given product are forthcoming do not take into consideration all of the (social) costs of obtaining these supplies.

Even though relative demand prices reflect relative social benefits accurately and relative costs include social costs, there are sectors of economic activity where certain institutional factors (particularly monopoly and monopsony) prevent benefits and costs from being equated. Each of these factors will be considered in the discussion which follows.

Government Production Better than Private in Some Areas

Government may be able to produce some services more efficiently than private producers because government may be able to eliminate some steps in getting the product to consumers.

Fiscally, it is not necessary for government to collect from the users of its services in the same way that private producers collect. Government may (and does) make some services available to all who wish to use them without reducing the incomes of each user by an amount necessary to cover production costs for the services. This is the net effect of general taxation to finance government services.[4]

The financing of private production is somewhat different from the financing of government production. Although a private producer may utilize funds which he already has on hand or may borrow from other economic units, in the long run he must plan his operations so that receipts are at least equal to expenditures. This means that he must collect from the buyers of the goods and services which he produces. In a free market the amount of money collected from each buyer must be related to the amount of product purchased. The product must be measured.

In some instances, the costs of measuring the product and collecting from buyers on the basis of the amount purchased by each may be high compared to the other costs involved in producing the service. In such instances, there is a case for governmental *distribution* of the product if it is not necessary for government to collect on the basis of individual use.

Imagine a situation in which all highways were privately operated and funds were collected on the basis of the amount of services used—the number of ton miles driven, for example. A large administrative staff would be required to see that consumers

---

[4] The funds needed by government (especially the national government) to produce these services can be secured from other sources, too. Direct creation of purchasing power through money issue or borrowing from banks can be utilized by the national government. When the level of employment is not affected by resort to these sources of funds, the effect upon the private economy is comparable to that of a tax. When the level of employment is expanded, however, the private economy will shrink less than when government production is financed from taxation. For a more complete discussion, refer to Chapter III.

paid to use the roads and that they paid according to amount of service received.   Checks would be required to assure that everyone paid to use a highway and that each user of the highway drove no farther than merited by his payment.   The costs of making such checks would be large compared to construction and maintenance costs (for our approximately 3 million miles of rural roads alone in the United States), considering the large number of exits and entrances to highways in this country.   The administrative costs might not be excessive for a particular highway,[5] but would become absurdly high if the highway system as a whole was operated on this basis.[6]

If efficiency in resource allocation is to be admitted as a consideration in determining the division of resource use between the public and private economies, there are cases where the superiority of methods available to government for distribution of the product should not be ignored.   *The major resulting benefit is that the resources which are needed to collect from consumers on the basis of amount of product used can be made available for other purposes, public or private.*   This is an evident benefit from the public distribution of highway services, as already indicated. Collecting for each use of streets and sidewalks would create an impossible administrative situation.   Again, where the (marginal) cost of getting water to users is low, metering and collecting on the basis of use may be more costly than providing water free of charge.

There may be other areas in which the techniques of production available to government are superior to those available to private producers.   However, the economy in getting products

[5] For the first full year of its operation (October, 1940, through October, 1941) even the Pennsylvania Turnpike had costs of fare collection and turnpike patrol that were 8.2 per cent of its revenue of $3,451,000.   Although publicly operated, this Turnpike is an illustration of excellent conditions for operation and administration that could be assumed for private enterprise.

[6] Sellers could develop other techniques than have been used in collecting for the services which they produce.   For example, if the cost of meters and their installation were so expensive that it was not economic to install them in every home or office, sellers of electricity might charge on the basis of the size and number of electrical appliances operated by each user.   Similarly, if highways were privately operated, collection for services might be made on the basis of such indices of highway use as the occupation of the auto owner, age of the vehicle, and its gross weight, among other things.   Opportunities for evasion and the accompanying overcharging of other users would be numerous, however.   Unless collections coincided fairly closely with the amount of services used, the amount produced might be considerably reduced.

into the hands of consumers is obvious and serves as an illustration of a more general case.

Relative Demand Prices Not Always an Accurate Index of Relative Social Benefits

Equality of the values of the marginal products of a resource in all of its various uses is a valid criterion for allocating resources so that the total product is maximized—when relative prices are an accurate index of relative social benefits. If our economy were solely private and each consumer were allocating his own income to maximize his own satisfaction, an individual's demand schedule for a product would represent a schedule of the sacrifices of *other* products which he would be willing to make in order to get various quantities of *this* product. Demand prices would represent estimates of expected individual benefits.

Some products, however, provide benefits to persons other than the immediate users of these products. For example, educational training may benefit other persons as well as the individuals receiving the training. Since individuals are unlikely to be willing to pay for things which they do not receive (as long as they can get other things by paying for them), services providing benefits to persons other than their users are likely to be undervalued in a strictly private economy. Their relative prices are likely to be lower than they would be if all benefits—those going to others as well as to the purchaser—were considered.

A rather large proportion of services produced by government are of the kind which provide benefits to persons other than the immediate users. Public education, national defense, public health, police and fire protection are among the many examples. The widespread benefits from public education are particularly evident. Although total productivity is increased as a result of education, the additional product is seldom entirely captured by persons who learned and now possess the skills. Part of the benefits of the skills acquired are passed on to the members of the economy as a whole. Education which consists of transmitting knowledge of the way in which our social and economic system functions is likely to result in improved economic and social institutions benefiting others in addition to those receiving the training.

In areas where the range of these "extra-buyer" benefits is

large—as in education—there is a case for government either producing these services or altering relative incentives to encourage additional production and use of them in the private economy. The latter procedure, however, is likely to be rather cumbersome. It would involve subsidies to producers to encourage production and discriminatory subsidies to consumers to encourage more widespread use of these goods and services which provide extra-buyer benefits. Consequently, governmental production and dissemination of such services appears the more desirable procedure.

Relative Supply Prices Not Always an Accurate Index of Relative Social Costs

A second kind of divergence between private and social interests is presented on the supply side of the market picture. Not only may demand prices underestimate social benefits, but supply prices may underestimate social costs.

Just as his demand schedule represents the buyer's willingness to sacrifice other opportunities in return for various amounts of a given good, the supply schedule represents what has to be sacrificed in order to induce sellers to part with various quantities of the good. Supply prices infrequently include costs to economic units other than those producing the product. For example, the supply prices of a metal are not likely to include the "smoke nuisance" costs to the persons residing near a smelter, or supply prices of lumber are unlikely to consider as costs the increased erosion resulting from the removal of the cover provided by the forests.

The problem posed in this situation where supply prices do not include all of the costs is one which has been given considerable attention by economists.[7] Finding solutions to these problems entails either discovering ways to force private producers to include all costs or having government take over production in these areas. Subsidies to producers conditional upon their reducing the smoke nuisance, conserving the soil, and the like may be one solution. However, this may prove an extremely cumbersome procedure. Governmental operation in these areas where these external diseconomies are relatively large may be desirable.

[7] See, for example, A. C. Pigou, The Economics of Welfare, 2nd edition, London: Macmillan & Co., Ltd., 1924.

Criterion for Maximum Production in the Private Economy
Not Always Satisfied

The general cases which we have been discussing are those where equality of the values of the marginal products of a resource in all of its various uses cannot be applied as a test for maximum product without qualification. In determining the division of resources between the public and private economies, it must be recognized that the products of the public economy are seldom "priced" in a free market, that government may have important advantages in producing some products, and that demand and supply prices in a free market may neglect important elements of social benefits and social costs.

In addition to these cases, there are situations to which this criterion of equality among the values of the marginal products of a resource in all of its various uses could be applied and yet is not satisfied. An important class of such cases has been labelled "monopoly."

A private producer will be maximizing his profits when his marginal revenue from output is equal to his marginal cost of output.[8] However, it is only under perfect competition that marginal revenue and price of the product will be identical. It is only under conditions where the price of the product is equal to marginal revenue (and the price of the resource is equal to its marginal cost) that equating marginal revenue and marginal cost of output will equate also the value of the marginal product of an increment of a resource and the price of that resource. Thus, if the product-demand schedules and resource-supply schedules that face the firm are not perfectly elastic, product prices will not be equal to marginal revenue of output and factor prices will not be equal to marginal cost of input. Unless the elasticities of the product-demand schedules facing every firm are exactly the same and the elasticities of the factor-supply schedules are also equal for every firm, the best allocation of resources will not result from each firm maximizing its profits.

For example, imagine that all (OA) of a specialized resoure, A, is being used in two industries, X and Y, and that both industries

---

[8] This is a necessary, but not a sufficient, condition. Marginal revenue must be falling more rapidly (or rising more slowly) than marginal costs in order for equality of marginal revenue and marginal cost to represent a position of maximum rather than minimum profit.

are "competitive," that is, there is free entry of firms into either industry and the product demand-schedule as well as the resource supply-schedule facing any firm is perfectly elastic. Assume that units of the resource are freely transferable (at no cost) between the two industries and that there are many resource owners competing with each other, unable to follow a price policy and selling always in the best market. Alternative uses for the factor are assumed to bring no return, and the resource owners have no reservation price. The price of the factor will then be the same in both industries, and, in the long run, the factor price will be equal to the value of the marginal product in both industries. The curves XK and YL in Figure 2 represent schedules of the value of the marginal products in the two industries, prices for X and Y changing as the division of the resource between the two industries makes possible the production of various combinations of X and Y. Assume that production and demand conditions in the two industries are such that OA_1 of A is used in producing X and A_1A is used in producing Y.

If the X industry is monopolized, its demand for A will no longer be a schedule of the value of the marginal product of A in producing X. Instead it will be the *marginal revenue product* —the curve XK' in Figure 2. OA_2 of A will now be employed in producing X and A_2A in producing Y. As a result of monopolization (there being no change in the production functions), A_2A_1 of A has been forced into the Y industry and the factor price has fallen.

Similarly, if the Y industry had been monopolized (there being no change in the production functions) the Y industry's demand schedule for A might be YL'. If the X industry were competitive OA_3 of A would be employed in X and A_3A in Y, A_1A_3 having been forced into the Y industry.

If both industries are monopolized, the division of A between the two industries will be the same as the competitive division only if the elasticity of demand for X at that output at which OA_1 is used in producing X is the same as the elasticity of demand for Y at that output where A_1A is used in producing Y.

Various prices which the producers of X will be willing to pay for various amounts of the factor of production (A) when the X industry is producing under competitive conditions, are represented by the line XK. These prices represent the values of the

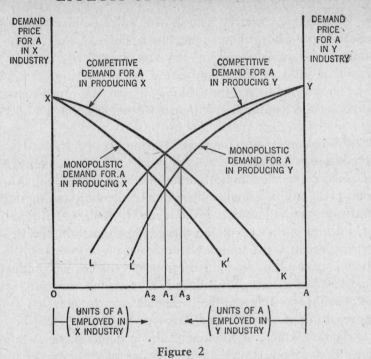

Figure 2

Effects of Monopoly on Resource Allocation

The competitive demand for A in X is $f_a P_x$, while the competitive demand for A in Y is $\phi_a P_y$, where f_a is the marginal physical product of A in X, ϕ_a is the marginal physical product of A in Y, P_x is the price of X, and P_y is the price of Y.

When X is monopolized (fa remaining unchanged), the demand for A in X becomes $f_a P_x\left(1 - \dfrac{1}{\eta x}\right)$ where $P_x\left(1 - \dfrac{1}{\eta x}\right)$ is the marginal revenue from X and η_x is the elasticity of demand for X. Similarly, the monopolistic demand for A in Y is $\phi_a\, P_y\left(1 - \dfrac{1}{\eta y}\right)$ where $P_y\left(1 - \dfrac{1}{\eta y}\right)$ is the marginal revenue from Y and η_y is the elasticity of demand for Y.

$$f_a\, P_x\left(1 - \frac{1}{\eta x}\right) = \phi_a\, P_y\left(1 - \frac{1}{\eta y}\right) \text{ at } A_1 \text{ only if } \eta_x = \eta_y.$$

marginal product of A in producing X. Similarly, the line YL represents prices which competitive producers of Y will be willing to pay for various amounts of A.

When the X industry is monopolized (on the assumption of no change in physical production conditions within the industry), the demand for A in producing X will fall (see line XK').   The monopolist will be willing to pay the factor owners the marginal revenue product (marginal revenue multiplied by the marginal physical product) rather than the value of the marginal product (price multiplied by marginal physical product).   Similarly, monopolizing the Y industry will reduce the demand for A in producing Y (see line YL').

The difference between marginal revenue and price depends on the elasticity of demand for the product.   The more elastic the demand, the smaller the difference between price and marginal revenue.   Thus, if both the X and Y industries were monopolized, the division of the factor (A) between the two industries would be the same as under competitive conditions only if the elasticities of demand for X and Y at the competitive outputs were equal. Note that the price for A would be lower under monopoly than under competition even though the division of the factor between the two industries remained unchanged.

Several ways have been suggested for dealing with the resource misallocation which results from monopoly.   Most of these solutions fall into one of the following categories: (1) restoring competition, (2) regulation, (3) subsidization, and (4) socialization.   We shall examine each briefly.

Restoring competition.   There are some areas of production where, by maintaining control of supplies of raw materials or productive processes, a few producers are able to dominate the field.   Before World War II, the Aluminum Company of America had almost complete control of the sources of bauxite for producing aluminum.[9]   The world's most complete monopoly was probably that of the DeBeers Company which controlled the mining of diamonds.   Taking steps to break the stranglehold over raw materials and patents, to achieve increased competition in the field through encouraging freedom of entry, to break down giant firms into a large number of smaller firms, and to increase competition in general—this has been the historic basis of our national antitrust policy since passage of the Sherman Act in 1890. Enforced with varying degrees of indifference since its passage,

---

[9] Production necessities of World War II resulted in the breaking of the aluminum monopoly and the creation of a handful of new firms.   Whether the new firms in the field will proceed much differently than did *Alcoa* before the war in price and production policy remains to be seen.

the Sherman Act has occasionally resulted in sensational dissolution of national combinations declared to be "in restraint of trade." Best known are the dissolution of the Standard Oil trust and the American Tobacco trust in 1910. It is doubtful, however, whether much restoration of competition can be attributed to either of these acts of "trust busting." [10]

Restoring competition may often work against efficient production. Increasing attention has been paid in recent years to the effects on efficiency in production of the traditional policy of breaking a large unit into a number of smaller ones. Numerous small firms can operate more efficiently than large ones in such a field as agriculture. In some fields other than agriculture, it may be that placing limitations upon the maximum scale of operations of any firm (so that no producer can alter the price at which he can sell the product by altering his output) would result in no loss in technical efficiency.

There are many other areas of production, however, where limitations on the size of firms will reduce efficiency—where the average costs of production of a given total output by small firms are in excess of those in large firms. It is easy to visualize this clearly if we think of the duplication of investment which would be involved in many firms supplying electricity to a city of 10,000. American economic history provides us with other examples of relatively few firms of some minimum size emerging as part of an industry. Thus, from an initial period in the early 1900's when there were several hundred firms, the automobile industry had "shaken down" to less than a dozen firms by 1940. One of the smallest (and most active) of these is the Studebaker Corporation, which indicated assets of about 38.5 million dollars at the end of 1940. In general, it appears that if we want to preserve the technological efficiencies which go with bigness in many industries, and still reduce the divergencies between social bene-

---

[10] Thus, the Standard Oil trust was dissolved, but control of the various Standard Oil companies remained in Rockefeller hands for many years. This was shown in 1929 when, in the famous proxy fight between Rockefeller and Stewart for control of Standard Oil of Indiana, the large bloc of stock which the Rockefeller interests owned plus the relatively small percentage of proxies which they obtained was more than enough to outvote the Stewart interests. The four great tobacco companies which emerged from the tobacco dissolution have continued to follow a fairly uniform price policy, and such competition as has arisen has come from small or new companies. Tobacco would appear to be a difficult field to monopolize, with the abundant sources of raw materials from small, individual producers. But competition on a price basis has not been noticeable.

fits and costs, we must look for techniques other than reducing the sizes of firms.

In situations where competition cannot be economically restored (where limitations on the size of firms cannot be established without markedly reducing the efficiency of production), it may be possible to redirect monopoly by altering the conditions facing the operator.   Conditions might be so changed that the producer would find it to his interest to act in a manner which would equate price with marginal cost (generally speaking, to expand output).   One such technique is through governmental enactment of maximum prices—the long-established technique of the *regulation* of public utility rates—and other practices.

Regulation.   This technique is used by state public utility commissions, by the Interstate Commerce Commission, and by other rate-making (and regulatory) bodies.   The price is fixed independently of the producer's output.   He cannot alter the price by changing the amount of his production.   If the price can be established so that it is equal to minimum average costs of production, the monopolist is forced to equate marginal social benefits with marginal private costs, or retire from production. Generally speaking, this will result in a fuller utilization of his plant, and a larger output at lower prices—somewhere around what would be the competitive level.

The regulatory approach, however, has long posed serious difficulties.   Even if the regulators have a strong sense of public interest (and are not too receptive to "courtesies" offered by the regulated) there may be relatively high costs entailed in getting the information and making the proper decisions for adequate regulation.   There has been constant dispute between public utilities and regulatory commissions over the valuation of utility property as a base for rates which would yield a "fair" return. A fair return has been one of the subjects of disagreement.

From a social point of view, prices should be set so that demand and supply are equated at the point of minimum average cost.   Consequently, the rate makers must know at least as much about the demands for a regulated product and its cost of production as do the producers.   Two complete sets of experts—one for the producer and one for government—are required.   This duplication may be an important cost in terms of the other things which one set of experts might be accomplishing.

Our experience with regulation bears out its limitations. Except in scattered areas, like Wisconsin, control of utility rates and practices has not been very successful from a welfare point of view. Some people have, in fact, given up the possibilities of making regulation effective;[11] others continue to argue that regulation has never been given a fair chance.[12] The numerous difficulties in redirecting monopoly through regulation are almost universally recognized.

Subsidization (and taxation). Another possible technique for redirecting monopoly production would be to utilize subsidies[13] so producers would be encouraged to expand their output to the point where price is equated with marginal costs. This would eliminate the waste of resources which is inherent in monopoly itself. Producers could be induced to produce at the point where marginal cost equals price by paying them a subsidy per unit of output equal to the difference between price and marginal revenue at this output (see Figure 3). Producers would be maximizing the difference between gross receipts (including subsidy) and gross expenses by producing at this level. They would, of course, be making rather large profits.

Presumably, it would then be possible to levy (and collect) a 100 per cent tax on *monopoly* profits without disturbing in any way the decision of the producer about subsequent amounts which he would produce or supply.[14] (See Figure 3.) Actually, it has been recognized that any given producer might be quite indifferent to expansion beyond his monopoly output if he faced the prospect of a tax confiscatory on all "extra-normal" profits which he might make. To meet this objection, it has been suggested that the rate of tax on monopoly profits might be decreased as the monopolist approached more closely to capacity (optimum) production beyond his monopoly output.[15]

[11] See, for example, Bauer, "Can Utility Rate Regulation Be Made Effective?" *Public Utilities Fortnightly,* 19:797 (June 24, 1937), and Henry C. Simons, "A Positive Program for Laissez Faire," *Public Policy Pamphlet No. 15,* 1934, page 11.

[12] See Thompson and Smith, *Public Utility Economics,* pages 622-624, New York: McGraw-Hill Book Co., Inc., 1941.

[13] Refer to Benjamin Higgins, "Postwar Tax Policy I," *Canadian Journal of Economics and Political Science,* 9:3 (August, 1943), pages 425 ff; D. B. Marsh, *Taxes Without Tears,* Chapters IX and X. Reference is also made to this possibility by Joan Robinson in *Economics of Imperfect Competition,* pages 163-165, The Macmillan Company, 1934. Somewhat similar proposals can be found in the writings of Edgeworth, Pigou, and Marshall.

[14] For an arithmetical example of the "all-out" subsidy-tax approach, see Marsh's note to Chapter X of *Taxes Without Tears.*

[15] See especially the treatment by Higgins, "Postwar Tax Policy I."

Limited possibilities of antimonopoly fiscal policy.   Criticisms of existing antimonopoly regulation may be admitted, yet the probability of fiscal action doing much better is not very great. First of all, it would be impossible (or nearly so) for monetary-fiscal agencies to make rational decisions as to the amount of subsidy to be given particular industries, or to firms within those industries.   Furthermore, it would be difficult to determine the rate of taxation which should be applied to recapture excess profits.   And it would not be easy to define a set of rules for subsidization and taxation which would prevent discriminatory treatment (favorable or unfavorable) of particular producers.

It is generally agreed that monopoly is a matter of degree, and that it is difficult to find business firms (with the possible exception of firms in agriculture) which do not enjoy, to some extent, elements of monopoly protection (either in selling goods and services or in buying them) which affect to some extent their pricing and output policies.[16]   For durable goods, an indicator of the adequacy of the subsidy might be provided by inventories. If inventories piled up, the subsidy would be too large and *vice versa*.   For services, however, there are no such guides.

The second criticism follows from the first.   Although the plan might get rid of regulatory rate-making commissions, the administration of the plan would require administrators to have much knowledge of the demand for any given product and costs of producing it.   *The cost of a double set of experts would be introduced all over again and the real costs of administration might remain relatively high.*[17]

The role of government operation (socialization).   We have already indicated several times that, in our economy, there is a strong preference in favor of private ownership and operation of business enterprises.   Yet if business enterprise cannot be made to operate in the social interest by any combination of the methods of regulation, "restoration of competition," and subsidization, government should carry out its responsibilities for the social welfare by taking over specific business enterprises when necessary.

---

[16] Even the established corner grocer gains to some extent from the fact that he has a clientele of customers who have some degree of preference for him over similar firms.

[17] It is interesting to note that Joan Robinson labeled the idea "ingenious, though impractical," *Economics of Imperfect Competition*, page 163.

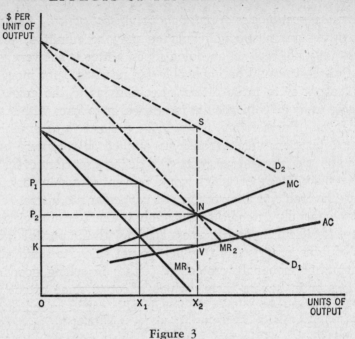

Figure 3

Effects of a Subsidy on Monopoly Output

D_1 is the demand schedule for the monopolists' product, MR_1 is the marginal revenue curve and MC is the marginal cost curve. Profit is maximized where $MC = MR_1$, *i.e.* at output OX_1, where the price will be OP_1. However, consumers' welfare would be increased if the amount which they are willing to give up (the price per unit of the product) is equal to the (marginal) cost per unit of output. At this point the amount OX_2 would be produced, and the price would be OP_2.

The monopolist could be induced to produce output OX_2 if he were to be paid a subsidy of NS ($= X_2N$) per unit of output. His new average revenue schedule would then be D_2, and his marginal revenue curve would be MR_2. His profit would be at a maximum where MR_2 $= MC$, *i.e.* at output OX_2, where his average receipts would be $OP_2 +$ NS, and his profit per unit of output would be VS.

This profit can be captured without reducing his output by levying a tax slightly less than $KVST$. The tax must be a fixed amount and be independent of output. At no level of production other than OX_2 is he as well off as at output OX_2, either before or after the tax.

Since government is not interested in maximizing profit from the production of goods and services, it could conduct its operations in such a way that price and marginal cost were equated. All of its costs of producing a particular good or service would be covered if it followed this rule. A governmentally operated enterprise need not be "subsidized" by transfers from general taxation. Duplication of administrative skills—one set in industry and another in government—would not be required.

Much of the benefits provided by governmental operation might follow from government production of only a part of the total output of the good or service. By equating price and marginal cost, the price charged by government would be lower than that previously charged by a private producer—assuming comparable cost conditions between governmental enterprise and private enterprise producing the same good or service. Governmental operation—subject to the condition that the administrator must always try to equate price and marginal cost—would alter considerably the character of the demand for the product of a competing private producer. Unless consumers were not willing to substitute governmentally produced goods for privately produced goods, the demand for the private producers' products would become considerably more elastic.[18]

Preferences for Private Production Can Be Considered

In the preceding analysis we have assumed that where there is a choice between production of a good or service in the public or the private economy the total product will be maximized when the job is done by the unit which can do it most efficiently. But the problem is more than just efficiency. We have assumed that there is a marked preference for having things done privately rather than by government in the United States. This means that people would be willing to sacrifice some product in order

[18] TVA had a marked influence in demonstrating that the demand for electricity was relatively elastic in addition to increasing the elasticity to private producers. The low-rate policy of the TVA has resulted in a sharp reduction in rates and a great expansion in the purchase of electricity from private power concerns in the areas of the Southeast adjoining those served by the TVA.

to have it produced in the private economy rather than by government.

The intensity of these preferences for privately produced products over government products can be readily determined where government and private producers are turning out the same things and are selling them in a free market. If the products are identifiable and consumers are willing to pay more for the privately produced products, the private products will sell at higher prices than the government products. If there were no such preferences and units of the product are otherwise identical except for their having been produced publicly instead of privately, there would be no price differences. If government products were preferred, they would bring higher prices.

Imagine that consumers in a given area had a choice between purchasing electric power from a government source or a private power company. If consumers were, on the average, willing to pay 3 cents per kilowatt hour for 100 kilowatts purchased from government and 4 cents per kilowatt hour for 100 kilowatts purchased from the private producer (the quality of the service being exactly the same in both instances), we could readily say that a decided preference existed for privately produced electric power. Government would have to be able to produce more than one and one-third times as efficiently as private producers before the total (value) product could be increased by shifting resources out of private electric power production and into government production of electric power.

Sometimes preferences may not be expressed by differences in relative prices which consumers are willing to pay for governmentally as compared with privately produced goods. However, such preferences may be indirectly expressed in an individual's willingness to pay additional taxes to give tax relief to private industry although he might not be willing to pay increased taxes to subsidize government operation.

For example, city dwellers might not be willing to pay additional fare to ride an electrified rather than a coal-burning train. Still, because of the smoke nuisance they would prefer the train to be electrified. They might be willing to encourage private industry to electrify its line through granting it tax relief for which they would compensate by paying higher taxes. At the same time they might not be willing to pay higher taxes to permit government to take over the line and electrify it.

Where the products of government are not being sold—as is true of most governmental services—these preferences for privately produced or governmentally produced products cannot be readily measured. Relative prices which consumers are willing to pay for given quantities cannot be compared. If such preferences can be determined, however, they can be considered in allocating resources between the private and public economies.

Government Expenditure and Full Employment

The assumption that the resources which are used by government otherwise would be used by the private economy may not always be realistic. Although in earlier chapters we have urged that fiscal measures to encourage full employment be primarily steps to assure adequate markets for the products of the private economy, we have also pointed out this approach could lead to inflation rather than full employment. In the event we in the United States choose to use the fiscal system to stabilize the general level of prices, direct action upon the level of employment may be necessary. Such direct action could be provided by government's expanding or contracting its role as producer and employer.

Planned flexibility in fiscal policy primarily through variations in tax revenue. As we have indicated previously, it probably is not desirable to vary expenditures for resources in order to affect employment, if the necessary surplus or deficit can be attained by altering tax collections. If efficiency in the allocation of resources is a consideration, governmental expenditure for resources should be determined by the relative contributions of governmentally and privately used resources. Assume that there is a generally agreed division between governmentally used and privately used resources so that the total product could be at a maximum when resources were fully employed. Governmental purchase of additional resources for the purpose of increasing employment would result in a smaller total product than could be achieved if these resources could be put to employment in the private sector of the economy by other techniques. Decreased governmental use of resources in order to reduce inflationary pressure would result in a smaller total product—if inflationary pressures could be diminished by draining off spending power.[19]

Increased taxation is certainly capable of draining off spending power and thus diminishing inflationary pressure. Reduced taxation *may* be capable of adding considerable strength to markets, thus promoting increased employment. Taking the various factors into consideration, we have concluded (Chapter VI) that reducing governmental expenditure appears undesirable as a means of combating inflationary tendencies. The same objective can be achieved by increasing taxes. As a way to encourage employment, tax reductions also appear more desirable than increases in expenditure—if tax reductions are effective in encouraging people to increase their expenditure for goods and services.

Outline of a public expenditure program. It was noted in Chapter VI, however, that tax reductions may not be capable of bringing the economy out of a deep depression. If a condition of serious depression is encountered, direct public employment may be necessary. This makes it desirable for us to outline a program for a flexible fiscal policy emphasizing expenditure as stated by perhaps its best known proponent of recent years, Professor Alvin H. Hansen.[20] His general position is that "public outlays—properly financed—may indirectly influence [Note: He means increase] the total volume of outlays (private and public) in that they tend to increase private consumption outlays and private investment outlays. Public outlays may have an effect very much greater than the income stream directly created."

This stimulation may be accomplished in several ways:

(*a*) Increasing private consumption by public outlays on free services, such as education, roads, parks, health facilities, and so forth. If there are many free services, an increase in mass consumption occurs as a result of the redistribution of income.

---

[19] So, too, the pattern of transfer payments should be designed to help achieve what social policy has defined as a "desirable" income distribution. (See Chapter X.)

[20] Of his many statements on fiscal policy and public expenditures, one of the most recent, and probably the best on the subject of expenditure is found in "Fiscal Policy for Full Employment," a pamphlet of 23 pages published in 1946 by the Institute of Economic Affairs (formerly the Institute on Postwar Reconstruction) of New York University. The remarks made here are a very brief statement of his program for public expenditures as outlined in that pamphlet, page 4.

(b) Subsidization of mass consumption. The possibilities here
center around expansion of public housing, grant of family allowances, underwriting of a minimum food budget, actual subsidization of low-income groups in depression periods to aid in
purchase of consumer durable goods (like furniture and refrigerators), focusing agricultural programs on income supplements.

(c) Expansion of public outlays on investment. Principally, these
areas are found in urban redevelopment and housing, resource
development along the lines established by the TVA, expansion
of road improvements and of government lending to finance
rural electrification, private housing, and international development.

Comparison and contrast between Hansen and this book.   It is
of some interest to note that much of what Hansen has suggested
has also been advocated as a productive use of resources in this
book.   Part of what he suggests relates to limitations on economic inequality through fiscal policy, which is the subject of the
next chapter.   The main difference is that we have urged that
public expenditures for resources be evaluated in terms of their
allocative effect upon the total product, and that flexible tax
policy be used to encourage employment.   Hansen is inclined to
doubt that reducing taxes will be very effective in combating
deflation.   He believes programs of government expenditure must
be blueprinted so that they can be rapidly expanded in times of
unemployment.   Apart from those who believe that the budget
should be balanced at all times, regardless of economic consequences, it may fairly be said that the two approaches contrasted
above are the main fiscal approaches of economists today to the
problem of full employment.

We wish to emphasize that a slump may develop so rapidly that
tax flexibility or variability in transfer payments may not be
sufficient to reverse this slump.   Direct action by government
upon the level of employment might be necessary.   Provisions
for such measures as a "second line of defense" should be made in
advance.   Such measures would include various public works
projects.   Plans for such projects as a "second line of defense"
should be made in advance.   However, these projects should be
such that they contribute to social productivity as well as em-

ployment. Highway improvement, in addition to that which otherwise would have been made, falls in this class.

Summary

In this analysis, we have not been able to indicate the exact proportion of the nation's total resources which should be used by government to produce goods and services.[21]   Decisions relating to this division are, in the final analysis, made politically.   But we have tried to indicate some of the relevant factors which enter into an evaluation of government expenditure.

In general, it can be said that the total product from a given amount of resources is maximized when the value of the marginal product of a resource is the same in all of its various uses.   This criterion is not satisfied in the private economy when monopoly prevails (unless the "degree of monopoly" is the same in all industries).   The techniques which we have discussed as ways of reducing the structural maladjustments resulting from monopoly included (1) restoration of competition, (2) regulation, (3) subsidization, and (4) government operation.   Where the efficiencies of large production units are not relatively greater than those of small units, restoration of competition by breaking down the large units into small ones would not interfere with efficient production.   However, where there are marked economies from large-scale production, the case for government operation—at least along the "yardstick" principle—is a strong one.   Although regulation and subsidization appear to offer opportunities for inducing producers to act more in the social interest, regulation has not proven satisfactory.   And subsidization poses important practical problems.

Other areas in which governmental use of resources which could be used by the private economy may yield high returns include (1) those in which government has definite advantages in production and (2) those in which social benefits are underestimated by the price mechanism in a free market.   Both of these are areas in which government is now participating.   Operation of the highway system is an example of an area in which government

---

[21] Nor have we tried to say what the level of transfer payments should be.   To the extent that we can draw conclusions about transfer payments, we shall do so in Chapter X.

production is likely to be more efficient than private production, while public education is an illustration of government operation in a field where social benefits are underestimated in the market. If the educational system were privately operated exclusively, the amount of educational services provided would be much smaller than would be socially desirable.   The benefits of education are widely disseminated, but the individuals being educated are willing to pay for only the benefits which they expect to receive. Other services of government—legislation, public health, and protection, for example—fall in the same category.

Where the resources *would be employed* in the private economy *but actually are not being utilized,* their use by government does not necessitate sacrificing other products.   Although we prefer to encourage full employment by acting upon markets, direct action upon employment may at some times be necessary.   A blueprint of a public expenditure to be used in the event markets cannot be strengthened through changes in tax collections was outlined in the final section of this chapter.

SELECTED READINGS

1. Hansen, Alvin H., *Fiscal Policy for Full Employment,* New York: Institute of Economic Affairs (formerly Institute on Postwar Reconstruction), New York University, 1946.
2. ———, *Economic Policy and Full Employment,* Chapter XVI, New York: McGraw-Hill Book Co., Inc., 1947.
3. Hicks, J. R., "The Foundations of Welfare Economics," *Economic Journal,* 49: (December, 1939), 696-712.
4. Higgins, Benjamin, "Postwar Tax Policy I," *Canadian Journal of Economics and Political Science,* 9:408-28 (August, 1943).
5. Lange, Oscar, "The Foundations of Welfare Economics," *Econometrica,* 10:215-28 (July–October, 1942).
6. Lerner, Abba P., *The Economics of Control,* Chapters 5, 6, 7, and 9, New York: The Macmillan Company, 1946.
7. Marsh, Donald B., *Taxes Without Tears,* Part II, Lancaster, Pennsylvania: Jaques Cattell Press, 1945.
8. Pigou, A. C., *The Economics of Welfare,* Part II, 4th edition, London: Macmillan & Co. Ltd., 1932.

9. Pigou, A. C., *A Study in Public Finance*, Part I, Chapters III and VII, London: Macmillan & Co. Ltd., 1928.
10. Scitovsky, T. de., "A Note on Welfare Propositions in Economics," *Review of Economic Studies*, 9:77-88 (November, 1941).

CHAPTER X

FISCAL POLICY AND ECONOMIC INEQUALITY[1]

EVERYONE is aware that all income[2] receivers in the United States do not receive incomes of the same size. The extent of income inequality in the United States during the middle 1930's is pointed out in a well known study of income distribution.[3] This study indicated that the top 1 per cent of consumer units received about 14 per cent of total consumer income. The top 2 per cent received about 18 per cent of the total. The bottom 46 per cent (consumer units with annual incomes averaging $1,000 or less) received only 18 per cent—the same proportion as the top 2 per cent. Although annual total consumer income during the war averaged more than twice total consumer income in the year during which this study was made, the upward movement of the total income did not remove the wide variations in the distribution of personal incomes.[4] This is true even after

[1] Although this chapter is primarily concerned with the distribution of personal incomes, the distribution of the ownership of resources—the distribution of "wealth"—must also be considered. Policies which influence the pattern of resource ownership also influence the personal income distribution. More equality in the pattern of resource ownership would automatically bring with it greater equality in the distribution of personal incomes. The largest single source of income for incomes of $100,000 per year and over is income from property. Some writers believe that fiscal controls to check inequality should center around "wealth control" and should rely heavily upon techniques such as inheritance taxation.

[2] The term *personal income* (except as otherwise indicated) is used in this chapter to describe the flow of money as well as the flow of goods and services involving no monetary exchange. For example, the income of a wage-earner owning the house in which he lives would include the net value of services provided by the house as well as the worker's money wage. The income of a farmer would include the value of goods produced for home consumption. Some elements of income, those frequently called "psychic" income and measurable in terms of differentials in income as we have defined it, are omitted by this definition.

[3] U. S. National Resources Committee, *Consumer Incomes in the United States, 1935-36*, Washington, 1938.

[4] No simple and acceptable measure of inequality in the distribution of income has as yet been devised. Inequality must be measured with reference to some standard or norm. The norm of absolute equality is frequently used. Graphic

the relatively high wartime income taxes have been accounted for. Statistical summaries of several studies on income distribution are given in Table 12.

TABLE 12

Distribution of Personal Incomes in the United States

Size of Income	Per Cent of Total Income Receivers				Per Cent of Total Income before Taxes		
	1935-36[a]	1941[b]	1944[c]	1946[d]	1935-36	1941[e]	1944
0-$1,000 . . .	46.5	35	32.1	17	18.2	9.0	12.2
$1,000- 2,000 . . .	35.3	30	36.2	23	33.0	21.0	27.0
2,000- 5,000 . . .	15.8	30	28.1	50	29.1	42.0	41.6
5,000 and over . .	2.4	5	3.6	10	19.7	28.0	19.1
Total	100.0	100.0	100.0	100.0	100.0	100.0	100.0

[a] Data are derived from United States National Resources Committee, *Consumer Income in the United States, 1935-36*.

[b] From "Spending and Saving of the Nation's Families in Wartime," *Monthly Labor Review*, October, 1942, page 701.

[c] Derived from estimates submitted by the Division of Research and Statistics, United States Treasury, and presented in House *Hearings* on Revenue Revision of 1943, page 21.

[d] Data are from "Survey of Consumer Finances," Federal Reserve Bulletin, June, 1947, page 652.

[e] Reference is to net money income.

It takes but a moment's reflection to realize that the collecting and spending of money by government tends to alter the distribution of personal income. For example, funds collected through progressive income or inheritance taxes and used to pay part of the costs of direct relief reduce the incomes of high-income receivers and increase the incomes of low-income receivers. When one considers the maze of activities involving governmental expenditure or taxation, it is clear that only by chance will an individual citizen's contribution to the public economy exactly equal the benefits he receives in money or in public services.

The most "desirable" income distribution is only in part an economic problem. Support for greater equality in income dis-

representations of given income distributions and comparisons with an equalitarian distribution can yield fairly good pictures of the extent of inequality. Refer to Mary Jean Bowman, "A Graphical Analysis of Personal Income Distribution in the United States," *The American Economic Review*, Vol. XXXV, No. 4 (December, 1945), pages 607-28 and to Dwight Yntema, "Measures of the Inequality in the Personal Distribution of Wealth of Income," *Journal of the American Statistical Association*, Vol. 28 (1933).

tribution in a democratic society stems largely from the wide-spread personal belief that gross inequalities are unfair and un-just.   Such beliefs must be recognized regardless of their validity if democracy is to continue to function.   Evidence of the exist-ence of such beliefs is presented in the popular support for political policies designed to reduce inequality.   Economics, however, may contribute to a determination of desirable income distribution in so far as income distribution may affect output and employment.

Before we discuss in more detail this problem of desirable income distribution we will briefly describe the distribution of personal income in the United States, indicate some factors which determine the relative sizes of personal incomes and thus lead to inequalities, and point out how fiscal activities have altered the distribution of personal incomes.   We can then discuss the problem of a desirable income distribution and indicate how fiscal policy can help to achieve this distribution.

Personal Income Distribution in the United States

We have already referred to the inequality in incomes noted by the study of consumer incomes in 1935-36.[5]   Although the increase in national income during the war years raised the level of income for many income receivers, it did not break the pattern of inequality which previously existed.   The consumer income study found that one third of total consumer units received less than $780 each per year in 1935-36.   A study made by the Bureau of Labor Statistics found that 35 per cent of income units received money income of less than $1,000 in 1941.[6]   For 1944, a year in which national income had increased to a new peak, the United States Treasury estimated that 32.1 per cent of income recipients would have incomes (before income taxes) of less than $1,000.[7]

There *was* a decided upward drift in national income during the war (as Table 12 clearly indicates), but this increase did not

[5] U. S. National Resources Committee, *Consumer Income in the United States, 1935-36*, Washington, 1938.

[6] "Spending and Saving of the Nation's Families in Wartime," *Monthly Labor Review*, October, 1942, page 701.

[7] The total income of recipients of less than $1,000 was expected to be 12.2 per cent of total income (before taxes).   See reference to these estimates in Table 12, *supra*.

eliminate either extremely high or extremely low incomes. During the war years, as in 1935-36, the bulk of national income continued to be received in the intermediate income brackets. In 1944, 68.6 per cent of the national income was received by those in income brackets between $1,000 and $5,000. This compares with 62.1 per cent for the same brackets in 1935-36.

Studies of income distribution in years prior to the 1930's indicate inequalities similar to those shown by the later studies.[8]

Factors Determining the Distribution of Personal Incomes

All of these studies suggest that there are basic personal or social factors which tend to produce inequalities in personal incomes. In an economy where income is received primarily from the sale of productive agents or the sale of the services of productive agents, two important factors tend to bring about inequalities: (1) differences among individuals in the value of personal talents or skills which each possesses and (2) differences in the amounts of income-producing property held by various individuals. Cinema actresses usually receive larger incomes than ditchdiggers because the movie actresses' "skills" are priced much higher than those of the ditchdigger. The income of a Rockefeller heir may be high because of his equity in income-producing property. In 1942, "property income" constituted the largest portion of our really large incomes and a substantial portion of incomes in excess of $10,000 per year. (See Table 13.)

In the absence of a government providing money or services to and collecting money from individuals (let us make this unrealistic assumption for a moment), the pattern of income distribution would depend entirely on the kinds and amounts of resources —income-producing property and personal skills owned by various individuals—and the prices they could get for making these resources available for production. Government, however, modifies this distribution pattern by acquiring resources and using them to perform a wide range of government services, often directed largely toward the lower-income groups. Government programs to underwrite a minimum level of nutrition, housing, or health are examples. Government may also add directly to the

---

[8] See National Bureau of Economic Research, *Income in the United States, Its Amount and Distribution, 1909-19*, New York: Harcourt, Brace & Company, 1921, and other studies made by the National Bureau.

money incomes of certain groups through such payments as pensions to veterans, benefit payments to agriculture, or provision of unemployment relief. To finance such activities, as well as its regular "general benefit" functions, government typically subtracts taxes from the incomes which individuals receive, although other forms of financing are also available.

How Government May Alter Income Distribution

This brief description of the manner in which personal incomes are determined suggests three basic techniques by which the government may alter the distribution of incomes. These will be

TABLE 13

Sources of Income Reported for Federal Taxation by Individuals and Fiduciaries for the Taxable Year 1942[a]

(in percentages of total income for each class)

Net Income Class	Personal Compensation	Property Income	Mixed Income	Other Income	Total[b]
Under $5,000......	79.9%	6.5%	13.2%	0.5%	100.0%
$5,000-...........	52.1	14.5	32.6	0.8	100.0
$10,000-..........	40.5	22.3	36.4	0.8	100.0
$25,000-..........	34.9	28.4	36.0	0.7	100.0
$50,000-..........	28.0	33.0	38.1	0.8	100.0
$100,000-.........	19.3	39.4	40.6	0.7	100.0
$150,000-.........	14.4	43.8	41.4	0.4	100.0
$300,000-.........	7.8	46.3	45.6	0.3	100.0
$500,000-.........	3.6	62.8	33.5	0.1	100.0
$1,000,000 up.....	1.2	73.0	25.8	0.1	100.0

[a] These data were derived from *Statistics of Income for 1942*, Part I, pages 160-165, issued by the United States Treasury Department, Bureau of Internal Revenue, Washington, D. C., 1945. They do not include a large number of returns filed for 1942 under short Form 1040A, optional for individuals whose gross income (from certain sources) did not exceed $3,000. *Statistics of Income* did not provide a detailed breakdown of income by sources for those using 1040A, nor differentiation between gross and net income. *Property Income* as defined above includes the sum of dividends from corporations; interest; rents and royalties; dividends on share interest in Federal building and loan associations; net gain or loss from sales of capital assets (reported figures on net gains minus reported figures on net losses); net gain or loss from sales of property other than capital assets (reported figures on net gains minus reported figures on net losses); and income from fiduciaries. *Mixed Income* is the sum of business profits minus business losses (for unincorporated business units, mainly proprietorships and partnerships). *Other Income* includes various miscellaneous sources, such as income from gambling profits and from prizes. All returns reported above are taxable returns. Property income was relatively unimportant in the nontaxable returns.

[b] Totals do not add exactly to 100, due to rounding.

described briefly here and appraised critically at the end of the chapter.

First of all, government may change the pattern of resource ownership—by levying death and gift taxes or by placing limits upon the amounts of income-producing property which an individual may own, for example. Thus, a socialist state sets sharp limits to the ownership of income-producing property since the state itself owns most of such resources, and distributes the income from income-producing property through a social dividend.

Second, government may try to alter the pattern of resource prices, through establishing minimum wages or minimum prices for certain products. Third, government may alter personal incomes independently of resource ownership or resource prices by personal income taxes or by creation of purchasing power on the one hand and by public expenditure on the other. Progressive personal-income taxes tend to reduce proportionately more the incomes of high-income receivers. Direct payments to or provision of government services for lower-income groups can be made.

Changing the pattern of resource ownership. The first of these methods—changing the pattern of resource ownership—can be accomplished chiefly through death and gift taxes. This technique of social policy has become increasingly acceptable during the last century.[9] It has been contended that death and gift taxation attacks an unjust type of inequality, based primarily on status. Thus, it has been suggested that B has no reasonable claim to a running head start over A *simply* because someone of an earlier generation accumulated a fortune through efficiency and industry and transmitted it to B. There has been the claim, too, that death taxation, as compared with income taxation, should have a smaller effect on incentives to invest or produce, because the tax does not currently reduce the fruits of economic activity.[10] On the other hand, it is generally agreed that not until existing loopholes (particularly in the use of various trust devices) are greatly reduced and exemptions sharply lowered

---

[9] See John Stuart Mill, *Principles of Political Economy*, and Adolph Wagner, *Lehrbuch der politischen Oekonomie*, VI, Theil II (2nd edition, 1890), pages 381-85 *et passim*.

[10] These arguments will be examined in some detail in Chapter XVII.

can Federal death and gift taxes be very effective in checking inequality.[11]

Acceptance of public policy to reduce inequalities in income and in wealth is further evidenced by a general recognition of public responsibility in providing equality of educational opportunity. There is a widespread belief that each citizen should be given an adequate opportunity to discover and develop his personal talents. Such opportunities can be expanded and divorced from income status through public education.[12] Education can be considered as a form of (immaterial) property. Equalization of educational opportunity may thus be looked upon as a means of equalizing property ownership.

Changing the pattern of resource prices. Changing the pattern of resource prices (the second technique by which government may alter income distribution) is accepted less among economists, but is relatively popular among politicians. Minimum wage legislation, parity prices for farm products, and similar techniques are all directed toward altering the distribution of personal incomes by altering relative product or resource prices. Minimum wages tend to reduce discrimination in rates of pay for comparable work. But minimum wages can be set so high as to interfere with the kind of allocation of labor which will result in the "best" production pattern.[13] Similarly, parity prices for agricultural products may encourage production of too much of some products and too little of others, since "parity" itself has been based on an historical price relationship which long ago has been outmoded by shifts in demands and costs.

In general, trying to alter income distribution by altering resource prices tends to interfere with an allocation of resources in line with current consumer preferences.[14] There is not even any assurance that a more equal distribution of income will result

[11] Thus, there is a flat exemption of $60,000 under the Federal estate tax, which automatically excludes most estates from taxation.

[12] This overlaps with public policy designed to reduce inequality by methods independent of resource ownership or resource prices.

[13] By "best" production pattern, we mean the one most in line with consumer preferences. Refer to Chapter I.

[14] "Interference" with prices, particularly where monopoly is prevalent or where prices are so uncertain that they do not adequately guide production, may improve resource allocation. Note, however, that resource allocation rather than income distribution should be the primary economic consideration in favor of price interference by government.

from such procedures. Individuals owning larger amounts of the resources whose prices are raised are made better off than individuals who own smaller amounts of these resources.[15] Unless it is possible to pay higher prices for the resources owned by the low-income groups than for the same kinds of resources owned by the high-income receivers, the distribution of income will not necessarily be made more equal.

Working directly on the size of income. The third approach— altering within limits the distribution of income independently of resource ownership and resource prices—may have the fewest unfavorable effects upon our ability to reach other goals of social policy. The increased acceptance of progressive income taxation in providing funds for governmental services conferring general benefits has characterized American public finance, particularly since the Federal income tax amendment of 1913.[16] Use of the progressive income tax carries with it implicit acceptance of the tax as an instrument of income redistribution. On the expenditure side, government outlays may operate directly to affect income distribution. Many such expenditures—those for "adequate" nutrition, health, and housing, for example—operate to reduce inequality. Other types of expenditure, especially interest payments on the national debt, tend to increase inequality. A direct advantage of working *directly* on the size of income is that this makes the size of income itself rather than the status of the income receiver as "worker," "farmer," or "capitalist," the central criterion for redistribution.

The Extent to Which Government Has Altered Distribution of Personal Incomes

The increasing ratio of governmental expenditure to total expenditure and the increasing reliance upon progressive personal-

---

[15] Dr. T. W. Schultz provided evidence of this when, in reporting on results of the 1939-1940 Iowa Farm Sample Survey, he pointed out that, in 1939, government payments to Iowa farm operators were distributed as follows: Upper third in net income, $350; middle third, $179; lower third, $152 (average amounts paid). See T. W. Schultz, "Economic Effects of Agricultural Programs," *American Economic Review*, 30: (February Supplement), 127-154, 1941.

[16] Strictly speaking, the present personal-income tax movement began with the Wisconsin state income tax of 1910, but received its major support with the passage of the income tax amendment. We have already mentioned the use of the tax at the Federal level between 1861 and 1872. Its use was again attempted in the income tax act of 1894—an act which had wide popular support but was declared unconstitutional.

income taxation in the United States have prompted investigation of the effects of governmental fiscal activities upon our distribution of income. One of these studies[17] analyzed the effect of Federal government expenditures and tax withdrawals upon income distribution for the decade 1930-1939. This study concluded that, during the thirties, the lowest third of income receivers obtained direct income from Federal expenditures amounting to about 27 per cent of these expenditures, although they paid only 5 per cent of all Federal taxes. Receiving 10.4 per cent of aggregate income in 1935-36, the bottom third also received an estimated 27.1 per cent of their total income from Federal expenditures during the thirties. On the other hand, the largest income group used by Stauffacher ($15,000 and over)[18] received about 17 per cent of Federal expenditures during the thirties, although paying nearly 40 per cent of total Federal taxes.[19] These data indicate that Federal fiscal activities exercised a considerable redistributional effect in favor of the low-income groups. This might have been expected in view of the relief and public works programs undertaken by the Federal government during this period.

A second conclusion reached by this study was that the real swing in favor of the low-income groups was primarily a result of income creation through government deficit financing. "The aggregate of the excess of income payments over tax withdrawals in the first five income groups (those below $5,000) is nearly

[17] See Charles Stauffacher, "The Effect of Governmental Expenditures and Tax Withdrawals Upon Income Distribution, 1930-39," *Public Policy*, Yearbook of the Graduate School of Public Administration, Harvard University, Cambridge, Massachusetts, 1941, pages 232-261.

[18] Taken from the study on *Consumer Incomes in the United States, 1935-36*, made by the National Resources Committee. Stauffacher relied heavily on the findings of this study.

[19] Charles Stauffacher, *ibid.* Stauffacher's methodology was briefly this: (*a*) he used the findings of the Consumer Income and expenditure study for 1935-36 as the anchor for his estimates on income distribution during the entire decade. (*b*) He followed rather orthodox assumptions as to tax incidence in estimating the distribution of the tax load. Thus, he placed the entire corporate income tax on the stockholders and assumed that internal revenue excises were shifted forward in their entirety. (*c*) He allocated government expenditures according to a pattern of direct flow. Thus, Stauffacher concerned himself with where government *money* went, in transfer payments, wages and salaries, and expenditures for materials and supplies. He could have gone on to analyze the distribution of benefits from government services, but chose not to do so (probably for reasons of analytical difficulty). Such analysis would doubtless have revealed a further redistributional effect beyond the one which Stauffacher isolated.

equal to the amount of Federal borrowing during the period." [20] This means that much of the improvement in the incomes of the low-income groups was made possible by an expansion in the size of the national income and consequently did not involve reducing the incomes of high-income receivers. In fact, the incomes of high-income receivers may have been increased as a result of the expansion in national income.

The other important recent study relating to income distribution deals with the incidence of taxation—Federal, state and local.[21] Some of the results of this study are summarized in Table 14. They indicate that when the *incidence* of state and local as well as Federal taxes is considered, the proportion of income taken from the low-income groups by taxes in 1941 was not very different from the proportion taken from the middle-income groups. In that year, the effects of an essentially progressive Federal tax structure were counteracted by the regressive character of state and local taxation, there being no *marked* over-all progression until income exceeded $5,000. The data in Table 12 indicate that only about 5 per cent of income receivers obtained as much as $5,000 in 1941. In more recent years, however, decreases in Federal personal-income tax exemptions and increases

TABLE 14 [22]

Estimated Consumer Income and Tax Incidence, 1941

Consumer Income Classes	Taxes as Percentage of Income[a]
Under $1,000	16.0
$1,000-2,000	15.5
$2,000-3,000	15.8
$3,000-4,000	16.2
$4,000-5,000	18.5
$10,000 and over	28.4

[a] Taxes include "imputed" taxes, especially death and corporate profits taxes, and income includes estimates of the value of home-produced food, rental values of owned homes. The acceptability of the percentages hinges largely upon the acceptability of the assumptions which are made in analyzing the incidence of various taxes.

[20] Charles Stauffacher, "The Effect of Governmental Expenditures and Tax Withdrawals Upon Income Distribution, 1930-39," page 260.

[21] Helen Tarasov, *Who Does Pay the Taxes?* New School for Social Research, 1942. Earlier work along this line was conducted by Gerhard Colm and Helen Tarasov. See "Who Pays the Taxes," *TNEC* Monograph 3, 1940. By "incidence" is meant the "final" resting place of a tax. For discussion of incidence in some detail, see Chapter XII.

[22] Data are from Helen Tarasov, *Who Does Pay the Taxes?* New School for Social Research, 1942, page 6.

in personal income tax rates together with stiffer corporate-profits taxation during the war period have made the over-all tax structure more progressive than it was in 1941.

With the Federal government collecting from 25 to 30 billion dollars annually in tax revenues during the 1950's, the progressive income tax will be of much greater relative importance in determining the character of our tax system than it was before the war.   Marked progression in the percentage of income taken by taxes (Federal, state and local) may begin around $3,000 instead of at $5,000 as was true in 1941.

A higher level of Federal expenditure will also tend to exercise a greater influence upon income distribution than did prewar Federal spending.   A considerable part of Federal expenditure will provide each citizen with essentially the same benefits.   Expenditures for national defense and for general government fall largely into this category.   With Federal expenditures at between 25 and 30 billion dollars annually, about one-half of this total probably will be kinds of expenditure that will exert relatively little redistributive influence.[23]

About half of total Federal expenditure, however, will have definite redistribution repercussions.   Some items will tend to be directed largely toward low-income groups such as pensions and other veteran costs, narrowing the dispersion of the distribution of income.   Other items will be directed largely toward high-income receivers and will tend to widen the dispersion of the income distribution.

Interest on debt and income distribution.   The main item of government expenditure which flows largely toward the upper-income groups is interest on government debt.   Interest on Federal debt has been estimated for fiscal year 1947 at about 5 billion dollars, and interest on state and local debt was running at about 650 million in 1945.   Data on the distribution of final ownership of public debt by income groups are quite incomplete. The data that are available, however, indicate that the bulk of government debt is held directly by individuals with larger than average incomes or by agencies in which persons with high incomes have controlling interests.   Analysis of consumer incomes indicates that families with less than $3,000 annual income saved

[23] See Lewis H. Kimmell *et al.*, *Postwar Fiscal Requirements*, Washington, D. C.; Brookings Institution, 1945.

relatively small amounts prior to the war.[24]   There is little to indicate that wartime spending and saving patterns have been altered toward a substantially larger volume of savings by low-income groups.[25]

Of the approximately 260 billion dollar interest-bearing Federal debt outstanding at the beginning of 1946, about three-fifths was held by banks, insurance companies, and other agencies in which the equities of large-income receivers exceed the equities of small-income earners.   Less than one-fifth of the debt (47.5 billion) was made up of savings bonds, the kind of issue mainly held by individuals.   Only about half of this 47.5 billion dollars of savings bonds was issued in denominations under $500.[26]   It seems unlikely that many income receivers with less than $3,000 annual income would invest in bonds of $500 denomination or greater. We might conclude that about one-tenth of the Federal debt was held directly by income earners with annual incomes of $3,000 or less.

[24] The study of *Consumer Incomes in the United States, 1935-36* showed that while consumer units (families and single individuals both included, separately counted) with incomes of $3,000 and over represented only 6.9 per cent of total units, they received 30.9 per cent of total income and made 78.7 per cent of total positive savings.   When the large "negative" savings of consumer units with incomes below $1,250 are taken into account, the units above $3,000 income made nearly all the *net* positive savings by individuals.   An early wartime study by the Bureau of Labor Statistics, covering calendar year 1941, is not entirely comparable, since the unit of income was *money* income only and consumer money income increased sharply during the intervening years.   Findings of the study confirm the pattern of income distribution and savings of the earlier study, however.   In more prosperous 1941, consumer units with net money income above $3,000 were 15 per cent of total income units, received 45.9 per cent of total net money income, and made 85.3 per cent of total *net* money savings.   See *Monthly Labor Review,* October, 1942, page 706.   Or see Bureau of Labor Statistics, *Bulletin 723,* March, 1943.

[25] A national survey of liquid asset holdings, spending, and saving near end of 1945 was made by the Division of Program Surveys, Bureau of Agricultural Economics, U. S. Department of Agriculture and was reported in the *Federal Reserve Bulletin* for June, July, and August, 1946.   Among other things, it indicated that, for 1945, the top 30 per cent of the spending units made 96 per cent of total net savings, and represented incomes of about $3,000 and over.   Only about 4 per cent of net savings were made by the 70 per cent of spending units with incomes under $3,000.   The concentration of liquid asset holdings (U. S. government bonds and bank accounts) was not as great as of net savings.   As of February, 1946, the bottom 47 per cent of spending units having incomes under $2,000 held about 21 per cent of liquid assets, but "the over-all interpretation still seems to be that a very large and probably preponderant share of accumulated assets are in the hands of groups who are normally large net savers, and who may therefore not be inclined to part with their wartime accumulations." From *The Survey of Current Business,* July, 1946, page 11, analyzing the study on liquid asset holdings.

[26] See *Treasury Bulletin,* February, 1946.

United States Savings bonds similar to the bonds sold during the war are still being issued. However, among the total of income receivers with annual incomes of $3,000 or less, redemptions of old bonds probably are exceeding purchases of new ones.[27] The absolute amount held by the lower-income groups appears to have passed its peak.

To these direct personal holdings of Federal debt—which we have estimated to be around 24 billion dollars for individuals with annual incomes of $3,000 or less—we should add the "investments" of Social Security trust funds. These were an additional 15 billion dollars in November, 1945, giving a total of about 39 billion as the estimated "minimum" stake of the lower-income groups in the national debt as of this date. These groups also have some stake in the national debt held by the banking system, and in the heavy investments in government securities by such savings institutions as insurance companies, savings banks, and so forth. Nevertheless, it seems undeniable that the stake in the national debt of what we have called the "lower"-income groups is relatively small and that the flow of interest payments on the national debt will go predominately to the income groups which make the bulk of the savings.[28] There is little in the nature of the relatively small flow of interest payments on state and local debt to alter this general conclusion. Furthermore, state and local obligations are seldom issued in denominations of less than $1,000, which strengthens the likelihood that few of these bonds are held by the lower-income groups.

Other expenditures affecting inequality. In contrast to the tendency of interest payments on the Federal debt to flow primarily to the upper-income groups, other items of Federal expenditure direct income toward the lower-income groups. Among these items are:

1. Veterans' pensions and benefits
2. Social security payments and public assistance
3. Expenditures to underwrite a minimum nutrition program
4. Expenditures to underwrite a housing program
5. Provision of public education

[27] This conclusion is based upon data presented in *Treasury Bulletin*, January, 1947.
[28] This is borne out by the data from *Statistics of Income* cited earlier in this chapter, which shows that the ratio of property income to total income is very low for those with net incomes below $5,000.

6. Some aids to agriculture

7. Certain quantitatively small expenditures, such as those for recreation, libraries, health, and hospitals.

The personnel of our armed forces in World War II represented a cross-section of our population. The bulk of the armed forces came from what we have called the low-income groups. Consequently, it seems reasonable to expect that expenditure for veterans' pensions and benefits will flow predominantly to the lower-income groups. The size of Federal expenditures for veterans' pensions and benefits cannot be predicted accurately at this time. However, 6.2 billion dollars have already been budgeted for the year 1947, and one study of postwar fiscal requirements estimates that these expenditures will run between 2.2 and 3.6 billions annually after demobilization has been completed.[29] Thus, a sizable flow of income will be directed from this source toward the lower-income groups.

Social security and assistance payments by the Federal government are budgeted at about 1.2 billion dollars for 1947. These include an estimated 500 million in old-age retirement payments (which are being more than covered at the present time by payroll taxes on employers and employees). They also include direct grants to the states of about 600 million dollars for a variety of welfare activities.[30] The direct grants are matched by the states as a prerequisite for obtaining the Federal funds. The social security and assistance payments estimated at 1.3 billion dollars for 1947, however, do not include possible withdrawals by the states of accumulated funds in the unemployment trust fund. These accumulations are regarded as state funds managed by the Federal government. They totaled 7.6 billions in November, 1945. Withdrawals from these funds, negligible during World War II, are now beginning to increase.[31] Part of the funds for financing retirement and unemployment compensation

[29] See Lewis H. Kimmell, et al., Postwar Fiscal Requirements.

[30] These grants are chiefly for old-age assistance and aid to dependent children. They also include aid to the blind, public health work, maternal and child health services, aid to crippled children, and child welfare service.

[31] Withdrawals in the first six months of 1946 were 725 million dollars, as compared with deposits of 503 million. This includes relatively small withdrawals and deposits for the Railroad Unemployment Insurance Account, directly administered by the Federal government. This compares with deposits of 721 million and withdrawals of 66 million for the last six months of the war ending in August, 1945. Sources: Treasury Bulletin, May, 1946, page 17 and August, 1946, page 17.

is contributed by those to whom the payments are made. Contributions are made in the form of payroll taxes. However, direct assistance payments by the Federal government, about 600 million dollars for 1947, are a factor redistributing income toward the lower-income groups.

Much attention has been directed during the last few years to the merit of Federal programs to assure a minimum level of nutrition for each family, regardless of the family's income. The food-stamp plan and school-lunch program of the New Deal were steps in this direction. Proposals expanding the extent of Federal aid in the maintenance of nutrition have been put before Congress since abandonment of the food-stamp plan in 1942. A new school-lunch program is. in operation at the time of writing (early 1947). It may be reduced in scope or eliminated under the proposals to reduce government expenditures which are being debated in early 1947. Expenditures to raise minimum nutritional levels are very likely to flow primarily to low-income groups, since it seems probable that low-income groups will be the primary participants in programs likely to be formulated.[32]

Similarly, expenditures to improve levels of housing probably will be channeled largely toward income receivers in the lower-income brackets. Programs providing Federal subsidies for slum clearance and for the construction of low-cost housing may not involve large Federal expenditures. But the participants in such programs are not likely to be in the high-income brackets.

More than 2.5 billion dollars were spent annually by government for public education during the past decade. These expenditures have important redistributive features. Education—at least through the high school years—might not be available to millions of children in low-income families if it were not publicly supported. Furthermore, the importance of state (and to a small extent, Federal) aid to local schools has been increasing, so that

[32] Only persons receiving "relief" were eligible to participate in the food-stamp plan. Because of the stigma associated with receiving subsidies from the government, current proposals usually provide no restrictions on eligibility. Nevertheless, participation would not be advantageous to a high-income earner. For example, the Aiken Bill proposed to sell to every family a claim to an adequate diet for 40 per cent of the family's income. A family of 4 with an annual income of $3,000 could purchase this same diet for less than 40 per cent of its income (1945 price levels assumed). Some students do not consider the Aiken proposal practicable, since it obviously provides each family with a tremendous incentive to understate its income in order to obtain government assistance.

during recent years state aids to local elementary and secondary
public education have grown to more than one-third of the total
costs of such education. The financing of these state aids
appears to bear less upon the low-income groups than does the
financing at the local level. The more extensive these aids become, the more important will be their redistributive character.

Aids to Agriculture amounted to approximately one billion
dollars annually in the years immediately preceding World War
II. About 1.2 billion dollars is budgeted for agricultural aid and
subsidies in 1947. This figure does not include the sizable
amount of expenditure for supporting agricultural prices which
is expected to be required after 1947 if the existing type of support for agricultural prices is continued. Total expenditures for
agriculture for later postwar years under existing legislation
have been estimated at between 2.3 and 2.8 billion dollars.[33]

The bulk of aids granted to agriculture have been of a kind
which has provided larger benefits to the farmers receiving the
larger incomes, as was pointed out earlier in this chapter. For
example, the size of the direct payments made to a farmer under
the Agricultural Adjustment Administration have been closely
correlated with his income from other sources.[34] Similarly, price
supports also associate governmental subsidies with other income,
since the amount of governmental aid varies directly with the
volume of marketings of the individual farmer. Nevertheless,
even though the bulk of aids to agriculture go to the middle- and
high-income farmers, the incomes of most of these income receivers have placed them in the low-income groups.[35]

Of less importance, in terms of total governmental expenditure,
has been governmental aid provided through the Farm Security
Administration. This agency was created during the thirties to
provide technological assistance to farmers, particularly those in
the low-income group, and to make loans to farmers who could
not obtain credit through other channels. In the fiscal year 1941,
FSA expended nearly 85 million dollars.

[33] See Kimmell, *et al., Postwar Fiscal Requirements.*
[34] Payments have been made on a per acre basis and are weighted directly with
productivity. The larger or the more productive a farm, the larger the payments
going to that farm.
[35] Available data indicate that average earnings in agriculture are considerably
below average industrial worker's earnings. The distribution of income within
agriculture is indicated by the fact that 15 per cent of the total number of farmers
produced only 50 per cent of total agricultural output.

How Should Income Be Distributed?

Our investigation thus far has indicated the extent of inequality in personal incomes in the United States, pointed out some of the causes of inequality, suggested some general techniques which might be used to reduce inequality, and indicated the direction in which the fiscal activities of the public economy have been leading the distribution of personal incomes.

Before we can evaluate more fully the way in which various fiscal techniques should be used to bring about greater (or less) equality in the distribution of income, we must consider the question, *"How much inequality should we have?"* There are two parts to this problem: (1) the distribution of a *given* total product, and (2) the impacts of income distribution—the conflicts and complementaries—upon the achievement of the other objectives of social policy. In particular, the way in which the product is divided may have important effects upon the size of the product to be divided.[36]

Unfortunately, there are no economic criteria which give us any clues to the way in which a given product should be distributed, if we are considering distribution of income independently of the other objectives of social policy. We probably can safely assume that adding a dollar to an individual's income will increase his welfare. Conversely, subtracting a dollar from an individual's income will reduce his welfare. But the amount by which welfare is increased or reduced cannot be determined. Consequently, we are not able to find out whether taking a dollar from one individual and transferring it to another individual will increase or diminish the total welfare from a given total product.

Although we are not able to shed any light on this problem of distributing a *given* total product, there are some things which can be said about the relationship between various kinds of income distributions and achievement of the other objectives of social policy. *The principal area of interdependence is between income distribution—the way in which the product is divided—and the size of the product to be distributed.*

It is generally recognized that a completely equalitarian dis-

[36] It has been pointed out in earlier chapters of this book that the problems of income inequality and full employment may complement each other to a degree, although the two problems may be attacked separately.

tribution of income would result in a smaller total production than some less equalitarian distributions. Compensation for production must be somewhat in line with differences in *personal* efficiency and productivity, if maximum effort is to be encouraged. For example, Soviet Russia introduced greater differentials in "rewards" to individuals after an initial practice of paying relatively equal wages.[37]

On the other hand, it is also recognized that raising the incomes of low-income receivers independently of their contributions might increase productivity. Providing them with a higher level of nutrition, housing, education, medical care, and the like could increase considerably the value of the output which they produce.

There is evidence that at least a part of the income of many high-income receivers could be reduced without diminishing their productivity. It is important, however, that the method used to decrease income does not completely reduce the opportunity to achieve additional income by additional effort. *Marginal* tax rates of 60 to 75 per cent on the highest incomes may have relatively small effects upon production. It is possible, however, that rates in effect during the latter part of World War II may have come close enough to confiscation to discourage effort, at least under peacetime conditions.[38]

It is recognized that averaging of incomes over a period of years may increase equity in personal income taxation. At the same time, averaging would also permit a given amount of tax to be collected with less injurious effects upon incentive than the current procedure of treating each year's income as independent

---

[37] Various supplementary devices are used by the Russians to introduce differences in "psychic" rewards as well as in money incomes. Greater recognition is awarded the more productive workers through such rewards as the assignment of responsible positions in the industrial plant and the awarding of medals. Wage rates are frequently piece rates and thus tie wages directly to output.

[38] World War II rates, mentioned above, applied to all taxable net income from $200,000 up for the taxable years 1944 and 1945. The top marginal surtax rate was 94 per cent, but there was also an over-all ceiling of 90 per cent of taxable net income. Rates were slightly reduced by the Revenue Act of 1945. Professor Groves has pointed out that the 25 per cent ceiling on capital gains taxation, combined with the distribution of capital gains in favor of upper-income groups, actually resulted in an effective top rate for all net income of about 71.5 per cent in 1944. See his *Postwar Taxation and Economic Progress,* page 183, New York: McGraw-Hill Book Co., Inc., 1946. For further discussion, see Chapters XIII and XIV.

of the income of previous (or subsequent) years. (Averaging procedures are discussed in Chapter XIV.)

These comments illustrate the nature of the conflict between various notions of desirable income distribution and maximum size of product to be distributed. If we are to maximize the size of the product, we may not be able to achieve the kind of income distribution generally considered desirable. Conversely, if we are to achieve the kind of income distribution which we consider most desirable, we may not be able to maximize the size of the product. Social policy must recognize the extent to which people are willing to depart from one goal in order to move toward the other.

The extent of the conflict thus depends largely upon our concept of desirable income distribution. The tendency to emphasize almost entirely the achievement of a maximum product from a given set of resources and to accept the resultant income distribution as most desirable probably reached its peak in the nineteenth century.[39] Pressure for "justice in distribution" has increased, however. It has been recognized that part of the variation in income is a sort of chance variation. The inheritance of property, for example, may bring income for which the inheritor is not directly responsible. A technical discovery or the discovery of mineral deposits on one's property may greatly augment one's income independently of his contribution. It is often very difficult to define the "productivity" or "contributions" on which rewards might be based.

Some people define "justice" as complete equality—everybody should have the same income. Others set the limits below which personal incomes should not be allowed to fall and above which personal incomes should not be allowed to rise. The bulk of concepts, however, appear to be framed in terms of basic minima below which people cannot "decently" exist. The notion of "decency" has itself secured a certain amount of objectivity in recent years by becoming closely identified with the notion of "working health and efficiency." Working health and

[39] It is true that leading economists and philosophers recognized that what people receive as income and what they "should" receive may get out of line if an adequate framework of rules is not established and enforced by the state. Still, there was a widespread attitude that "rewards" and "productivity" were not far out of line. This attitude is still held by many people.

efficiency can be given content in terms of minimum levels of nutrition, housing, education, medical care, and the like.

This provision of a basic minimum income for everybody undoubtedly would raise the productivity of a number of those to whom income was transferred. If the increase in productivity was greater than the decrease among those from whom income was taken, we could then redistribute income in a way which would leave everybody at least as well off as he was before. Such a situation would represent a definite improvement in social welfare.[40] If, however, no such redistribution was brought about or the size of the product actually fell, we could not say whether social welfare had been diminished or increased.

The limitations of economics in contributing a solution to the problem "How should income be distributed?" are suggested in this brief discussion. The economist can point out the kinds of conflicts and complementaries which may arise between various notions of appropriate income distribution and the other objectives of social policy. But it is up to society to decide in the light of available information about these conflicts and complementaries, how income should be distributed.

How to Alter Income Distribution?

We have already suggested three general approaches to the alteration of the distribution of personal income by government: (1) altering relative prices, (2) changing the pattern of resource ownership, and (3) taking income away or adding to income independently of changes in prices or the pattern of resource ownership. These general techniques can be applied to the achievement of any kind of income distribution, whether the dispersion is greater or smaller than at present.

Most fiscal devices which can be used to alter the distribution of personal incomes fit into one of these three categories. Resource prices can be changed by sales, or occupation taxes, or by subsidizing particular products. The pattern of resource ownership can be modified to some extent by death and gift taxes. Progressive income taxation also tends to change the relative pattern of resource ownership, since it probably modifies the

[40] See N. Kaldor, "Welfare Propositions of Economics and Interpersonal Comparisons of Utility," *Economic Journal*, 49: (September, 1939) 549-52, and J. R. Hicks, "The Foundations of Welfare Economics," *Economic Journal*, 49: (December, 1939) 696-712.

pattern of savings proportionately more than it modifies the pattern of consumption. Progressive income taxation, however, may also alter somewhat the distribution of income independently of prices or resource ownership. Also payments to individuals or the provision of government services can be made independently of the amounts of resources owned or the prices of these resources.

Taxation. Some form of taxation is very likely to be used by government in taking income away from those individuals whose incomes are to be reduced, whether they be rich or poor.

If it is considered desirable to achieve a given distribution of income and, at the same time, to maintain a minimum of impediments to reaching the other objectives of social policy, taxes which bring about the desired relative income distribution with a minimum of alteration in relative prices are to be preferred. For example, increasing prices by sales taxes on items purchased by the high-income groups might reduce their income sufficiently, but the same amount of income could be taken from them by other kinds of taxes. It can be demonstrated that their welfare would not be reduced as much as it would be through sales taxation.[41] Although other kinds of taxation may indirectly affect prices, their price effects are likely to be smaller. Hence the reduction in the welfare of those taxed is not likely to be as great as when taxes which directly affect prices are used to reduce their incomes.

Death and gift taxation designed to disperse relatively large accumulations of income-yielding property probably has a minor effect upon prices and consequently upon resource allocation. The importance of accumulation for one's heirs as an incentive has not yet been adequately determined. If it is not important, the knowledge that a large proportion of one's accumulation will pass out of the family may have little effect upon the production pattern. Certainly fiscal writers as far back as John Stuart Mill have argued in favor of severe taxation of the transfer of property at time of death (and presumably their arguments would apply in part to gift taxation).[42]

The effectiveness of death and gift taxation in altering the

---

[41] This will be treated in Chapter XVI on Commodity Taxation.

[42] Some aspects of their position have been outlined earlier in this chapter and will be examined in more detail in Chapter XVII.

relative distribution of income-producing property is difficult to estimate. In some cases, heavy death taxes may break up particular concentrations of property. The net result may be primarily a transfer of property from one high-income receiver to others. But death and gift taxes with a sharp reduction in present loopholes (examined in Chapter XVII) could not be avoided by some individuals in the present generation who plan to transmit property to those in succeeding generations. Our existing system of death and gift taxation suffers from high exemptions and many loopholes, and its present effectiveness in reducing the dispersion of property ownership is limited. It probably has relatively minor effects upon resource allocation.

Progressive personal-income taxation tends to reduce inequality in personal income distribution in two ways: (1) it reduces inequalities in current disposable income, and thus (2) decreases the potentiality of amassing large concentrations of wealth. Carried too far, it may reduce the size of the total product more than is considered desirable in view of other social ends. This potential effect of high income-tax rates has already been referred to, and will be the subject of analysis later. It is of interest that even those who have pointed out this conflict between taxation and product have continued to hold to the personal income tax as the primary tax in the tax structure.

The analyses that have been made and the evidence that has been assembled imply that whatever we do about reducing income dispersion through taxation, taxes which work directly on the size of income rather than the allocation of resources are to be preferred. This means primary reliance upon income taxes and upon death and gift taxation. The effects upon relative personal income distribution can be the same as if other forms of taxation were used. But the adverse effects upon the allocation of resources will be smaller.

Expenditures. What has been said about the kinds of taxes to use in reducing incomes also applies to the techniques used for increasing incomes. Wherever it is possible, supplementary income provided by government—through cash grants or the provision of services—should be made in a manner which interferes least with resource allocation. For example, farm incomes might be increased by action which would forcibly raise farm prices. Consumers paying these higher prices would substitute, wherever they could, other commodities for farm products. These consumers would be better off to pay to farmers the same amount that they would lose through increased prices, but to make the payments in a manner which does not affect prices. It can be demonstrated that, if increasing a given individual's income is the objective, techniques should be used which do not tie the receipt of income to the production of given products or the ownership of particular productive agents.[43]

The bulk of governmental expenditures have been, and probably will continue to be, for the provision of services—not for cash grants. The provision of services may not be as effective as cash grants (per dollar of expenditure) in achieving the desired income distribution. Nevertheless, as we have suggested in Chapter IX, government may be able to provide some services more efficiently than they could be provided by nongovernmental procedures. The size of the product as well as the distribution of income may be improved. These services, like cash grants, should be made available wherever feasible, independently of the kind of production in which the recipient is engaged, as long as the redistribution of income is the objective.

SELECTED READINGS

1. Boulding, Kenneth, *The Economics of Peace,* Chapter 6, New York: Prentice-Hall, Inc., 1945.
2. Chapman, Sidney J., "The Utility of Income and Progressive Income Taxation," *Economic Journal,* 23:25-35, 1913.
3. Kimmell, Lewis H., *et al., Postwar Fiscal Requirements,* Washington, D. C.: Brookings Institution, 1945.
4. Lerner, Abba P., *The Economics of Control,* Chapter 3, New York: The Macmillan Company, 1946.
5. Pigou, A. C., *The Economics of Welfare,* Part 1, Chapter 8 and Part 4, 4th edition, London: Macmillan & Co. Ltd., 1932.
6. Pigou, A. C., *A Study in Public Finance,* Part 2, London: Macmillan & Co. Ltd., 1928.
7. Stauffacher, Charles, "The Effect of Governmental Expenditures and Tax Withdrawals upon Income Distribution, 1930-

[43] See, for example, T. W. Schultz, "Economic Effects of Agricultural Programs," *American Economic Review,* 30: (February Supplement) 127-154, 1941.

39," *Public Policy,* pages 232-61, Yearbook of the Graduate School of Public Administration, Harvard University, Cambridge, Massachusetts, 1941.

8. Tarasov, Helen, *Who Does Pay the Taxes?* New School for Social Research, 1942.

9. United States National Resources Committee, *Consumer Incomes in the United States,* Washington, 1938.

10. Young, Allyn, "Public Finance," *Economic Journal,* 39:78-83, 1929.

PART FOUR

PUBLIC REVENUES AND
PUBLIC BORROWING

CHAPTER XI

THE STRUCTURE OF TAXATION: GENERAL CONSIDERATIONS

THE nation's annual tax collections increased by over five times —from 10.2 billion dollars to about 54.3 billion dollars—between 1929 and 1945. During the same period, the yearly gross national product approximately doubled, increasing from 99.4 billions to about 200 billions. The increasing importance of taxes relative to national income and product since 1902 was described in Chapter II.

Scarcely a day passes for a given individual during which he is not made aware of the extensiveness of our present tax system. He may come into contact with the income tax, the property tax, sales taxes, gasoline taxes, or social security taxes, to indicate but a few. Even in 1941, a year in which tax collections were far below the amount which they reached in 1945, Tarasov concluded that a consuming unit with yearly income between $2,000 and $3,000 paid nearly one-sixth of its income in taxes.[1]

Of additional interest to the student of fiscal policy is the recent development in *ideas* about taxation. There has been a growing recognition that tax policy is an important tool which the government may employ in keeping the general level of prices from advancing too rapidly or in maintaining a high level of production and employment. From this point of view, the most important aspect of taxation is not the amount of revenue which it produces, but its effect on the level of income and employment. Increased attention has also been directed to the role of taxation in promoting equity in the distribution of income and efficiency in the allocation of resources. We will examine taxation primarily as a means of achieving these three major objectives of economic policy.

These objectives are not independent of each other: there are

[1] See Chapter X, Table 14.

187

both conflicts and complementaries between them. Consequently, a tax system which will help to achieve one of these objectives will not necessarily help most in achieving the others. Sales taxes and personal income taxes will both subtract from the disposable incomes of consumers. But sales taxes may operate to increase inequality in income distribution, while the progressive personal-income tax is an effective instrument for lessening inequality.

Over a period of time, the relative importance attached to the major objectives in taxation may change. With this change will also come an alteration in the character of the desired tax system. During World War II, the greatest increase took place in income and profits taxes, but there was an extended use of nearly all kinds of taxation, partly to fight inflation. Objectives like an equitable distribution of income and efficient allocation of resources played a less important role in tax policy than they can in a peacetime economy, where the over-all objective itself is not so simply defined as "winning the war."

National Government Best Able to Use Broad Tax Policies

Framing a tax structure which will simultaneously consider all of these objectives is more practicable for the national government than for state and local governments. Using fiscal (including tax) policy to encourage full employment, as we have pointed out earlier in this book, may require direct creation of purchasing power. Only the national government is empowered under the Constitution to issue money.

Furthermore, it does not seem realistic to expect any state to shape its fiscal policies primarily to further the national interest, if the interest of the residents of the state is in conflict with the national interest. The pressures of interstate competition for industry and investment are too strong, and the powers of any single state are insufficient to counter general inflationary or deflationary tendencies adequately.[2]

These limitations of governmental units other than the Federal government are even more apparent at the local level. Not only is the tax base smaller than for the state, but the variations

[2] The state governments acting in concert, however, might be able to do more than they have done to counter general inflationary or deflationary tendencies. Leadership along this line might be exercised by an agency such as the *Council of State Governments*.

in the tax base among taxing units is much greater than among the states.[3] To date, the principal tax which has been practicable for local units of government to employ is the property tax. Relatively little experimentation with different types of taxes has been feasible for these local units.

Thus state and local governments are more inclined to think of living within their tax revenues over a period, than is the national government. This restricts, but does not eliminate the effective steps which the Federal government may take to follow broad goals in fiscal policy. After all, the most likely postwar level of Federal expenditures (around 25 to 30 billions) is itself two or three times the level of total state-local spending which will probably take place. To show how state and local units of government are to fit into the over-all purposes of fiscal policy is, nevertheless, an important problem in fiscal planning. It is one to which considerable attention has been devoted recently[4] and one which will especially concern us in the final section of this book.

The Tax System and Full Employment: Tax Flexibility

As we have emphasized in previous chapters, the tax system can contribute to full employment if tax collections are reduced sufficiently to strengthen markets, or can help check inflation if they are increased to drain off excess spending power.[5] This implies that tax collections should be flexible.

With a given schedule of rates and exemptions, a reduction (or increase) in aggregate money income automatically brings a decrease (or increase) in tax collections. This, however, has not strengthened (or restricted) markets sufficiently in the past. Further flexibility could be built into the fiscal structure.

[3] In 1945, per capita income in the state having the highest per capita figure (Nevada) was about three times per capita income in the state having the lowest per capita income (Mississippi). Average per capita income in Nevada was $1,480 while in Mississippi it was $556. See *The Survey of Current Business*, August, 1946, page 16.

At the local level some school districts in Iowa, for instance, have 25 times as much assessed value of property per person as do others. The highest district has 250 times per person as much assessed value as the lowest.

[4] One prominent study is by Alvin H. Hansen and Harvey S. Perloff, *State and Local Finance in the National Economy*, New York: W. W. Norton & Co., Inc., 1944. Another is the report of the Committee on Intergovernmental Fiscal Relations, "Federal, State and Local Government Fiscal Relations," Senate Document No. 69, 78th Congress, 1st Session, 1943.

[5] See particularly Chapter VI.

Greater flexibility also could be accomplished by deliberately altering either tax rates or exemptions.

The need for tax flexibility has to be explicitly recognized, and provisions for greater flexibility have to be incorporated into the tax pattern, if the fiscal system is to make its maximum contribution to full employment. Reducing the time lag between the receipt of income and the collection of taxes (refer to Chapter XIII) has increased the flexibility that has been built into the personal income tax. However, this flexibility may not be sufficient. The exact amount by which taxes should be reduced or increased cannot be specified for every situation in advance. Further flexibility (though it is not automatic) can be incorporated into the tax system if monetary-fiscal agencies are granted the power to decrease taxes or to increase them in an attempt to encourage a greater or smaller money expenditure for goods and services.

Several kinds of taxes lend themselves to flexibility. Rates on excises or general sales taxes could be changed and would be almost immediately reflected in disposable income available for private expenditure on goods and services. Tax rates or exemptions for the personal income tax collected currently upon current incomes could be altered and would soon be reflected in changes in disposable income. In fact, as we have suggested, changes could be extended backwards in time to reduce past taxes as well as present ones, thereby adding further to disposable income available for current expenditure.

There are strong arguments in favor of the personal income tax as the most desirable tax. These relate in part to personal income taxation as the most consistent with tax equity, as explained later in this chapter. Other major considerations favoring income over sales taxation are examined in Chapters XIII, XIV, and XVI.

Flexibility a modernized version of tax adequacy. Flexibility in tax collections may be viewed as a modernized concept of the old idea of "tax adequacy." In this modernization, however, adequacy is evaluated in terms of the contribution which taxes make to sustaining full employment or discouraging inflation.

If this concept of adequacy is to be extended to state and local levels as well as the national level, it implies an extension of Federal grants-in-aid to state and local units of government.

These units cannot look at adequacy in terms of the impact of taxes upon employment or prices unless they have sources of revenue other than their own tax collections.

Equity in Taxation

Equity in taxation, though an ethical rather than an economic concept, has come to represent substantial agreement on certain important things.   Thus, equity means taxation either according to "ability to pay" or "benefits received."   Ability to pay is central when our interest lies in the impact of taxation on income distribution.   Benefits received can be applied where the benefits of public expenditures can readily be traced, although the scope for the use of the benefit principle is limited, as we shall see.   Further, tax equity is generally accepted to mean that equal tax treatment should be given to persons similarly situated as to income and as to benefits from government activities.[6]

A place for benefits received has already been recognized. The nature of most public activities, however, makes application of the benefit principle rather limited.   A case can be made for apportioning the costs of social insurance and of highway maintenance through the collection of social security and highway taxes.[7]   But relatively few public activities in a private enterprise system can be sold.   No one would suggest, for instance, the marketing of the services of the legislatures and the courts.   Consequently, even though the benefit principle has applications, the area left for application of ability to pay is very large.

The ability-to-pay theory of taxation.   One of the first formulations of ability to pay was made by Adam Smith, who stated in *The Wealth of Nations:*

> The subjects of every state ought to contribute to the support of government as nearly as possible in proportion to their respective abilities, that is, in proportion to the revenue which they respectively derive under the protection of the state.[8]

Although this statement fits fairly closely our general ethical concepts, it still leaves unanswered the real meaning of ability

[6] Our present tax laws violate this criterion in several ways.   One of the most obvious lies in the discrimination against an individual with a fluctuating income.

[7] Certain nontax revenues—license and privilege fees, special assessments, and the like—may be established somewhat in line with benefits received.   Such revenues are collected, for the most part, by state and local governments.

[8] Adam Smith, *The Wealth of Nations,* Book V, Chapter 2.

to pay or how to measure such ability in the application of such a principle. Today, however, ability-to-pay taxation seems to be based on the following hypotheses:

(1) The benefits of most public activities are widely scattered throughout the population. Where costs are involved in providing those activities and some of such costs are financed by taxation, such costs should be apportioned in a manner which will impose the smallest "real" burdens.

(2) The real burden imposed by a tax of a given size will be inversely correlated with ability to pay.

(3) Although no single measure of an individual's[9] ability to pay is entirely satisfactory, ability is best measured by net income over a given period of time, adjusted for the number of persons dependent upon the individual. Some discrimination according to the source of income may be warranted. Windfalls such as inheritances, for example, might be taxed more heavily than other kinds of income, since supposedly nothing was given up in order to get such income.[10] Property income might be taxed at a higher rate than income from wages and salaries, since property income is more nearly net income—deductions for maintenance of the property being permitted. The Federal government, however, abandoned distinction between earned (wage and salary) and unearned (property) income for tax purposes in 1943.

(4) The mere receipt of *some* income by an individual does not indicate ability. Ability (in a positive sense) does not emerge until there is an amount of income which exceeds some minimum generally considered to be sufficient to permit a standard of consumption which will at least permit working health and efficiency.[11]

[9] It is generally accepted that ability to pay is strictly an attribute of persons or households and that it is nonsense to talk about the ability to pay of a corporation. The ability to pay is an attribute of the stockholders, managers, employees, and buyers of products of the corporation.

[10] Inheritances are not considered income under present tax laws. They may reasonably be considered income under another income concept for tax purposes. These various concepts are examined in Chapter XIII.

[11] It must be recognized, however, that the existence of *any* income is often considered "fair game" by those who frame tax laws. A good illustration is found in the wave of general sales taxes enacted by many states during the thirties. Indiana and West Virginia also have low-rate gross income taxes which

Progressive taxation. The second of the hypotheses we have listed above—that the "real burden" of a given percentage of income paid in taxes is less if the tax is collected from an individual whose income is high than if it is collected from an individual whose income is low—has formed the basis for progressive taxation. By progressive tax we mean that the tax rate increases as the tax base rises. The realism of this hypothesis, however, cannot be tested. Although it appears reasonable that the ten thousandth dollar of income means less to either individual *A* or *B* than the one thousandth dollar of income, we cannot say whether the ten thousandth dollar means more or less to individual *A* than the one thousandth dollar means to individual *B*. This inability to measure utility, however, does not mean that the tax structure should be regressive. People's needs probably are more alike than their incomes.

Progressive taxation need not be founded on any assumptions about people's utility functions. Progression can be defended for what it is: *a direct fiscal attack upon inequality.* If such inequality as exists is considered undesirable in principle by the bulk of the population, progression in the tax structure is a way to reduce this inequality. No pseudoscientific principle need be presented to justify the use of progressive taxation in such a case.[12]

Acceptance of progression as an idea does not imply general agreement as to the exact tax rate schedule. In fact, the acceptance of ability to pay and of progression exists principally at the Federal level. Concurrently, most state and local taxes bear down with relative severity on the lower-income groups.[13]

Resource Allocation and the Tax System

We have consistently urged that taxes should have a minimum influence in determining the allocation of economic resources—in relatively free markets. Such allocation, in our private enter-

---

have effects similar to those of sales taxes. These taxes were regressive in effect, that is, took a larger per cent of the income of people with small incomes than with large incomes.

[12] See S. J. Chapman, "The Utility of Income and Progressive Taxation," *Economic Journal*, 23:25-35 (March, 1913).

[13] Refer to Helen Tarasov, *Who Does Pay the Taxes?* New School for Social Research, 1942.

prise economy, will best be determined according to the pattern
of consumer preferences and relative costs.[14] It is, however,
possible that a frontal attack on monopoly through appropriate
fiscal action might improve resource allocation, as was indicated
in Chapter IX.

The tax system may affect resource allocation in several ways.
The kinds of taxes levied may encourage the production or consumption of some commodities and discourage production and
consumption of others. Also, more or less resources may be
required by government to collect the tax, and by taxpayers to
comply with payment of the tax.

**The tax system and the production pattern in the private econ-
omy.**[15] Taxation which purposely discourages the production and
consumption of particular commodities or of certain types of
economic activities finds but a limited place within the social
goals accepted in this book, which have stressed (among other
things) both the full use of resources and their best allocation.
On the one hand, prohibitory Federal taxes on such articles as
opium, marijuana, and similar drugs may be accepted as helping
to prevent consumption which is generally recognized to impair
health and working efficiency. Both the latter are among the
prerequisites for maximum total product. Similarly, taxes to
collect social damages from certain external diseconomies—smoke
from burning soft coal, for example—can be justified. Such taxes
will encourage reducing the smoke nuisance, and their proceeds
can be used to compensate those who are damaged. On the
other hand, the many discriminatory taxes of the states against
efficient forms of merchandising, such as chain stores, or against
healthful products, such as margarine, cannot be reconciled with
the goals either of maximum product or of minimum interference
in the allocation of resources.

In general, it is recognized that taxes should be of the type
which *directly* discourage production, employment, and exchange
as little as possible. We recognize, with Hansen and Perloff,

[14] See Chapter I for a brief discussion of this position, and for recognition that
the role to be played by the public economy in resource use must generally be
determined according to other than relative price considerations.

[15] Many of the ideas discussed in this section will be developed more fully in
Chapter XVI.

that "in general, all taxes are more or less restrictive on consumption or investment" (taken by themselves).[16] But some taxes are more restrictive than others. A good example is any tax which varies with total output and thus acts to raise marginal unit-costs of production. A tax of some given amount per package of cigarettes, per bottle of beer, or per package of playing cards will illustrate. Such a tax—in contrast to one on personal net income—directly results in a new equilibrium between supply and demand which is usually at a higher price and provides smaller employment opportunities in the taxed industry.[17]

There are heavy taxes on articles of common consumption, such as those on alcoholic beverages and on tobacco products, which are difficult to rationalize. On the one hand, such taxes are heavy enough to carry implications that their aim is "sumptuary," to discourage consumption. On the other hand, demand appears to be relatively inelastic, and the taxes have not been made so heavy that consumption expenditure is actually cut. The result is that the government gets much "revenue" and low-income consumers are penalized compared to other income groups.

No simple problem is involved here. These so-called "sumptuary" taxes are actually used to collect large revenues, so that use of the taxes tries to serve two inconsistent purposes at the same time. They are not actually used primarily for sumptuary purposes; otherwise, the revenues would not make these taxes the Number 1 and Number 2 sources of Federal excise tax revenues, as they are. Furthermore, the taxes represent an interference with the allocation of economic resources which works directly against one of the primary tax objectives which we have set up. Yet, the number of suppliers of tobacco and liquor products is small and price competition is almost absent, so that removal of these taxes might not be expected to alter prices to

[16] Reprinted from *State and Local Finance in the National Economy,* page 248, by Alvin H. Hansen and Harvey S. Perloff by permission of W. W. Norton & Co., Inc., New York. Copyright, 1944 by the publishers.

[17] Unless specialized resources are used which must absorb the tax for lack of alternative opportunities, this result is more likely to be true in short-run than in long-run periods. The above statement does not overlook the possibility that "outside" influences operating on incomes generally may increase demand by enough or more than enough to offset the effects of such a tax on the volume sold. Refer to Chapter XII.

the consumer very much.[18] Political difficulties to removal of such taxes would be great and cannot be ignored. Economically, the excess profits resulting from removal of the taxes could be recovered by some kind of an excess-profits tax or would show up in larger receipts from corporate-net-income and personal-net-income taxes.[19]

The tax system and antimonopoly policy. A frontal attack on monopoly could be made through fiscal policy which would combine subsidization and taxation. If successful, such a policy would clearly improve the pattern of resource allocation. The limitations of such a policy were judged to outweigh its possibilities in Chapter IX, and the possible role of fiscal policy in this area will not be analyzed again in this chapter.[20]

Tax administration. A minimum amount of resources devoted to the collection of taxes and to compliance with tax regulations means that more resources can be devoted to other pursuits in either the public or the private economy. Thus *economy* and *simplicity* in tax administration contribute to minimizing the effects of taxation on the allocation of resources. The implications of economy and simplicity will be examined in detail in this section.[21]

The development of our complex society, operating under the Federal system, has made it increasingly difficult to attain desired administrative goals. In particular, it has restricted the amount of simplicity and economy which it has been possible to attain and works directly against our goal of minimizing the effect of tax administration on the allocation of resources.

(1) *The gains from simplicity in the tax structure.* The achievement of greater *simplicity* in our tax structure would reduce the impact of tax administration on resource allocation.

---

[18] Because of past public action, tobacco manufacturers may be particularly vulnerable to antitrust action. Consequently, it is possible that reduction in tobacco taxes would lead to reduction in prices to consumers.

[19] There is implied here some integration of corporate and personal net income taxes, a subject to be discussed in Chapters XII-XV. See also Chapter XVI.

[20] The reader should refer to the analysis in Chapter IX, pages 144-153.

[21] For a thorough treatment of tax administration refer to such well known public-finance texts as W. J. Shultz, *American Public Finance*, 3rd edition, New York: Prentice-Hall, 1942, and Harley L. Lutz, *Public Finance*, 3rd edition, New York: Appleton-Century, 1936. For a recent, fresh treatment of certain aspects of tax administration, see a series of articles by James W. Martin on "Costs of Tax Administration," *Bulletin of the National Tax Association*, Vol. 29 (January–April, 1944).

For example, it would reduce the amount of legal talent now needed by business firms for tax purposes; it would reduce the amount of resources now used by the printing industry for tax purposes; it would release thousands of people at the clerical level for other occupations.

Complexity in our tax structure has risen primarily from the development of the United States within a political framework of many taxing units.[22]   Under our Constitution, only the taxation of property is forbidden the national government.   Only the taxation of imports (and exports) is forbidden the states.[23]

Within these restrictions, the property tax has come to center almost exclusively with local units of government,[24] but states and the Federal government have reached out to levy "overlapping" taxes of many types. About the only important field the Federal government has not chosen to enter is that of "general sales taxation," but the fiscal importance of this abstinence is very doubtful, in view of a variety of goods and services taxed by the Federal government. Federal taxation of business, however, remains relatively simple. As it impinged on businessmen in 1946, Federal taxation consisted chiefly of: (1) a graduated tax on corporate net profit, (2) employment taxes under the Social Security Act, (3) the administration of tax payments on the sale of selected goods and services, especially alcoholic beverages, tobacco, gasoline, and sugar, and (4) partial administration of withholding techniques under the personal income tax.

States, for the most part, have felt few inhibitions about the types of taxes which they have employed. During the thirties especially they provided for or increased the taxation of corporate and personal incomes, general sales, alcoholic beverages, and

[22] Under our Federal constitution, the 48 states and the national government are all sovereign taxing jurisdictions, and in 1942 there were about 155,000 government units possessing at least limited taxing powers.

[23] The taxation of property is, in practical effect, denied the Federal government by the clause in the Constitution which forbids direct property taxation by the national government except in proportion to the population of the various states.   States are forbidden to tax imports or exports except with the consent of Congress.   For Constitutional references, see Article 1, section 8 and Article 1, section 10.   The 21st Amendment also gives the states control over liquor in its various aspects.

[24] This is true except for a few states, notably New Jersey and Texas. As a percentage of total state tax revenues in fiscal 1945, however, the property tax was but 5 per cent.

employment taxes (the last under the Social Security Act) to mention a few of the more obvious developments.[25]

The net result is a very complex tax system especially in the field of business taxation by the States. State business taxes, in fact, have been aptly described by Hansen and Perloff as a "chaos." [26]

They remark:

> Business taxes in the states are a conglomeration of heterogeneous taxes imposed for different purposes, on different bases, under many forms of rate schedules, and with many types of administrative machinery. . . . Businesses are subject not only to property taxes, net income taxes, excise taxes, sales taxes, capital-stock taxes and severance taxes, but also to a great variety of special charges, including privilege, license and occupation taxes. [There are over 200 occupation taxes alone in some of the southern states.]

(2) *Simplicity largely forgotten in American tax system.* From this brief summary, it is clear that simplicity as an administrative canon of taxation in the American tax system has largely been forgotten. Space does not permit a study of the many administrative complexities in state business taxation, but one example may be given. In 1946, 33 states employed some form of a corporate net income tax. For a corporation doing only part of its business in State A, the state may not legally tax more than such portion of the corporate net income as may "reasonably" be allocated to the state. An interstate business operating in all 33 states (perhaps a mail-order house) must thus understand the varying tax laws of these 33 states and allocate its net income among them according to formulas prescribed by the various states.

There is no simplicity in the administration of 33 different income taxes, besides the Federal tax, but a measure of equity might be retained if the formulas for allocating net income among the states were relatively uniform. Unfortunately, the last available study of the interstate allocation of business income for

[25] For a brief survey of developments in Federal and state taxation since 1900, see Chapter II. For specific discussion of developments in overlapping taxation, see the same chapter.

[26] Reprinted from *State and Local Finance in the National Economy,* Chapter 3, especially pages 44-47. The quotation given is from pages 44-45. By permission of W. W. Norton & Co., Inc., New York. Copyright, 1944 by the publishers.

state income-tax purposes indicated that ten different factors, or combinations thereof, were being employed.[27]   The result is that such interstate corporations may find themselves taxed on an allocated net income which exceeds their total net income, and will be placed at a competitive disadvantage to this extent, compared to corporations doing business over a more restricted area.

(3) *Recent simplification in Federal income tax.*   In one major area, we made definite progress in tax simplification between 1940 and 1945.   We refer to the Federal personal income tax, which was converted during this period from what we have called a "class" tax to a "mass" tax.   In 1940, potential taxpayers were required to work through a rather long tax form, compute their tax liability (if any) for the *preceding* year, and mail the return with tax payment (in quarterly portions if desired) to a Collector of Internal Revenue.   In 1945, at the income peak for World War II, simplification in procedure had been carried to the point where, of over 47 million returns filed, 20 million represented withholding receipts which authorized the Collector to compute the tax, and another 17 million were based on a short form combined with a tax table using standard deductions.   Nevertheless, 11 million returns were based on the traditional, complete tax form.[28]

This simplification in procedure was a tremendous, though necessary, step in applying the income tax to the bulk of income receivers.   To work out the new procedures, however, cooperation was required from employers to make the withholding procedures effective, and a further cost of tax compliance was placed on them.

On the whole, this simplification in procedure which it was possible to accomplish in the income tax in so short a time is encouraging for the future.   Too much, however, should not be expected from simplification in procedures.   Federal tax authorities have commented on several occasions that simplification itself has limitations under present-day complexities in the definition of the tax base,[29] such as the interstate allocation of corporate

---

[27] Tax Research Foundation, *Tax Systems of the World*, pages 146-151, 9th edition, Chicago: Commerce Clearing House, Inc., 1942.

[28] See Summary Report of Secretary of the Treasury, Washington, D. C., July 21, 1945, page 23.

[29] See the remarks of Roy Blough, formerly Assistant to the Secretary of the Treasury, before the American Institute of Accountants on "Simplification of Corporate Tax Structure," St. Louis, Mo., October 19, 1944.

net income mentioned above, for instance.   More is to be anticipated for the future from reduction in the present number of
our overlapping taxes, as well as simplification of tax structures
within the states and greater uniformity among states.

(4) *Costs of tax administration heavy in our tax system.*   This
brings us to the second administrative goal which we have recognized as important to the attainment of our basic tax objectives: economy.   Most simply expressed, this means that a minimum amount of resources should be tied up in collecting, and
complying with, taxes.   Our present complex tax system cannot
expect to achieve this goal.   Overlapping Federal and state taxes
mean a considerable waste of resources in the collection of taxes
and in taxpayer effort to comply with (or to avoid) the taxes imposed on him.   From another point of view, it has frequently
been said that tax collection (along with other functions of government) should conform to the rule of allocating to a governmental unit that which it can do most efficiently.[30]

In the last two decades, it has been increasingly recognized
that economy in tax administration includes two elements: (1)
costs of collecting taxes from the governmental viewpoint, (2)
costs of complying with taxes from the taxpayer's viewpoint.
Economy broadly conceived involves something more than simply the ratios of cost to collections.   It involves getting the
most for money spent by government units in carefully chosen,
well-trained administrators.   It involves willingness on the part
of society to incur expenses which will bring about *effectiveness*
of tax collection beyond the first 90 per cent of almost any tax.
Such portion of almost any tax is likely to be forthcoming with
little outlay for administration.   This, of course, requires some
agreement on what level of effectiveness to achieve (beyond this
first 90 per cent), and then the determination of the maximum
economy in the costs of getting this effectiveness.   Obviously,
the last dollar of tax liability cannot be collected.   Yet, as a
recent Fiscal Relations Report observes:[31]

---

[30] It is pointed out in Chapter XXIII that available evidence indicates a margin
of superiority for the Federal government in the collection of most overlapping
taxes.   This means that the Federal government should become the "fund source"
for governmental activities even more than at present.

[31] "Federal, State and Local Government Fiscal Relations," Senate Document
69, 78th Congress, 1st Session, 1943, page 310.   This will be referred to subsequently as the Fiscal Relations Report or simply as the Report.

It may well be . . . that the social interest requires an investment in tax administration well beyond the point of diminishing returns. Tax administration is a policing job as well as a means of collecting revenue, and the justice of effective tax collections has value in terms of public morale and may even be an end in itself.

Keeping a broad interpretation of economy in mind, we may profitably examine the elements of cost in tax administration which were distinguished above. A major limitation shows up immediately. Reliable data on costs of administration and compliance are difficult to obtain and are lacking entirely in the field of taxpayer compliance, except for one or two pioneer studies in this field. So important did the recent Fiscal Relations Report consider this lack that it recommended a research project on this subject as the most important in the field of intergovernmental fiscal relations.[32]

(5) *Costs of collecting American taxes*. The Fiscal Relations Report gives data on the over-all cost of collecting Federal internal revenue from 1941 back to 1934. These data indicated a postdepression peak of $1.54 per $100 of taxes collected, and an almost steady drop, as tax revenues increased, to $0.89 per $100 in 1941. Between 1941 and 1944, the over-all figure dropped from 89 cents to 32 cents per $100. Although expenditures of the Bureau of Internal Revenue nearly doubled during these three years (increasing from 65.3 millions to 129.9 millions), revenues increased between five and six times (from 7,370 millions to 40,122 millions). This revenue figure cannot be held —probably should not be held (on the basis of our previous analysis)—as a regular, annual goal in the postwar period, but it is relevant that the President's 1947 budget (revised) forecasted internal revenue of about 37.0 billion dollars. At revenue levels so far above prewar tax collections, the administrative costs per dollar of taxes collected by the Bureau of Internal Revenue would continue much below those of prewar years.[33]

---

[32] See Fiscal Relations Report, page 307. Such a project, aimed directly at costs of taxpayer compliance, was set up and ready to start when World War II broke out and forced its abandonment.

[33] There are, of course, other administrative costs at the Federal level than those of the Bureau of Internal Revenue. These are mainly those of the Bureau of Customs and the Federal judiciary. The Bureau of Customs does other things than simply collect duties on imported goods; in 1944, its expense of $25,045,000 on $434,259,000 of imports credited to the BOC gave the highest tax collection

For the year 1941, the Bureau of Internal Revenue has provided a detailed breakdown of the cost of collecting different types of Federal taxes per $100 of revenue, ranging from $1.68 for individual income taxes to 10 cents for manufacturers' and retailers' excise taxes.[34] It is of interest to note that, in 1941, the fiscal experts writing the Report considered the over-all cost of administering all taxes (89¢ per $100) to be impressively low and the figure for the personal income tax moderate, considering "its elaborate law and equally elaborate machinery of administration and collection." [35] From 1941 to 1944, the personal income tax increased 13 times, while the total cost of the Bureau was doubling. This was the period when techniques already noted were being developed, and when, as a result, the cost of income-tax administration fell sharply.

The limitations of these data should be observed. They are all average cost figures, and tell us nothing about the marginal cost of collecting that part of tax revenue in excess of the 90 per cent which has been suggested as the return for almost any tax without much expense for enforcement. It may well be that the marginal cost of collecting the last 10 per cent of tax revenue may have remained relatively high. This would be consistent with the past practice of the Bureau of Internal Revenue in concentrating its resources for enforcement on the larger income returns and following the trail of these returns down to the last dollar, if possible.

More than one tax expert has urged that the Bureau use its limited funds to greater advantage by selecting a random sample of *all* tax returns for some broadly based tax such as the personal income tax, and investigating this sample of returns, regardless of *apparent* accuracy or inaccuracy in the returns themselves. This kind of investigation would strengthen taxpayer morale and probably lead to the filing of more complete returns, and the report of more taxable income, even if the last dollar of taxable income were not discovered and listed for a relatively few large returns. The proposal would have much less strength for the days when the income tax reached less than 4,000,000

ratio at the Federal level. Much of the time of the judiciary is occupied with tax cases; total cost of the Federal judiciary in 1944 was $13,075,000.

[34] See Fiscal Relations Report, page 307.

[35] *Ibid.*, page 308.

people, as it did a few years ago, than it does for recent years, when the Federal personal income tax resulted in taxation of over 40,000,000 people.

At the state-local level, the Fiscal Relations Report comments that "available data on the cost of administration of state taxes are notoriously fragmentary, ill-defined, and unreliable." [36] The Report nevertheless presents the best available data concerning costs of administering state and local taxes. For all state and local tax receipts, it estimated the average cost per $100 of taxes at $2.32, and for specific major taxes on which data were gathered from only a portion of the states in some instances, the Report placed the cost per $100 of taxes at a low of 50 cents for gasoline and a high of 8 dollars for motor vehicle licenses.[37] Total estimated costs of tax collection in 1941, including the Bureau of Customs but not those of the judiciary, were about $305,000,-000. The costs in 1944 were about $375,000,000. In both cases, state and local costs account for about $220,000,000. After pointing out the limitations of cost of administration data, unless accompanied by such qualitative considerations as "adequacy of administration," the Report nevertheless concludes that "in few, if any, cases of overlapping taxes can the States administer their laws as efficiently in terms of a ratio of outlays to collections as can the federal government." [38]

(6) *Costs of taxpayer compliance.* It has already been emphasized that economy in tax administration includes the cost of compliance from the taxpayers' point of view as well as the costs of collecting taxes by governmental agencies. Little investigation of these costs has yet been made, however. The principal available study was made by Professor Haig for the year 1934,[39] which he himself characterized as "a pioneering expedition into unexplored territory." It was based on a sample of 163 corporations which responded in detail to a questionnaire originally sent to 1,600. Despite various biases toward overstatement, Haig

[36] See the Report, page 308. The writers continue: ". . . the cost of the tax mechanism is a major consideration in the case for tax coordination."

[37] In some instances this 8 dollars may have included expenditures for highway policing functions.

[38] See the Report, page 310, where some of the reasons for this are also noted.

[39] See Robert Murray Haig, "The Cost to Business Concerns of Compliance with Tax Laws," *The Management Review*, Vol. 24 (November, 1935), American Management Association, pages 323-333.

concluded that "actual contact with the individual returns has led me to the belief that the costs of compliance are understated in more instances than they are exaggerated."[40] Cost of compliance was:

1. For state corporation income tax (median of 76 corporations), 9.5 per cent of tax.
2. For Federal corporation income tax (median of 95 corporations), 4.7 per cent.
3. State sales tax (arithmetic mean for 91 corporations), 3.7 per cent.
4. Property tax (arithmetic mean for 122 corporations), 1.04 per cent.
5. The 163 corporations in the sample filed 31,100 primary tax returns (basis for determining liability), 6,268 Federal and 24,782 state and local. In addition, they made over 160,000 informational returns and other reports to tax officials.

No quantitative data on the costs of taxpayer compliance yet exist, although Professor Martin, in his studies of tax administration for the Senate committee on "Federal, State and Local Fiscal Relations," "guessed" these costs as high as 200 million dollars in 1941, and total costs of tax administration (collection and compliance) as about half a billion dollars.

With reference to the Haig study, it is of interest that after pointing out limitations arising especially from the fact that the year studied was a late depression year (1934), the committee report concluded: "Even making all due allowances for important elements of uncertainty and probable exaggeration in (Haig's) figures, they carry enough weight to make an impressive case for doing something about compliance costs."[41]

(7) *Taxpayer costs and interstate trade barriers.* In view of the interest during the last decade in the subject of interstate trade barriers, it is of interest that Haig was himself especially impressed by the relatively high compliance costs of corporations doing business in more than one state. Thus, he found that of 63 corporations that paid state corporation-income taxes, and furnished sufficient information for analysis, businesses confined to one state had a typical compliance cost of 3.5 per cent where the typical cost for concerns doing business in more than one

[40] Haig, "The Cost to Business Concerns," page 326.
[41] See the Report, page 312.

state was 10.5 per cent.[42]   He attributed this differential to the lack of uniformity in state laws and found in these high costs of doing business in more than one state an important barrier to the extension of a genuine free-trading area within the economy.

Haig, of course, was only touching on the fiscal barriers set up by the states to discourage interstate trade.   Under the 21st Amendment (which repealed the 18th Amendment establishing prohibition), control over liquor manufacture and its sale was given to the states, along with control of importation from other states.   The result has been a nation-wide movement on the part of the states to give especially favorable treatment to home producers rather than foreign producers.   Better known are special tax restrictions placed by some states on the sale of margarine and operation of chain stores, and the imposition of especially heavy taxes and restrictions on trucks and buses engaged in interstate commerce.   These restrictions all operate to impair what we have called "the best allocation of productive resources."   It is encouraging to note that influential bodies like the Council of State Governments have begun to move against these trade barriers in recent years.

(8) *Other administrative aspects of taxation.*   A complex tax system necessarily makes it difficult to attain desired administrative goals in taxation, as we have seen in examining such goals as *simplicity* and *economy.*   To the latter, Adam Smith added the canons of *certainty* and *convenience,* both of which merit brief consideration.[43]   The nature of certainty is fairly clear.   In a democratic society, rules governing the tax structure should be laid down by the representatives of the people and should be enforced without discrimination among persons similarly situated with respect to liability for any given tax.   Tax legislation should

---

[42] See Haig, "The Cost to Business Concerns," pages 328-330.

[43] Smith laid down his administrative canons as follows, in the *Wealth of Nations,* Book V, Chapter 2:

    a. The tax which each individual is bound to pay ought to be certain and not arbitrary.   The time of payment, manner of payment, quantity to be paid, ought all to be clear and plain to the contributor and to every other person. (*certainty*)

    b. Every tax ought to be levied at the time, or in the manner, in which it is most likely to be convenient for the contributor and to every other person. (*convenience*)

    c. Every tax ought to be so contrived as both to take out and keep out of the pockets of the people as little as possible, over and above what it brings into the public treasury of the state. (*economy*)

be made as understandable and simple as possible for those taxes which are used. In this sense, taxes which are used should be certain, clear, and not arbitrary.

But attaining certainty in our tax system is more difficult than stating its nature. Thus, in Federal taxation alone, "no less than thirteen sources, with diverse aims, backgrounds and equipment, contribute to the stream of tax law vexing and confusing federal taxpayers . . . . Uncertainty is part of the price paid to protect individual liberties and rights from arbitrary encroachment by government action." [44] These sources are a combination of the actions of legislative, administrative, and judicial agencies, and all contribute to making certainty of tax liability a goal difficult to attain.

Convenience is a less important criterion for tax administration.[45] Other things being equal, there is certainly a case for collecting a tax at the time, and in the manner, most convenient to the taxpayer. For instance, a major development of Federal income taxation since 1942 has been to adjust the time of payment more closely to the current economic capacity of the taxpayer by shifting toward a current collection system. This is in line both with greater convenience (and compliance) for the taxpayer and with the goal of flexibility in tax collections discussed earlier in this chapter.

However, other things are not always equal. Thus, it would appear that under our present system of collecting Federal per-

[44] W. J. Shultz, *American Public Finance*, page 309. Shultz summarizes the problem as follows: "Legislators are not the sole contributors to the taxpayers' bewilderment. After Congress enacts a tax statute, the Treasury supplements the law with regulations, and amends the regulations with frequent 'decisions.' The Bureau of Internal Revenue and the General Counsel make both published and unpublished rulings and interpretations, and mimeographs attempt to convey to officials the policy and attitude of the administration. Judicial interpretation then enters. Every federal district court, the Board of Tax Appeals [now the Tax Court], and the Court of Claims, establish the law in those cases over which they have original jurisdiction. Circuit Courts of Appeals hand down binding interpretations. The Attorney-General's opinions on tax matters are controlling on the administrative authorities; and the Solicitor-General governs the Bureau by determining the cases in which to apply for or consent to review, and the cases in which to acquiesce in lower court decisions. And the Supreme Court has final word in the limited class of cases which reach hearing there." Words in the brackets have been added by the writers. Reprinted by permission of Prentice-Hall, Inc., New York. Copyright 1942 by publishers.

[45] The canon of convenience is discussed here in a somewhat different framework from that considered by Adam Smith. Smith related convenience to compliance. Although we acknowledge this relationship, compliance has been treated as a separate problem (see the sections on tax administration).

sonal income taxes, the factor of convenience has been too heavily weighted in favor of the farmer. Whereas most self-employed persons (potentially taxable) must make an estimate of annual tax liability every three months (which they can subsequently revise) and pay a quarterly share on that basis, the farmer is not required even to declare his estimated liability until the first month of the next year (January 15). Recognizing the imperfections and difficulties of farm bookkeeping, we still feel that present regulations represent an undue concession to the farmer.

Again, commodity taxes falling largely on consumers may be relatively convenient to pay, coming in small driblets and generally not requiring a return from the consumer. This, however, is not enough to tip the scales in favor of regressive commodity taxes as opposed to the objections to them which can be raised.

(9) *Conclusions on tax administration.* The remarks we have made on tax administration may be summarized as follows: (1) Such goals as relative simplicity and economy tie in directly with major objectives of taxation which we have advocated. (2) These goals, along with others, are themselves difficult to attain in a fiscal system which permits the operation of 49 sovereign government units and 155,000 total government units having some taxing power. (3) True economy in tax administration includes more than just the money costs of administration. It also includes the maximization of public and taxpayer morale by widespread and nondiscriminatory use of resources devoted to enforcement. Nevertheless, economy does include costs of taxpayer compliance as well as costs of tax collection. Together, these probably tie up resources aggregating half a billion dollars a year. Reduction in the use of resources for this purpose should be possible and to the extent accomplished, the national product available for private use could be increased.[46] (4) Substantial reduction in the use of resources for tax administration (including costs both of tax collection and of compliance) can probably

---

[46] It is recognized that (*a*) reducing the cost of compliance is concerned with the attitude of the taxpayer toward government as well as with actual lowering in compliance costs, (*b*) the compliance problem is by no means confined to corporations, though most easily subject to measurement at the corporate level. The aggregate of time and energy used by individuals in keeping and supplying tax information—especially information on the income tax—is substantial, although recent progress in simplifying income tax procedure is impressive.

be maximized only through a gradual, but quite complete recasting of Federal-state-fiscal relations. This recasting would, among other things, increase the relative role of the Federal government in tax collections and administration.[47] (5) Such other traditional goals of administration as relative certainty and convenience cannot be ignored. But relative certainty is restricted by the complex tax system which we have built and by the provision for its continuous alteration by a combination of legislative, administrative, and judicial agencies. Convenience must be evaluated in the light of the major tax policies which have been advocated in this book. It conforms with some, but conflicts with others. This weakens its usefulness as a tenet of sound tax administration.

Summary

From this discussion of fundamental considerations in taxation, it is apparent that a "good" tax system is one which will contribute to the achievement of the major objectives of fiscal policy emphasized throughout this book. Such objectives have centered about: (1) promoting full employment, (2) obtaining equity in income distribution, (3) minimizing interference with the allocation of economic resources—unless antimonopoly fiscal policy is utilized. In terms of taxation, it has been indicated that achieving the first objective means principally *planned flexibility* in taxation at the national level. Achieving the second objective centers largely around ability to pay taxation, while obtaining the third goal is related to important aspects of tax administration, especially relative simplicity and economy.

It was also pointed out that minimizing interference with resource allocation would mean a reduction in taxes on specific commodities and occupations, such as taxes on cigarettes and on chain stores, but the problems involved in such tax reduction were recognized. The possibility that a combination of subsidies and taxes might make a direct means of attack on monopoly elements was recognized, but upon analysis the possibilities of such fiscal policy were found to be limited.

In the course of our discussion, it became apparent that major

---

[47] One of the final conclusions of the Fiscal Relations Report on tax administration was that "if the fiscal independence of the states is to be maintained even at its present level, other interests than those of strictly administrative advantage must be weighed in the balance." See the Report, page 315.

revisions in our tax structure will be required if taxation is to make a substantial contribution toward achieving our stated objectives of fiscal policy in the future. These revisions will be discussed in succeeding chapters, in the light of our recognized objectives for fiscal policy. They will emphasize, in turn:

(1) Personal income taxation as the heart of the future tax structure.

(2) Drastic simplification in business taxation, in two main respects: (a) a great deal of integration of business taxation and taxes on owners of business, (b) simplification of the complicated business tax system of the states.

(3) Declining emphasis on the taxation of commodities and services.

(4) An overhauling of death and gift taxation, with recognition of the increasing role which death taxes should play in controlling inequality.

(5) Modernization of the property tax, along lines indicated by recent trends and developments.

(6) A continued growth in intergovernmental grants from larger to smaller units, both (a) to promote greater equalization of resources among governmental units, and (b) as a natural consequence of the most efficient method of collecting most taxes, that is, through the Federal government.

This adds up to a reorganized over-all tax structure, centering around a flexible, centrally collected, progressive personal-income tax.

SELECTED READINGS

1. Committee on Federal, State, and Local Government Fiscal Relations, "Federal, State, and Local Government Fiscal Relations," Chapter 5, Washington, D. C., Senate Document No. 69, 78th Congress, 1st Session, 1943.

2. Groves, Harold M., *Postwar Taxation and Economic Progress*, Chapter 1, New York: McGraw-Hill Book Co., Inc.

3. Haig, Robert Murray, "The Cost to Business Concerns of Compliance with Tax Laws," *The Management Review*, 24:323-33 (November, 1935).

4. Hansen, Alvin H. and Perloff, Harvey S., *State and Local*

210 PUBLIC REVENUES AND PUBLIC BORROWING

Finance in the National Economy, Part 1 and Chapter 12, New York: W. W. Norton & Co., Inc., 1944.

5. Lerner, Abba P., *The Economics of Control*, Chapters 19 and 23-25, New York: The Macmillan Company, 1946.
6. Martin, James W., "Costs of Tax Administration," *Bulletin of the National Tax Association*, Vol. 29 (January, February, March, April, 1944).
7. Simons, Henry C., *Personal Income Taxation*, Chapter 1, Chicago: The University of Chicago Press, 1938.
8. Smith, Adam, *The Wealth of Nations*, Book 5.

CHAPTER XII

SHIFTING AND INCIDENCE OF TAXATION[1]

The Problem

IN ANALYZING the impacts of various kinds and amounts of taxes upon the allocation of resources, the distribution of income, or the level of production and employment, it is important to know how these taxes affect relative prices for products and productive agents. If a tax changes the price pattern, it is usually said that this tax—or at least a part of it—has been shifted. The economic unit paying the tax money to the Treasury is not the economic unit upon whom the entire burden of the tax rests. If buyers of the goods or services which this unit sells pay higher prices for these goods or services, a part of the *incidence* of the tax has fallen upon them. The tax has been shifted *forward*. If sellers of goods or services which this unit purchases receive lower prices, at least a part of the burden of the tax has been shifted to them. The tax has been shifted *backward*.

It has already been pointed out that tax collections, viewed independently of the way in which tax revenues are spent (the pattern of government expenditure) are deflationary. They tend to reduce money expenditure for goods and services. If this reduction in money expenditure weakens markets sufficiently to bring increased unemployment, the burden of the tax is widely diffused. However in this analysis of shifting and incidence, it will be assumed (unless otherwise specified) that employment

[1] The theory of shifting and incidence of taxation has received extensive treatment in economic literature. Refer to such studies as Otto Von Mering, *The Shifting and Incidence of Taxation*, Philadelphia: Blakiston Co., 1942; Edwin R. A. Seligman, *The Shifting and Incidence of Taxation*, 5th edition revised, New York: Columbia University Press, 1926; F. Y. Edgeworth, "The Pure Theory of Taxation," *The Economic Journal*, VII (March, June, and December, 1897), 46-70, 226-238, and 550-571; Duncan Black, *The Incidence of Income Taxes*, London: The Macmillan Company, 1939; and Marion H. Gillim, "The Incidence of Excess Profits Taxation," *Columbia University Studies in History, Economics and Public Law*, No. 514.

and total money expenditure are unaffected. This could be the situation if tax and other policies were formulated with an eye toward maintaining full employment. Within such a framework we can view the effects of taxes upon relative prices and the consequent effects on the allocation of resources and the distribution of income.

Basic Assumptions

Economic units act "rationally." In order to analyze the incidence of different kinds of taxes, it is necessary to know how various economic units will act in response to changes in their economic environment. Although we can not formulate a general theory describing exactly how the firm, the resource owner, or the consuming unit behave, we can estimate the *direction* of the response—if we can assume that the economic unit acts consistently in trying to attain some preferred position.

(1) *The firm.* The firm is the unit of production organization. It buys or leases the services of productive agents and mobilizes these services in turning out products (goods and services) which it sells. Within the firm are made decisions regarding what to produce, how much to produce, what techniques of production to utilize, and what and how much of the various productive agents to employ. These decisions are made in the light of such factors as expected demand conditions for products and expected supply conditions for productive agents.[2]

In most analyses of shifting and incidence of taxation, it is assumed that the firm attempts to maximize expected profit.[3] It

[2] For analysis of the theory of the firm refer to such works as J. R. Hicks, *Value and Capital*, New York: Oxford University Press, 1939; George J. Stigler, *The Theory of Price*, New York: The Macmillan Company, 1945; or Kenneth E. Boulding, *Economic Analysis*.

[3] In most situations demand conditions for products, supply conditions for productive agents, and even the technical rates of conversion of productive agents into products are not anticipated with certainty by the firm. For example, the firm knows that a number of different prices may be received for products or paid for productive agents, but just which price will be received or paid is not known. The entrepreneur may make certain estimates of the probability of each of these prices holding at different dates in the future when he may buy or sell. Not only the most probable price but also other factors such as the range of expected prices may influence the firm's plans. A tax may not alter the most probable profit position, but may reduce the probability of large profits and induce the firm to change its plans.

See, for example, Gerhard Tintner, "The Theory of Production Under Non-Static Conditions," *The Journal of Political Economy*, Vol. I, No. 5 (October, 1942); George J. Stigler, "Production and Distribution in the Short Run," *The Journal of*

is also assumed that the firm had reached its preferred position before the imposition of the tax, and that if the tax changes the conditions facing the firm, it will adjust its operations to achieve the preferred position after the tax had been imposed.

Considerations other than profits may also be of importance in motivating the firm.   An entrepreneur may, for example, wish to preserve a minimum liquidity position or to maximize some combination of liquidity and profits, or he may be interested in expanding the size (net worth) of the business even though lower profits will be the result.   Some combination of size, liquidity, and profits may be maximized.

Ignoring these other factors and assuming that the firm is motivated only by profit considerations is an oversimplification. However it does not invalidate estimates of the *direction* of changes induced by taxes as long as factors which change profits do not alter liquidity or size, or as long as changes in profits are accompanied by changes of the same direction in liquidity or size. It seems reasonable to expect that factors reducing profits would also work toward reducing liquidity and the net worth (size) of the enterprise.   Also changes increasing profits would tend to increase liquidity or net worth.

(2) *The resource owner.*   Like the firm, the resource owner is interested in achieving some preferred position.   If he is the owner of capital agents, he may be interested in maximizing returns from the sale of these agents or their services.   If he sells only his labor, he may be interested in maximizing some combination of real wages and leisure.

In analyzing the impact of taxes upon the resource owner, it must be assumed that he had achieved his preferred position before the tax was levied and that he, too, will adjust his conduct if a new preferred position emerges after the tax is imposed.   As long as the various components of the preferred position are substitutes (for example, more leisure can compensate for a smaller real wage), our analysis is not invalidated by assuming that the resource owner attempts to maximize returns from the sale of the services of the agents which he owns.

Political Economy, Vol. XLVII, 1939; A. G. Hart, "Anticipations, Uncertainty and Dynamic Planning," *Studies in Business Administration,* The School of Business, University of Chicago, Vol. XI, No. 1, 1940; H. Makower and J. Marschak, "Assets, Prices and Monetary Theory," *Economica* (new series), Vol. V, 1938; and Oscar Lange, *Price Flexibility and Employment.*

(3) *The consumer.* The consuming unit makes decisions regarding how its given income should be allocated in the purchase of various goods and services. Just what the consuming unit is attempting to maximize is not subject to measurement. However, it is not necessary to know exactly what is being maximized. It is necessary only to assume that the consumer is attempting to reach some preferred position and that he is acting consistently.[4]

(4) *Implications for analysis of tax shifting and incidence.* These assumptions regarding rational action by the various economic units are basic for analysis of tax shifting and incidence. The firm may try to shift a tax through increasing the selling prices for its products or through reducing the purchase prices for resources which it employs. The resource owner may try to shift a tax through increasing the selling prices of his resources. The consumer may try to shift the tax through reducing his buying prices. It follows from our definition of shifting that a transaction involving a price is necessary for a tax to be shifted.[5] The conditions under which relative prices may be changed will be the center of our analysis of shifting and incidence of taxation.

The test of whether a tax actually has been shifted is not whether the price pattern has changed *after* the tax but whether the price pattern is different from what it would have been in the absence of the tax. Changes in tastes and in technology may work toward changing prices in an opposite direction from that which the tax is causing. For example, a tax of one cent per gallon may be imposed on gasoline. At the same time there may occur a technological improvement in gasoline production. Prices to consumers may be unchanged even though the tax has been shifted to them. The empirical difficulties in determining shifting and incidence are quite like those encountered in deriving empirical supply and demand functions for commodities.[6]

---

[4] Implying that the consumer is attempting to achieve some preferred position and that he acts consistently means that he is able to rank various combinations of goods according to preferability and that, in indifference-curve analysis, indifference curves do not intersect. It is not necessary that specific values be assignable to various indifference curves.

[5] The consumer is likely to seek to avoid a tax by altering his consumption pattern. This may throw part of the burden of a tax back to firms and resource owners even though the effect of the consumer's action prevents the tax from being collected. The economic effects of a tax are by no means confined to those which follow from the actual collection of the tax itself.

[6] Progress has been made in solving the problems posed in deriving empirical supply and demand functions. For example, a system of equations, rather than a

Government expenditure for resources unchanged.   In order to separate the effects of the taxes from the effects of the way in which the tax money is being spent,[7] we shall first assume that the level of government expenditure for resources is independent of tax collections and is unchanged.   This is not a very realistic assumption for cases where the taxes are being collected by the state and local governments.   These units usually try to match tax collections and expenditures and they spend mostly to purchase resources.   But, if the Federal government taxed only to avoid inflation or to redistribute money incomes, Federal expenditures for resources would need to be altered.   This assumption will be relaxed at a later stage in the analysis.

Constant total money expenditure per unit of time.   A further simplification will aid us in abstracting from the general deflationary impacts of taxation.   We shall assume (unless otherwise specified) that the total volume of money expenditure for goods and services is unchanged.   This assumption is not unreasonable if we are comparing the effects of various kinds of taxes.   For example, the funds from increased tax collections might all be transferred to income receivers having the same propensity to spend as those from whom the funds were taken.   Or, a sales tax might be removed as an income tax was inaugurated.   Although relative prices probably would be altered by such a change, the amounts of tax collected by the levy on personal incomes could be adjusted so that the total volume of money expenditure in the economy would remain unchanged.

General Principles of Shifting and Incidence

The shifting of a tax comes about through price transactions. A change in equilibrium price for a good or service must be brought about by a shift in either the supply or demand for that good or service, since, by definition, market equilibrium exists

---

single equation, expresses price-quantity relationships and may be derived with existing statistical methods.   Refer to J. Marschak and W. H. Andrews, "Random Simultaneous Equations and the Theory of Production," *Econometrica*, XII, 1944, and to Trygve Haavelmo, "The Probability Approach in Econometrica," *Econometrica*, XII (Supplement, July, 1944).   It is possible that in the future we may be able to estimate with increasing accuracy the way in which a tax is shifted.

[7] This permits us to neglect changes in the cost positions of various firms as a result of changes in government expenditures and to simplify the analysis.   Note, in contrast, the assumptions made by De Viti de Marco.   See Antonio De Viti de Marco, *First Principles of Public Finance,* translated by E. Marget, pages 150-51, New York: Harcourt, Brace & Co., 1936.

only when supply and demand are equated. Consequently, if the imposition of a tax induces a seller to shift upward his supply schedules, all or a part of the tax may be shifted to buyers. Analysis of shifting and incidence thus becomes an investigation of the conditions under which the imposition of a tax induces changes in demand or supply which would not have been made prior to the tax.

Increases in selling prices—forward shifting. A tax collected from a seller will reduce the seller's net receipts unless, as a result of the imposition of the tax and its impact upon supplies of other sellers, he is in some way able to increase the prices for the goods and services which he sells.[8] If the seller will not absorb this reduction in net receipts without contracting his supply schedule, and if the demand for the good or service is unchanged, an increase in the prices of the things which he sells, and a reduction in the amount exchanged will be the result.

(1) *Taxes upon the resource owner.* For the resource owner, a tax upon sales of his resources for particular uses would encourage him to sell more of these resources for untaxed uses. The same amounts of these resources would be sold for taxed uses only at a higher price.

If all uses are taxed, or the tax is independent of the use of the resources, relative opportunities are unchanged. There is no gain to the resource owner from altering the pattern of sale.[9]

(2) *Taxes collected from the firm.* Imagine that the producers of a given good or service employ only unspecialized productive agents which have many other uses. Assume also that the percentage of the total supply of resources used in this industry is so small that the prices of productive agents are unchanged even though the industry's output is doubled or cut to zero. Factor supplies, in other words, are perfectly elastic for the industry as a whole or for any single firm in the industry. If the firms offer lower prices for the resources, none will be made available to them.

---

[8] The adjustments in selling prices as a result of the tax must be made more or less simultaneously by all sellers. This means a gradual increase in price if the tax is shifted forward.

[9] Since it is a bit difficult to tax leisure—the alternative to work—a tax upon wages may encourage laborers to devote less time to work and more to leisure. Similarly, a high tax upon the incomes of professional, managerial, and entrepreneurial groups may encourage these people to devote less time to work and more time to spending their money and seeking additional noncash income.

(a) *Perfect competition.* It is conceivable that the demand curve facing any firm in the industry is perfectly elastic and that each firm is making only enough profit to induce the operator to maintain his investment in the production of this good or service. This condition, together with the specifications made above regarding the supplies of productive agents, constitutes important elements of the situation known as *long-run equilibrium in perfect competition.*

A tax collected from a single firm in the industry—whether the tax is related to the quantity of output, the quantity of inputs, or a fixed fee such as a license tax—will eventually drive this firm out of business.[10] The firm cannot increase its selling prices or it will sell none of its products. Its net receipts will be reduced by the amount of the tax. Although it may continue to produce as long as current operating costs can be met from current receipts, output will be contracted when important elements of plant and equipment must be replaced. (See Figures 4a and 4b.)

If the tax is levied upon all firms in the industry, the supply of the product must eventually be contracted—unless, of course, there are compensating improvements in technology or reductions in the prices of productive agents. This will be the tendency regardless of the kind of tax, as long as the tax is collected only from firms in this industry. For production to continue in the long run, the price must rise.

(b) *Imperfect competition.* In situations where the firm has a conscious price policy and where profits are in excess of the minimum necessary to keep the firm producing at the pretax level of output, a tax collected from a firm may not alter its supply schedule, even in the long run, as long as such a tax is not in excess of abnormal profits and as long as the tax is not tied to the level of output.[11] Such a tax is similar to an excess-profits tax

---

[10] It is recognized that singling out one firm for taxation from the many firms in a competitive industry is very unlikely and would be difficult administratively. This example is introduced to illustrate that what is true in the taxation of a single firm in an industry is not necessarily true for taxation of all firms in the industry.

[11] Even though the product-demand and factor-supply schedules facing the firm are perfectly elastic, profits may be greater than normal because of impediments to the movement of resources or ignorance of relative profit opportunities. This situation is frequently called "pure" competition. *Cf.* Edward H. Chamberlain, *Theory of Monopolistic Competition,* 4th edition, Cambridge, Mass.: Harvard University Press. Imperfections of this variety represent a relatively

and would be essentially one upon a rent. The entrepreneur could achieve no higher return in other lines of enterprise. He

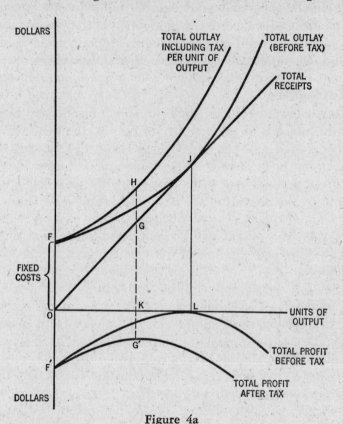

Figure 4a

Effect of a Tax Levied Upon the Output of a Single Firm Under Perfect Competition

OL is the pre-tax long-run level of output, while OK is the short-run output after the tax. At OL, total profit (in excess of "normal" profit) is zero. At OK, total loss is $KG' = HG$, the minimum loss possible under the new conditions. As long as total loss is less than fixed costs ($OF = OF'$), the firm will contract output, but will continue to produce in the short run. In the long run, losses cannot be avoided, and output must be contracted to zero unless the price is increased to cover the tax.

unimportant sort of situation in present-day markets, largely because there are few instances where product demands and resource supplies are perfectly elastic. However, for analysis of tax shifting and incidence, this case can be treated approximately the same as the case to be treated in this section under imperfect competition.

would not be induced to stop investment in his current enterprise and reinvest in another. If, however, the tax is related to the level of output, it will pay the firm to contract output, regardless of the size of the tax or the level of profits. (See Figures 5a and 5b.)

Thus, under the conditions postulated in this portion of the discussion of forward shifting—supplies of productive agents perfectly elastic to the industry and each firm achieving profits in

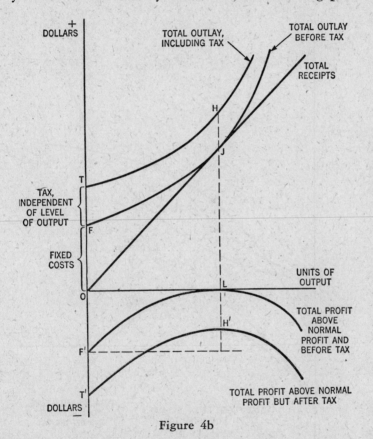

Figure 4b

Effect of a Tax Collected from a Single Firm Under Perfect Competition, if Tax Is Independent of Output

OL is the pre-tax, long-run level of output. As long as the tax is less than fixed costs, $OF = OF'$, the firm will continue to produce output, OL, since at no other level can losses be reduced below $LH' = JH$. In the long run, unless price is adjusted to cover cost including the tax, output will be reduced to zero.

excess of those necessary to keep it from disinvesting—a tax collected from the firm will not alter the firm's supply schedule as long as the tax does not exceed these abnormal profits and is independent of the level of output. A license tax would be of this variety. A tax related to the level of output—an excise, for example—will induce the firm to contract its output and consequently will alter supply. A higher price will be needed to induce the pretax level of output.

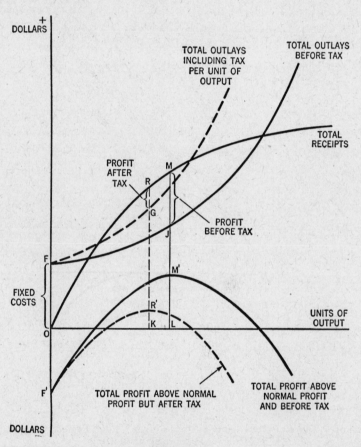

Figure 5a

Effect of a Tax Upon Output and Collected From a Single Firm Under Imperfect Competition

OL is the output at which profit is at a maximum before the tax, while *OK* is the output at which profit is at a maximum after the tax.

(3) *Effect upon price.* In order to determine the impact upon price of a tax which is collected from firms and which can be shifted only forward, it is necessary to know only the *total* demand schedule as well as the *total* supply schedule for the product. This means that we need not worry about whether the firms are operating under conditions of perfect competition, monopolistic competition, oligopoly, or monopoly, for we are concerned only with the supply-and-demand conditions facing the industry.

Given a reduction in supply, the increase in price will be greater the more inelastic the demand (see Figure 6).

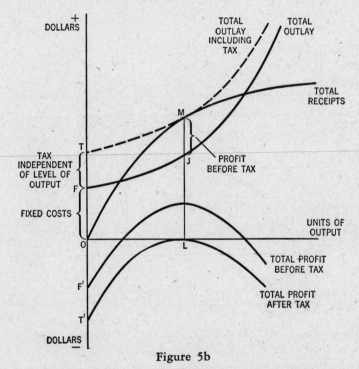

Figure 5b

Effect of a Tax Collected From a Single Firm, but Independent of the Level of Output, Under Imperfect Competition

As is true in the other situations, a tax collected from a firm but independent of output, will not alter the short-run level of output as long as it does not exceed the sum of fixed costs and profit. In the situation portrayed above, the long-run level of output also would be unaffected, since all costs can be covered.

Reductions in buying prices—backward shifting. In addition to shifting a tax forward through increasing the selling prices for products, a firm or industry may shift a tax backward through reducing the buying prices for productive agents. If the supplies of productive agents are completely elastic to the aggregate of firms from which the tax is being collected, no reduction in the prices of these resources can result. However, if as the firms reduce their purchases of an agent its price falls backward, shift-

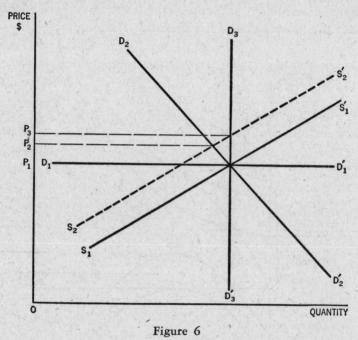

Figure 6

Effects of Changes in Supply Upon Price Under Various Demand Conditions

$S_1S'_1$ represents the supply schedule before the tax. After the imposition of the tax, the supply schedule shifts to the position $S_2S'_2$.

If the demand is perfectly elastic $(D_1D'_1)$, there will be no change in price. Only the quantity exchanged will be reduced. If the demand is perfectly inelastic $(D_3D'_3)$, price will increase by the full amount of the shift in supply and there will be no reduction in the quantity exchanged. If the demand schedule is $D_2D'_2$ price will increase—but less than if the demand were $D_3D'_3$—and the quantity exchanged will decrease, but less than if the demand were $D_1D'_1$.

ing may be the result.   Some laborers, for example, may be relatively immobile because of their high degree of specialization, costs of moving to other communities, attachment to the com-

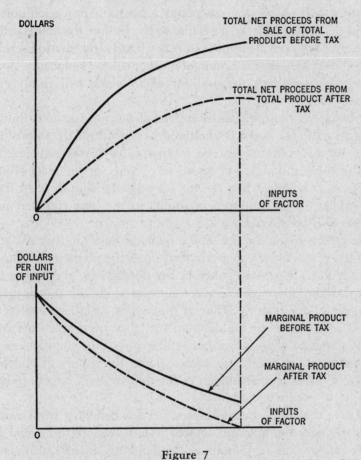

Figure 7

Effects of a Tax Upon Demand for Productive Agents

The total product curves represent the relationships between inputs of a factor (inputs of other factors remaining unchanged) and the total sale value of the product.

The marginal product curves represent the firm's demand for the productive agent.   Obviously, if the tax is dependent upon output, the demand for the factor will be reduced.   If the tax is independent of output, the factor demand is unchanged.   (See figures 4b and 5b.)

munity in which they live, and other factors. Such immobility permits backward shifting.

Assume that each firm was equating the marginal revenue productivity of each factor with its marginal cost. A tax related to output will reduce the proceeds (after tax) from each unit of output and consequently the value to the firm of the contribution made by each unit of input. In other words, the marginal revenue productivity of each unit of input will be reduced. A reduction in the firm's demand for each factor will result (see Figure 7).

If, however, the tax is independent of output, the contribution of any productive agent is unaltered as a result of the imposition of the tax. Profits cannot be increased, or losses reduced, by altering the combination of inputs or outputs, or the level of production. It is only when the tax exceeds the sum of fixed costs plus profits in the short run or profits in the long run that production will be altered.

The effects of a reduction in the demand for a productive agent upon the prices of this agent depend upon the elasticity of supply of the factor. Given a change in the demand for the factor, the change in the price will be inversely correlated with the elasticity of supply of the factor. Thus, if the supply of labor is perfectly elastic, a reduction in the demand for labor by a given industry will not reduce wage rates, but will reduce only employment in that industry. For a factor such as land, the supply of which is relatively inelastic, a reduction in the demand will largely reduce the rate of return to land.

Backward shifting by consumers. A tax collected from a consumer reduces the amounts which he has available to spend for goods and services or to build up his holdings of cash and securities. Some rearrangement of the allocation of his expenditure is thus necessitated. The kind of change in the pattern of expenditure (including changes in cash balances) depends upon the way in which the tax is collected—that is, the kind of tax—as well as the size of the tax.

If the tax is levied upon purchases of particular commodities—as is the Iowa "use" tax on purchases from mail-order houses, for example—this is equivalent, in the eyes of the consumer, to an increase in the price of the taxed commodity relative to prices of other goods and services. Although purchases of nearly all items are likely to be reduced, the consumer will substitute untaxed goods and services for the taxed one. A proportionately greater reduction in the amount of the taxed product purchased, and consequently, a relatively greater reduction in its price, is to be expected. In a sense, a part of the tax is being shifted to the sellers; or, inversely, all of such a tax cannot be shifted forward to buyers (see Figure 8).

If the tax is independent of the pattern of consumption—as is a personal income tax, for example—purchases of all goods and services (as well as cash holdings) may be reduced. A lowering of the general level of prices is to be expected. Some prices, however, will be reduced proportionately more than others. The prices of those goods and services which are the poorest substitutes for money—durable consumers' goods, for example—will be reduced relative to the prices of goods and services which are the best substitutes for money—bonds, for example.

Obviously, if the tax is levied upon only a single consumer, it usually cannot be shifted. His purchases constitute such a small percentage of total purchases that he could double them or reduce them without affecting at all the prices of goods and services. But, if the tax is collected from consumers, and it is levied upon purchases of a particular good or service, the kind of shifting described above is likely to take place. Sellers of the product will find the relative demand for that product reduced independently of the general level of money expenditure. An income tax collected from all consumers, however, will have the impacts described above only if it reduces total real income. If the general level of money expenditure is unchanged—as could be the case if some people were taxed and the proceeds transferred to others —the impacts of the tax would be wholly the result of differences between the preferencs of those taxed and those receiving the proceeds.

Forward 'and backward shifting. In many instances in which a tax is shifted, it is shifted both forward and backward. Economic units such as the firm are both buyers and sellers. When a tax is collected from them, prices for products may be increased and buying prices for productive agents may be reduced. The extent to which a tax is shifted forward or backward depends primarily upon the elasticities of demand for the things being sold and the elasticities of supply of the things being purchased. If

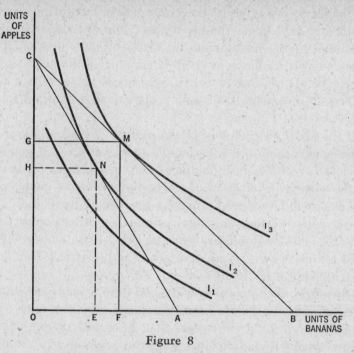

Figure 8

Effects of An Excise Tax Upon Consumer Welfare

In the above illustration, we have been given the consumer's income, a sector of his preference system and the relative prices for apples and bananas. The consumer's income is represented by the quantities of apples and bananas which he could purchase (the combinations on the line CB). The curves I_1, I_2 and I_3 represent sectors of contours of his preference system. Any combination of apples and bananas represented by any point on I_1 is equivalent, in the eyes of the consumer, to any other combination represented by any other point on I_1. Combinations on I_2 are preferable to those on I_1, and combinations on I_3 are preferable to those on I_2. The price ratio—the ratio of the number of apples which has to be given up in order to get a given number of bananas—is the ratio $\frac{OC}{OB}$. Under the conditions postulated, the consumer will purchase OG of apples and OF of bananas. A tax (AB/OB) on purchases of bananas raises the number of apples that he must forego in order to obtain a given number of bananas. He is induced to reduce his purchases of both apples and bananas. But, in this example, his purchases of bananas are reduced proportionately more $\left(\frac{EF}{OF} > \frac{HG}{OG}\right)$.

the supply of a productive agent purchased by the firms from which the tax is being collected is relatively inelastic while the demand for the firms' products is relatively elastic, the bulk of the tax will be shifted backward. Prices of productive agents will be reduced proportionately more than prices of products are increased. On the other hand, if the demand for the firms' products is relatively inelastic while the supplies of productive agents are relatively elastic, the bulk of the tax will be shifted forward. Prices of products will be increased proportionately more than prices of productive agents are reduced.

The relative difficulties of shifting a tax thus depend upon the way in which various opportunities are affected. A specific tax—a tax upon the use of a particular productive agent in a particular line of production—is more likely to be shifted than is a general tax which affects all opportunities for using the resource in the same manner.

For example, a tax upon land used in producing tobacco is unlikely to be shifted if the land is adaptable only to tobacco production. No more favorable opportunities for using the land in producing commodities other than tobacco exist after the tax than before. If, however, the land can be used to produce corn as well as tobacco, and only its use in producing tobacco is taxed, the tax is likely to be reflected in higher tobacco prices. Unless the return from producing tobacco is equal to that from producing corn, the land will be used to produce corn.

Long-run and short-run adjustments. In the preceding analysis, we have referred to long-run and short-run effects of taxes. Since it takes time for adjustments to be made after relative prices have been altered, the short-run adjustment as a result of a tax will be different from the ultimate adjustment. For example, an excise tax collected from manufacturers may induce relatively little immediate shift in output or price. A manufacturer may try to increase his price to cover the entire tax, but he will find that he is making less profit (or a greater loss) than if he equated marginal net returns (considering the tax) with marginal current operating costs. For a time, indeed, total returns may be insufficient to cover total costs.

Eventually, however, a decision must be made with respect to incurring additional fixed costs—the replacement of a piece of equipment, for example. Unless the product price is expected to be increased or resource prices are expected to be reduced, the decision will be against the replacement. As more time passes, other similar decisions involving this and other firms will have to be made.   Each decision against incurring costs which would permit output to be maintained will result in a reduction in output.

As output is contracted, the price for the product will increase, or prices for resources will fall. Ultimately, unless there are other changes, prices will be altered so that there will be no further incentive for changing output.   This is the position of long-run equilibrium.   Intermediate positions between decisions will be positions of short-run equilibrium.

The element of time as it is related to adjustments induced by taxes is thus of primary importance in cases where specialized resources are used in production. Highly specialized machines or laborers with skills adapted to a particular industry may accept lower returns for a time without moving from the industry.   The machine may have no alternative use.   The capital invested in it cannot be moved except by allowing the machine to depreciate through use.   For specialized laborers to retrain for another job takes time and involves some expense.   Such factors as attachment to the home, community, and even the particular kind of job that he has been doing may deter a laborer from moving even though he could get higher wages in other employment.

Where the resources are not specialized and can be moved rapidly, their supply schedules to any industry may be highly elastic.   The long-run and short-run distinction in such a case is unimportant, for the two equilibrium positions tend to coincide.

Impacts of changes in government expenditures.   Thus far in the analysis it has been assumed that various kinds of taxes are being turned on and off without any change in government expenditure.   The analysis may be made more general by discarding this assumption of no change in government expenditure. Changes in the level of government expenditure may counteract or reinforce the effects of taxation upon relative prices.

Increases in government expenditure, since they will increase demand, will, in general, tend to move the price level in a direction opposite to that brought about by taxation, whereas decreases in government expenditure will reinforce taxation.   There may be two other kinds of impacts: (1) a change in relative demands; (2) a change in relative costs and hence in relative supplies.

An increase in government expenditure, the level of tax collections being held stable, will result in more disposable income for the private economy. This will tend to increase the general level of money prices. But, proportionately it will increase most of all the prices of those commodities which are the poorest substitutes for money—durable consumers goods, for example. Thus, for a commodity whose relative price has been increased as a result of a tax but which is a closer substitute for money than the untaxed commodities, the impact of additional government expenditure is to reduce its *relative* price. For a commodity which is a poor substitute for money and upon which an excise has been levied, additional government expenditure will increase further its *relative* price. Decreases in expenditure will have reverse effects.

If the increased government expenditure is for goods upon which excises are levied, the prices of these goods compared to the prices of other goods are further increased. When the increased government expenditure is for untaxed goods, the result is a fall in the *relative* prices of taxed goods.

Additional money may also be spent by government to improve roads, waterways, power facilities, and the like. This improvement may reduce the costs of producing certain taxed goods, thereby reducing their prices relative to those whose costs are not influenced by the change in government expenditure. For example, improvements in highways may reduce consumers' costs of goods which are transported over public roads, or construction of hydroelectric plants may reduce costs of electricity and consequently the prices of goods in which electricity consumption is a cost.

Government expenditure in subsidies conditional upon the production of certain goods which are also taxed is likely to counteract the impacts of the tax upon the prices of these goods. A state, for example, might tax potatoes and this tax might be shifted forward. At the same time, the Federal government might be paying farmers a subsidy on potatoes. The subsidy and the tax pull prices in opposite directions. Similarly, a tax upon coal may be shifted backward to coal miners.[12] But a subsidy to

[12] Both in England and in the United States, the coal miner has been a worker whose skill is specialized and who has clung tenaciously to the mining region in spite of changes in the attractiveness of other opportunities. Thus, shifting a tax on coal backward to the miners would be relatively easy, if it were not for miners' unions.

mine operators paid on the basis of the number of miners employed would tend to increase miners' wages and counteract the tax.

Illustrations from Various Forms of Taxation

From our analysis of general principles of shifting and incidence of taxation we may conclude that the incidence of a tax depends both upon the kind of tax and the position of the economic unit from which government collects this tax. The way in which a tax is shifted depends upon the way in which various opportunities are changed as a result of the tax.

For example, taxes related to the level of sales of a firm or resource owner are likely to induce these sellers to alter their sales pattern. Such taxes are very likely to be shifted—to alter the price pattern. Taxes independent of the firm's output may not be shifted, even in the long run, if they do not exceed "abnormal" profits. Other opportunities for investment may not be taxed, but they are still no more profitable than the taxed ones. In the short run, such taxes may not be shifted if they do not exceed the sum of "abnormal" profits and fixed costs. An opportunity to move the fixed investment does not exist (by definition) in the short run.

Similarly, taxes collected from consumers and independent of the pattern of purchases—as the Federal personal income tax— are difficult to shift. They do not change the relative positions of various opportunities, all being affected more or less in the same manner.

These general principles can be applied to analysis of the incidence of various kinds of taxes, if we know the position of the units from which the government is collecting the tax money. In this section we shall apply our analysis to some of the major forms of taxation—excise taxes and import duties, general sales taxes, "use" taxes, personal income taxes, license fees, corporate income taxes, excess-profits taxes, undistributed-profits taxes, and payroll taxes. Aspects of these taxes other than their incidence will be discussed in subsequent chapters.

Excise taxes and import duties. An excise is a tax upon a domestically produced good or service. It is usually levied as a specified amount per unit of the commodity produced or sold— as so many cents per package of cigarettes, per gallon of gasoline, and so forth—or as a percentage of the selling price of the commodity.   The tax money is collected from a seller—the manufacturer, wholesaler, or retailer.   Most states and the Federal government levy excises on a wide variety of products.

A tax levied upon a single commodity or group of commodities narrows the gap between the sellers' receipts and the expenditures related to the sale of the taxed commodity.   It induces sellers to contract sales, selling the product at a higher price per unit.   At least a part of the tax is shifted forward to buyers of the product.   A part of the tax, however, may be shifted to the sellers of productive agents—if the supply schedules for productive agents to the industry are less than perfectly elastic.   Profits will be reduced.   However, shifting of the tax will take place regardless of the level of profits made by the sellers.

Import duties are taxes upon foreign-produced commodities. They are usually collected from importers.   Like excises, at least a part of such duties will be shifted to buyers.   If the importing country makes up a sufficient sector of the market for the imported good to be able to influence prices by the level of purchases of such goods within the country, a part of the tax may be shifted backward, falling in turn upon foreign producers and resource owners.

General Sales Taxes.   A general sales tax is an *ad valorem* (percentage of dollar selling-price) tax levied upon sales of a large collection of goods and services.   Occasionally such items as food, or services, or rents are excluded.   In 1946, 32 states were employing some type of general sales taxation.   The tax is usually collected from those who sell to ultimate consumers—from retailers, for example.

The incidence of such a tax depends largely upon its generality. If the tax were levied only within a single state, consumers would, wherever possible, substitute out-of-state purchases for purchases within the state.   This would be particularly important in the border regions where the costs of making such substitutions are likely to be small.[13]   If the costs of making purchases out of the state were zero, the tax could not be shifted to consumers.

[13] For example, Iowa has a general sales tax, while the bordering states of Minnesota and Wisconsin do not.   Although Iowa also has a "use" tax, it is not enforced against individual consumers who make purchases outside the state, except in the cases of out-of-state auto purchases and purchases from mail-order houses.   Consequently, Iowa merchants selling near the Iowa-Wisconsin or Iowa-Minnesota border probably have some difficulty in shifting the general sales tax to consumers.   Part of the burden of the Iowa tax is undoubtedly borne by Iowa retailers in these border areas.

Either sellers in the state levying the tax would suffer reduced net receipts—some of them being forced out of business in the long run—or resource owners would find their returns reduced. A reduction in the returns received by resource owners could take place only if the owners had been selling at prices in excess of those at which they were willing to sell.

If the costs of substituting purchases that are not taxed for taxed purchases are in excess of the amount of the tax—the situation which usually exists—the tax will be shifted. It will be shifted only forward if the supply schedules for resources are perfectly elastic. But it will be shifted both forward and backward if these supply schedules are less than perfectly elastic. Thus, a nation-wide general sales tax is likely to result in increased prices to consumers and reduced returns to some resource owners.

"Use" taxes. In an effort to minimize opportunities for buyers to substitute out-of-state purchases for purchases which, in the absence of the tax, would have been made within a state where there is a general sales tax, "use" taxes have been invoked. These taxes are levied against all commodities purchased for use in the state, except that goods already subject to state sales taxes are usually exempt. Thus, if state A has a "use" tax while a neighboring state does not, a buyer residing in state A and purchasing in another state an auto, a refrigerator, or any other commodity subject to tax, must pay the tax if he uses the good in state A. The tax was made applicable to purchases from out-of-state mail-order houses by a Supreme Court decision in 1944.

The incidence of such a tax is exactly the same as that of a generalized sales tax where costs of substitution are in excess of the amount of the tax. The tax will be shifted backward if total expenditure upon the commodity (including the tax) is not increased. It will be shifted partially forward if total expenditure on the commodity (including the tax) is increased.

Property taxes. Nearly all units of local government collect a property tax from owners. Real estate—land, buildings, and other improvements—constitutes the largest class of taxed property. Some other items of personal property, however, usually are subject to tax also. The tax is levied as a percentage of value—value being determined in accordance with specified rules by a tax assessor.

In the short run, this tax is unlikely to be shifted. The property already exists independently of the return to it.   The short-run supply is not affected.   Reducing the net return to property may, however, discourage maintenance of the property and also deter the building of new houses, office buildings, and the like. The long-run supply schedule will be reduced.   At least part of the tax will be shifted forward—to renters and to buyers of goods and services where the use of rented property enters as a cost.

Two of the elements giving land its productivity may be distinguished: (1) its fertility, and (2) its geographic location.   In so far as the maintenance of the fertility of agricultural land requires the continual replacement of capital, the effect of a land tax will be to discourage such reinvestment and to reduce the long-run supply of land.   As in the case of other capital improvements on property, at least part of the tax will be shifted in the long run.

In the case where the value of urban land is dependent on its location, the tax cannot affect supply.   Consequently, it will not be shifted in either the long run or the short run.

Tax capitalization.   Imagine that a tax, at least a part of which cannot be shifted, is levied upon the income received from ownership of a certain asset.   Since the size of the income stream going to the holder of this asset has been diminished, the amount which any buyer will be willing to pay for that asset will be reduced.   If the owner bought the asset the day before the tax was levied and did not anticipate the tax levy, he has suffered a substantial capital loss.

Inversely, if a tax (all of which was not shifted) has been levied upon the income from a certain asset and is removed, the size of the income stream from that asset has been augmented. The relative price of that asset will be increased.

For example, if you have title to a salable annuity yielding $3,000 annually, and the rate of return on other investments of comparable risk is 3 per cent, the sale value of the annuity should be $100,000.   Assume that a tax upon the income from your annuity reduces this income to $1,500 annually but does not reduce the rate of return on other investments.   The sale value of your annuity has been reduced to $50,000.

This change in the price of the asset is calculated on the assumption that the gross yield from the annuity, the tax, and the rates of return on other comparable investments are all *expected* to remain unchanged. If all these conditions are not fulfilled, the price of the asset will fall, but will not be halved. For example, if half the tax is shifted, the price will be reduced by $25,-000; if the tax is expected to last for only 10 years, the prices of the asset will be reduced by about 25 per cent; if rates of return in other lines are also reduced, the price of the asset will fall by less than $50,000.

The change in the price of assets which results from changes in taxes is known as *tax capitalization.*[14]

Tax capitalization is particularly important in connection with property taxes. Through forcing down the capitalized value of land or other property *at the time the tax is levied,* subsequent buyers of the property will not bear the burden of the tax because they will be able to discount it in determining the price which they will pay for the property. The existence of property taxes on land in the United States for a relatively long period of time means that these taxes have already been "capitalized" and existing land owners have not been burdened except to the extent that tax rates have risen since they acquired their land. Additional land taxes—higher tax rates or rises in the ratio of assessed valuation to true valuation, for example—would result in further reductions in land values, unless there are other counteracting changes.

Of greater importance are the problems posed in connection with increases in property values which would result from discarding or reducing property taxes. A high capital-gains tax on land transfers might be desirable in order to capture such windfalls as would arise in changing from property taxation to personal income taxation.

Similarly, if a corporation tax were levied after the corporation was established, the capitalized value of the corporation would be forced down, since corporate income would be taxed at a higher effective rate than income from other sources. However, the

---

[14] A general formula for determining the present value of an asset is as follows:

$$P = \frac{V_1 - T_1}{(1 + r_1)} + \frac{V_2 - T_2}{(1 + r_2)^2} + \frac{V_3 - T_3}{(1 + r_3)^3} + \cdots + \frac{V_n - T_n}{(1 + r_n)^n} = \sum_{i=1}^{n} \frac{V_i - T_i}{(1 + r_i)^i}$$

Where P is the present value, V_i is the amount of income expected from the asset during the year i, T_i is the expected amount of the tax which cannot be shifted, r_i is the expected rate of return on other investments during the year i, and n is the number of years relevant to the decision.

existence of corporate income taxes (providing that there are no expected changes in tax rates) will have little effect upon the capitalized value of new corporations.   The tax will be taken into consideration in decisions about alternative investment opportunities.   In the event that effective corporation income tax rates are reduced, the capitalized value of existing corporate equities is likely to increase.   Consequently, it is desirable to consider provisions for capital gains taxes at the time that reductions in corporate income taxation are contemplated.

Personal income taxes.   A personal income tax is a tax collected from an income receiver and based on the size of his income. Only money income is usually taxed, and occasionally certain kinds of money income—pensions, for example—are exempted from income taxation.   The personal income tax is the most important single tax in the Federal tax structure.

It is commonly asserted that a general tax on personal money-incomes cannot be shifted as long as it does not discriminate between different sources of income.   This conclusion is based on the assumption that neither *relative* supplies of goods and services nor demands for goods and services are altered as a result of the tax.   Unless the demand for a good or service has been increased, resource users will not pay higher prices for the quantities of resources they have been using.   The resources have no greater productivity than before the tax.

An income tax may, however, shift the supply schedules of some resources.   Marginal money incomes of those being taxed are reduced.   The alternative of more leisure and less work may become relatively more attractive to workers or to enterpreneurs. In order to secure the same amount of labor, a higher wage may have to be offered.   Wartime experience with income taxation in the United States indicates that income receivers are becoming increasingly conscious of comparisons of income *after* rather than *before* taxes.   Increased taxes may be used by labor unions as a basis for demands for increased wages.   It is conceivable that the long-run result will be a shifting of some of the tax burden from the worker to the consumers of products in which his labor is used.

Some changes in the relative price pattern may occur as a result of changes on the demand side.   If total money expenditures for goods and services remain unchanged, then decreases in expenditure by those being taxed must be offset by increases in expenditure by other economic units—perhaps by those to whom the tax money has been transferred. It is unlikely that the new expenditure pattern will be exactly the same as the old, since the preferences of those receiving additional income probably will not be the same as the preferences of those paying the taxes. Consequently, some prices will be higher than before the tax while others will be lower. If total money expenditure falls, it is unlikely that all prices will be reduced by the same proportion. Prices of goods and services which are the poorest substitutes for money are likely to fall most. Also certain institutional factors make some prices relatively inflexible in the downward direction —for example, labor unions tend to resist wage cuts, and there are administered prices for the products of some corporations.

Among those taxes whose incidence may be predicted with a relatively high degree of accuracy, the personal income tax stands high. Two important factors which make it difficult to shift this tax are: (1) The general character of the tax and the relatively uniform treatment accorded income from various sources for tax purposes. Tax-free fields are few, and the treatment accorded to the bulk of income payments—wages, salaries, rents, interest, and dividends—is uniform. (2) The independence of the income tax and production costs minimizes change in relative supplies.

Corporation income taxes. The corporation income tax is a levy against the net incomes of corporations. The Federal government and many states employ this form of taxation.

The incidence of this tax is somewhat difficult to determine. Since the tax is upon the total of a firm's profits, it need not be related directly to output. Consequently, a short-run reduction in output, like that induced by an excise tax, appears unlikely. Of course, some firms may not have been trying to maximize profits, having been satisfied with some minimum rate of return. If the corporate income tax reduced profits below this minimum, the tax might be considered as a cost. The price of the product might be increased, and a reduction in output, even in the short run, might be expected.

The tax, it is true, discriminates between corporate and noncorporate income, taxing only the former. It might be expected that a lower percentage of business would be conducted under

the corporate form. Actually, the advantages of the corporation
—principally in raising capital and in the range of powers which
it can exercise—have been sufficient to offset the tax disadvantage. This has been particularly true for corporations of sufficient size to make the problem of raising capital an important
one, or for businesses desiring the wide range of powers typically
available under the corporate charter.[15] It is possible that a
heavy corporate-income tax hinders the entry of new firms into
a given field of production. Hence, the tax may fail to exercise
a potential check on high prices through limitation of added competition.

If the corporate form of doing business has advantages which
can be translated into lower costs, taxing the net income of corporations would mean lower returns to the management, the stockholders, or the owners of other resources employed by the corporation. It could also mean higher prices to the buyers of products
sold by corporations.

In the short run, a reduction in returns to stockholders or to
management is to be expected. In the long run, decisions about
methods of doing business are of some relevance, and both backward and forward shifting of the tax appears likely. The bulk
of business in the United States is conducted by corporations.
Consequently, neither the supplies of productive agents nor the
demands for products are perfectly elastic for the aggregate of
corporations. An increase in costs of doing business in the corporate form, and the consequent shift in the demand for productive
agents and in the supply of products will thus affect both sets of
prices.

License taxes. Many businesses—manufacturers, wholesalers,
retailers, and some professional workers—pay fees for the privilege of doing business in a particular state or city. The businesses are *licensed,* and the fees paid in obtaining the licenses are
license taxes.

These fees are usually not related to the volume of output, although occasionally fees are graduated according to the size of
the business or the number of outlets. Consequently, it is usually
not in the interest of the business to alter its output as a result of
the tax.

In cases where the license is graduated according to the size

[15] Refer to Chapter XV.

of the business or the number of outlets, the effect may be to drive some firms partly out of business—to reduce their sizes or numbers of sales outlets. This, in turn, may make it easier for remaining outlets to raise prices. An example of the way in which a heavy license fee per sales outlet may affect prices is found in Iowa where the license to sell cigarettes is relatively high. Sales outlets are relatively fewer and cigarette prices exceed those in adjoining states where excises are as heavy but where licenses are not so high.

If the tax is less than the amount of abnormal profits—profits in excess of those necessary to induce the firm to remain in business—it will not be shifted, even in the long run. It will reduce profits but will not increase product prices or reduce resource prices. The firm cannot increase profits by altering its input or output position. If only normal profits—those profits just necessary to keep the firm operating in the long run—were being made before the tax was imposed, short-run prices will not be affected. Shifting of the tax will take place in the long run, however.

Where the tax is levied against professional workers—such as lawyers, doctors, and dentists—short-run prices will not be affected. Long-run prices will be unchanged as long as the tax does not exceed rents—the difference between the return received and the return at which the professional worker would be willing to engage in that profession.

Payroll taxes. To secure funds for financing certain social security programs—old-age retirement, for example—"contributions" are made by both employers and employees. These "contributions" are collected from the employers, the employee's portion being deducted from his wage. The size of the tax is proportional to the size of the wage.

Another major social security program, unemployment insurance, is financed entirely by a payroll levy on employers. It falls on employers who hire eight or more people, and whose employees are "covered" by the provisions of the law. Thus, a manufacturer will probably have to meet the payroll tax, but an employer of agricultural workers will not.

There is little question but that the employee's portion of the tax is *not* shifted. His productivity is unchanged. He cannot charge his employer more for the same amount of labor. His "contribution" is essentially a form of compulsory saving. It is very likely that the portion of the tax paid by employers is at least partially shifted. The tax is proportional to the employer's wage payments. It will induce him to substitute other productive agents for labor wherever feasible. A contraction in his demand for labor (with accompanying decreases in employment and/or wages) and a reduction in the supply of his product probably will be the result, although the tax may also reduce his profits.

Excess-profits taxation. A tax upon business profits in excess of a legally defined "normal" has been collected from businesses in the United States, Great Britain, Canada, and some other countries. The tax was extensively employed during the war. In the United States it applied only to the "excess" profits of corporations. "Normal" profits usually have been defined as the average rate received during some past time-period. The wartime law in the United States defined "normal" for any business as 95 per cent of the average rate of profit received by that business in the period 1936-1939, or 8 per cent on a legally defined capitalization during this period.

The incidence of excess-profits taxes depends partially on the definition of normal profits. If the normal is established below the average or the modal level of expected profits necessary to induce a firm to maintain its investment, and the tax is expected to be permanent, a part of the tax may be shifted in the long run. If the normal is defined above the modal level, the tax has many of the characteristics of a tax on economic rent and is difficult to shift.

It is necessary to point out, however, that even though normal is defined above the modal level, a part of the tax may also be shifted in the long run. The tax has the effect of chopping off the possibility of large gains, but at the same time it does not reduce the probability of losses. Consequently, a higher most-probable profit may be necessary to induce the firm to remain in business in the long run.[16] In order to achieve this higher most-probable profit, some shifting of the tax would have to occur.

[16] Offsetting this possibility is the fact that, when applied, excess-profits taxes have been used as wartime, emergency levies. Thus, our wartime levy for World War II became effective on 1942 corporate income, but was repealed in November, 1945, almost immediately after the war, to be effective January 1, 1946.

Taxation of undistributed profits. In 1936, the Federal government levied a tax upon the undistributed profits of corporations. This tax was graduated according to the relative size of undistributed profits and was designed to induce corporate management to distribute these undistributed profits to stockholders.[17]

Such a tax has no immediate impact upon the profit position of the firm and from this point of view is non-shiftable. But it does reduce the firm's liquidity position. To guard against the consequences of an unfavorable (but possible) credit market or to reduce costs of physical expansion, corporate management may at some times wish to maintain a relatively high liquidity position. Taxation of undistributed profits increases the costs of achieving such a position. Higher expected long-run net returns may be necessary to compensate for such taxation. *If* liquidity considerations are of any importance to the firm, the tax probably will be at least partially shifted.

Summary

In this analysis we have tried to show how taxation may affect relative prices. The impact of a tax upon the price pattern depend primarily on the way in which the tax shifts the supplies and demands for various goods and services. This, in turn, depends upon the manner in which various opportunities have been affected by the tax.

For example, if a single industry is taxed, resources may be expected to move into other industries altering the price pattern by raising prices in the taxed industry and perhaps reducing them in other industries. When all industries are taxed in the same manner, relative opportunities may be changed very little.

If consumers must pay a tax on one commodity, they will try to allocate their incomes in another way. If all commodities are taxed in the same manner, the price pattern is likely to be relatively unchanged.

Thus, the more *general* the tax—the more it affects every opportunity in the same way—the less likely it is that the tax will be shifted. The personal income tax, of all the various taxes which the Federal government uses, most approximates this requirement

---

[17] This tax aroused so much opposition in the United States that it was repealed effective in 1940.

for non-shiftability.   It is virtually impossible to devise a tax which will not affect relative prices in some way.

SELECTED READINGS

1. Black, Duncan, *The Incidence of Income Taxes,* London: Macmillan & Co. Ltd., 1939.
2. Edgeworth, Francis Y., "The Pure Theory of Taxation," *Economic Journal,* VII:46-70, 226-38, and 550-71 (March, June, and December, 1897).
3. Gillim, Marion H., "The Incidence of Excess Profits Taxation," *Columbia University Studies in History, Economics and Public Law,* No. 514.
4. Hicks, J. R., *Value and Capital,* Chapters 6-9 and 15-17, Oxford: The Clarendon Press, 1939.
5. Mering, Otto Von, *The Shifting and Incidence of Taxation,* Philadelphia: Blakiston Co., 1942.

THE PERSONAL INCOME TAX

TAXES on the personal net incomes of individuals (and of fiduciaries) have grown, in about 30 years, from relative insignificance to the most important single source of tax revenue in our tax system. In 1946, these taxes provided 19.1 billion dollars out of 51.7 billion, or about 37 per cent[2] of our total tax revenues.

Introduction

Personal income taxes have been called "the outstanding contribution of popular government and liberal political philosophy to modern fiscal practice."[3] The personal income tax deserves its relatively high rating as a tax primarily because it lends itself to the achievement of the major objectives of fiscal policy better than do most other taxes. (1) A general personal income tax has fewer unfavorable impacts upon resource allocation than do most of the other taxes in our tax system. (2) It is relatively easy to determine the incidence of a general personal income tax and consequently to forecast how this tax will affect the income

[1] This is the first of two chapters on the personal income tax, which will attempt to outline the characteristics of our present income-tax system, especially at the Federal level. Chapter XIV will examine critically some of the problems of our income-tax system. The writers have received substantial assistance from the recent book of Professor Harold M. Groves, *Postwar Taxation and Economic Progress*, a research study for the Committee on Economic Development, New York: McGraw-Hill Book Co., Inc., 1946. See especially Chapters VII and VIII in his book.

[2] These tax data are for all units of government. Sources: For Federal taxes, *Treasury Bulletin*, August, 1946; for state taxes, *State Tax Collections in 1946*, Bureau of the Census, August, 1946; for local taxes, *Government Finances in the United States, 1942*, Bureau of the Census, 1946, with estimates for increase in property taxes and for scattered local income taxes. For the Federal total of 40.3 billion dollars in tax revenue, personal income taxes were 46.4 per cent of total collections.

[3] Henry C. Simons, *Personal Income Taxation*, page 41, Chicago: University of Chicago Press, 1938, reprinted by permission of the publisher.

distribution. (3) The personal income tax can be made a relatively flexible tax, thus permitting flexibility in the fiscal system to be gained through taxation.

Although it may influence "incentives" adversely and hence reduce supplies of some resources, personal income taxation can be formulated so that it affects all income opportunities in about the same fashion. If incomes from all sources are taxed at the same rates, the tax tends to have relatively little influence upon the price pattern and upon resource allocation.

The importance of the progressive income tax as an instrument for attacking income inequality has already been discussed in Chapter X. Once the kind of income distribution which is most desirable for a given time has been determined, income-tax rates can be established to help achieve this distribution.

Changes in commodity-tax levies probably could bring about more immediate impacts in the level of expenditure for goods and services than could changes in personal income-tax rates. However, recent changes in the personal income tax have reduced the lag between changes in individuals' incomes and changes in their income-tax payments. The personal income tax could be made to synchronize income-tax payments with income even more than these recent changes have made possible. As we shall point out in Chapter XVI, income taxation is superior to commodity taxation in its effect upon consumer welfare and resource allocation.

There are, however, certain practical problems—problems of administration, in particular—which must be faced in making the personal income tax in practice the kind of tax which we have indicated it might be in theory. These problems arise in (1) defining income for tax purposes, (2) minimizing evasion and avoidance of taxation, (3) determining the proper rate structure, and (4) coordinating personal income taxes with other taxes in the tax system. These problems and the practices which have been utilized to solve them will be discussed in this and the following chapter.[4]

---

[4] Problems which involve questions of tax policy are principally problems of tax avoidance. Many also involve considerations of tax equity. They include treatment of capital gains and losses, tax-exempt securities, the reduction in existing tax discrimination against fluctuating incomes, the taxation of nonmoney (imputed) realized income, personal exemptions and deductions, and certain other problems of tax policy.

Historical Development[5]

After brief experiments with income taxation during the period 1861-1872 and in the 1890's, the Federal government did not settle down to the taxation of personal net income until 1913.[6] In 1915, soon after the Federal tax was established, it provided but 6.5 per cent of Federal tax revenues, drawn from about 337,-000 returns.[7] A personal exemption of $4,000 for married couples was granted. The "normal" tax was 1 per cent on all taxable net income,[8] and no surtaxes applied until taxable income exceeded $20,000. Surtax rates ranged from 1 to 6 per cent on taxable net income in excess of $20,000.

After a period of extension and refinement, the Federal income tax raised nearly 20 billion dollars in (calendar) 1945, reaching about 42.5 million taxpayers, and providing the Federal government with about 45.5 per cent of its total tax revenue (see Table 15). Meanwhile personal exemptions had been reduced to $1,000 (for a married couple), national income had grown tremendously, and tax rates began at 23 per cent on the first dollar of taxable income (including both normal and surtax), increasing to 94 per cent on taxable net income in excess of $200,000.[9] The most impressive changes in the Federal income tax, as was pointed out in Chapter II, came during the years 1939-1945. During these years the levy was converted from a "class" tax

[5] The remarks which follow are only a sketch of developments of income taxation in the United States. For fuller treatments of this subject, see Sidney Ratner, *American Taxation*, New York: W. W. Norton & Co., Inc., 1942; Roy G. and Gladys C. Blakey, *The Federal Income Tax*, New York: Longmans, Green & Co., 1940; and Roy G. Blakey and Violet Johnson, *State Income Taxes*, Chicago: Commerce Clearing House, Inc., 1942.

[6] Under power granted by the 16th Amendment to the Constitution.

[7] Not classified as to taxability by the Bureau of Internal Revenue.

[8] The early personal income taxes were linked with the 1 per cent corporation net income tax passed in 1909. This was done by making dividends received exempt from the tax base of the "normal" tax. Thus, in the early years of the present Federal income tax, the corporation tax was used as a partial means of collection at source. This linkage, which did not apply to surtax, is responsible for the original division of Federal income tax liability into "normal" tax and "surtax," a division which has continued to the present. Linkage with the corporation tax was gradually weakened, however, by the growth of a separate corporate-tax structure, and was finally eliminated in 1936, when dividends received (except most stock dividends) became part of the personal tax base for Federal income tax.

[9] An over-all ceiling of 90 per cent of net income subject to taxation was also in effect. The Revenue Act of 1945, effective in 1946, reduced rates to a range of 19 to 86.5 per cent, and lowered the over-all ceiling to 85.5 per cent.

Table 15[10]

Federal Tax Collections (Calendar) 1945

(in millions of dollars)

Type of Tax	Amount Collected	Percentage of Collections
1. Taxes on individual net incomes..........	$19,885	45.5%
2. Taxes on corporation profits.............	14,472	33.1
3. Taxes on goods and services[a]...........	6,582	15.0
4. Employment taxes.....................	1,751	4.0
5. Estate and gift taxes....................	663	1.5
6. Taxes on imports......................	388	0.9
7. Total tax collections...................	$43,741	100.0

[a] Includes capital stock on corporations amounting to 352 million dollars.

reaching only about 4 million taxpayers on 1939 incomes to a "mass" tax reaching more than 42 million taxpayers in 1945, and from a tax which could be paid (in part) until nearly a year after the year in which income was earned to a tax which was collected much sooner after the income was received. Both of these developments were important for the effective use of personal income taxation as an instrument of fiscal policy.

Even the expansion of recent years, however, left American income tax rates far below those imposed in the United Kingdom on incomes of comparable amounts during the years of World War II. This is indicated in Table 16.

State income taxes have been collected for a long period of time, but have not been very important in state tax revenues. Relatively unsuccessful experiments with income taxation were made by the states before 1911. However, the foundation for present state income-tax systems was firmly laid by Wisconsin in 1911. In 1913, five states employed the income tax. A total of only about $314,000 was raised by four of these states.[11]

By 1946, 33 states employed personal income taxation, collecting about 395 million dollars or about 6.6 per cent of state tax revenues. Using relatively low personal exemptions and much

[10] Sources: *Statement of Internal Revenue Collections During the Calendar Year 1945*, Bureau of Internal Revenue, Washington, D. C., February 18, 1946; *Treasury Bulletins*, February, 1946; August, 1945; and February, 1945.

[11] Separate data were not given for North Carolina by the Bureau of the Census in its decennial *Wealth, Debt and Taxation, 1913*, Vol. 2, pages 12, 24. The other four were Wisconsin, Virginia, South Carolina, and Oklahoma.

TABLE 16[12]

"Effective" [a] Income-Tax Rates on 1942 Incomes in the United States
and the United Kingdom[b]

Net Income of a married couple without dependents	Net Tax Rate	
	United States	United Kingdom
$1,000............................	2%	5%
2,500............................	13	23
5,000............................	20	33
10,000............................	28	42
50,000............................	57	72

[a] "Effective" tax rates mean total income tax as a percentage of net income. The rate structure employed in computing the tax rates was approximately the peak of wartime tax rates, although nominal increases were made in the United States by the Revenue Act of 1943.

[b] *Net* tax includes all provisions for postwar refunds of part of the tax. British estimates assume the exchange ratio between British and American currency to be £1 = $4.00.

the same definition of income for taxation as the Federal government's, the states have nevertheless found that the Federal government has largely preempted the income tax field, and rely for the bulk of their tax revenues on a variety of commodity, gross receipts, and business taxes.[13]

Defining Income for Tax Purposes

One of the most important problems in personal income taxation is that of defining income for tax purposes. Several concepts of income have been suggested. As we shall see, our legal identification of taxable income has some similarities to two of these income concepts. Discussion of these academic concepts should not be interpreted as suggesting that practical definitions of taxable income rest on any well-defined, academic base. The practical definition of income is largely one of enumeration in which these academic concepts have had some influence, but in which it has been taken for granted that what was or was not income was self-evident. Among the concepts of taxable income

[12] Estimates for the United Kingdom are from data published in the *Treasury Bulletin*, December, 1942, page 74. Data for the United States are from the same source. In addition, state income taxes are included in United States figures, at the rates levied in Iowa on 1942 incomes, 1 to 5 per cent.

[13] The city of Philadelphia uses a 1½ per cent tax on income earned in Philadelphia, whether by residents or nonresidents. Dividends and interest received are exempt from tax, but there is no personal exemption.

which will be considered are: (1) income as a "service-flow" in consumption, (2) income as "recurrent" receipts, and (3) income as the *net* addition to an individual's economic power within a specified period of time.[14]

Under the "service-flow" concept, income is thought of as the value of goods and services consumed by an individual in a given time period. An individual's income is thus defined as his consumption. The monetary equivalent would be money expenditures for personal and family consumption (of non-durable goods and services) plus the estimated money value of services received from durable consumers' goods and from the unpaid labor of individual and family members for their own comfort and welfare. Under this definition of income, expenditures on durable goods, whether capital or consumer goods, would constitute savings and would not be subject to taxation. The value of the service yielded by such holdings of consumer goods would be taxed in the period in which the services were enjoyed.[15]

The "service-flow" concept of income is a logical and consistent definition of consumption, but does not lend itself very well to a definition of taxable income. If it were applied, a large portion of the current money incomes of upper income groups would escape personal income taxation, since personal savings are concentrated in these groups. Such savings are generally conceded to represent increases in power and elements of ability to pay and should be taxed. Adoption of the service-flow concept for income taxation would, in large part, convert the income tax into a spendings, or consumption, tax. Such a tax may, in fact, be useful to curb consumption—an objective which we try to achieve in wartime. But it would not accomplish the objective of taxing according to ability to pay.

Further, it would be almost impossible to determine a monetary equivalent to many of the items included in this concept. It would be desirable—and probably feasible—to include the money

[14] Reference to the idea of income as national income or product was made earlier in this book in Chapter I, Table 1, and in Appendix A. The concepts and values of gross national product, net national income, and income payments to individuals were defined and distinguished. While the concept of national income or product is useful for other purposes, it has only limited uses for discussion of taxable income.

[15] Irving Fisher was a persistent advocate of this concept of taxable income. See, for example, his "Income in Theory and Income Taxation in Practice," *Econometrica*, January, 1937.

values of certain items of real income in the tax base (such as the rental value of owned homes). It would be much more difficult to establish annual monetary values for the services of some other durable consumers' goods. It would violate accepted social patterns to tax on the basis of some arbitrary value, the services performed by housewives. The administrative problems of applying the tax base to most of our items of real income would be almost insuperable. The writers doubt that ability-to-pay personal income taxes could be successfully applied where income would be determined according to the service-flow concept.

A second concept is that of "recurrent, consumable receipts." The late Professor Carl Plehn was the principal advocate of this concept of income. He stressed three characteristics of income: receipt, anticipated recurrence, and expendability.[16] On the basis of these characteristics, he included in income wages and salaries, interest and rents, annuities and pensions, and probably dividends on shares of stock in a corporation. Since it is possible that income defined in this way may be only partly spent in consumption, it includes current savings out of income by implication. On the other hand, Professor Plehn specifically excluded as nonrecurrent such items affecting individual assets as gains and losses on capital transactions, and receipts from bequests and gifts.[17]

Plehn's ideas about income partly conform to our current description of taxable income (which includes savings, for instance), but the ideas are weak in several respects. While contending that anticipated recurrence over some period of time was one essential attribute of income, Plehn did not indicate what *length* of time-period or what probability of income receipt over time was a sufficient prerequisite for anticipated recurrence. Neither did he deny that any item of receipt which increases the economic power of an individual between two points in time is just as expendable as the items of receipt which he chose to include in his definition of income.

[16] See Carl Plehn, "Income as Recurrent, Consumable Receipts," *American Economic Review,* Vol. XIV, 1924, pages 1-12.
[17] Plehn's reasoning in the exclusion of bequests and gifts from income is somewhat strange. He agreed that what counts as income for purposes of taxation is the private, personal income of the individual. But he also contended that the receipt of an inheritance or gift cannot be counted as income, because "it is not considered wise [writer's underlining] to spend these receipts." See his discussion, *ibid.,* pages 1-12.

These inherent weaknesses in his concept of income show up when we examine some of the economic transactions with which he was concerned. Thus, it is clearly incorrect to call interest and dividends a recurrent item of income for an individual, when in fact he may enjoy such a receipt only occasionally or perhaps only once. It is questionable to exclude capital gains and losses from income on the grounds of nonrecurrence when, for some individuals, such gains or losses may show up nearly every year as a result of trading in capital assets. As we shall see in Chapter XIV, capital gains (or losses) may be important elements in the disposable income which a particular individual may (or may not) enjoy and such gains (or losses) are properly included in determining *his* taxable capacity. Again, the windfall receipt of an inheritance by some individual is just as much income to him as if money assets had been received in one of the ways which Plehn labeled "income," because of "recurrence." Further, such receipt may well increase his economic power.

This brings us to the "net accretion" concept of income, which is also partially embodied in our laws specifying the nature of taxable income. From many points of view, the net accretion view of income would be the most satisfactory basis for a definition of taxable income.

Under the "net-accretion" concept[18] all types of receipt or accrual in purchasing power to the individual between two points of time would be included in income—less expenditures necessary to obtain this income. Completely applied, net accretion in income would include not only what has been called "recurrent, consumable receipts," but also receipts from inheritances and gifts, appreciation or depreciation in capital assets (whether realized or not), and the money value of the various types of real income also included under the "service-flow" income concept discussed above. Attention would be focused on net accretion in income or economic power, and not on the disposition of this income, whether for consumption, savings, or gifts.

This way of looking at income has real advantages where the purpose is to apply a tax based on relative *personal* ability to pay.

[18] The most frequently cited American proponent of this income concept is Robert Murray Haig. See his *The Federal Income Tax*, New York: Columbia University Press, 1921.

Firstly, it is an inclusive concept which would make it unnecessary to set up separate schedules for the treatment of capital gains (or losses) or for the treatment of receipts from inheritances or gifts. It would, in other words, provide the basis for most inclusive definition of the tax base for purposes of personal income taxation which would be possible. Secondly, it recognizes that where personal income taxation is involved, the question whether capital gains should or should not be taxed is largely irrelevant, since the receipt of a capital gain is definitely an addition to the economic power of an individual. While it is true that other individuals may simultaneously suffer capital losses (which reduce *their* economic power), and that such gains and losses may (at least over time) tend to cancel out for society as a whole, this ignores the fact that, for particular individuals, capital gains may *never* be offset by compensating losses (or *vice versa*). If what we want to do is to tax personal net incomes, then we should not try to combine some kind of an additive process for society with recognition of the varying economic status of different *persons*. Losses, of course, should be fully recognized as deductions from income.[19]

On the other hand, it is impossible to apply this concept of income entirely to determination of taxable income. Part of this follows from the administrative difficulties of measuring the value of "income in kind." This type of income receives little recognition for Federal income taxation in this country, and for most state income taxation.[20] Further, it is generally agreed that the taxation of unrealized capital gains (or deduction for unrealized losses) would be administratively impracticable, so that a realization test for income is more practicable. This has been recognized both in our tax laws and in various expedients which have been applied to give more favorable treatment when capital gains (or losses) have accrued over a period of years as opposed to the

[19] The British have largely ignored capital gains and losses in their taxation of personal income, although not entirely, as Robert Murray Haig pointed out in a series of articles, "Taxation of Capital Gains," *The Wall Street Journal*, 1937. Mention of the treatment of capital gains and losses is given later in this chapter and the problems of including such gains (or deducting such losses) in the tax base receive critical analysis in Chapter XIV.

[20] The difficulties are not dissimilar to those discussed in connection with the service-flow concept of income earlier in the chapter. On the other hand, a case can be made—both in precedent (largely British) and in feasibility—for taxing certain types of income in kind. This problem will receive more detailed consideration in Chapter XIV.

acquisition or disposition of capital assets which occur within some taxable period.

Finally—although this is not a disadvantage of the net-accretion concept as such—it must be recognized that the taxation of bequests and gifts has long taken place in this country under laws and rate schedules which have set these particular components of income apart from the receipt of income from other sources. The practical difficulties of reversing our practices and integrating the disposition (or receipt) of these types of assets with other assets included in the income tax base cannot be ignored.   Nevertheless, in the writers' opinion, the net accretion concept offers the best available basis (with necessary modifications) for definition of the personal income-tax base, considering administrative practicability and accepted social patterns.[21]

This brief survey of alternative income concepts has led to the place where there is merit in comparing our legal (Federal) description of income[22] with the net-accretion and current-receipts concepts.   This type of comparison is made briefly in Table 17, together with a brief explanation of the main items compared.

Large Amounts of Personal Income Escape Taxation

We have pointed to the need for subjecting a large percentage of income to potential taxation, if the personal income tax is to be most effective in combating inflation or deflation. With a primary interest in the volume of tax revenue, Professor Groves has recently emphasized the continuing necessity of a broad base for the personal income tax in the postwar period, if it is to remain the principal source of Federal tax revenue.[23]   He cites estimates to show that, even with a net national income of 140 billion dollars only about 41.2 per cent (57.6 billion) would be taxable if 1944 (surtax) exemptions were maintained.   Assuming approximate accuracy of his estimates, for a national income of 140 billion dollars, his conclusions are that (1) even a tax with as low personal exemption as the 1944 income tax would eliminate from

[21] The net-accretion concept of income is not concerned with such personal exemptions for taxation as might be used if tax laws were based on this concept. This does not preclude the use of a personal exemption system if this income concept were made the basis of tax law, however.

[22] It is generally recognized that no definition of income exists in present income tax laws, but simply an enumeration of taxable and nontaxable receipts.

[23] See Harold M. Groves, *Postwar Taxation and Economic Progress*, Chapter VII, New York: McGraw-Hill Book Co., Inc., 1946.

TABLE 17

Comparison of the Legal, Net-Accretion and Recurrent-Receipts Concepts
of Income, Applied to Federal Taxation

Item Compared	Federal Law	Treatment Under	
		Net-Accretion Concept	Recurrent-Receipts Concept
1. Receipts or accruals from all sources included in *gross* tax base....................	No[a]	Yes	No[b]
2. *Gross* tax base includes realized income only................	Yes[c]	No	Yes
3. *Gross* tax base includes only money income.................	Yes[d]	No	No
4. Only net income is taxed......	Yes[e]	Yes[f]	Yes[f]
5. Savings are included as a portion of income..............	Yes	Yes	Yes
6. Capital gains are taxed; capital losses are treated as deductions from other income.......	Yes[g]	Yes	No

[a] Certain types of receipts or accruals are excluded from the gross tax base, for a variety of reasons. These will be examined subsequently.

[b] Among other things, the income must be realized money income and capital gains and losses are excluded.

[c] Or when persons are compensated in goods and services for personal services rendered or goods exchanged, as when a farmer exchanges eggs for groceries.

[d] With a few exceptions. See footnote[c].

[e] Both business expenses and specified personal expenses may be deducted. This excludes expenses for personal consumption, except in a few cases of which the opportunity to make a deduction for extraordinary medical expenses is the most important.

[f] Assumes deduction for expenses incurred in obtaining the income, but has nothing to say about exemptions to be allowed in disposal of the income.

[g] Especially favorable treatment is provided for capital gains. Treatment accorded to losses is much less favorable.

any (income) taxes over one-third of American income recipients and would not tax between one-half and two-thirds of the income of all recipients, and (2) such taxation "cannot be said to err on the side of harshness or to sap unduly the purchasing power of the low-income groups."[24]

Groves concludes that much of our national income is not in-

[24] By permission from Harold M. Groves, *Postwar Taxation and Economic Progress,* pages 168-169. Copyrighted, 1946, by McGraw-Hill Book Co., Inc.

cluded in the tax base upon which the income-tax structure is
ultimately built.   He indicates that much of the income not subject to taxation may be accounted for by a combination of miscellaneous nonreported income, permitted tax deductions, and personal exemptions. An estimate of the proportion of income
payments included in the tax base for a situation in which income
payments total 166 billion dollars is presented in Table 18.

TABLE 18[25]

Estimated 1947 Personal Income Tax Base

(1945 surtax exemptions)

Use of Income	Estimates Amount (in billions of dollars)	Estimates Per Cent of Total
1. Total income payments.........	$166.0	100.0
2. Deductions from reported income	17.0	10.2
3. Personal exemptions from re- ported income.................	58.0	34.9
4. Income not reported............	22.0	13.3
5. Net taxable income.............	69.0	41.6

"Income not reported" is made up of income which avoids the
tax base "because it is below the personal exemption level, because it is privileged (as in the case of tax-exempt interest), because there is administrative leakage, because it is reinvested by
corporations (corporate savings), and because differences appear
in calculating national income and in measuring income for tax
purposes." [26]   "Personal deductions from reported gross income"
(after allowing for business and professional expenses) are permitted by income-tax laws, and include other taxes paid (principally state and local taxes in the case of Federal income tax),
interest on debts, extraordinary medical expenses (with a specified maximum deduction), and contributions (also with a
limited maximum), as their main components.[27]

[25] These data were derived from a Treasury release, March 13, 1947.
[26] Groves, *Postwar Taxation and Economic Progress,* page 168. Copyrighted,
1946, by McGraw-Hill Book Co., Inc.   The substantial size of nonreported income
was indicated by the study of *Consumer Incomes in the United States, 1935-36,*
National Resources Planning Board, Washington, D. C., 1938.
[27] Deductions are listed in more detail later in this chapter and are examined
critically in the following chapter.   A brief study of *Statistics of Income for 1942,
Part I,* bears out the main conclusions of Professor Groves on the "disappearance"
of a large portion of national income from the tax base.   In 1942, net national

Personal exemptions, reduced from $2,500 for a married couple with no children in 1939 to $1,000 in 1944 (from $3,300 to $2,000 for a family of four, all eligible for exemption, and from $1,000 to $500 for a single person), are very important in reducing the size of the tax base. At their 1939 level, such exemptions would reduce the tax base of 57.6 billion dollars, which Professor Groves has estimated for a national income of 140 billions, to 29.2 billions. Granting the need for a large postwar tax base, such estimates indicate that the retention of relatively low personal exemptions (as in 1946) is desirable. It is generally agreed that personal exemptions, varying with the number of dependents, are necessary to the continuance of the personal income tax as an ability-to-pay tax, and perhaps for other reasons.[28] The writers would especially emphasize the need for a broad tax base as necessary in the use of the personal income tax as an efficient instrument for planned flexibility in fiscal policy.

Special problems of the tax return. The methods whereby the process of computing Federal income-tax liability has been simplified in recent years are summarized in the following sections. There still remain two main complexities. One is the ability of taxpayers to submit separate returns if a joint return would increase tax liability, and where more than one person in a family has sufficient income to require the filing of a tax return. The other is the ability of husband and wife in certain "community-property" tax states (Arizona, California, Idaho, Louisiana, New Mexico, Texas, Washington, and Wyoming) to divide income for purposes of tax reporting, whether or not the income has been earned by more than one person. Some *net* tax avoidance may be possible if larger tax rates on larger incomes, an integral feature of our tax-rate structure, are escaped in part.

---

income, as reported by the Department of Commerce, was 121.6 billion dollars. Of this amount, 86.6 billions were reported on tax returns, or about 35 billions (27.9 per cent) were unreported. Deductions, after business expenses, amounted to 7.9 billion dollars, about 9 per cent of reported income, and about 6.5 per cent of national income. A special deduction item to be noted is the 10 per cent deduction (after business expenses) which is automatically allowed by the government in the computation of its tax table for "shortcut" determination of tax liability. This tax table is referred to later in this chapter. Personal exemptions on 1942 income were—to the point where nontaxable income was reduced to zero—41.4 billion dollars, or about 34 per cent of national income. This left 37.3 billions as the tax base, only about 31.6 per cent of national income in 1942.

[28] Brief examination of personal exemptions will be made in the following chapter. Professor Groves has outlined his reasons for such exemptions on pages 171-174 of *Postwar Taxation and Economic Progress*.

The ability of taxpayers to use these options enables certain taxpayers to obtain net savings which increase with the size of the income and with the relative share received by one of the taxpayers. To take an hypothetical example, suppose a husband and wife receive a total income of $10,000, of which $1,000 is legally deductible, and of which $1,000 was received by the wife. For a net income of $9,000 filed under a joint return, total taxes (1946) would have been $2,185. If, however, the husband chose to take the deductions of $1,000 against his income, and husband and wife agreed to split their $1,000 exemption, the total tax would have been $1,957.

In any of the community-property states these two individuals can split total income received, whether or not the income has actually been received by more than one person. Continuing with our previous example, let us suppose that the husband and wife split the net income of $9,000 and each report $4,500. In this case, total tax liability would have been $1,843 (1946)—less than if either separate returns were filed as in our second example, and still less than under a joint return. If, in fact, total income received by either husband or wife were greater than in our example, there would be an even greater tax advantage in splitting the income, especially where the relative share of income received by one of the two persons was large.

The potential income-tax loss which results from the practice of separate returns, especially in community-property tax states, cannot be ignored. For the income year 1942, for example, individual income-tax returns from the eight community-property tax states were about 15.6 per cent of all returns, and represented about 15.4 per cent of total net income reported for taxation.[29] On these returns, the Treasury suffered substantial loss in income-tax revenues, because of the special practice of splitting income permitted in these states. The potential loss in tax revenue due to the permissive filing of separate returns where there is more than one person receiving income within a family is more difficult to estimate.

There is no completely equitable solution to the problems of separate returns. A case can be made for compulsory joint returns, which the Treasury has proposed on several occasions, but

---

[29] Based on *Statistics of Income for 1942, Part 1,* page 90, Treasury Department, Washington, D. C., 1945.

which has never been enacted into law. This procedure is embodied in British income-tax law. Yet it can be objected that such a compulsory practice would be unfair where, in fact, several persons within a family have substantial income secured from independent sources. Separate computation of tax for each member of a family has also been proposed, under which the income secured by all members of the family would be added, with tax computation per member being based on total net income divided by the number of persons in the family. The separate tax so computed for each member would then be multiplied by the number of persons in the family to obtain the total tax reported on one tax return. Such a system of reporting would be a definite improvement over the system permitted in the community-property tax states, but would obviously benefit families with dependents. Every member of the family could claim exemption regardless of his income. Whether or not this is desirable depends in part on the stimulus to larger families which is wanted, but the analysis of this social end is not one which will be undertaken by the writers.

In any event, some improvement could be made in our present requirements for types of tax returns which may be filed. Compulsory joint returns would probably represent such an improvement, as also would the separate computation of tax liability along the lines explained above, although it might prove desirable to limit such tax computation to husband and wife. Another improvement would be the requirement that community-property tax returns be filed by all those required to file income-tax returns. Any of these suggestions would remove the differential advantage which now exists for individuals living in the community-property tax states.

Determining Federal Income-Tax Liability

During recent years, we have simplified the Federal income-tax process for the majority of individuals required to file returns. The bulk of individuals affected by the income tax are now able either to turn over their withholding receipts to the government and let the Bureau of Internal Revenue compute their final tax liability, or to use a short-form tax return which enables them to determine their tax liability by the inspection of a prepared table. Thus, individuals with wage-salary income not exceeding $5,000 plus $500 for each personal exemption (including the taxpayer) and with income from other sources not in excess of $100 are able to supply information on this miscellaneous income, sign their withholding receipts, and let the government compute their tax liability. Whether they are subject to withholding or not, individuals with gross income not over $5,000 may use a short-form tax return which enables them to determine their tax liability readily by inspection of a table which allows for personal exemptions and for deductions which are 10 per cent of gross income.[30] Some individuals, however, are either compelled to use the complete tax form 1040 to determine tax liability or, for reasons to be indicated shortly, find it to their advantage to do so.

By a combination of collection at source for the payment of the bulk of wages and salaries, and of current declaration of estimated annual income and payment of tax thereon in installments, the time involved between receipt of income and payment of tax has been substantially reduced.

Let us begin our explanation of the income-tax process by following the steps from calculation of the sum of gross money values received by an individual (or increase in the value of assets held) to the calculation of final tax liability. We will assume that it will be necessary for such an individual (whom we shall call "X") to use the full tax form, and that he is a self-employed businessman whose net business profits for the year are $10,000. The path which he will follow in determining tax liability is described below.[31]

1. He begins with a sum of gross money values received during the year from all sources and perhaps with a change in the value of capital assets which he owns.
2. From these, he will first exclude certain "non-income" items as defined by law. This will leave a sum of gross money receipts which may be thought of as the gross tax base.
3. From the gross tax base, he will subtract business expenses, including an allowance for depreciation and/or depletion, to obtain *adjusted gross income*.[32]

[30] Strictly speaking, the table is made available for individuals whose *adjusted* gross income does not exceed $5,000. The (downward) adjustments which are permitted are chiefly those for business expenses.

[31] The steps described do not include those which he must follow in complying with the requirements of tax declaration, as part of our current-collection system. Explanation of these additional steps will follow immediately after the steps in determining tax liability have been indicated.

[32] "Business expenses" is a general term to cover the deduction of various specified items listed in amendment of Section 22 of the Internal Revenue Code

4. From adjusted gross income, he will obtain net income by subtracting permitted *personal deductions*.

5. His net income will be decreased by the amount of his personal exemption, varying with the number of dependents, to obtain *net taxable income*.

6. This net taxable income was subject in 1946 to both normal tax (3 per cent in 1946), and to progressive surtax rates applicable to his taxable net income (these rates varied from 17 to 88 per cent in 1946).

7. From the tax so computed, the Revenue Act of 1945 permitted him to deduct 5 per cent, and set the maximum of net taxable income which could be taken in tax at 85.5 per cent.[33]

In explaining the application of these steps to Individual X, we need more data than we have so far. We have assumed that X is a self-employed businessman whose net profits reported on the accrual basis are $10,000. We will now assume, in full, that:

1. For items increasing the money value of his assets:
   a. His gross receipts from the sale of goods and services in his business during the year are $100,000.
   b. He receives $3,000 cash in interest and dividends on investments in corporate securities.
   c. He receives a bequest of $25,000.
   d. He also receives $5,000 as the proceeds of a life insurance policy from the death of a child in the family just prior to the end of the preceding year.
   e. He receives $2,000 interest on investments in state and local securities which he owns.
   f. He receives dividends in stock shares instead of in cash from a corporation, such shares having a market value of $500.
   g. The value of a tract of land which he owns increases from $5,000 to $8,000.
   h. Merchandise which he holds for business purposes rises in value by $2,000.

---

by the Individual Income Tax Act of 1944. Deductions allowed for depreciation, depletion, and obsolescence are explained in *Bulletin F* of the Bureau of Internal Revenue. This bulletin is revised from time to time.

[33] For the majority of income receivers who derive their incomes from wages or salaries, gross income and adjusted gross income are the same, so that the adjustment in Step 3 above is not necessary. Apart from this adjustment, derivation of taxable net income and determination of tax liability are based on essentially the same steps as those indicated above, even though the government has provided "short-cut" processes by which the tax liability (if any) of most income receivers may be determined.

2. For items decreasing the money value of his assets:
   a. His business expenses are $90,000, including a charge for depreciation and anticipated bad debts.
   b. He pays state and local taxes amounting to $2,000.
   c. He incurs and pays medical and dental expenses of $3,000 for himself and dependents.
   d. He contributes $3,000 for religious and charitable purposes.
   e. He pays $500 interest on funds borrowed.
   f. He makes a gift of $1,000 to a friend.
   g. He expends $5,000 for the living expenses of himself and family.
   h. He repays debts of $1,000.
3. He makes a capital investment of $15,000 in land and buildings, partly out of accumulated funds, in expectation of personal profit from this investment.
4. He is married and head of a family consisting of a wife and one minor child, none of whom are income earners during the year. He is therefore entitled to a personal exemption of $500 for each member of the family, including himself, or a total of $1,500.

On the basis of these data, and the prevailing schedule of tax rates (here taken to be the tax-rate schedule effective in 1946)[34] what will be the income-tax liability of Mr. *X*? To answer this question, we must follow through the steps in tax computation previously listed, as well as revert to the legal definition of income for taxation from time to time.

First, the data include certain "non-income" items which are not relevant for our purpose, as well as certain deductions from income permitted by law. The non-income items are of several types. Since our Federal tax law is based largely upon realized money income, his unrealized appreciation of $3,000 in the value of land which he owns, as well as the real income enjoyed from living in an owned home, are excluded. The increase of $2,000 in the value of his merchandise will be included if *X* reports on the accrual basis. Certain items increasing the money value of assets have been excluded from gross income for several reasons: (1) Because of constitutional interpretation. Thus, income on such instrumentalities of one level of government as government securities are exempt from income taxation by another level of government (such as the exemption of the interest on Federal

[34] See Appendix C for this rate schedule.

securities from state income taxes and *vice versa*). Again, the Supreme Court has held that stock dividends which do not alter the proportionate ownership of stockholders in a corporation are tax-exempt. (2) Certain receipts are subject to other forms of taxation. The receipt of bequests and gifts is not called "income." This may be because we also have Federal taxation of bequests and gifts. (3) Because of prevailing social and economic attitudes. Thus, the proceeds of a life insurance policy are not income for tax purposes.[35] In our particular example, non-income items total $35,500.[36]

Set against the total of items increasing assets by $140,500, this subtraction of $35,500 leaves $105,000. The next step is to secure adjusted gross income, which permits the deduction of business expenses, which amount to $90,000 in this instance, leaving $15,000. Specified personal deductions may then be subtracted from adjusted gross income. Deductions permitted are mainly for state and local taxes (except special assessments); interest on indebtedness; contributions for religious, charitable, educational, or scientific purposes up to 15 per cent of (adjusted) gross income; and for "extraordinary" medical or dental expenses —those in excess of 5 per cent of adjusted gross income up to a specified maximum.[37] Deductions for ordinary living expenses,

---

[35] For a more complete list of non-income items for tax purposes, see the Internal Revenue Code, Section 22. Based primarily on the concept of realized money receipts, however, this section does not mention such income as unrealized appreciation (or depreciation) in capital assets or real income with a monetary equivalent, such as income from the use of an owned home. Receipts from insurance due to other reasons than the death of the insured, or from annuities, are included in gross income to the extent that such receipts (when added to amounts received before a particular income year) exceed the aggregate premiums or consideration paid by beneficiaries in order to obtain such receipts.

[36] This amount is the sum of the bequest of $25,000; $5,000 in life insurance; $2,000 tax-exempt interest; $3,000 unrealized appreciation; and $500 in stock dividends.

[37] For a quite complete statement of permitted deductions, see Internal Revenue Code, Section 24. The Code lists these deductions, among others:

1. Trade or business expenses.
2. For individuals: all non-business expenses paid or incurred during the taxable year for the production or collection of income, or for management of property held for the production of income.
3. All interest paid or accrued within the taxable year: except that interest on tax-exempt securities is not deductible.
4. Taxes, except death, gift, Federal income and excise taxes, and taxes assessed against local benefits (special assessments).
5. Business losses and other losses arising from fires, other casualties, or theft— to the extent not covered by insurance.
6. Bad debts, or a reasonable addition to reserve for bad debts.

expenditures for capital investment or repayment of capital indebtedness are not permitted, nor are outright gifts (for other than contributory purposes already mentioned).[38]

In the case of Individual X, permitted personal deductions total $7,250,[39] leaving a net income of $7,750. Having three personal exemptions (counting himself) Individual X is entitled to a personal exemption of $1,500 before tax. This leaves him with a taxable net income of $6,250, to all of which both normal tax (3 per cent) and surtax (beginning at 17 per cent on the first $2,000) apply. His "tentative" tax can now be calculated (with the aid of tax rate and exemption data). It is $1,455, but the Revenue Act of 1945 permitted "tentative" tax to be reduced by 5 per cent to obtain final tax liability, which is $1,416, or 18.3 per cent of his net income of $7,750. This effective rate, it should be noted, is much lower than the highest marginal rate which X has to pay. On the part of his taxable net income over $6,000, his combined normal and surtax rate is 30 per cent[40] (28.5 per cent after the permitted 5 per cent reduction).

7. A reasonable allowance for depreciation (including obsolescence) arising from property used in the trade or business or held for the production of income; likewise, a reasonable allowance for depletion.

8. Gifts and contributions for religious, charitable, scientific, or educational purposes to the extent of 15 per cent of adjusted gross income.

9. Deduction for extraordinary medical and dental expenses paid during the year, not otherwise compensated by insurance.

[38] Under the Federal Gift Tax (1946) an individual is entitled to an exemption of $30,000 plus $3,000 to any one person in a given year.

[39] Determined as follows: state and local taxes $2,000; allowance for medical costs $2,250; allowance for contributions $2,500; payment of interest on debts $500. Deduction for medical-dental expenses was determined as follows: 5 per cent of adjusted gross income of $15,000 is $750. Medical expenses to the extent of $3,000 were incurred, or $2,250 above the 5 per cent figure. This much is deductible, since it is still below the ceiling amount of $2,500 permitted as a deduction for this type of expense for an individual with more than one personal exemption. The allowance for contributions was determined as follows: 15 per cent of $15,000 is $2,500. While Individual X made contributions in excess of this amount, only $2,500 is an allowable deduction under the law.

[40] The "effective" rate is pulled below the top marginal rate by the taxation of parts of his taxable net income at lower marginal rates. Thus, the first $2,000 of his taxable net income is taxed at 20 per cent, the next $2,000 at 23 per cent, the next $2,000 at 26 per cent and the portion of his net income over $6,000 is taxed at 30 per cent. (These rates are prior to the final subtraction of 5 per cent of tax.) For purposes of simplicity, gains or losses on the sale of property have been excluded in the above example. To the limited extent that tradings in property are defined as transactions involving "capital assets" by the (1946) law, net capital gains were taxed at a top rate of 25 per cent, while capital losses could be deducted only against gains, plus the lesser of $1,000 or net income (exclusive of such capital gains or losses), with a limited provision for carry-over of net capital loss.

Relatively few individuals have as large a net income as our hypothetical X. Where the adjusted gross income of such an individual is below $5,000, he may use a "short-cut" tax process, with a tax table to determine his tax, or he may be able simply to sign a withholding receipt from his employer and let the government compute his tax liability, if any, for the year. These alternatives have been mentioned previously. Two things need to be pointed out, however:

1. There are many cases where the system of withholding and declaration (and payment) of estimated tax results in some overpayment of tax, giving an option of a refund payment to the individual or application of his "overpayment" against his tax liability for the following year. Such overpayments may come about in several ways: (a) because tax has been withheld where an individual has earned a total amount below his personal exemptions (and permitted deductions), (b) because of errors of estimate in tax liability not completely removed at the time that the individual files his final tax return for one year by March 15 of the following year, or (c) because of the roughness of the income brackets which are employed in applying different rates to different sized incomes. This latter factor results in overestimation of the tax rate to be applied on an individual's income rather than taxation of a larger income than was actually received. In 1945, of 47,000,000 returns filed for the taxable year 1944 over 30,000,000 were entitled to total refunds amounting to 1.4 billion dollars.

2. There are cases where individuals with adjusted gross income below $5,000 may find it more profitable to list their permitted deductions than to take the 10 per cent deduction allowed in the tax table (Supplement Table T) included with the tax form. Conversely, there are cases for individuals with gross income above $5,000 where it may be more profitable to use the maximum deduction allowed in the tax table ($500) than to list total deductions which may total less than $500. In both cases, the option may be exercised. (The $500 maximum deduction in the tax table is called the "optional standard deduction" for those with adjusted gross income above $5,000.)

The "Current-Collection" System

Scattered observations have already been made about the reduction of time between the receipt of income and the payment of the tax which has been achieved in Federal income taxation in recent years.   It is the purpose of this section to summarize the main features of our present system (1946), which began with the Revenue Act of 1942 and culminated in the Individual Income Tax Act of 1944.

Steps toward currency in tax payments operating in 1946 began with the initiation of a withholding system for wages and salaries (excluding those of a few groups, chiefly agricultural laborers and those employed in domestic service). This system began in January, 1943, with a 5 per cent wartime Victory Tax on wages over $12 a week. It was subsequently revised and broadened. In 1946, it withheld most of the income tax on gross wages and salaries up to $5,000 for individuals, plus $500 for each "personal exemption."

An important phase of "current" collection in 1946 was a system of tax declaration and current payment by two main economic groups (apart from those engaged in agriculture and a few other wage-earning groups): (1) Individuals whose wages or salary subject to withholding could reasonably be expected to exceed $5,000, plus $500 for each exemption, and (2) Individuals whose gross income from sources other than wages or salary could reasonably be expected to exceed $100 and whose gross income might be expected to exceed $500.   Both groups of persons were required to make advance estimates of annual tax liability by March 15 of a given year and to pay one-quarter of any indicated tax liability by successive payments on March 15, June 15, September 15, and on January 15 of the following year.   If part of his income was subject to withholding at the source, an individual falling in either of these two groups was expected (in 1946) to estimate the tax to be withheld at the source in a given year and could deduct this tax from his total estimated tax liability.

The functioning of this system of tax declaration and payment can be clearly illustrated by an hypothetical case of a self-employed businessman (unincorporated and outside agriculture) who, in both 1942 and 1946, had a net taxable income of $10,000. We shall assume that, in both years, his income was earned from January 1 throughout the year, although not necessarily with the same regularity day by day.   On his 1942 income, this businessman was not required to state his income to the Federal government at all until March 15, 1943, the deadline for filing his tax return for the previous year. He could then, if desired, meet his tax liability in four quarterly installments ending December 15, 1943. This meant that a portion of his tax liability which was actually incurred in early January, 1942, might not be met until nearly two years later, although the average lag probably was about 7 months.

In 1946, this maximum period for meeting any portion of tax liability had been reduced to less than fifteen months, and most of such liability was met within three to four months after it had been incurred. Tax payments which followed March 15 could be accompanied by amended declarations, with alterations in such tax payments. Provided that his adjusted estimates of annual income (and tax liability) came within 80 per cent of the final tax liability, as indicated by a tax return filed not later than March 15, 1947, the individual was not subject to any penalty (assuming, of course, that taxes due were paid within the time intervals permitted by the tax law).

Especially favorable treatment given farmers[41] in the current collection system has already been mentioned (Chapter XI). The lag between receipt of income and payment of tax has been reduced least of all for this class of taxpayer. A farmer is not required to make a declaration and payment of estimated tax for the income of one calendar year until January 15 of the following year. Even then, he may avoid a declaration if he files his final income tax return by January 15. If he does not choose this option, he may still file his tax return by March 15, and avoids penalty for understatement of tax liability if his final return indicates that his estimate (as of January 15) was not below final tax liability by more than $33\frac{1}{3}$ per cent.[42]

The especially favorable treatment accorded farmers probably arises both from the comparatively poor bookkeeping methods which farmers generally use[43] and from the inherent nature of their businesses, which may be subject to sudden changes in

[41] An individual may qualify as a farmer if at least two-thirds of his gross income comes from farming.

[42] The system which is used to encourage accuracy in tax estimates imposes this penalty: the lesser of (1) 6 per cent of the excess of final tax over the sum of estimated tax and tax withheld at source, and (2) the excess of 80 per cent of final tax ($66\frac{3}{3}$ per cent in the case of farmers) over estimated tax.

[43] The requirement that a farmer submit a schedule of farm income and expenses (Form 1040 F) with his tax return both recognizes this fact and probably requires many farmers who are potential taxpayers to keep better business records than they would otherwise do.

weather and disease beyond their control, affecting their final income for the year both rapidly and substantially.[44] It seems to the writers that the requirements for advance estimates of income and payment of anticipated tax and the imposition of penalties for underestimation of income which are applied to other economic groups should be applied to farmers. This appears reasonable since the current declaration system permits amendments of original estimated income (and tax liability) at four successive intervals during the course of a year.

Our current collection system has developed to the point where part of tax liabilities incurred on the income of one month becomes tax receipts to the Federal government in the following month. For taxes withheld on wage-salary income, the process of tax collection has a lag of only slightly more than one month. An employer with a monthly wage bill of over $100 is required to turn over taxes collected in any month to the government within 10 days after this period has ended.

Summary of the Federal Income Tax Collection System (1946)

I. Filing of Returns:
   A. Under the withholding system:
      1. One of the following types of tax return is required of any individual from whom some portion of his annual wages or salary have been deducted in taxes by an employer:
         a. If wage or salary received does not exceed $5,000, plus $500 for each dependent, and if gross taxable income from other sources is not over $100, the individual may sign his withholding receipt from his employer, supply information as to miscellaneous income received, and let the government determine his final tax liability.
         b. If such wage or salary exceeded $5,000, plus $500 for each exemption or, even if less than this, the individual receives gross taxable income (such as interest and dividends) from other sources over $100, the individual must use a tax form (rather than his withholding receipt) as a basis of indicating tax liability.
         c. If an individual who may file a withholding receipt desires to do so and if his gross income does not exceed $5,000 he may file instead a tax return based on a "shortcut" method of determining tax which uses a tax table

---

[44] It may also be due in part to the political pressure which organized farm groups have been able to exercise in affecting the kind of current collection system which the Federal government has set up.

for incomes of varying size and varying numbers of personal exemptions. This table, which accompanies the tax form, allows for personal exemptions and for an assumed 10 per cent deduction from gross income.

   d. If he wishes, such an individual may ignore the tax table and file a full-length tax return. In this case, he lists all permitted deductions against income. This will be advantageous if his allowable deductions exceed the 10 per cent allowed by the tax table.

2. If wage-salary income in excess of $5,000 (plus $500 for each exemption) or income from other sources greater than $100 is anticipated, the taxpayer must file an advance declaration and pay estimated excess taxes over and above estimated taxes which will be withheld. If such excess was not anticipated, but actually is received after September 15 of a given year, an estimate must be made by January 15 of the following year, and any excess taxes over those withheld at source must be paid. (See description of the declaration system in the following sub-section.)

3. All final tax returns, in whatever form, are due by March 15 of the year following the receipt of income.

4. If any tax return indicates that amounts withheld, for instance for work during only part of the year, exceed the tax-free annual income permitted by personal exemptions and deductions, the individual is entitled to a tax refund, or to apply excess taxes paid against income-tax liability in the succeeding year.

5. Withholding of wage or salary income is not required for a few classes of workers, especially those engaged in agriculture, domestic service, or casual labor.

B. Under the system of income estimate (declaration) and current tax payments:

1. For individuals not engaged in agriculture:

   a. An individual not affected by withholding must file an advance declaration of anticipated income and tax liability by March 15 of the year in which income is being received if: (1) his gross income is expected to exceed $500, or (2) his income from sources other than wages or salary is expected to exceed $100.

   b. Under certain conditions explained above, an individual affected by the withholding process may still have to file a tax declaration by March 15 of the year in which income is being received.

c. For both classes of individuals, payment of one-quarter of any indicated tax liability (over and above amounts withheld) must be made on March 15, June 15, September 15, and on January 15 of the following year. At each of these dates after March 15, opportunity is given for an amended declaration of estimated annual income, and for adjustment of tax payments which may be indicated.

d. Final tax returns must be filed by both classes of individuals by March 15 of the year following receipt of income. Such returns may use the short-form tax return, with tax table, if adjusted gross income (gross income minus specified business expenses) does not exceed $5,000. For returns showing an adjusted gross income over $5,000, a detailed tax return, without use of the tax table, must be used. On such returns, personal deductions may be listed, or an optional standard deduction of $500 against income may be used.

2. For individuals engaged in agriculture:

a. Such individuals are defined as those persons who derive 80 per cent or more of their gross income from agricultural pursuits.

b. Unless such individuals expect to receive "outside" income from nonagricultural sources in excess of $100, they are not required to file an estimate of annual income (and tax liability) until January 15 of the year following the receipt of income. Any tax due on the basis of this estimate must be paid at this time. The January 15 estimate may also be made the final tax return, if the farmer desires, or a final return may be made by March 15.

c. Individuals engaged in agriculture have the same opportunity for use of the short-form tax return, with tax table, or for use of a full-length return, as do others who make tax returns. But businessmen engaged in farming are also required to fill out and append to the tax return a statement of farm income and expenses.

3. A system of penalties is provided by law to obtain the maximum accuracy in (adjusted) estimates of tax liability. This penalty is the lesser of:

a. 6 per cent of the excess of the final tax over the sum of (adjusted) estimated tax and tax withheld at source, or *b.* The excess of 80 per cent of the final tax (66⅔ per cent in the case of those engaged in agriculture) over the estimated tax.

    C. Informational returns are also required:

        1. From all employers engaged in withholding taxes from employees, information is required on the amount paid each employee during the year, his personal exemption status, and the amount of tax collected.

        2. From persons or corporations paying interest, dividends, and royalties, information is required as to the amount paid to each individual.

II. Collection of Tax:

    A. Each employer who withholds taxes on wages or salaries in excess of $100 is required to turn over funds collected to a depositary bank of the Federal government not more than ten days after the end of the month for which the tax was withheld.

    B. Individuals—except those engaged in agriculture—are required to make any additional tax payments (over and above withholding) indicated for a given year on March 15, June 15, and September 15 of that year, and by January 15 of the following year.

    C. Those engaged in agriculture are required to make estimated total tax payments for a given year by January 15 of the following year. They may pay this tax then, or by the following March 15.

III. Settlement of Tax Liability:

    A. Any taxpayer may make a final tax return by March 15 of the following year, by submitting his withholding receipt, using a tax return with a tax table, or a tax return without the use of a tax table, as the individual case may indicate.

    B. No matter what type of return may be used by the taxpayer, his final tax liability allows a personal exemption of $500 for himself and each dependent, deductions of 10 per cent of gross income up to $5,000 of (adjusted) gross income and permissive deductions above $5,000, with an option to take a standard deduction of $500, if the taxpayer desires.

    C. If the final tax return indicates that the taxpayer has made payments in excess of tax liabilities, tax refunds are due, or the refund may be applied against tax liability in the following year. If the final return indicates substantial understatement of annual tax liability by the taxpayer, penalties may be imposed. The outline of this penalty system has been given.

D. An important effect of the current-collection system has been
to bring most tax revenues for one income year into the hands
of the Treasury by March 15 of the following year. The final
tax return is now chiefly a means to settle accounts with the
government on taxes already paid, rather than to make the tax
return the occasion for the first payment (perhaps only a
portion) of tax liability on income of the preceding year.

Some Methods for Evading or Avoiding Federal Income Tax

Despite the conversion of the Federal income tax into a "mass"
tax which, in 1946, covered the majority of our income receivers,
some methods for avoiding or reducing the tax still remain.[45]
Some of the most important of these loopholes include tax-
exempt securities and taxes on capital gains on assets held until
after death of a taxpayer.

One of the most prominent methods of tax avoidance is the
reinvestment of corporate earnings to avoid payment of personal
income taxes. This loophole gave rise to a Federal tax on undistributed profits in 1936, which was sufficiently unpopular to
be repealed, effective in 1940. However, the desirability of
reaching undistributed profits through personal income taxation is
widely accepted by students of taxation, and proposals to inte-
grate corporate and personal income taxes have been widely
discussed in recent years. Consideration of the problem of undistributed corporate profits will be a major subject of Chapter
XV.

There are two other loopholes which will be mentioned. One
is the use of the trust fund and the other is the personal holding
company. It is legally possible for a taxpayer to create almost
any number of trust funds for the benefit of family members and
others. The taxpayer's income-yielding property is committed
to these trust funds, operated by trustees. These trustees, in
turn, make payments to beneficiaries of the trust funds according
to the provisions of varying agreements. By this device, it is
legally possible for an individual with a large income to split it
so successfully that he avoids progressive rates of the income tax,
yet may manage to retain working control over property which

---

[45] *Evasion* of tax occurs when a taxpayer fails to comply with the laws, as
when he fails to report a portion of taxable income. The primary check for
evasion is administrative vigilance. *Avoidance* occurs when the taxpayer has
made use of available legal loopholes to reduce or completely avoid the tax.

provides the basis of income for the trust funds. Equitably, the income of all such trust funds should be consolidated for purposes of a tax return by the creator of the trusts.

Another device which taxpayer ingenuity has produced is the personal holding company. Under this arrangement, if A received a large income, he incorporates a holding company, to which all his income-yielding property may be delegated. Without penalty restrictions, this company would not be subject to tax rates higher than those imposed on other corporations, which fall far below the top rates of the personal income tax.[46] Meanwhile, the incorporator may also be the sole owner of the company.

This method of tax avoidance has received special attention, and if legally held to be a personal holding company, such a corporation is now subject to almost confiscatory rates of tax. Under 1946 laws, if 50 per cent of a corporation's stock is owned, directly or indirectly, by not over five persons, and if 80 per cent or more of its income is derived from investments, it is considered a personal holding company. As such, it is subject to penalty tax rates (in addition to taxes applicable to ordinary corporations) of 75 per cent of undistributed income not over $2,000 and of 85 per cent of undistributed income in excess of $2,000. These provisions, together with refusal to permit foreign incorporation of a personal holding company (by resident taxpayers) to escape penalty rates on such holding companies, have been quite effective in reducing the importance of this particular loophole from personal income-tax liability.

State Income Taxes

Reference has already been made to the fact that, while 33 states (including the District of Columbia) made use of personal income taxation in 1946, tax revenues from this particular source were less than 7 per cent of total state tax revenues (page 245). A few additional comments on state income taxation will be made here. Such taxation really had a firm beginning with the adoption of the Wisconsin income tax in 1911. Such personal taxes were imposed by 15 states by 1930. The depression years of the early thirties gave a substantial push to the adoption

---

[46] Under 1946 Federal laws, the top corporation rate was 38 per cent, while the highest tax rate applicable to the income of an individual was 88.5 per cent on taxable net income over $200,000.

of the tax by more states, and by 1935, 27 of the 33 states which imposed such taxes in 1941 had begun such taxation.

Some of the states with largest incomes, such as Illinois and Pennsylvania, are among those which do not impose personal-income taxation. On the other hand, New York state alone collected half of all such tax revenue in 1941, the last prewar year. In 1946, despite wartime reduction in its income-tax rates, New York collected about 37.5 per cent of personal income-tax revenue. Four states (New York, California, Massachusetts, and Wisconsin) accounted for 71.9 per cent of total personal income-tax revenue in 1941 and for 62.5 per cent in 1946.

Income for purposes of state income taxation is defined in much the same way as for Federal taxation. Capital gains and losses for purposes of taxation are part of the tax base in all except three states (Iowa, South Dakota, and Maryland), although the methods used to apply income taxation in the area of capital gains and losses are varied, resembling changing Federal practices over a period of years. While the (1946) Federal law allowed no exemptions for income received from corporate cash dividends—paid out of corporate net income previously subject to Federal taxation—the practices of the states with respect to the treatment of corporate dividends received by individuals has been varied. For instance, in 1942, six states (Iowa, North Carolina, North Dakota, South Dakota, Vermont, and Virginia) permitted the exemption of corporate dividends paid out of (allocated) corporate income which had been used as the measure of the state corporation income-tax base. But this dividend credit was allowed only to the extent that the corporate income was taxed by the state.[47] Deductions of other taxes from gross income are permitted, as in the case of the Federal income tax. But Federal income taxes for the tax period preceding the filing of the state tax returns may be deducted, rather than state income taxes.[48] Unlike the Federal government, the states have

---

[47] For a summary on treatment of corporate dividends for personal income taxation by all income-taxing states in 1942, see Roy G. Blakey and Violet Johnson, *State Income Taxes*, pages 10-11, Chicago: Commerce Clearing House, Inc., 1942.

[48] The significance of reciprocal deduction of income taxes for the continuance of reasonable equity in Federal and state income taxes is discussed briefly in the following chapter. A few states with state income taxes do not permit deduction of Federal-tax liability; among them are two of the six most important state income-tax states, New York and California.

not moved toward current collection of income taxes, so that income received in one year is uniformly not reported for taxation until the following year.

Personal exemptions under state laws tended to follow Federal practices until 1941, although a few state personal exemptions were lower than prevailing Federal exemptions. Thus, in 1941, the most common personal exemptions for state income taxes were $1,000 for a single person, $2,500 for a head of family, and $400 for a dependent. These were the same as Federal exemptions for the income year 1940. State income-tax exemptions have not undergone much change since 1941, although Federal exemptions were reduced after 1940 and, in 1946, were uniformly $500 a person, including dependents.

Five states (Arizona, Iowa, Minnesota, South Dakota, and Wisconsin) use a system of "tax credits" to grant the personal exemptions which they give. Thus, in Iowa, the head of a family was (in 1942) allowed a tax credit against tax of $20. Under Iowa rates in 1942, this was equivalent to the personal exemption of $1,500. The tax-credit system has one main contrast with the more commonly used system of personal exemptions. Income-tax liability on *all* net income at the highest rate applicable is computed before the tax credit is allowed. With a progressive-rate structure, the application of the tax-credit system results in a somewhat larger tax for a net income of any given size than does the application of tax rates *after* a stated personal exemption has been deducted from net income.

Tax-rate structures under state income taxes have been progressive, but the progression has been moderate. In 1941, the tax rate on the first $1,000 of taxable income in most income-tax states was 1 per cent, and only four states (California, Minnesota, Wisconsin, and North Dakota) imposed tax rates which equaled or exceeded 10 per cent on the largest taxable incomes. The most severe rate applied was that of North Dakota—15 per cent on taxable net income over $15,000.

There are important problems of state income taxation relating to the application of tax to an individual residing in one state who receives his income from sources partly outside the state. Discussion of these interstate problems, however, is postponed until the final section of the book, which deals specifically with intergovernmental fiscal relations.

CHAPTER XIV

THE PERSONAL INCOME TAX II

IN THE previous chapter, some of the practices followed in personal income taxation in the United States were examined. This chapter is devoted to examining some of the problems associated with personal income taxation.

Reducing Discrimination Against Irregular Income

The discrimination of our existing income-tax system against fluctuating incomes is one of its most serious weaknesses. For example, if an individual's taxable income is $13,000 in each of 10 years, he will pay about 26 per cent less in taxes during the ten-year period than he would if his taxable income alternated between nothing and $26,000. Such a situation is undesirable, both from the standpoint of fairness (*equity*) and from the standpoint of the stimulation of incentives to undertake risky new enterprises. The penalty on fluctuating incomes arises from our failure to permit a carry forward of unused personal exemptions and of losses incurred in any one year.

The penalty on fluctuating income is made more severe because of increasing tax rates as income increases. Fluctuations in incomes are due to many factors, only a portion of which are fluctuations in business, employment, and national income. The more uncertain movements in our society become, the greater income fluctuations may be. If our tax system impinges severely on fluctuating income, it will also hamper processes of change and development of new enterprises in the economy.

One solution for reducing the tax discrimination against fluctuating income might be to make the tax base a simple moving average of annual incomes over a period of years. However, experience with such averaging, where it has been tried (for example, in Great Britain), has not proven satisfactory. A simple moving average which would smooth income would include in the tax base data which are several years old. It may shift the burden of a tax to a depression year, when income and taxable capacity may actually be very low. As an alternative, Professor Simons has suggested that a taxpayer be permitted to compute his average taxable income for some period of years (say five years), to determine what his total taxes would have been if his average income had been his actual income in each year, and then to claim a rebate if such taxes exceeded his five actual payments by more than a certain per cent (say 5 to 10 per cent). No one year could appear in more than one averaging computation.[1]

Another alternative is to make increased use of carry-forward provisions—to postpone until more prosperous years the tax liabilities which are incurred in low-income years. This implies tax payments in years of prosperity which are higher than they otherwise would be since such current payments would include taxes carried forward. Such tax policy would supplement tax flexibility gained by reduced rates in low-income years and higher rates in higher-income years. Although this procedure would have a more favorable impact upon markets than do existing procedures, it would not reduce the discrimination against fluctuating income. Furthermore, such a procedure would increase the complexity of a tax policy which also utilized refunds and flexibility in tax rates.

Professor Groves has suggested that, with our present broad income-tax base, such averaging (and refunds) might be limited to relatively large incomes—say over $5,000—and that for smaller incomes, a carry-over of unused personal exemptions and of losses might be allowed for a limited period, with no refunds. Such a system, he believes, would greatly reduce the tax discrimination against fluctuating income for all taxpayers. Admitting the difficulties in any system of averaging, he believes that attempts to refine income-tax procedure along the above lines would be worth a trial. He also believes that such a system should accom-

---

[1] Henry C. Simons, *Personal Income Taxation*, page 154, Chicago: University of Chicago Press, 1938. Simons points out that the percentage margin necessary to claim a rebate is introduced to keep the number of rebate claims down and that the exact percentage figure should be fixed with regard to questions of administrative cost. Considerations of simplicity also argue for the use of fixed periods, "opportunity to file claims being granted simultaneously to all taxpayers, say every fifth year."

pany any attempt to apply income taxation to capital gains and losses along the lines indicated in a subsequent section of this chapter.[2]

Capital gains and losses. At first glance, the problem of treating capital gains and losses for purposes of income taxation seems relatively simple. Thus, if an individual purchases 10 shares of stock for $1,000 and later sells them for $1,500, it would appear that his gain of $500 was an addition of $500 to his capital assets during the period in which he held the stock. It should be subject to taxation along with his other items of income. (Similarly a $500 loss should be deductible from income.) Yet problems arising in connection with capital gains and losses for income-tax purposes have been the source of continuous debate and of legislative experimentation since our income-tax system was established in this country. It is the purpose of this section to examine some of these problems.

The writers consider that a valid basis exists for including capital gains and losses in determining net income for taxation. However, it must be recognized that, as a matter of administration, a *realization* test—conversion of the asset into cash—is necessary before such gains and losses can be considered for tax purposes.[3] The writers believe that gains and losses included in the tax base should be consolidated with other sources of income in the tax base. Such treatment does not preclude attempts to allocate realized gains and losses on capital assets according to the period of time during which the asset may have been held.[4] It does imply that realized losses not deductible against capital gains or other income in a particular year may be carried forward and applied against income of future years, until such losses are "used up."

Such proposed treatment for capital gains and losses has never been fully incorporated in our Federal (or state) income-tax

[2] See Harold M. Groves, *Postwar Taxation and Economic Progress*, pages 227-236. These pages contain data on the quantitative significance of income fluctuations and of proposed rebates.

[3] Problems of equity in applying this realization test to capital assets held for varying lengths of time have caused much debate and various legislative changes in the application of income taxation to capital gains and losses in the United States.

[4] Attempts to do this have been made under the law, such as the Federal Revenue Act of 1934 (see Table 20) and proposals for such allocation not yet enacted into law have been made by various students of taxation.

laws.[5] But the Federal government and most of our 33 income-tax states (as of 1946) have been much more active in applying the income tax to capital gains and losses than have many foreign countries, such as Great Britain.[6] Acceptance of equality in the method of treatment for gains and losses is important if private investors are to be encouraged to assume risks on long-term investments in new enterprises. Along with such treatment should go provisions for mitigating fluctuations in taxable income from all sources, as well as an over-all tax structure which will be favorable to private enterprise.[7]

As an introduction to some of the issues connected with capital gains and losses in income taxation, several things may be pointed out:[8] (1) Capital gains have provided a minor source of total individual income in the economy. Nevertheless, they have provided a substantial, but very unstable, portion of total income-tax revenues. (2) While capital gains are received by a relatively small number of taxpayers, they are often an important source of income for particular taxpayers. (3) Capital gains tend to be concentrated in the higher-income groups and to be taxed at relatively low maximum rates, while capital losses are concentrated in smaller incomes.[9] Having capital gains puts people higher on the income scale than they otherwise would be. (4) Our tax policy, particularly since 1933, of allowing deductions of capital losses only against capital gains (plus $1,000 to $2,000 in excess of such gain), has kept many of these losses out of Federal tax returns, so that statistical evidence on total capital losses is not

[5] Equality in method of treatment for all gains and losses was granted for Federal taxation only for income years 1918 through 1921. Even during this period, the carry-over of unused losses was limited to one year.

[6] Neither Iowa, South Dakota, nor Maryland recognize capital gains and losses for income-tax purposes. The British have consistently held that capital gains and losses are not income. Nevertheless, they have reduced the number of types of transactions from which capital gains or losses can be said to arise. The result has been to introduce a degree of arbitrariness in the definition of capital gains and losses which it is difficult to defend. For summary and criticism of the British practices, see R. M. Haig, "Taxation of Capital Gains," six articles in the *Wall Street Journal* (March and April, 1937).

[7] Comment on these accompanying features of the tax structure in so far as they pertain to other taxes, will be made in subsequent chapters.

[8] Most of these have been emphasized by Professor Harold M. Groves in his recent book, *Postwar Taxation and Economic Progress*, Chapter 8, pages 206-223.

[9] See *Statistics of Income for 1942, Part I,* pages 25-36 for statistical evidence on this and preceding statement.

available.[10] (5) Capital assets were first recognized as a separate class of asset by the Revenue Act of 1921. An increasingly large number of capital assets have been excluded from special taxation by revenue acts. Such items are treated as other items of income for tax purposes.

The *TNEC* study covering the years 1918 through 1937 estimated that realized gains and losses were only 1 to 2 per cent of total individual incomes over this period. Only in years of great prosperity and of great depression did such gains and losses approach substantial percentages of total individual incomes.[11] Nevertheless, under our (Federal) tax laws, taxation of net capital gains provided 15.2 per cent of total individual income-tax revenue from 1926 through 1940. In 1928, nearly half the income-tax revenue came from capital gains. In 1931, however, income-tax revenues would have been one-third greater had deduction of net capital losses from net taxable income not been permitted.[12]

While capital gains provide a minor source of income for the economy, and are received by relatively few individuals, nevertheless such gains are often an important source of income for particular individuals. On Federal income-tax returns for the income year 1936, capital gains were 26.2 per cent of the total net income of those who reported net capital gains.[13] Since capital gains tend to be concentrated in higher-income brackets, and were taxed at relatively low "ceiling" rates (while capital losses exceeded capital gains in lower-income brackets), the "effective" tax rates—ratio of total tax to total net income—of the

[10] Although estimates, based primarily on *Treasury Statistics of Income,* have been made. See Temporary National Economic Committee, "Concentration and Composition of Individual Incomes, 1918-1937," Monograph 4, pages 37-40. Washington, D. C.: United States Government Printing Office, 1941.

[11] In 1928, net gains were estimated to be 5.6 per cent of total individual incomes and in 1931, net losses were placed at 4.7 per cent. See *TNEC* monograph, *ibid.,* pages 37-40.

[12] These figures were derived from data presented by the Treasury to the Ways and Means Committee of the House of Representatives on March 30, 1942. See H. R. 6358, Exhibit 3, of the Treasury Department. It has been pointed out that, because of limited deduction for capital losses permitted from 1934 to 1947, it is impossible to say what the ratio of gains and losses to total revenues would have otherwise been.

[13] See study of capital gains and losses on all Federal income-tax returns for 1936 conducted by the Treasury Department, Division of Tax Research, working with the WPA.

recent war period were actually much lower for large incomes than the "nominal" ceiling rates imposed by the tax-rate structure. Thus, Groves has shown that the top effective rate on a million-dollar income in 1944—of which over a third was typically capital gains—was not really 90 per cent (as set by law) during the war period, but about 70.9 per cent.[14]

The varying treatments which have been given capital gains and losses make it impossible to give a statistical summary of what realized gains and losses actually have been during the income-tax period. This is more true of losses than of gains, since not all losses could be deducted from income while all gains had to be reported. It is even impossible to say what taxes from such capital items might have been if losses and gains had been treated similarly during the income-tax period. Neither is it known to what degree realization (sale of the asset) itself has been affected by the tax rate.

It is not possible to take firm hold on the problems arising in connection with capital gains and losses for tax purposes unless we have some idea of the ways in which capital assets have been defined for taxation during our income-tax period, and some knowledge of the principal ways in which we have treated capital assets for tax purposes under our income-tax laws. Turning first to the definition of capital assets, we find that the concept of capital assets for taxation (1) is quite different from the most widely accepted concepts of capital in either economics or accounting, and that (2) the definition of capital assets for tax purposes has become increasingly restricted with the passage of time.

Prevailing accounting practice is to consider as capital assets only "fixed assets"—tangible and intangible assets, more or less permanent in their nature, which aid production and sales. Tangible assets commonly included are: land, machinery, tools, furniture and fixtures, and equipment; intangible assets generally include: patents, copyrights, trade-marks, and goodwill. In economics, consumers' durable goods as well as the various producers' goods listed above are generally called capital assets.

Beginning with a broad, if somewhat hazy, concept of gains and losses including most of the assets listed above, Federal Revenue Acts have gradually delimited the legal meaning of capital assets until, in 1946, such assets included only the following: (1)

---

[14] See Groves, *Postwar Taxation and Economic Progress*, page 183.

stocks and bonds, (2) real estate not used in the trade or business,[15] (3) intangible business assets not subject to depreciation under tax laws, such as trade-marks and goodwill, (4) gains on the sale of property held for consumption purposes (such as a residence), (5) miscellaneous transactions carried on with the intent of speculating. Gains and losses from the sale of securities or real estate represent most gains and losses from capital transactions for tax purposes.

The process of delimiting the sphere of capital gains and losses for tax purposes is summarized in Table 19. Here only the main developments will be summarized:

1. Up until the Revenue Act of 1921, the Federal income tax did not specifically recognize capital assets as a distinct type of asset. Gains and losses from all sources except transactions in consumption goods were included in the income base.[16]

2. The Revenue Act of 1921 first formally defined capital assets, and specifically excluded property held for the personal use of the taxpayer (such as a house or automobile), as well as property normally included in the inventory of the taxpayer at the end of the taxable year (such as stock-in-trade).

3. The Revenue Act of 1934 gave a more formal statement of the exclusion of goods held as stock-in-trade, or primarily for sale to customers. It also specifically included gains on the sale of (durable) consumption goods (such as sale of a residence) in the tax base, although it declined to recognize realized losses on such property.

4. The Revenue Act of 1938 excluded property subject to depreciation from capital assets if used in the trade or business. This provision excluded such items as business buildings, machinery, and patents from treatment as capital assets, although net gains from the sale of such items remained taxable, under full income-tax rates.

5. The Revenue Act of 1942 excluded all real property used in the trade or business from capital assets (such as farm land), and subjected net gains from sales of such property to full income-tax rates. (Real estate held less than six months is included as a capital asset under the Revenue Act of 1943.)

[15] Profits and losses from the sale of real estate used in the taxpayer's business were excluded from capital gains and losses only if the real estate had been held less than 6 months. (1946 law.)

[16] The Revenue Acts of 1916 and 1918 did include the existence of gains and losses from transactions outside the taxpayer's business. The 1918 Act permitted losses to be deducted from income of any kind.

TABLE 19

The Definition of Capital Assets for Purposes of Federal Income Tax,
1913-1946

I. There was no formal definition of capital assets until the Revenue Act of
1921. For earlier years:
  A. Gains on sale of capital assets were treated like other income.
  B. Under the Revenue Act of 1913, effective through the income year
     1915, net losses could not be deducted against capital gains nor other
     income, and could not be carried forward.
  C. For the income years 1916 and 1917, all capital losses could be de-
     ducted against capital gains. Stock dividends were made taxable at
     their cash value. (Such taxation was held unconstitutional in 1920.)
  D. For the income years 1918 through 1921, capital losses could be de-
     ducted against income of any kind, with a one-year carry-over of any
     unused loss.

II. Under the Revenue Act of 1921, effective for the income years 1922 and
1923:
  A. Capital assets were made to include property acquired and held by the
     taxpayer for profit or investment for more than two years, whether or
     not connected with the business, but not property held for the personal
     use of the taxpayer or property of a type which would properly be in-
     cluded in inventory at the end of the taxable year.
  B. Realized gains and losses on assets held less than two years were also
     made subject to taxation (see Table 20).

III. Under the Revenue Act of 1934, effective for the income years 1934 through
1937:
  A. The definition of capital assets does not differ materially from that
     given under the 1921 act, except that gains on assets held for consump-
     tion purposes were made subject to taxation, although losses on such
     property were not made deductible.
  B. For treatment of capital assets held for varying periods of time, see
     Table 20.

IV. Under the Revenue Act of 1938, effective for the income years 1938-1939,
the definition of capital assets for taxation was substantially narrowed:
  A. Property subject to (legal) depreciation and used in the trade or busi-
     ness was excluded from the definition of capital assets.
  B. The effect of this provision was to exclude from taxation as capital
     assets such items as business buildings, machinery and equipment, and
     patents. Capital assets for taxation were confined mainly to securi-
     ties, land, and transactions carried on with the purpose of speculation.

V. Under the Revenue Act of 1942, effective in 1943, the scope of capital
assets for taxation was further narrowed:
  A. Real property used in the trade or business was excluded from capital
     assets, except that
    1. Gains and losses on real estate used in the taxpayer's business were
       excluded from capital assets only if such real estate had been held
       less than six months.
    2. Gains and losses on property not defined as capital assets are con-
       solidated with other income for purposes of taxation.

Apart from the legal definition of capital assets, the question of treating realized gains and losses from such assets for taxation has been a source of almost continuous disagreement, and of many alterations, as the summary in Table 20 indicates. The simplicity and equity of a plan which taxes gains at full income-tax rates, and permits deduction of realized losses against other income, with a carry-over of unused loss deductions to future years (until fully deducted), seems obvious as a first choice. In order to avoid discrimination against income from capital gains, averaging of income for tax purposes would be necessary.

Three methods of treating capital gains and losses for income-tax purposes have been (1) to classify gains according to length of time held, allowing deduction of losses only against gains of a similar class; (2) to tax capital gains, with full allowance of losses against gains and other income, although with a very limited carry-over period of unused losses (as in the income years 1918 through 1921); (3) to treat capital gains like other income with no, or limited, deduction for losses. Valuation of the gains and losses that were dependent on length of time the capital assets were held by the taxpayer first appeared in the Revenue Act of 1934 and the principle was retained under the 1946 law. Application of relatively low maximum rates for taxation of capital gains was in effect between 1922 and 1933 (inclusive), and from 1938 to the present time. Carry-forward periods for "unused" losses in any given year have varied from nothing to five years.

Under the present law, capital assets are divided into two classes, those held six months or less (short-term) and those held over six months (long-term). Short-term gains are taxed at full income-tax rates. Long-term gains may either be reduced to 50 per cent for income-tax purposes and included with other income, or may be taxed at a maximum effective rate of 25 per cent. Losses are given similar treatment except that—whether long-term or short-term—they may be deducted from capital gains in full, and other income up to a maximum of $1,000 and "unused" losses may be carried forward for a maximum period of five years. It is clear that present laws give relatively favorable treatment to taxpayers with relatively large incomes and with substantial capital gains (the 1946 law benefited taxpayers with taxable net income including net capital gains when such income exceeded $16,000).

TABLE 20

Summary of Provisions for Reporting Capital Gains and Losses Under the
Federal Income Tax, 1913-1946

I. Income Years 1913-1915
    A. Capital gains were treated like other income.
    B. Capital losses were not deductible.

II. Income Year 1916
    A. Capital gains were treated like other income.
    B. Capital losses were deductible against gains to the extent of such
    gains.
       1. The 1916 Act broadened the concept of deductible losses to in-
       clude losses incurred in transactions not connected with the trade
       or business, as well as losses connected with trade or business.
       2. Capital gains (or losses) from sale of property acquired before
       March 1, 1913, were to be determined by the fair market price or
       value of the property on March 1, 1913 (whichever was greater).
       3. Until 1924, the law made no distinction between current ordinary
       losses and losses from sales of capital gains.
       4. Stock dividends were made taxable at cash value (until held un-
       constitutional in 1920).

III. Income Years 1918-1921
    A. Capital gains were treated like other income.
    B. Capital losses were allowed in full against income of any kind.
       1. Losses could be allowed even if not charged off within the year.
       If the loss exceeded the income for the year, the excess might be
       deducted in computing the tax for the next year.

IV. Income Years 1922-1923
    A. For assets held two years or less: (such assets were not defined as
    capital assets).
       1. Gains: Included with other income subject to full rates.
       2. Losses: Allowed in full against other income, but not against capi-
       tal gains (on assets held over two years).
    B. For assets held over two years:
       1. Gains: At option of taxpayer, capital net gains were taxable at
       $12\frac{1}{2}\%$ in lieu of other income tax, except that the total tax (in-
       cluding tax on net capital gains) could not be less than $12\frac{1}{2}\%$ of
       total net income.
       2. Losses: Allowed in full against income of any kind.
    C. A carry-over of net losses for two years was granted.

V. Income Years 1924-1931
    A. For assets held two years or less:
       1. Gains: Same as 1921 Act.
       2. Losses: Allowed in full against income of any kind.
    B. For assets held over two years:
       1. Gains: Same as 1921 Act.
       2. Losses: Could be segregated from ordinary net income, and a tax
       credit of $12\frac{1}{2}\%$ of the capital net loss could be taken.
    C. Carry-over of losses granted.

TABLE 20 (*continued*)

VI. Income Years 1932-1933

    A. For assets held two years or less:

        1. Gains: Same as 1924 Act.

        2. Losses: (*a*) Losses from sales or exchanges of stocks and bonds were limited to gains from such sales. (*b*) Other losses were allowed in full against income of any kind. (*c*) Carry-over of short-term losses was abolished.

    B. For assets held over two years:

        1. Provisions remained same as for 1924 Act.

VII. Income Years 1934-1937

    A. The special 12½% rate (option) was abolished, and a system of percentage gains subject to taxation at the following rates was inaugurated:

        1. Where asset was held one year or less.......100%

        2. Where asset was held over 1, not over 2..... 80

        3. Where asset was held over 2, not over 5..... 60

        4. Where asset was held over 5, not over 10.... 40

        5. Where asset was held over 10............. 30

    B. For losses (with Act of 1934): Deduction of losses, on basis of foregoing percentages, allowed against gains plus $2,000 in computing net income; no carry-over.

VIII. Income Years 1938-1941 (Revenue Act of 1938)

    A. Three percentage classes for gains or losses were now established instead of the previous five:

        1. For assets held 18 months or less...........100%

        2. For assets held more than 18 months but not more than 24 months.................. 66⅔

        3. For assets held over 24 months............. 50

    B. For assets held 18 months or less:

        1. Gains: To extent not offset by allowed losses, subject to full tax rates.

        2. Losses: Allowed only against gains on similar transactions, with a one-year carry-over, $2,000 net loss allowance eliminated.

    C. For assets held more than 18 months:

        1. Gains: Net gains computed on basis of foregoing percentages may be included with other income, or segregated and taxed at 30%, whichever method resulted in smaller total tax.

        2. Losses: Net losses on basis of foregoing percentages may be deducted from other income or 30% of such losses may be credited against tax computed on net income before loss deduction, whichever gave larger tax. Net loss deduction against other income (than capital gains) was limited to $2,000.

        3. The 30% tax was not computed on the total amount of such gain, but on the fraction of the taxable gain. The tax could not exceed (therefore) 20% of the actual gain in case of assets held 18 months to 2 years, and 15% in case of assets held over two years. Similarly, the maximum loss deduction was either 20% or 15%.

        4. The $2,000 net loss allowance against other income was retained.

        5. Carry-over: none.

TABLE 20 (*continued*)

IX. Income Years 1942 to 1947

   A. Capital assets are now divided into two classes: Those held over 6 months, those held less.

   B. For assets held six months or less, all gains are included in taxable income; for losses, they may be offset against gains with offset against other income up to $1,000 (unless net income without such losses is less than $1,000).

   C. For assets held over six months: there is taxation of 50% of gains at maximum rate of 50%; a ceiling rate of 25% of gains. Losses may be applied against gains, whether short- or long-term (but long-term losses must be computed on a 50% basis), plus "ordinary" income up to $1,000).

   D. Any net loss carry-over—whether of short- or long-term losses—becomes a carry-over for the following five years against any future capital gains, and against other income up to $1,000 in each year (or against net income smaller than $1,000).

   E. Up until 1942, the gain realized by a stockholder on redemption by the corporation was arbitrarily a short-term gain; such gain is now classified as to time and treated as any other capital gain.

   F. Net capital gain for any one year is the excess of capital gains plus "ordinary" net income (adjusted gross income if Supplement Table T is used) up to $1,000, whichever is smaller, over capital losses.

Methods for treatment of capital assets for tax purposes have naturally shifted over the years with shifts in the relative influence of those influencing tax legislation. Thus, the Federal government, interested in tax revenue, has often favored limitations on loss deductions.[17] This attitude is especially evident in the stringent limitations on loss deductions prevalent since the Revenue Act of 1934 (see Table 2). Again, taxpayers have often argued that, under a progressive income tax, assets held for long periods of time should be given relatively favorable treatment. For example, a realized gain may result from an accrual over a relatively long period of time, so that taxation with a progressive-tax structure of the entire gain in a particular year might well result in overtaxation. (Logically, the same reasoning holds for deduction of capital losses.) This system of taxing capital gains (and deducting losses) on a declining percentage basis was embodied in the Revenue Act of 1934, and remains today in a more simplified form.

Again, it has been argued that the possibility of capital gains is sufficiently important as an incentive to business enterprise so

---

[17] This attitude also conforms roughly to that of those who regard the purchase and sale of capital assets as essentially speculative transactions which ought to be penalized.

that especially low maximum rates should be applied to the taxation of such gains. Such treatment was given from 1922 through 1933, and from 1938 to the present. The writers' point of view with respect to tax treatment of gains and losses has been stated previously. Such treatment might weight gains and losses as taxable income according to the length of time the asset has been held.

Proposals to give more favorable tax treatment to gains and losses which result from assets held for varying periods of time have been written into our income-tax laws since the Revenue Act of 1934. Under this act (see Table 20), the percentage of gain or loss included for taxation declined from 100 per cent where an asset had been held less than one year to 30 per cent where the asset had been held over 10 years. The use of a percentage system can be defended where there is a progressive-tax structure, although systems of percentages written into law have been somewhat arbitrary. Less arbitrary is the proposal that, in the year when the capital gain or loss is realized: (1) the total gain or loss should be divided by the number of years during which the asset has been held by the seller, (2) one year's portion of the gain or loss so determined should be included with the seller's other net income in the year of sale, (3) the prevailing marginal tax rate applicable to the taxpayer on his entire taxable net income in the year of sale (so determined) should be applied to the balance of the gain or loss.[18]

The proposals for treatment of capital gains and losses which the writers have advocated would be an improvement upon present practices, but by themselves would not be sufficient. For one thing, the present system of permitting capital gains to be canceled at the time of a taxpayer's death (or through gifts) needs revision. Transfers by gift and at death should be treated as "realizations" at the time of transfer, on the basis of current market values.[19] Only in this way is it possible that all corporate income, much of which, when undistributed, is the basis for appreciation in the value of corporate securities, will be taxed as personal income. Such a change would partly answer the claim that taxation of capital gains at full personal income-tax rates

[18] This proposal was outlined by Harold M. Groves in *Proceedings of the National Tax Association*, page 124, 1939.

[19] The present basis for taxing such assets received is the value existing at the time of transfer, and not cost to the donor or deceased.

would sharply reduce the exchanges of investment capital. The possibility of wiping out capital gains at time of death is unquestionably one important factor that discourages the exchange of capital assets under our existing tax provisions. Willingness to make exchanges also depends in part on the tax-rate schedule which exists. It may be that a broadly based income tax would make desirable and possible a lower tax-rate structure, particularly for incomes of intermediate size (say between $10,000 and $100,000) than we now have.[20] Finally, no proposal for revision of our system of treating capital gains and losses for income taxation can neglect the desirability of mitigating fluctuations in income over a period of years (by some system of averaging).

It might be costly to collect some taxes on capital gains if such gains were taxed at the same rates as other income. High rates, applicable to some capital gains, might make the reporting of such gains unreliable. If experience demonstrated that high rates encouraged widespread evasion in the taxation of capital gains, it might be more equitable to tax these gains at lower rates than to tax heavily an honest minority who reported all their gains, while other taxpayers escaped.

Tax-Exempt Securities

One of the major items of income excluded from income taxation by one level of government (such as state and local governments) is the interest on securities issued by other levels of government (such as the Federal government). Quantitatively, the percentage of publicly held Federal securities outstanding which were partially or wholly exempt from Federal income taxation on June 30, 1945, was relatively small, being only 11.7 per cent (24.1 billion dollars out of 205.9 billion).[21] But such securities are wholly exempt from state and local income or property taxation. In addition, there were outstanding on the same date about 16.5 billion dollars of state and local securities entirely exempt from income taxation by either Federal or state governments.

The issues connected with tax exemption are complex, but it will be argued in this section that tax exemption should be abolished because it (1) tends to nullify the progressive rates of our

---

[20] See discussion in final section of this chapter.
[21] As of March, 1941, the Federal government ceased to issue additional securities not subject to Federal income tax.

income tax, and to undermine the ability-to-pay principle of taxation, (2) tends to interfere with the normal flow of investments, and (3) results in a net loss of revenue to government units as a whole.

Tax-exempt securities have become part of our investment pattern in the United States for two main reasons. First, by reason of constitutional interpretation, the taxation of the instrumentalities of one sovereign unit of government by another has been forbidden since 1819.[22] Second, government units have issued tax-exempt securities for the purpose of securing lower interest rates and a broader market for their securities.

Turning to the simplest of the main issues connected with tax exemption, it might appear that the loss in revenue from not taxing the interest from government securities would be exactly offset by the lower interest rates (cost of borrowing) paid by government units. However, for government units in the aggregate, lower interest rates probably do not offset the loss in revenues. The interest rate may need to be high enough to attract marginal buyers, to whom the tax-exemption privilege may mean little. The incomes of some of these buyers may be so small that the tax rate is small. Hence, the saving from tax exemption is negligible. This will tend to keep up the interest rate when a se-

[22] The constitutional decision which has governed this policy was made by the Supreme Court in McCulloch vs. Maryland in 1819. (4 Wheaton, 431-36, 1819) Taxation of the incomes of state and local government employees was initiated by the Federal government in 1939 and has since been continued. At the same time, the states began to tax incomes of Federal employees. The constitutionality of such (nondiscriminatory) taxation has been upheld. A definite constitutional basis for such taxation by the Federal government was clearly established by the 16th Amendment, which authorized the taxation of income from all sources. There are many who feel that similar reciprocal taxation, of a nondiscriminatory type, would also be constitutionally upheld if applied to income from government securities. It has already been pointed out that the Federal government no longer issues securities exempt from Federal taxation. It should also be pointed out that government securities are not exempt from all taxes under all circumstances. Thus (1) one state can tax its residents on the income or property value of securities which it may issue and on securities issued by other states or by local governments; (2) tax-exempt securities may be included in the gross estate for purposes of computing death taxes—the tax is considered to be on the privilege of transfer; (3) the income from tax-exempt securities may be included under state corporation-income taxes set up as franchise taxes measured by net income. As of 1942, all personal-income tax states taxed the income from obligations of other states and the political subdivisions of these states. As to obligations of the home state, 9 states taxed the obligations, 24 did not. 12 states taxed the interest on obligations of their own political subdivisions. Treatment of interest on Federal-state-local obligations under state corporation-income taxes showed considerable diversity.

curity issue is of sufficient size to require a considerable number of small income buyers, such as United States savings bonds. As a corollary, whether the amount of securities issued is large or small, the progressive character of our income-tax structure (together with the fact that purchases of government securities are typically in many income groups) permits recipients of large incomes to avoid taxation by *some* net amount. Thus, the Treasury has shown that an individual who purchased $100,000 of 4 per cent tax-exempt bonds in 1942 had an equivalent return to that of a taxable security of 33⅓ per cent.[23]

A net loss in revenue is more easily demonstrable for the Federal than for state and local governments, due to the more steeply progressive rate structure of the Federal income tax. In 1942 the Treasury estimated its annual fiscal loss from tax-exempt state and local securities at $275,000,000. The Federal government has little gain from its own borrowing with which to offset this loss, since no Federal securities have been issued exempt from Federal taxes since March, 1941. As of June 30, 1945, Federal securities publicly held which were partially or wholly exempt from Federal taxes were only about 24.1 billion dollars, as compared with 12.9 billions of state and local securities privately held. This was a relatively small figure compared with the more than 181 billion dollars of Federal publicly held marketable debt outstanding on this date.

Local governments probably enjoy a net gain from tax exemption. Not only are their own securities typically exempt from their own local taxes, and often from taxes of their own state government, but their securities are exempt from the relatively high rates of the Federal income tax. The result is probably a broader market for their securities and a decrease in interest rates which they have to pay. From a tax standpoint, reciprocal taxation of securities by Federal, state, and local governments would be of little advantage to local governments, whose percentage of

[23] See *Hearings on Revenue Revision of 1942*, statements of the Treasury Department before the Ways and Means Committee of the House of Representatives, Vol. 3, April 16, 1942, pages 3079 and 3087. To express the advantage differently suppose that Individual X with a taxable net income of $100,000 in 1942, derived $4,000 income from investments of $100,000 in taxable securities. At 1942 rates, this $4,000 was subject to a top-bracket tax of $3,320 (83%). Assume that X shifted his $100,000 into tax-exempt securities, with an interest rate of 3 per cent. His loss in interest income would have been $1,000, against a former tax of $3,320, with a net saving of $2,320.

total state and local debt in 1945 was over 85 per cent. These units of government would have little tax compensation for the higher interest rates which they would have to pay since they do not utilize the income tax, except in a few cases, and do not rely heavily on taxation of intangible property.

The net gain or loss to state governments from tax exemption depends upon comparative Federal and state income-tax rates and upon the ratio of publicly held Federal securities to state securities. The 33 state governments which use the income tax have relatively modest rate structures as compared with the Federal government. Except in four instances (California, Minnesota, Wisconsin, and North Dakota) tax rates in 1941 did not go above 10 per cent, as compared with 81 per cent for the Federal government in the same year. Even the top rate did not exceed 15 per cent of net income. Under such comparative rate structures, state governments using the income tax would gain much less in revenues from taxation of interest from Federal securities than the Federal government would gain from taxation of the same amount of interest from state securities. However, the extremely high ratio of publicly held Federal securities to state securities more than offsets this comparative disadvantage. On June 30, 1945, total state debt outstanding (less sinking-fund assets held by the states) was only about 1.8 billion dollars. At the same time, publicly held Federal debt totaled about 237.6 billions. Given such a differential in outstanding debt, the states lose a considerable amount by the continuance of reciprocal exemption. As long as their "effective" tax rate is at least .76 per cent ($\frac{1}{132}$) as high as that of the Federal government, the states in the aggregate stand to gain from discontinuing reciprocal exemption.

In terms of generally accepted concepts of equity, nothing can be said for the continuance of tax exemption. It has already been pointed out that individuals with large incomes are able to reduce their tax liabilities by investing in tax-exempt securities. This tends to nullify the progressive tax rates of our income-tax system, and is clearly contrary to application of the ability-to-pay principle of taxation.[24] On another count, tax exemption inter-

[24] At the same time, it is only fair to point out that, from the most recent data available, individuals do not own the bulk of government securities which are partially or entirely tax exempt. As of June 30, 1945, more than half was held by commercial banks, insurance companies, and other corporations. Most of these

feres with the flow of new investment vital to the maintenance of an enterprise system. Individuals who would otherwise assume risk-bearing investments are now able to obtain a relatively safe and profitable haven from risk-assumption through holding tax-exempt securities. With respect to the various social disadvantages of tax exemption which stand out, "exemption does things which would seem preposterous if done straight-forwardly," as Professor Simons has pointed out.[25]

Various solutions for the tax-exemption problem have been offered. A Constitutional Amendment providing for reciprocal, nondiscriminatory taxation by the Federal government and by state and local governments has been suggested by some writers. This solution can probably be dismissed as very improbable of acceptance. It is unlikely that, with the benefits of tax exemption which accrue particularly to local governments, such an amendment would be adopted without an extended period of education on the disadvantages of tax exemption. Another proposal is that various units of government cease issuing securities exempt from taxes and that, with respect to securities already outstanding, holders of such securities should be paid annually the difference between the yield of tax-exempt securities and taxable securities of similar degree of risk until such time as existing tax-exempt securities are retired.

This "bonus" idea has no serious objection in principle (although the difficulties of ascertaining the yield-differences as basis for such bonuses would be great) if it were actually a sure step toward abolition of tax-exempt securities. It is true that, the Federal government has already ceased issuing securities which are exempt from its own taxes, and that less than 12 per cent of outstanding, publicly held Federal securities carried partial or complete income-tax exemption from Federal taxes as of June 30, 1945. It is unlikely, however, that local units of government, in particular, will abandon the practice of selling securities which are exempt from local taxes or that all states will begin to tax the securities of their own subdivisions.

---

securities would become subject to some forms of Federal, state, and local taxation, but at rates far below the top rates applicable under Federal and state income taxes for individuals. Source: *Annual Report,* U. S. Secretary of the Treasury, 1945.

[25] See Henry C. Simons, *Personal Income Taxation,* pages 178-179, Chicago: University of Chicago Press, 1938.

It is unrealistic to expect that the issue of new securities exempt from their own taxes will be abandoned by all local and by state governments in any future period which can now be foreseen. About the most that can reasonably be expected in the reduction of tax exemption is that the reciprocal and nondiscriminatory taxation of Federal securities by state and local governments and of state and local securities by the Federal government will be initiated and upheld as constitutional. Along with this, it is to be hoped that the present Federal practice of selling no additional securities exempt from Federal taxes will be followed gradually by the adoption of similar practices by state and local governments with respect to their own securities. Quantitively, the percentage of public debt outstanding which is Federal debt —about 94 per cent in June, 1945—is so large that the relative magnitude of the tax-exemption problem is much less than a few years ago. The small and declining percentage of Federal debt which is exempt (in part or in whole) from Federal taxes makes this especially true.

Other Important Problems in Income-Tax Policy

If adjustments in our personal income taxes were made which would improve the treatment of capital gains and losses for tax purposes, mitigate the discriminatory effects of fluctuations in income, and eliminate tax exemption, in so far as is possible, some of the major defects in our present income taxes would be greatly reduced. There remain a number of other problems which deserve brief attention.

Integration of personal and corporate taxation. Not until our personal and corporate taxes are so set up that a much larger proportion of our taxes are paid through personal income taxes than now occurs will it be possible to make a really close approach to the ability-to-pay principle of taxation through personal taxation. Solution of this problem might require a very high undistributed-profits tax on corporations. It also may be possible that less reliance on business taxes as such is the most practicable approach to ability-to-pay taxation. In any event, such changes would require a closer integration of corporate and of personal income taxation than is now achieved.

Coordination of Federal and state income taxes. Despite the relatively small portion of our income-tax revenue that comes from state income taxes, it is probable that greater coordination of Federal and state income taxes will be necessary in the future in the interest of simplicity and the maximum success for the use of the personal income tax as the major tax in the tax system. Achieving greater coordination of these taxes will be part of the subject matter of the final section of the book, but two related facts may be pointed out here. On the one hand, the Federal government permits deduction of state income taxes for purposes of determining net income and (in 1942), 25 out of 33 income-tax states (including the District of Columbia) also permitted deduction of Federal taxes for state income-tax purposes.[26] Reciprocal deduction assures that no combination of Federal and state income taxes will actually confiscate income for tax purposes. On the other hand, the need for greater coordination can be seen from the actions of state and Federal governments during the recent war period. While the Federal government was endeavoring to check inflation through fiscal policy, including high income-tax rates, several states used the period of large tax revenues to reduce their income taxes.[27]

Taxation on non-money ("imputed") income. An attempt should be made to tax substantial elements of real income that now escape the tax base. Taxation of such income would expand the tax base and make possible a reduction in marginal tax rates required to collect a given amount of revenue. Favorable effects upon incentives might be the result.

It is recognized that not all imputed income could equitably be made subject to taxation and that an arbitrary line must be drawn somewhere. Thus, it would clearly be unfair to tax one housewife who did all her own work more than another housewife who hired part of her work done—unless it was desired to penalize industry. When probable administrative problems are added to tax equity in this field of human endeavor, we have a good illustration of an area to which it is not desirable to extend the income tax. Nevertheless, there are at least two types of imputed income which probably should be in our income-tax base. One is the value of products grown and consumed on farms, estimated to be about 2.14 billion dollars or 8.7 per cent of gross

[26] Massachusetts is not included, because it permits the deduction of certain items reported for Federal income tax, and not of others.

[27] For example, New York reduced its personal income-tax rates effective on 1942 income while Iowa reduced rates effective on 1943 income.

income from agriculture (including government payments) in 1945.[28] The other is the net rental value of owner-occupied homes, estimated to total about 1.9 billion dollars in 1940.[29]

The reporting of products consumed on the farm would depend largely on the honesty of the taxpayer, but the accumulation of information on such income by the Bureau of Agricultural Economics and other government agencies suggests that a reasonable estimate of the value of such produce could be assigned for farms of a given type and with various numbers in families. The taxpayer could always be given an opportunity to make a sufficiently complete declaration of products grown and consumed at home to prove that the arbitrary figure was too high.

Inclusion of the rental value of owner-occupied homes has a precedent in British income-tax practice. If it proved administratively difficult and expensive to check such values as were included, an arbitrary value could be assigned by tax administrators, as in the case of farm-grown and consumed produce, subject to the desire of the taxpayer to take sufficient time to demonstrate that his assigned rental value was too high. At the very least, it would appear that deduction of property taxes from gross income for income-tax purposes should not be permitted.

Exemptions and deductions. The reasons for the use of personal exemptions in our income-tax systems are partly economic, partly administrative, partly political. From an economic viewpoint, there is merit in sufficient exemption from taxation to maintain working health and efficiency of the taxpayer. This also means that the amount exempted must be allowed to vary with the number of dependents, the majority of whom will themselves become the income-earners of tomorrow. Furthermore, the exemption of some minimum income helps to underwrite the markets for consumer goods and thus the successful operation of

---

[28] See the *Farm Income Situation,* Bureau of Agricultural Economics, U. S. Department of Agriculture, June, 1946, page 27. A substantially lower tax rate probably should be applied to such income because of the impacts which taxation may have upon the size of the total product. People may be willing to work in their own gardens if they do not have to pay too much for the privilege. Valuing home-produced food at market values and taxing it at the same rates as are applied to other income might substantially increase the cash outlay for gardening and reduce the amount of gardening.

[29] See Donald B. Marsh, "The Taxation of Imputed Income," *Political Science Quarterly,* Vol. 58 (December, 1943), pages 514-536. The above net figure allows for deductions for repairs, depreciation, insurance, interest, and real-estate taxes.

our private enterprise system. (Refer to page 253 of Chapter XIII and page 290 of Chapter XIV.)

From an administrative standpoint, the merit of trying to apply income taxes to individuals with very small incomes can be questioned. The cost which would be incurred might exceed the tax yield which would be obtained. From an economic standpoint, such a result would clearly be a waste of resources. Political pressure to retain the personal income tax, not as a "mass" tax, but as a "class" tax, as before 1940 will continue. It cannot be ignored by those who wish to see the personal income tax retained as the major source of government tax revenue.

Much has already been said about personal deductions from income in computing statutory net income. On the one hand, deductions which are permitted represented about 8.7 per cent of total income reported by individuals for Federal taxation for 1942. In the tax simplification which was developed during the war years, the bulk of the taxpayers—with incomes up to $5,000 —are now permitted to assume a personal deduction of 10 per cent in calculation of tax liability, unless they wish to list specific deductions which exceed 10 per cent. Living expenses are not deductible in obtaining statutory net income, except for a limited deduction for unusually high medical-dental expenses. A tenant cannot deduct rent which he pays. Greater equity would be achieved between home-owners and renters if home-owners were not allowed to deduct property taxes paid on such homes. Some increase in equity could be achieved, however, if tenants were permitted to deduct rents.

The reciprocal allowance of deduction for state income taxes by the Federal government and of Federal income taxes by state governments which use the income tax is important in the co-ordination of Federal and state taxes. Deductions for interest paid are probably more liberal than are required. Accepting the general concept that living expenses are not to be deducted from taxable income, there seems no reason why an interest deduction should be allowed on consumption loans.

The tax-rate structure. The problem of the "best" tax-rate structure is one which comes up for continuous discussion. What we are concerned with is the tax-rate structure which is actually effective, and not the "apparent" tax structure which we now have because of our especially low ceiling on the taxation of capital gains.   We can say that a tax structure, effective in reaching taxable income at the various rates used, should not be so sharply progressive that, for a person with a given income, it would not appear desirable to enter into economic activities which might increase that income still further.

It can be argued that 1946 tax rates, though a little below peak wartime rates, may have been so great as to discourage incentive and risk-assumption by those receiving moderately large and very large incomes.   Thus, at 1946 rates, a person with a taxable net income of $50,000 (not from capital gains) was already paying 68.4 per cent of his net income above $44,000 in the form of income tax.   The 31.6 per cent remaining after taxes may have been so small as to discourage such individuals from undertaking additional ventures which might have increased his income before tax to a still higher figure.   The over-all tax rate was permitted to rise as high as 85.5 per cent.[30]

It is generally recognized that virtually any tax (unless it comes out of economic rent) reduces the size of the total product.   Our society has been willing to sacrifice some product in order to achieve a more equal distribution of that which was produced. However, there are limits to the amount of product which society will be willing to give up in order to achieve this desired end. The 1946 tax rates may have reduced the product more than is socially desirable for peacetime purposes.   The writers do not have sufficient information to draft a (peacetime) tax structure which would bring about the desired combination of equity and incentive.

In terms of simplicity, it is also reasonably clear that the Federal government should adopt one tax-rate structure for its personal income taxes, instead of continuing the division between normal and surtax rates.   The original reason for the distinction —to exempt from a 1 per cent normal tax corporate dividends previously subject to a 1 per cent corporation tax—has long since ceased to have any meaning.   There is now a separate structure of corporate-tax rates which (in 1946) rose to 38 per cent,[31] and all corporate cash dividends are now taxable to the individual.

[30] This was reinforced by the fact that, although the maximum tax rate on capital gains alone was 25 per cent, the possibilities for deduction of capital losses were very limited.

[31] This is not to say that we should not achieve greater integration between present personal and corporate taxation.

The only remaining reason for the distinction between normal tax and surtax is the continued existence of a relatively small amount of Federal securities which have been issued exempt from normal, but not from surtax (about 23.2 billion dollars worth on June 30, 1945, as compared with 205.9 billions of publicly held Federal securities). The problems connected with adjusting compensation on these securities should not be insuperable.

Retention of a substantial standard or beginning rate on taxable income (which amounted to about 19 per cent in 1946) is desirable if we are to use the personal income tax as a means of relatively effective integration with Federal corporation taxes in the future. The 1946 beginning rate may be too low to permit effective integration of personal and corporate income taxes.

Taxation of stock dividends. Dividends on owned stock which are received in shares of stock of a similar type rather than in cash or other property have been exempt from income taxation since a Supreme Court decision of 1920 holding such dividends nontaxable. This decision[32] and later ones held essentially that stock dividends which do not alter the proportionate ownership in a corporation are not taxable. Partial basis of the reasoning was that any stockholder, under such circumstances, had no greater proportionate equity in the corporation than before, and hence no greater value. Yet resort to the market, where most values are determined for purposes of taxation, does not always bear out the idea that the stockholder does not have a greater realization in economic value than before. Especially where the payment of a stock dividend is actually and obviously a means of retaining and reinvesting earnings in the corporate business, the market often gives a value to each share of the enlarged stock issue which makes the total market value of the issue greater than before. When this happens, a particular stockholder finds that his shares of the particular stock have increased in aggregate value which can be realized. It seems equitable that any such increases in total value should certainly be made subject to income taxation.

It is now believed that if a case involving the attempted taxa-

---

[32] Eisner V. McComber, 252 U. S. 189, 1920. Such dividends were taxable at market value from 1916 to 1920 and may provide a taxable capital gain if and when the stock is sold.

tion of stock dividends came before the Supreme Court, and if the economic implications were similar to those in the illustration just given, a much more favorable attitude toward the taxation of stock dividends might be taken by the Supreme Court than in the twenties. If stock dividends were declared taxable by the Supreme Court, one of the strongest arguments for taxing undistributed profits would disappear.

Summary

The personal income tax has been recognized as the chief tax instrument which should be used for (1) planned flexibility in tax revenues, and (2) equity in taxation. By processes of simplification, the tax has been adapted to mass use in recent years. At the same time, our existing income taxes fall short of the degree of perfection as tax instruments which they might attain. For the future, our income taxes—and particularly the Federal income tax—should have some of these characteristics:

1. A broad tax base, with relatively low personal exemptions, should be retained. The current collection system should be retained and further developed.
2. A broader concept of income for taxation should be developed in some of the following ways:
   a. Realized capital gains and losses should be taxed at full tax rates, with no limitations on the period for carry-over of unused losses, and with similar treatment being accorded losses and gains in any one year.
   b. Reciprocal and nondiscriminatory taxation of income from government securities by Federal and by state governments should begin. Further, new issues of government securities should not be exempt from taxes by the issuing government.
   c. The taxation of important elements of "imputed" (real) income such as the value of products grown and consumed on farms, and the rental value of owner-occupied homes should be attempted.
   d. Gains from bequests and from the receipt of inheritances or gifts should be recognized as elements of taxable income. (This would make separate tax-rate schedules for inheritances and gifts unnecessary.)
   e. Taxes should be applied to the increased value of corporation stocks due to the payment of stock dividends.

3. There should be reduction in the differential advantages which now exist for the use of income-tax returns, particularly to those living in community-property states. This could mean the use of compulsory joint returns, as in Great Britain, or of taxation based on per capita tax liability.

4. Tax-rate schedules should be used which:

   a. impinge less severely on upper-income groups than at present,

   b. make it unnecessary for the taxpayer to use more than one tax-rate schedule in the preparation of a tax return,

   c. retain a "substantial" beginning or standard rate of tax.

5. There should be reduction of present discrimination against irregular and fluctuating income by some appropriate type of "averaging" over a period of years.

6. Steps should be taken toward the integration of personal and corporate taxation, which will lessen emphasis on business taxes as such (See Chapter XV).

7. There should be more complete integration of Federal and state income taxes (See Chapters XXIII and XXIV).

SELECTED READINGS

1. Blakey, Roy G. and Gladys C. *The Federal Income Tax*, New York: Longmans, Green & Co., Inc., 1940.

2. ——— and Johnson, Violet, *State Income Taxes*, Chicago: Commerce Clearing House, Inc., 1942.

3. Groves, Harold M., *Postwar Taxation and Economic Progress*, Chapters 7 and 8, New York: McGraw-Hill Book Co., Inc., 1946.

4. ———, *Proceedings of the National Tax Association, 1939,* pages 124-125, Columbia, South Carolina, 1940.

5. Haig, Robert Murray, *The Federal Income Tax*, New York: The Columbia University Press, 1921.

6. ———, "Taxation of Capital Gains," *The Wall Street Journal*, 1937.

7. Marsh, Donald B., "The Taxation of Imputed Income," *The Political Science Quarterly*, 1943.

8. Ratner, Sidney, *American Taxation*, New York: W. W. Norton & Co., Inc., 1942.

9. Simons, Henry C., *Personal Income Taxation*, Chicago: University of Chicago Press, 1938.

10. *Statistics of Income for 1942. Part 1*, Washington, D. C.: United States Government Printing Office, 1944.

11. Temporary National Economic Committee, *Concentration and Composition of Individual Incomes, 1918-1937*, Monograph 4. Washington, D. C.: United States Government Printing Office, 1941.

CHAPTER XV

THE ROLE OF BUSINESS TAXATION [1]

Definition of a Business Tax

WE SHALL include within the meaning of the term "business taxes" those taxes which are imposed on types or classes of profit-seeking enterprises.[2] This will embrace not only taxes on business net income and excess profits, but such taxes as those on premiums of life insurance companies, capital-stock taxes, severance taxes (imposed by some states when natural resources, such as iron and oil, are being used up), special taxes on public utilities, and taxes on the privilege of doing business (franchise or license taxes). Such a classification cuts across other general classifications of taxes (such as sales and gross-receipts taxes on insurance and public utility companies), but some overlapping in tax classification is difficult to avoid.

For several reasons business activity is a favored target for taxation by legislative bodies. Many business taxes, such as state taxes on insurance companies, may be imposed on relatively few firms and cost little to administer. It is undoubtedly anticipated by the "tax makers" that some or all of such taxes will be shifted to purchasers of the good or service. But it is also anticipated that such taxes will provide a relatively constant yield in tax revenue, besides minimizing taxpayer resistance because the taxes are hidden. The reduction in purchasing power by this method is not as obvious to the taxpayer as it is when he pays a direct personal income tax.

It is widely believed that business as such derives benefits from government for which some payment should be made. Also the courts have been very favorable toward business taxes. This is

---

[1] A brief summary of Federal taxation of business net income in 1946 is given in Appendix E.

[2] It is recognized that, from the broadest point of view, nearly all taxes could be called "business taxes," since the receipt of most wealth and income is followed, eventually, by the expenditure of funds for goods and services.

important because most taxes which are imposed must ultimately be upheld by the courts before they become part of our tax structure. The taxation of business by states has grown to include so many types of taxes, imposed on so many different bases, that state business taxation cannot be rationalized on any basis except that of obtaining some additional tax revenue.

Business Taxes in Federal, State, and Local Government

Federal business taxation has been relatively simple. Confined to a few types of business taxation, principally the taxation of general-corporation net incomes and to wartime excess profits in both World Wars I and II, Federal business taxes have provided about 20-35 per cent of total Federal tax revenues since about 1920. Beginning with a 1 per cent excise tax (as measured by net income) on corporations in 1909, Federal business taxation has centered around corporation income ever since. By 1920, the Federal corporation-income tax, exclusive of a temporary excess-profits tax, provided about 12 per cent of total Federal tax revenue.[3] In the years since, it has provided from 10.3 to 38.5 per cent of total Federal tax revenue. Even in the peak of Federal tax collections (calendar year 1945), the corporate-net-income tax did not fall below 10.3 per cent of total tax revenues (4.7 billion dollars) despite the rapid rise of personal income taxes to 19.9 billions and of excess-profits tax revenue to 9.8 billion dollars. With the repeal of excess-profits taxes (and of capital-stock taxes) in the Revenue Act of 1945, the main issue in Federal business taxation (1946) was the future of the corporation-income tax. We will examine some of the issues in corporation-income taxation in a later section of the chapter.

When we turn to the areas of business taxation occupied by Federal, state, and local governments, we soon encounter a jungle of state business taxation, which is partially reflected in Table 21.

The existing situation in state business taxation has aptly been called a "chaos" by Hansen and Perloff in their recent book, *State and Local Finance in the National Economy*. They summarize the "chaos" as follows:

---

[3] This is necessarily an approximation based on *Statistics of Income for Income Tax Year, 1919*. The statistics for fiscal years ending June 30 did not separate individual and corporate-income taxes from 1918 through 1924.

. . . a conglomeration of heterogeneous taxes imposed for different purposes, on different bases, under many forms of rate schedules, and with many types of administrative machinery. They are characterized in general, by arbitrariness, complexity and lack of coordination. . . .[4]

The height of arbitrariness is probably reached in the occupation taxes, imposed in one form or another by all 48 states in 1946. These taxes, which have been made the subject of special study in recent years,[5] do not rest on any identifiable principle (except to produce some revenue) and employ at least 11 measures (used singly or in combination) to define the tax base. Used primarily in the southern states, where they sometimes cover 200 or more separate occupations, these taxes have never provided more than 13.4 million dollars, or less than .25 of 1 per cent, of total state tax revenues (1946). Only slightly less arbitrary are the various forms of capital-stock taxes now used in the various states. To determine the correct valuation of capital stock has proven almost impossible for tax administrators.

The determination of the value of the corporate franchise as the basis of widely used franchise taxes also has little consistency. However, of the 33 states which imposed corporate-net-income taxes, 7 used corporate net income (allocated to the state) as a measure of the value of the franchise (1946). Severance taxes were levied by 23 states (1946). Such taxes were generally imposed on natural resources extracted in the state. Such resources are often irreplaceable, as are petroleum, coal, and iron, and the products in which such resources are used are frequently sold outside the state.

The net effects of "the chaotic state tax structures" which have resulted from the "wild scramble for tax sources," as Hansen and Perloff have said,[6] are (1) to "increase the difficulty and uncertainty of business planning," and (2) to increase the costs of tax-

---

[4] See Hansen and Perloff, pages 44-45. A more complete statement of their conclusions on state business taxes was given in Chapter XI of this book, page 198. Reprinted by permission of W. W. Norton & Co., Inc., New York. Copyright 1944 by the publishers.

[5] Roscoe Arant, "Business Taxation in the Southern States," *The Tax Magazine*, Vol. 16, Chicago: Commerce Clearing House, Inc., 1938.

[6] See Hansen and Perloff, *State and Local Finance in the National Economy*, pages 46-47.

payer compliance with state laws. At the same time, the multiplicity of state business taxes have yielded relatively little tax revenue. In 1946, outside of 436 million dollars in corporate-net-income taxes, all the other business taxes (as we have defined them) yielded only 615 million dollars, or about 10.3 per cent of total state tax revenues.

A great deal of simplification in state business taxes is to be desired. But such simplification probably depends on greater centralization of tax collection in the Federal government and on expanded Federal grants to the states. Without this, it is unlikely that the states will be willing to give up the lucrative sources of tax revenues which they have managed to devise.[7]

TABLE 21[8]

State Business Taxes, 1942

Type of Tax	Tax Revenue (in millions of dollars)	Number of States Using Tax
1. General Corporation Net Income Tax[a]..	$274.0	32
2. Taxes on Specific Businesses		
a. Insurance Companies..............	113.0	48
b. Public Utilities....................	99.4	33
c. Corporation Franchise and Privilege..	87.8	47
d. Privilege of Selling Alcoholic Beverages............................	55.6	46
e. Motor Vehicle, Commercial Transportation......................	49.5	47
f. Occupations.....................	10.1	44
g. Chain Stores.....................	3.9	21
h. Miscellaneous...................	71.2	48
i. Sub-total of Taxes on Specific Businesses.........................	$490.5	
3. Severance Taxes....................	62.4	23
4. Total Business Taxes................	826.9	
5. Total State Taxes...................	$4,974.8	
6. Ratio of Business Taxes to all State Taxes	16.6%	

a The $274.0 million in general corporation net income taxes does not include the combined yield from corporate- and individual-income taxes in three states (Missouri, New Mexico, and North Dakota) where division of total tax into the two portions was not made.

[7] Some of the problems of intergovernmental fiscal relationships that are involved will be examined in the final chapters of this book, XXIII and XXIV.

[8] These data are derived from *State Tax Collections in 1942*, Bureau of the Census, Washington, D. C., July, 1943, pages 3-7.

As for business taxes levied by municipal governments, the existing situation is much less complicated than at the state level. Municipal governments do impose many business-license taxes, but these are generally related to costs of inspection designed to protect consumers from "fraud," "shoddiness," and "impurities" in the sale of products offered for sale. Quantitatively, local business taxes provide less than 5 per cent of local tax revenues.

Some of the statements which have been made indicate why much attention has been paid in recent years to the whole question as to whether "business" as such, apart from the owners of business, should be subject to separate taxes. The main issues involved in this discussion will be analyzed.

Analysis of Reasons Advanced for Continuance of Business Taxes

Several reasons for retaining taxes on business, apart from taxes on their owners, in the tax system have been advanced. Among them are these: (1) Because of special benefits received, especially the privilege to conduct business in the corporate form; (2) because business may have a special ability to pay; (3) because taxes can be used to prevent the growth of giant corporations, operating on a scale that is considered too large from a social standpoint; (4) because business taxes can be used to restrict the operation of business in ways that are considered economically or socially undesirable; (5) because business taxes can be used to cover the administrative costs of keeping business operations within laws governing the production and distribution of goods and services; (6) because abandoning taxation of businesses would result in windfalls to the owners of business equities; (7) because business taxes provide tax revenues without which it is not possible to provide the desired range of governmental activities. As we shall see, none of these reasons establishes a firm basis for any substantial amount of business taxes.

Taxation of business for benefits received. One of the most commonly cited reasons for the use of business taxes is that business should pay for special benefits received from government. It is argued that business should pay its share of the costs incurred by government in maintaining the orderly operation of market processes (such as the costs of protecting private wealth and property through the operation of police protection and of the courts, in providing market information, and so forth). It is also argued that business corporations should pay for some of the special privileges of doing business in the corporate form.

Special-benefit arguments do not justify collecting a very large amount of business taxes. If all of the costs of special government services could be allocated, the total would be a small percentage of present business tax collections. In 1944, a report for the National Planning Association[9] proposed a 5 per cent net-income tax for corporations to cover the costs of special benefits received by business. Granting to economic units the privilege of doing business in the corporate form probably permits an expansion in the total national product and hardly can be considered as imposing net costs upon society. But (gross) costs are involved in extending the corporate privilege. Various fees for corporate organization are collected by the states, partly for this reason.

Business may be provided some special benefits by public highways and certain other services. The costs of providing such benefits, however, can be covered by specific benefit taxes.[10]

Taxation of business ability to pay. Ownership of business does not establish a special ability to pay for taxation. Ability to pay, as we have seen, refers to the relative abilities of natural persons, not to some artificial entity such as a corporation which is owned by individuals. The application of ability to pay can be furthered, however, if our personal income taxes can be made to reach effectively full personal shares in corporate incomes. Means of effective integration of personal- and corporate-income taxes are available.

It is true that property income—deriving in large part from dividends and interest—does constitute an increasing proportion of total incomes as the size of income rises, but individuals receiving such income are already taxed at more severe rates under our personal income taxes. Individuals with small incomes, owning a few shares of stock, may have negative ability to pay for tax purposes.

Taxation of business to penalize business. Some people believe that the development of giant corporations is socially undesirable because: (1) of the resulting concentration of economic and

---

[9] See Beardsley Ruml and H. Christian Sonne, *Fiscal-Monetary Policy,* National Planning Association Pamphlet No. 35, Washington, D. C., 1944.
[10] Refer to Chapter XVIII.

political power, and (2) these giants do not always produce as efficiently as smaller firms. Taxation of business has been suggested as a means of discouraging undue bigness.

Our experience in the United States does not indicate that the development of substantial corporate-income taxes since 1909 has prevented the growth of such corporate giants as General Motors, United States Steel, and American Telephone and Telegraph Corporations, each with assets of over 1.8 billion dollars at the end of 1945.[11]

Since, over a period of years, corporation income taxes have not had an identifiable influence in preventing the growth of large business units, other factors which might make large-scale business units preferable may have more than counterbalanced the restrictive effects on business growth which corporate-net-income taxes could have imposed. For example, it is generally agreed that there are certain economies in large-scale production and distribution of some goods and services. Taxation itself is too limited and crude a means with which to combat the many factors which may result in the growth of large-scale business units.

Taxation of business to obtain a more desirable production pattern. The argument that business taxes can be used to restrict the operation of business in ways considered economically and socially undesirable covers a number of situations, most of which can not be rationalized with one or more of the economic goals of fiscal policy which we have accepted throughout this book. For example, 20 states in 1946 penalized efficiency in merchandising methods by imposing special taxes on chain-stores. All 48 states levied privilege taxes on dealers in alcoholic beverages. In both cases, the allocation of resources which resulted was different from that which would have occurred without such taxes.

Severance taxes were imposed by 23 states in 1946. (Most of these taxes were collected by Texas, Louisiana, Oklahoma, and Minnesota.) These taxes, imposed as so much per 100 gallons of petroleum drawn from the ground or as so much per ton of iron ore mined, are unquestionably shifted forward to purchasers, in

---

[11] Theoretically, as we pointed out in Chapter IX, a combination of subsidies and taxes might be used which would encourage expanded production by a monopolistic firm. It was concluded that the limitations in applying such a subsidy-tax plan would be very great.

whole or in part. They eventually fall on users of finished products, many of which are outside the states which levy such taxes. They reduce the amount of resources used in the particular industries which are taxed, and in most cases tend to increase inequality in the distribution of consumer incomes, since the resources most frequently taxed (petroleum, wood, iron, and coal) enter into many final consumer products.

On the other hand, most of such taxes are imposed on limited (often irreplaceable) natural resources within particular states. Such states may be justified in conserving their limited natural resources, not only from the standpoint of those living within the state, but also from the standpoint of general public welfare.[12] Although there are other (nonfiscal) ways of inducing conservation of natural resources, severance taxes may be more consistent with long-run economic progress than many other business taxes.

Taxation of business to cover costs of supervision. Business-license fees imposed to cover the costs to governments of inspection and administration of business units in order to insure business honesty, compliance with pure food and drug laws, and so forth, are very common, especially with municipal units of government. They will be briefly discussed in Chapter XVIII.

Taxation of business to prevent windfalls. The argument that eliminating taxes on business would result in windfalls to owners of business equities assumes that the incidence of business taxes falls at least partially upon business owners. Granting this assumption, the argument would not be valid if we had adequate taxation of capital gains. Even though stock prices would tend to rise when business taxes were eliminated, the windfalls which might result could be recaptured.

Taxation of business to obtain tax revenue. This brings us to the final goal of business taxation which we have mentioned—the possibility of securing some tax revenue with which to support the desired amount of governmental activities. This goal has

[12] Whether or not conservation of resources occurs will depend partly on the amount and effects of the tax. A relatively high tax on petroleum, for example, may encourage the rapid and incomplete exploitation of only the richest sources of petroleum. Yet it may be socially desired to exploit the limited natural resource at a relatively rapid rate, if present gains are considered as more than outweighing future social losses from such rapid exploitation. Economics of conservation can not do much more than indicate the consequences of such policy on present and future costs, prices, and volume of product. See: Pigou, *Economics of Welfare*, 4th edition, pages 29-30.

not been emphasized in our discussion of Federal tax policy, where taxation has been emphasized as a technique for preventing such developments as inflation and for securing the desired income distribution. Given the present organization of our fiscal system, however, the goal of adequate revenue at the state and local levels must be recognized as unavoidable.

From an economic standpoint, Federal and state local-tax systems should be dovetailed in the following major ways: (1) Taxation should be used at the Federal level primarily to accomplish the major objectives which can be accomplished by fiscal devices and which have been set forth in our preceding discussion. Its use for raising Federal revenues may become a means of implementing these objectives, but revenue as an end itself should be subordinated. (2) State (and probably local) revenues should depend to a much greater extent than at present upon Federal grants which, in turn, might, or might not, derive from tax revenue.

Such adjustments may involve a considerable period of time, and to make them will require much recasting of our present attitudes toward the role which the Federal government should play in the fiscal system. Meanwhile, considerations on how to raise revenue may have to be given more weight than previous analysis indicates. During this period, we will probably continue to place emphasis on some of our business taxes. Given our present system of state and local (particularly state) business taxation, it is clear that substantial simplification in our state business tax systems is economically desirable.

Among existing business taxes, the Federal corporation-income tax is probably the least undesirable, both because it does fall on most forms of corporate business activity at the same rate (for any given net income) and because the incidence of the corporation-income tax is more predictable than business taxes which vary directly with volume of sales.[13] The relatively general applica-

---

[13] The statement about the uniformity of a general corporation tax does not, of course, apply to the 32 state corporation income taxes, whose rates varied in 1942, though through a relatively small range of 1 per cent to 8 per cent. Moreover, there are 16 states which relied in 1946 on other sources of business tax revenue than a corporation income tax. Nevertheless, there is evidence that variation in state taxes falling on business has not been sufficiently great to be a primary factor in determining the location of business enterprise. See George A. Steiner, *The Tax System and Industrial Development*, Bureau of Business Research, University of Illinois, Vol. XXXV, No. 581, 1938, pages 45-46.

tion of the Federal tax at rates (1946) varying from 21 per cent to 38 per cent (depending on the amount of net income) greatly reduces the impact of the tax on the allocation of resources. The fact that the incidence of a net income tax will fall somewhat on corporate stockholders means that the effects of the tax on the distribution of income may be estimated to some extent in advance.

Despite the recent conclusion of Butters and Lintner that high *corporate* taxes do impede corporate expansion, they recommend that Federal corporation-income taxation should be retained—although at lower rates.[14]

Although there is a high probability of their continuance, the case which can be made for substantial business taxes is not very strong, even if we concentrate our attention primarily on only corporation-income taxation. Arguments against the taxation of business as such become more convincing when we examine some of the reasons which have been advanced for "untaxing" business in recent years.[15]

Analysis of Reasons for "Untaxing" Business

It has been urged in recent years that taxes on business are undesirable in peacetime because such taxes: (1) Reduce incentives and opportunity for new business investment, (2) increase inequality in the distribution of income, (3) reduce consumer expenditures, and (4) increase seriously the costs of taxpayer compliance. These reasons, while not all equally subject to empirical verification, do establish a case for reduction in emphasis on business taxation. The case for "untaxing" business is strengthened by the negative conclusions reached in the preceding section, where most of the alleged reasons for the taxation of business were examined and were found to lack much content.

In this connection it should be noted that there are some forms of business enterprise organized in the corporate form which, under certain conditions, are exempt from Federal and most state corporation income taxes, such as farmers' marketing and purchasing cooperatives. (Section 101 of the Internal Revenue Code).

[14] J. Keith Butters and John Lintner, *Effect of Federal Taxes on Growing Enterprises, A Case Study.* Graduate School of Business Administration, Harvard University, 1945.

[15] Some of these arguments have been presented clearly in two studies by Professor Harold M. Groves for the Committee on Economic Development, *Production, Jobs and Taxes*, Chapter III, 1944, and *Postwar Taxation and Economic Progress*, Chapter II, 1946. Both were published by McGraw-Hill Book Co., Inc., New York.

Business taxes discourage additional business investment.   The incentives argument has been directed for the most part toward the corporation-income tax.   Assuming that in corporations of considerable size, corporate managements make most decisions as to whether corporations shall invest resources in new or risky processes, existing tax laws probably work against such innovations.   Such corporate managers probably are dependent for economic advancement on the profits which they are able to show stockholders; further, they enjoy considerable satisfaction in increasing the size of the business which they operate.   To the extent that these statements are true, the amount of corporate profits *after income taxes* is an important factor motivating corporate management.   Since existing tax laws also penalize incentive by limiting the carry-back and carry-over of operating losses and of capital losses, the case for revision in our present tax laws affecting corporate income is further strengthened.[16]

Professor Lerner has contended that income taxation should not affect business operations as long as losses and profits are given the same treatment in determining taxable income and the marginal rate of taxation is the same for all levels of income.[17] Under our present laws, government does not compensate the business for losses at the same rate as it taxes profits.   For losses to be treated equally with profits in the determination of taxable income, more liberal carry-forward and carry-back provisions would be required than we now have in our Federal tax laws.   Furthermore, taxation of corporate income at progressive rates violates the criterion that the marginal rate of taxation should be unchanged if income taxation is to have no effect on business operations.

It is possible that our present corporate-income taxes do not seriously check corporate investment and expansion for our large corporations, since such corporations still have relatively free

---

[16] Some of the main provisions of our tax laws with respect to the deduction and carry-over of business losses are summarized in the final section of this chapter. Professor Groves has summarized the attitude of many corporate managements toward corporate earnings and their disposition as follows: "The company's success, with which management identifies personal success, is measured first by corporate net earnings, next by dividends, and least by dividends net of personal tax."   By permission from *Production, Jobs and Taxes,* page 25 by Harold M. Groves.   Copyrighted, 1944, by McGraw-Hill Book Co., Inc.

[17] Abba P. Lerner, *The Economics of Control,* pages 238-239, New York: The Macmillan Company, 1944.

access to the capital market for the sale of new securities. But the same cannot be said of new (or very young) and growing corporations, which are especially dependent on the reinvestment of earnings for growth. Existing corporation-income taxes, including "tipping of the scales" against corporate taxpayers on account of operating losses or capital losses which they may suffer, are a drawback to the development and expansion of new products and processes, in so far as the corporate form is adopted as desired form of business organization.[18] Yet, government cannot share in the business losses of firms that never become profitable without increasing the danger that this would adversely influence resource allocation. To the extent that the present maze of state business taxes does operate to increase the uncertainties and difficulties of business planning, these taxes also undermine incentives to undertake additional commitment of business resources for expansion in production.

This general line of reasoning is borne out by the recent case study by Butters and Lintner.[19] They concluded that while tax considerations do not often dominate decisions to *organize* new and independent corporate enterprises, tax considerations do become important when expansion is contemplated. They found that this is true particularly of high *corporate* taxes (as contrasted with high *personal* taxes), especially when applied to young and growing enterprises.

An outstanding attempt to check investment of resources in a particular line of economic activity is found in the special chain-store taxes imposed by nearly half our states. Under these laws, which act both to penalize customers and to check the use of efficient methods of merchandizing, average taxes per store vary directly with the number of stores. In levying the tax, usually only stores within the state are counted, but Louisiana graduates its rates according to the number of stores of a particular company in the entire country. One effect of the tax has been to cause many chains to close small units and to develop large or "super-market" units.

Despite the scarcity of quantitative proof for the incentive

---

[18] Some of the special problems of business-income taxation which arise in connection with new and small business are examined in the final section of this chapter.

[19] J. Keith Butters and John Lintner, *Effect of Federal Taxes on Growing Enterprises*.

arguments against business taxation, we are probably justified in saying that the restrictive effects of business taxes on the employment of resources in new enterprises must be recognized as a positive deficiency of our business taxation.

Other reasons for "untaxing" business. The other arguments for "untaxing" business may be summarized briefly. All business taxes which increase marginal unit costs of production and which vary with the volume of business tend to be shifted forward or backward. Such taxes tend to increase inequality in the distribution of personal (real) incomes.

Some shifting may also occur through the operation of corporate-net-income taxes, especially in the long run, as we pointed out in Chapter XII. To the extent that shifting does occur, the net volume of consumer expenditures will be cut. But the maintenance of such expenditures is likely to be a desired end in a peacetime economy, except when inflationary pressures, accompanied by relatively full employment, are present. Finally, the amount of resources used to administer efficiently and to comply with our many business taxes (especially our state business taxes) may be relatively large.[20] All the reasons for "untaxing" business, when considered along with the weaknesses of the various reasons for taxing business, make a powerful case for a reduction in the relative importance of business taxes in our economy.

Major Problems in Reducing Business Taxation

If reliance on business taxes is to be reduced, two major problems (in addition to the one of preventing holders of business equities from reaping large windfalls) will arise. These are the problems of (1) taxing undistributed corporate profits, and (2) simplifying state business-tax structure. The second problem is postponed for discussion until the final chapters of the book, although its importance in the arguments to "untax" business is not to be minimized.

The problem of undistributed corporate profits. Undistributed corporate profits are a problem because they permit certain people to avoid some taxation of personal incomes. The result is discriminatory treatment of personal incomes for tax purposes. Undistributed profits have become a tax problem largely because we have set up both corporate- and personal-income taxes with

[20] See reference to the costs of tax administration in Chapter XI, pages 201-205.

rate structures which differ greatly. Thus, in 1946, the top rate of our Federal corporation-income tax was 38 per cent, while the top rate of our tax on individual incomes was 91 per cent. Substantial variation in the top income-tax rates on corporations and individuals has existed since the first Federal income tax enacted in 1913, when the corporate tax rate was 1 per cent and the top individual rate was 7 per cent. The effect has been to give large stockholders with large incomes the opportunity to avoid part of personal income-tax liability by having corporations in which they are influential follow conservative dividend policies.

Thus, in 1946, an individual with a taxable net income of $205,-000 was subject to a tax of 91 per cent on the $5,000 of income in excess of $200,000. Such a tax would have been $4,550. But if this individual was entitled to receive $5,000 in dividends from a corporation in which he owned enough stock to affect corporate policy, the tax of $4,550 on his 1946 income was entirely avoidable by having the corporation decide not to pay dividends in 1946. Of course, he might be taxed later. For example, if the corporation decided to retain net income for expansion and improvement, the same individual might be faced with subsequent taxes on realized capital gains (if and when he disposed of his stock). On the other hand, there is no certainty that such retained corporate income will ever become subject to personal-income taxation.[21]

The principal arguments for discouraging large accumulations of undistributed profits have been that: (1) keeping undistributed profits at a low figure would make the personal income tax much more effective, and equity in taxation would be increased, and (2) retained corporate earnings are less likely to be actively used (spent) than if such earnings become available to stockholders for disposition. They are therefore more likely to produce a deflationary force on the flow of national income.[22] These are also the principal reasons for the use of an undistributed-profits tax which will "force" corporate earnings into the hands of stockholders.

[21] For example, the investment might turn out unfavorably and result in a capital loss. Moreover, if such stock were bequeathed to heirs, then (under 1946 laws) any existing capital gains to the person making the bequest were canceled at the time of death.

[22] As was indicated in Chapter III, offsetting fiscal steps could be taken to neutralize the deflationary impact of increased cash holdings by businesses.

To indicate the over-all size of undistributed corporate profits, we have chosen the income years 1938-1941—the period just before the full impact of the war. Data reported in *Statistics of Income* for these years indicate that, for all corporations reporting net income in these years, 69.3 per cent of net income after taxes was paid to stockholders in the form of cash dividends and assets other than the stock of the corporations, whereas retained net earnings were 30.7 per cent. Although retained net earnings were less than one third of net income in the four income years 1938-1941, such retained earnings were about 10.1 billion dollars.

Such data present only the barest outline of the undistributed-profits picture. For one thing, they include corporations paying no dividends out of net earnings as well as corporations paying 100 per cent or more of net earnings. They do not mention various motives for retention of net earnings, of which the possibility of personal tax avoidance is only one. Some corporations retain net earnings to build liquid reserves in anticipation of future operating periods when a net loss will be incurred. Others (such as small and growing corporations) find retained net earnings the major source of funds for expansion and development. Included within the 30.7 per cent retained net earnings, however, are also earnings of corporations who did use dividend policies as a means of limiting the personal income-tax liabilities of stockholders.

The national government has relied primarily upon three methods to minimize the retention of profits for purposes of tax avoidance. One, the application of "penalty" tax rates in the case of personal holding companies has been relatively successful in closing this particular tax loophole. Another, enacted in 1921, applies penalty rates to corporations which "improperly" accumulate surpluses. This method has not been very successful, since the motives for reinvesting corporate earnings are mixed, and it is difficult to prove that a functioning business corporation has not had a defensible motive in retaining net earnings, even if such earnings have not been invested in additional producing facilities. The third method tried was that of an undistributed-profits tax, at a peak rate of 27 per cent, in addition to other corporate taxes.

An undistributed-profits tax was proposed by the late President Roosevelt in 1936. His proposal, however, was to substitute this tax at a high rate for all other Federal taxes on corporate income.

Instead of enacting the President's proposal, Congress passed a law taxing undistributed profits at moderate rates (7 to 27 per cent) and maintained other Federal corporate taxes. The tax as enacted was collected during the income years 1936-1937. The rate schedule was greatly reduced in 1938 and the tax was repealed, effective in 1940.

While there is some evidence that the tax did increase dividend payments on 1936 and 1937 incomes,[23] it was bitterly assailed by business executives as an interference with their "legitimate" prerogatives in the disposition of net income, as well as on other grounds. An undistributed-profits tax, at very high rates, and in lieu of other taxes on profits, is nevertheless one instrument which might be used as a means of integrating corporate and personal taxation. As such an instrument, its use will be examined in the following section. Up to 1946, however, the undistributed-profits tax had not been used effectively as a means of integrating corporate- and personal-income taxes, and we still have not adapted our tax structure to accomplish this purpose.

Main Proposals for Integration of Corporate and Personal Taxes

Proceeding on the assumption that it is desirable to "untax" business income if personal-tax avoidance can be minimized or eliminated, some of the major proposals for necessary tax revision which have been made are: (1) Treat corporations like partnerships. Allocate corporate earnings (or losses) among stockholders on a pro rata basis, according to ownership of corporation stock, and consolidate such earnings (or losses) with other personal income for personal income taxation. (2) Remove corporation-income taxes, but tax stockholders rigorously on the basis of realized capital gains, even if such gains are not realized until death (of the stockholder). (3) Use some adaptation of the British income-tax system, under which a corporation acts primarily as a withholding agent for tax due on the individual incomes of its stockholders. (4) Use an undistributed-profits tax at very high rates in lieu of other corporation-income taxes. (5)

[23] According to *Statistics of Income* for the years 1936 through 1940, the percentage of corporate net income available for stockholders which was paid out in dividends (other than company stock) in 1936 and 1937 was 87.3 per cent. In the following three years, just before the United States began operation under a wartime economy, the percentage of dividends to corporate net income was 74.1 per cent.

Free the corporation from income taxes on income which it distributes in dividends, but impose a heavy tax on retained earnings which are "uninvested."

Prorata personal taxation of corporate income. The proposal for the prorata taxation of corporate income in the hands of individual stockholders is one of the oldest proposals for "untaxing" business. It is also one of the most logical, if a major end is to impose taxes on the basis of individuals' ability to pay, but it has limitations which will probably prevent its generalized application to the taxation of business income. The administrative costs of including all prorata gains (or losses) in the tax returns of several million stockholders would be very great. Assuming that the Supreme Court would be willing to modify its long-standing position that taxable income must be *realized* income, many stockholders might find themselves with allocated prorata corporate earnings at a time when a cash-dividend policy was not being followed and when total income received from all sources might be insufficient to meet both living expenses and tax liabilities. Conversely, the prorata method of taxation would still leave corporate managements relatively free to determine dividend policy and could leave undistributed and uninvested income at a socially undesirable high level.

Finally, we have come to accept the idea of the corporate business entity as not just a collection of individuals in a partnership. It is unlikely that we will abandon this idea of a corporate entity for purposes of taxation. There may still be a limited sphere in which prorata taxation could be successfully used without running counter to accepted objectives of economic policy and to social patterns of behavior. This sphere might be the small, closely held corporations, which operate largely as a family affair, and where there is an (almost) complete identity in the composition of the corporate management and the group of stockholders.

Taxation of capital gains in lieu of taxes on business. The late Professor Simons[24] was a proponent of the idea that business should be "untaxed" by considering the realized capital gains from holding corporate stock as personal income. Under the proposal, realized capital gains from holding corporate stock

[24] This proposal was made in an unpublished manuscript submitted to Professor Harold M. Groves and cited in *Production, Jobs and Taxes,* pages 25-26 and page 40.

would be taxed at the same rates as other personal income. Upon death of the stockholder, capital gains would not be canceled, as they are under present laws.

To implement Simons' proposals, existing Federal tax laws would have to be revised. Capital gains at time of death on assets in the hands of heirs are now canceled. Such gains would have to be called a realization for tax purposes. Beyond this, we question that the government as tax-collector should leave the timing of tax payments to individual discretion as much as this proposal would permit. During a period of years while a corporate security was owned, the whole tax-rate schedule applicable to income might rise and fall (or *vice versa*). An individual holding such a security might be able to dispose of his holding at a tax advantage.

Nevertheless, as in the case of proposed prorata taxation of corporate earnings in the hands of individuals, there are some situations where Professor Simons' proposal could reasonably apply. It might provide the best type of tax policy in the case of new businesses which definitely need aid in obtaining new capital. The application of Simons' proposals to this class of business enterprises would relieve such businesses of profits taxes at a time when growth requires that such businesses plough back earnings into the enterprises. At the same time it would attract additional investors to whom the prospect of freedom from immediate taxation on corporate income would appeal.

Even in this selective area, however, it would be necessary to define certain characteristics of a business enterprise which would make it eligible for such special tax treatment. For example, it would be necessary to decide for how many years a business should be classed as a "new" business, and how much invested capital it should be permitted to accumulate before its need for special aid in accumulating capital was no longer deemed important enough to warrant the proposed treatment for taxation. Any such demarcation would necessarily be arbitrary, but the proposed treatment for taxation might apply to businesses not over five years old nor having assets in excess of $100,000.

Using corporations as withholding agents for personal taxes. A proposal for the integration of personal and corporate taxes which has recently enjoyed considerable favor in this country is to adapt the present British system of income taxation to the United

States. Under this system, the corporation pays at some established flat tax rate on its entire net income, and acts as a withholding agent for taxes on individual incomes, also making an advance payment of taxes for stockholders while earnings are retained for reinvestment. This frees individuals from further taxes at the established corporate rate on corporate income. Depending on the size of their total personal incomes, some individuals would be entitled to tax credits under this system, while others would still have additional personal taxes to pay under a progressive tax-rate structure.

This is how such a system would work. Let us assume that Corporation X has a net income of $500,000 and that the lowest personal-income tax rate is 20 per cent. On this $500,000, the corporation would pay withheld taxes of $100,000; of the remaining $400,000, the corporation distributes $300,000 in dividends. On his share of this $300,000 the individual owes no additional taxes, unless the surtax rates applicable to him exceed 20 per cent. In determining the base for his personal income tax, the individual would include not only dividends received, but withheld tax on such dividends. However, he could subtract as a tax credit the amount of tax which has been withheld.

Let us assume that A has a net income for the year from all sources of $3,000, including $100 dividends received ($20 of which has been withheld as tax). His net taxable income will depend on the level of personal exemptions which we will assume will total $2,000. On his net income after personal exemptions, he would be subject to the beginning tax rate on $1,000. If this were 20 per cent, his gross tax would be $200. From this, he would be permitted to deduct $20 for tax already withheld and paid, leaving his remaining tax liability as $180. If and when his share of the $100,000 reinvested by the corporation becomes available in dividends, he will be subject to the same procedure with respect to calculation of tax liability in an ensuing period. If his taxable income exceeded (or fell below) the net income to which the initial (withholding) tax rate had been applied by the corporation, he would be subject to additional personal-tax liability (or eligible for a tax refund) with a progressive personal tax-rate structure.

Adoption of such a tax system for the bulk of our corporate enterprises would get rid of the corporation-income tax as such.

Application of the proposal as applied to corporations would not represent a revival of an undistributed-profits tax—whatever the merits of such a tax might be. Taxes paid by corporations on undistributed profits would simply be an advance payment of individual taxes. In order to facilitate individuals' later settlement of tax liabilities on dividends paid out of earlier net earnings, it would be desirable to require each corporation to compute and report annually the tax on undistributed profits for each share of stock outstanding.

In order to obtain substantial integration of corporate and individual taxes, it probably would be desirable that the tax rate applied to corporate income should be considerably above the lowest standard rate of tax on individual net income which we have employed in the United States. The use of the lowest standard rate of tax—19 per cent in 1946—would give many stockholders with taxable net incomes subject to higher rates a continuing motive to use corporations as "savings banks" in order to avoid full personal tax liabilities. To avoid a large number of refunds, it would not be desirable to apply the highest effective marginal tax rates for individuals to corporate income under this plan (about 86.5 per cent in 1946), since relatively few individuals and stockholders are affected by the maximum rate. The use of an intermediate tax rate for corporations which would be in the neighborhood of our 1946 top corporate tax rate of 38 per cent might be the highest tax rate which it would be desirable to apply to corporations under the proposed plan.

Even so high a tax rate imposed on corporations would not entirely remove the tax advantage of corporate reinvestment for high-income stockholders. A corporate tax rate of 35-40 per cent under the proposed plan would, however, eliminate the taxation of corporations as such and would be an important step in the direction of the maximum integration of personal and corporate taxes which might prove adaptable to our business environment. Before anyone is tempted to regard the proposal under discussion as utopian, he should reflect that a model for operation of such an integrated business-personal tax system has been successfully functioning in another major country (United Kingdom). The use of such a plan would not preclude the use of other devices previously described for "untaxing" closely held, small, and growing corporate enterprises.

Imposing an undistributed-profits tax in lieu of other corporation taxes. A fourth proposal for "untaxing" business that has been made is the imposition of a high undistributed-profits tax on corporations in lieu of other corporate taxes. In 1936, when President Roosevelt proposed such a tax, the Treasury estimated that corporate dividends withheld were sufficient to deprive it of over 600 million dollars in individual income-tax revenue. The fate of the 1936 proposal has already been described, but an undistributed-profits tax, in lieu of other corporation taxes, still remains a possible tax tool.

In support of their opposition to undistributed-profits taxation, managements contend that decisions as to reinvestment of corporate earnings should be their prerogative and not that of the government. They contend that there are many circumstances where it is necessary for business to accumulate considerable liquid reserves, even if such reserves are not immediately reinvested. Often, they contend, a group of stockholders which is widely dispersed and which is interested in stock ownership chiefly from the investment point of view is not best fitted to decide whether a given corporation should increase its assets by reinvestment of earnings or not.[25] In any event, they would argue, such stockholders generally have a chance to dispose of shares held on the market if they do not like the corporate policies which are being followed.

Valid arguments can be cited for and against a high undistributed-profits tax as a means of integrating business and personal taxation. On the one hand, those who criticize this tax cannot demonstrate that a considerable amount of current income is not withdrawn from the income stream as a result of withheld corporate earnings which are not reinvested. But the great unpopularity which accompanied our earlier attempt to use the undistributed-profits tax cannot be ignored. Presumably, the opposition to such a tax will be equally as great if it is proposed in the future. The strength of the argument that an undistributed-profits tax is desirable to prevent increases in corporate liquidity from becoming a means for income receivers to avoid personal income taxes would be reduced if all stock dividends were taxable as personal income. Such treatment of stock divi-

[25] This point of view was recognized by A. G. Buehler, *The Undistributed Profits Tax*, pages 183-184, New York: McGraw-Hill Book Co., Inc., 1937.

dends would permit corporations to build up liquidity for business purposes and at the same time minimize the use of the corporation as a refuge for tax avoidance by stockholders.

Taxing corporations only on uninvested profits. Among the many other proposals for integration of corporate and personal income taxes, we shall state only one—a variation of the un-distributed-profits tax. Under this proposal, a corporation would be freed from taxation of income which it distributes in dividends. It also would not be taxed on that portion of income retained and invested. But the portion retained and not invested would be subject to a heavy tax.

Back of this proposal is the belief that withheld corporate earnings may drain off a substantial portion of the income stream to increase corporate liquidity in various ways. The proposal has appeal, but would run into difficulties in defining "investment."

In order not to penalize corporations for building up a legitimate liquidity position, corporations must be permitted to hold some cash and securities. In order to prevent corporations from becoming "savings banks" for high-income stockholders, however, this liquidity position would have to be limited. Defining the maximum permissible ratio of liquid to total assets would be extremely difficult. There is considerable variability in liquidity requirements between firms. For example, electric power producers and railways require lower liquidity ratios than do retail grocers. Seasonal industries probably require higher liquidity than do industries unaffected by seasonal variations.

The right of a private corporation to make a self-protecting use of funds over a period of business fluctuations can scarcely be subject to a tax penalty if the private enterprise is to be granted relative freedom in its business actions. Such freedom, in the sense being discussed here, is probably necessary to the continued successful functioning of private enterprise units. We consider this particular proposal one of the least promising for integration of personal and business taxation.

Conclusions on methods of corporate-personal tax integration. The proposals for integration which we have briefly examined lead us to these conclusions: (1) For the bulk of corporations, the most promising step toward integration would be to convert corporations into withholding agents for individual income taxes. Such tax liabilities would be current, to the extent that corporate dividends are paid from earnings, and would be postponed to the extent that current earnings became the basis for future dividends. (2) For closely held corporations, business could be "untaxed" by applying taxes to prorata shares of corporate income (or losses) as part of personal income in the hands of individuals. For several reasons, it is not desirable to apply the prorata method of taxation to the income (or losses) of corporations generally, but the prorata method is logically unassailable from the standpoint of preventing tax avoidance by individuals. (3) For small, new businesses in need of additional capital, enterprises could be "untaxed" by applying only personal taxes on the basis of realized capital gains (or losses) in the corporate investments. But the problems of defining when an enterprise is "small" and when it ceases to be "new" would not be simple.

Major Problems of Business Income Taxation

Since the writers have found little cause for taxes on business in addition to taxes on their owners, it might be deemed unnecessary to discuss major problems in business-income taxation. However, it has also been recognized that taxes on business income, particularly on the income of corporations, may remain a part of our tax structure for a considerable period of time, in which case a discussion of the major problems in business-income taxation is relevant. In analyzing the corporation-income tax in 1946, Dr. Howard Bowen was sufficiently impressed by the probability of a search for Federal tax revenue in the near future that he urged retention of the corporation-income tax at rates sufficient to yield around 8 billion dollars annually in the years ahead.[26]

On the assumption that taxes on business will not be eliminated simply because there is little economic logic in retaining them, this section will be devoted to a brief analysis of the problems of business taxation. Most of the discussion in this section will be directed to Federal business taxation, and particularly to the taxation of business income.

The following problems of business-income taxation will be briefly examined, or mentioned:

[26] See Howard R. Bowen, "The Future of the Corporation Income Tax," New York: Irving Trust Company, 1946.

1. Should major tax emphasis be placed on a net income tax rather than some other form of tax, such as a gross income tax, a capital-stock tax, or an excess-profits tax?
2. Should a business tax cover only corporations or also unincorporated forms of business enterprise?
3. Should a business tax be imposed at some flat rate or have a rate structure which increases with income?
4. Should net income for taxation be defined as the entire entrepreneurial income available for both interest and dividends or, as at present, apply only to net income available to stockholders of a corporation?
5. What provisions should there be to reduce discrimination among businesses due to fluctuations in income?
6. Should changes be made in current practices for deductions of depreciation, depletion, and obsolescence from gross business income?
7. Should taxation be on the basis of a consolidated return for all corporate entities which make up a business firm or on the basis of separate returns for each corporate segment of the firm?
8. Should dividends received by one corporate entity from another (intercorporate dividends) be subject to additional taxation?
9. What lines of state policy should be followed in the interstate allocation of corporate income for purposes of taxation?
10. What are the outlines of increased coordination of Federal and state fiscal systems which would make states agree to simplification in the business-tax structure?

Why net-income tax is better than other types of business taxes. Net-income taxation is the most widely supported and is considered the least undesirable form of business-income taxation. As compared with gross-income taxation or taxation on the basis of capital stock, for example, uncertainties as to final incidence of the tax are less with a general net-income tax. This is a positive advantage if it is desired to plan the final incidence of the tax in advance. There is more likelihood that a general business net-income tax will rest on those who pay it in the first place— the owners of the business—than is true in the case of the other types of taxes which have been mentioned. As compared with a gross-income tax, a net-income tax places a lighter tax load on those who are attempting to establish new business enterprises on a relatively permanent basis. During the first few years, such an enterprise may show no net income at all, and the necessity of absorbing or of shifting a gross-income tax may prove to be the deciding factor in the success or failure of such a business enterprise. As a generalization, a gross-income tax or a capital-stock tax is likely to be partly or completely shifted over a longer-run period, and to result in a more unequal distribution of individual incomes than without such a tax.

A business net-income tax has a further advantage over a capital-stock tax. Assuming a given tax-rate structure and reasonable honesty in accounting practices, a net-income tax may be administered much more simply and with less opportunity for discrimination among business units than a capital-stock tax. Any thorough attempt to determine the base for a capital-stock tax necessarily involves an examination of several hundred thousand corporation balance sheets, in which it is possible to state the valuation of capital stock all the way from a nominal amount per share to the actual amount per share invested by stockholders in a corporate enterprise. From 1916 through 1926, the Federal government actually attempted to make a capital-stock tax workable, and then gave up the attempt as a failure.[27]

(1) *Special aspects of excess-profits taxes.* The net-income tax also has advantages over an excess-profits tax, such as was employed in both World Wars I and II. Probably necessary as part of a wartime control structure, this tax has less to commend it for peacetime use. Excess-profits taxation might help to check continuing monopolistic accumulation of capital which leads to further concentration of economic and political power. Such taxation would make such accumulation more difficult. However, the existing concentration would be little disturbed by excess-profits taxation.

The following deficiencies of a peacetime excess-profits tax stand out: (1) It does not take account of those varying degrees of risk among business enterprises which must be recognized in order to secure the investment of business funds and expansion in various enterprises. (2) It discriminates unfairly among various

---

[27] The so-called "capital stock" tax which was in force between 1934 and 1945 was a capital-stock tax in name only. The tax was combined with a "declared value" excess-profits tax in such a way that the higher the valuation for purposes of the capital-stock tax which the corporation gave, the lower was the rate of return on the basis of which the so-called "excess-profits" tax was calculated. This tax "team" was removed from the Federal tax structure by the Revenue Act of 1945.

types of competitive enterprise. (3) It presents many difficult questions about the definition of capital investment. It has not proved easy to work out the answers to these problems.

As it has been applied, the excess-profits tax relies heavily on the definition of some return on capital investment, above which it is considered that "excess" profits exist which should be subject to a special tax. (A net return of 8 per cent was not deemed excessive during the years of operation of the excess-profits tax from 1940-1945.) The basic trouble with the idea of an excess return on capital investment is that it does not allow for variations in the degree of risk among enterprises. The prospect of a relatively stable annual return of 6 per cent may be sufficient to attract capital for investment in public service enterprises, but the prospect of a return much above 8 per cent may be required in order to obtain capital for the development of mineral resources of uncertain quality and quantity. From this point of view, an excess-profits tax is a rather crude instrument of public policy which penalizes risk-assumption.

As they have been applied, excess-profits taxes are discriminatory against new business enterprises and against those whose net incomes fluctuated widely. For example, a business equipment concern which has very low (or even negative) net income in one year may escape the tax, but may be subject to it a year or two later, when recovery in the demand for its products may be very sharp. But a public service enterprise with relatively stable, but not excessive, returns on its capital investment may escape the tax year in and year out. Again, a relatively new enterprise may have succeeded in building up a large net income, after early years of operating losses, and may become subject to the excess-profits tax. The equity of excess-profits taxation under these conditions may be questioned.

As has already been indicated, excess profits have generally been regarded as those which exceed some established return on invested capital. To determine just what the invested capital "base" is has always proved difficult in the use of the excess-profits tax. In 1940, for instance, when an excess-profits tax was being discussed for World War II, there were still undecided cases in the courts dealing with the determination of invested capital under the 1918 World War I excess-profits tax law. The tax itself was repealed, effective in 1922. Almost immediately after the end of World War II, the Federal government repealed the wartime excess-profits tax, and set up a special tax body to speed the settlement of tax disputes arising out of the excess-profits tax of 1940-1945.

One of the consequences of the use of excess-profits taxes in wartime has been to make easier the formulation and renegotiation of wartime contracts between government and businesses. If the contracts appeared unduly profitable to business from the public point of view, an opportunity to capture excess profits through renegotiation of contracts has been presented by the tax. Under renegotiation in World War II, businessmen were able to capture only a portion of excess profits and were bound to give up a part of revenues. Thus, in 1945, government refunds on renegotiated war contracts exceeded 2 billion dollars.

Largely because of the limitations which have been mentioned, wartime excess-profits taxation has not been considered suitable for peacetime use. A general business net-income tax does not escape all the problems inherent in an excess-profits tax, but its application among business firms is less discriminatory and it avoids the technical problems of measuring invested capital. It is both more equitable among business firms and much easier to administer as part of our tax system.

Should a business-income tax apply only to corporations? Another problem in business net-income taxation relates to its coverage of different forms of business enterprise. Except in the case of the New York and Connecticut state taxes on business incomes, the tax has been confined to the net incomes of corporations. Logically, it is difficult to defend this tax classification. If there is any solid basis for the taxation of business, it lies in a payment for benefits received, and such benefits accrue to partnerships and proprietorships as well as to corporations. We have already indicated that, under our laws, we have made the price of the corporate privilege itself very small. Taxation of income growing out of the "corporate privilege" seems inconsistent with the favorable social and legal pattern for the use of the corporate device which we have established.

The reluctance to establish a Federal business net-income tax applicable to partnerships and proprietorships has been due partly to the administrative problems which would be involved in applying such a tax to several million unincorporated business enterprises.   New York state had faced this administrative problem (1943) by eliminating professional and personal service firms (unincorporated) from its state tax, and by granting a general $5,000 exemption from the tax. As of 1944, the result was that only about 39,000 unincorporated firms were required to file returns on 1943 incomes and had total tax liability of 26.2 million dollars. Connecticut also has a general unincorporated-business tax, imposed at very low rates, on a gross-income basis.

Aside from administrative difficulties, we see no good reason why net corporate income should be subject to business-income taxation while net income from other business forms should not be so taxed. For example, under existing laws, if an individual operates an enterprise as an unincorporated proprietor, he may pay a personal-income tax but pay no Federal corporate-income tax. However, if he incorporates, he is subject to the corporate-income tax as well as the personal-income tax even though he holds all of the stock. The exclusion (from taxation) of income from noncorporate business forms highlights the inconsistency of business-income taxation. Recognizing current practice, our further discussion of business net-income taxation will be confined to the discussion of corporation income taxes.

Should a business-income tax be imposed at progressive rates? Another problem in taxation of corporate net income is whether or not the tax-rate structure employed should be a progressive-rate structure. From 1909 through 1934, the Federal government taxed corporate net income at a flat rate; beginning with 1935 it has used progressive rates which, in 1946, increased from 21 per cent on the first $5,000 of taxable net income to 38 per cent on the entire net income over $50,000. As of 1942, 8 of the 33 states (including the District of Columbia) imposing a corporation net-income tax used progressive tax rates which varied from 2 per cent on the first $1,000 of taxable net income to 8 per cent on taxable net income over $5,000. The remaining states imposed flat rate taxes of from 2 to 8 per cent on taxable net income.

Progression in rates on corporation net income cannot be regarded as an application of ability-to-pay taxation. The notion of ability has no content unless it is applied to the varying incomes of different natural persons, not artificial corporate entities. Neither does corporate income-tax progression provide any assurance that the business enterprise with a large amount of invested capital will be subject to the highest tax rates; it is entirely possible that even large business corporations, such as United States Steel Corporation, may operate at a net loss during years of business depression. (This was the actual history of U. S. Steel during the years 1932-1934.)

Two arguments for relatively lighter taxes on small-business net incomes are: (1) such a tax policy may provide assistance to new business enterprises in the early years of their operation, years when profits may be small (or negligible) and when access to additional capital may be largely limited to the reinvestment of earnings which they are able to make, and (2) heavier taxes upon larger business incomes may help to check the concentration of economic and political power.

Differential rates of corporation-income taxes are a crude way of supplying assistance to new enterprises, however. Specially favorable tax treatment for new business firms can also be provided by exempting such businesses from income taxation in their early years. Although tax relief for new business enterprises is desirable, there is no assurance that everything which appears to be new business is actually new. Old businesses may set up subsidiaries (which are regarded as new) in order to obtain more favorable tax treatment.

How broadly should net income be defined for taxation? An important issue in corporate net-income taxation in the United States is the net-income base to which net-income taxes should be applied. Unlike the British, our corporation net-income taxes have uniformly been made applicable only to net income *after* interest on loan capital, with the result that we have encouraged financing through fixed-income, interest-bearing obligations. It is widely agreed that such financing tends to accentuate economic instability in times of business depression, since it is necessary to meet interest payments on borrowed funds to maintain corporate solvency. The presence of a substantial fixed charge in the form of interest is likely to receive primary business attention when net income is low (or negative) at the expense of corporate outlays for maintenance, replacement, and technological improvements. Such outlays, however, are necessary in order to maintain efficient production at lowest unit costs, and their contraction during business depression in favor of meeting fixed interest charges further decreases expenditure in the economy which may give rise to new production and employment.

The most obvious correction for our present tax policies in this particular area would be defining net income for taxation to include rather than to exclude interest on loan capital. However, in such economic units as our railroads, the proportion of interest-bearing bonds in the total capitalization of bonds and stocks averages 60 per cent. Since such units have been under increasing pressure to earn enough to meet interest charges since about 1930, the application of our corporate net-income taxes to interest, as well as to net income available for stockholders, would further increase their financial problems. Probably the most that is desirable in solving this problem of tax policy is to make interest on new borrowed capital (other than security issues to refund existing capital issues which are maturing or to make possible corporate reorganization following insolvency) subject to corporate net-income taxation. This much revision in the application of our corporate net-income taxes would increase future incentives to finance corporate business through selling stock rather than through borrowing.

More liberal treatment of business losses. Another problem in business-income taxation is the treatment of business losses for tax purposes. Our policy of using an annual accounting period tends to penalize businesses with fluctuating net incomes, unless our laws could allow very liberal consideration of the carry-forward (or carry-back) of net losses incurred in one year to determine tax liability in other years. Over a complete business cycle (1922-1939, for instance) it has been calculated that the effective Federal income tax in various lines of economic activity varied all the way from a tax of more than 100 per cent on the aggregate net income of agricultural and similar industries to about 16.2 per cent for industries manufacturing food products, beverages, and tobacco. During that period, the average Federal income-tax rate on incomes reported annually was about 13 per cent.

During the years 1938-1942, Federal corporation-tax laws were amended to allow a two-year carry-forward or carry-back of unused business losses in a particular year. The opportunity to carry-back losses was introduced in this country by the Revenue Act of 1942, and was still in effect in 1946. Its major purpose was to permit corporations which incurred losses in reconversion from wartime to peacetime production to charge any such net losses against the preceding period of wartime production. Our treatment of tax losses (1946) was still less liberal than that provided in the British income tax, which allows a 6-year carry-forward of business losses for the purpose of determining the income-tax base.

As a continuing peacetime provision, the opportunity to carry-forward losses for several years is preferable to a carry-back provision. The latter makes it necessary to reopen tax accounts which have once been settled and opens the possibilities of dispute, litigation, and the use of a larger administrative staff for tax enforcement. Carry-forward provisions at least as liberal as those which are allowed in the British tax system should be part of our corporation tax laws.

The general problem of taxation for capital gains and losses has already been outlined for individual income taxation. The application of Federal laws to corporate capital gains and losses, effective in 1946, did not differ greatly from the laws applicable to individuals. Long-term gains were taxable at a maximum effective rate of 25 per cent. But, unlike the treatment accorded under individual income taxation, such gains were not subject to a reduction of 50 per cent for tax purposes simply because capital assets had been held more than six months.[28]

Tax treatment of depreciation, depletion, and obsolescence. There has been considerable pressure in recent years for a revision in the current treatment (1946) of depreciation, obsolescence, and depletion for tax purposes. Current tax laws recognize that charges for depreciation (including obsolescence) are a "reasonable" deduction against gross income from the use of tangible real assets (except inventories) and intangibles such as patents and copyrights, in order to determine net income. Depletion charges against gross income from natural resources such as a mineral deposit, are also permitted.

The chief pressures for changes in Federal tax laws are devoted to depreciation, where it is argued that existing provisions are too rigid, and to depletion, where it is contended that existing pro-

[28] There were other minor differences in application of the 1946 laws to capital gains and losses of individuals, as compared with corporations.

visions are excessively liberal. The rates of depreciation for various classes of business assets are defined by the Bureau of Internal Revenue, which maintains a schedule (Bulletin F) of permitted annual rates of depreciation, depending on estimated economic life for such varied types of assets as machine tools and buildings. The Bureau also favors the use of "straight-line" depreciation accounting (which is most widely used by business), under which an equal annual deduction is made over the recognized economic life of an asset.

Presumably, the sum of depreciation deductions will, when added to salvage value, equal the cost of the business asset, or be sufficient to replace the particular business asset when its economic life has been exhausted. The Bureau also recognizes the rather hazy concept of "normal" obsolescence as part of permissive depreciation deductions. "Normal" obsolescence is supposed to refer to the impairment of capital which results from improvements or changes in the productive process which are predictable. Since most obsolescence, resulting from unforeseen inventions or changes in demand, is necessarily unpredictable, it is difficult to find much content in permissive deductions for normal obsolescence.

When we examine depreciation which is due to wear, tear, and general using-up of a relatively durable business asset, we find that there is a considerable case, on economic grounds, for greater flexibility in depreciation charges, especially in the opportunity for "accelerated depreciation" during the early years of service life of business assets. Accelerated depreciation charges would permit the cost of business assets to be charged off during the early period of their use and would make it possible for businessmen to accumulate more rapidly for the replacement of one business asset with a better one. It might lighten the load of depreciation charges in a period of general business depression and at the same time make possible the acquisition of new operating assets at relatively low cost in such a period. The "bunching" of capital outlays for business assets in time of business depression could provide a useful business stimulant to production, employment, and business recovery.

Depletion offers another set of problems. A depletion charge logically arises in the using-up of any wasting natural asset, such as oil deposits, minerals, and timber. Part of the gross return from the business exploitation of such assets is a return from the sale of the capital assets themselves. Unless depletion were recognized in the gross return and segregated for new investment or for reinvestment, the owners of a business would find themselves with no remaining business investment at the end of a period of years.

In an attempt to recognize the economic character of depletion, Congress has set up, and the Bureau of Internal Revenue allows, a schedule of depletion allowances which is based on some percentage of gross income depending on the character of the depleting asset.[29] The Bureau has often underestimated the economic life of wasting assets, and the allowances which it has set up are generally considered to be unnecessarily generous. The Treasury recommended twice in 1942 that depletion allowances should be based on percentages of the recovery of cost of investment in depleting assets. It has also been urged that if the period over which such allowances could be made were shorter than the economic life of the asset, some carry-back of excessive depletion charges could equitably be employed.

Use of consolidated returns and taxation of intercorporate dividends. A final major problem for business net-income taxation by the Federal government which will be discussed is the use of consolidated corporate returns and the taxation of intercorporate dividends. This problem has grown directly out of the rise of the holding company in our economic structure. Such a company is a type of corporation which owns the majority, or all, of the voting stock in a varying number of other corporations. It may be a "pure" holding company whose only assets are the stocks of operating companies (as often occurs in the public utility field). It may be partly a holding company, partly an operating unit, such as the large Northern States Power Company[30] in the utility field. It may simply be a parent corporation coordinating the operations of a number of operating subsidiaries, which may be organized as separate corporations principally for maximizing operating efficiency within the over-all corporate firm. This type

---

[29] Thus, Federal laws in 1946 allowed a percentage depletion charge of 27½ per cent on oil and gas properties, 5 per cent on coal mines; in no case was the allowance permitted to exceed 50 per cent of net income before depletion.

[30] Reference is to the Northern States Power Company incorporated in Minnesota.

of business organization is common in manufacturing industries—
General Motors is a good example.

During the thirties many actual and alleged abuses of public
utility holding-company systems were emphasized. The outcome was regulation of the practices of interstate holding companies, under the Public Utility Act of 1935. Unfavorable governmental reaction to practices attributed to these companies,
however, has appeared also in tax legislation. Under 1946 laws
the privilege of making a consolidated corporate return was subject to a payment of 2 per cent of consolidated corporate surtax
net income. Since 1936, 15 per cent of intercorporate dividends
received by a corporation not making a consolidated return have
been a part of taxable income. Assuming efficient regulation of
public utility holding companies by the Securities and Exchange
Commission and of railroads by the Interstate Commerce Commission, the writers find no logical reason why consolidated tax
returns should not be permitted without payment for the privilege or why intercorporate dividends should not be excluded
from taxable income.

Special problems of state business taxation. With the present
maze of state business taxes, a major fiscal consideration is to outline some fiscal system which would make the states willing to
forego most of the special business taxes which they now have.
As has been suggested earlier, such a system will require finding
revenues for the states to replace revenues from tax sources which
they might abandon. Such revenues would have to come from
Federal grants. At the Federal level it would be necessary that
reliance on tax revenue as a source of funds should not interfere
with the major objectives of economic policy such as we have outlined in this book. The inauguration of any such system of revenue for state governments would involve various political as well
as economic considerations. Discussion of these problems, as
well as some indication of how such a system of Federal-state relationships might function will be postponed until the final chapters of the book.

Descriptions of taxable income by the 33 states which impose
general corporation-income taxes resemble that of the Federal
government, although the types of business corporations uniformly affected are only mercantile and manufacturing enterprises. Special types of taxes are frequently applied to such

kinds of business enterprises as banks, public utilities, railroads, and insurance companies.[31] A special problem in state business-income taxation which will be discussed in some detail in the final chapters of the book, but will be mentioned here, is the interstate allocation of corporate income for purposes of taxation. Under accepted constitutional interpretation, no state is permitted to tax a larger portion of the net income of a corporation operating in more than one state than may "reasonably" be attributed to that state.

At least eight different indices of business done within state borders are used in state corporation-income taxation, but three are most widely used and have the endorsement of the National Tax Association as factors which it is reasonably equitable to use in combination to allocate interstate corporate income. These are the relative percentages within one state of total corporate payroll, tangible property, and gross sales. Any allocation formula which is used is arbitrary to some extent; the most to be hoped for if state corporation-income taxation is retained is that uniformity in the type of allocation formula which is used will become increasingly common.

SELECTED READINGS

1. Arant, Roscoe, "Business Taxation in the Southern States," *The Tax Magazine,* Chicago: Commerce Clearing House, Inc., 1938.

2. Buehler, A. G., *The Undistributed Profits Tax,* New York: The McGraw-Hill Book Co., Inc., 1937.

3. Butters, J. Keith and Lintner, John, *Effect of Federal Taxes on Growing Enterprises, A Case Study,* Cambridge, Massachusetts: Graduate School of Business Administration, Harvard University, 1945.

4. Groves, Harold M., *Postwar Taxation and Economic Progress,* Chapter 2, New York: The McGraw-Hill Book Co., Inc., 1946.

[31] Description of these special types of state business taxes is provided in considerable detail in such standard public-finance textbooks as Harley L. Lutz, *Public Finance,* Chapter XXVI, 4th edition, New York: Appleton-Century Co., 1946; W. J. Schultz, *American Public Finance,* Chapters XX and XXI, 3rd edition, New York: Prentice-Hall, Inc., 1941; Harold M. Groves, *Financing Government,* Chapters XI and XII, 2nd edition, New York: Henry Holt & Co., 1944.

5. ———, *Financing Government,* 2nd edition, Chapters 11 and 12, New York: Henry Holt & Co., Inc., 1945.

6. Hansen, Alvin H. and Perloff, Harvey S., *State and Local Finance in the National Economy,* Chapters 3 and 4, New York: W. W. Norton & Co., Inc., 1944.

7. Lerner, Abba P., *The Economics of Control,* Chapters 22, 23, and 24, New York: The Macmillan Company, 1944.

8. Lutz, Harley L., *Public Finance,* Chapter 26, 4th edition, New York: Appleton-Century Co., Inc., 1946.

9. Pigou, A. C., *Economics of Welfare,* Part 2, Chapter 9 and Part 1, pages 29-30, 4th edition, London: Macmillan & Co., Ltd., 1932.

10. Ruml, Beardsley and Sonne, H. Christian, *Fiscal and Monetary Policy,* Washington, D. C.: National Planning Association, Bulletin No. 35, 1944.

11. Shultz, W. J., *American Public Finance,* 3rd edition, Chapters 20 and 21, New York: Prentice-Hall, Inc., 1941.

12. United States Treasury Department, *Statistics of Income, Part II,* 1936 through 1940, Washington, D. C.: United States Government Printing Office. Published yearly 1938 through 1942.

CHAPTER XVI

COMMODITY TAXATION

A N IMPORTANT proportion of the tax revenues collected in the United States is derived from such levies as excises —particularly on gasoline, tobacco, and alcoholic beverages— general sales taxes, and customs duties. Although they usually are collected from sellers of goods and services (that is, the sellers pay the tax money to the government treasury) these taxes are frequently shifted to the buyers of these goods and services as well as to the sellers of the resources used in producing taxed commodities. Because a part of their incidence rests with consumers, such taxes are frequently called *consumption taxes*. However, since such taxes are levied upon commodities independently of whether or not these commodities are consumed, and because a part of them may be shifted backward we shall call these taxes *commodity taxes*.

Commodity taxation has played an important role in the United States' tax system since the formation of the Union. Receipts from customs duties made up more than one-half of Federal tax revenues in every year between the inception of the Federal tax system and 1864. During the Civil War, manufacturers' and sales taxes as well as excises upon tobacco and liquor were added to the sources of Federal tax revenue. After the Civil War and until the first World War, commodity taxes continued to provide a large proportion of Federal tax revenue. For example, in 1910, receipts from customs duties and liquor and tobacco excises brought in more than 95 per cent of total Federal tax collections.

The increase in the level of Federal tax collections during and after World War I, together with the introduction of personal- and corporate-income taxes at the Federal level, reduced the *relative* importance of commodity taxes in the Federal tax system. However, a variety of internal excise taxes imposed during the depression of the thirties helped to revive commodity taxation.

In the period 1935-1939 Federal excises, sales and documentary stamp taxes, and customs duties brought in around two-fifths of total Federal tax receipts.

Since 1939, there has been a further expansion in Federal commodity taxation. In 1944, about 5 billion dollars were collected from Federal excise taxes. In addition, there were revenues from customs duties. Excise tax rates (as of 1946, recently extended through 1948) on some of the more frequently consumed items are shown in Table 22.

The constitution denied to the states the right to levy customs duties. In 1900, the bulk of state revenues was obtained from property taxes. As indicated in Chapter XIX, state property taxes steadily decreased in relative importance after 1900 and represented less than 4 per cent of total state tax revenue in 1946. Commodity taxation was not an important source of revenue to the states until the widespread adoption of the automobile. As the use of motor vehicles increased, taxes on these vehicles (principally in the form of registration fees and gasoline taxes) became increasingly important. Throughout the thirties, for example, gasoline taxes represented more than one-fifth of state tax revenues. The repeal of prohibition and the occurrence of the depression prompted all the states to tax liquor and many of them to levy general sales taxes. By 1940, nearly half the states were using some form of general sales taxation. In 1940, general sales, tobacco, and liquor taxes yielded more than two-fifths of total state tax revenues.

Only a few local taxing units employ commodity taxation. Although a few cities (New York City and Denver, Colorado are examples) have a general sales tax, the bulk of local tax revenues has been obtained from the taxation of property. (Taxes on highway users and property taxes receive special attention in Chapters XVIII, XIX and XX.)

Incidence of Commodity Taxes

Even though taxes on commodities are usually collected from the sellers of taxed commodities, it is generally conceded that such taxes are shifted—that the economic unit from which the tax money is collected does not bear all of the tax. As was indicated in the discussion of shifting and incidence in Chapter XII, the way in which a tax is shifted depends upon the way in which

Table 22[1]

Rates and Yields of Federal Excise Taxes on Selected Items,
Fiscal Year 1946

Item	Tax Rate	Revenue, Fiscal Year 1946 (in thousands of dollars)
All Internal Excises		6,683,999
Tobacco Taxes		1,165,519
Cigarettes (small)	$3.50 per 1,000	1,072,799
Alcoholic Beverage Taxes		2,526,162
Distilled spirits	$9.00 per proof gal.	1,788,457
Beer and other fermented malt liquors	$8.00 per barrel	650,824
Manufacturers and Retailers Excises		1,414,717
Cosmetics, toilet preparations, furs, jewelry, and luggage	20 per cent	492,045
Gasoline	1½¢ per gal.	405,695
Tires and tubes	5¢ per lb.—tires 9¢ per lb.—tubes	118,072
Lubricating oils	6¢ per gal.	74,602
Auto parts and accessories	5 per cent	68,871
Other Taxes on Services		
Admissions	20 per cent (approx.)	415,268
Transportation of persons, seats and berths	15 per cent	226,750
Transportation of property	3 per cent	220,121
Local telephone service	15 per cent	145,689
Telephone, telegraph, radio and cable, leased wires, etc.		234,393

other opportunities are affected. An excise tax levied upon a single commodity is likely to induce additional purchases of other untaxed commodities. Buyers of the taxed good probably will have to pay higher prices for this good, but sellers also may be receiving lower profits. Also, if a significant proportion of a given resource is used in producing the taxed commodity, returns to the owners of this resource will be reduced.

A nationwide general sales tax upon all goods and services, however, would affect all goods and services. Since holdings of cash and securities are not likely to be taxed, a general sales tax would be likely to alter the relationship between commodity

[1] Data are compiled from the Treasury Bulletin, U. S. Treasury Department (November, 1946), pages 63, 64; and from the Revenue Acts of 1943 and 1946.

purchases and these holdings, encouraging relatively smaller expenditure on goods and services.

Thus, selective excises are likely to be shifted both forward and backward, to increase the relative prices of taxed goods and reduce the prices of resources used in producing taxed goods. Customs duties are also likely to increase relative prices of the kinds of goods that are imported. A nationwide general sales tax is unlikely to affect significantly the relative commodity-price pattern, if the relationship between government expenditure and government receipts is adjusted so that total money expenditure (after the tax) for goods and services is unchanged.

General sales taxation, however, has been primarily utilized by the states. Unless all states employ the tax and use the same rates, the geographic price pattern is likely to be altered. (Refer to Chapter XII.)

Effects Upon Resource Allocation

The impact of commodity taxation upon the allocation of resources depends on the effects of such taxes upon the pattern of relative prices. Unless the demand for the taxed commodity is perfectly inelastic, a reduction in consumers' purchases of this commodity is to be expected as a result of the increased price encouraged by the tax. Less of the commodity will be produced. If total employment in the economy is not reduced, resources will be moved out of the taxed industry and into other lines of production.

Suppose that an excise tax is levied upon potatoes. The price which the consumer will have to pay for potatoes is likely to increase, and the amounts which potato producers can afford to pay for resources are likely to fall. Some resources will be moved out of potato production and into production of other crops.

Specific excise taxes may thus tend to alter the production pattern. More of some commodities and less of others will be produced if the treatment is not the same for all commodities. The resulting production pattern is likely to be inferior to that which would prevail in the absence of such taxes. The taxes are costs which must be considered by producers. Such taxes are not costs, however, in the sense that they represent the value of alternative goods and services which must be sacrificed in order to get production of the taxed good. Consequently, the value to consumers of the goods and services produced by the resources which are moved out of the taxed industry is likely to be smaller than the value to the consumer of the taxed good which those resources could have produced had there been no tax.[2]

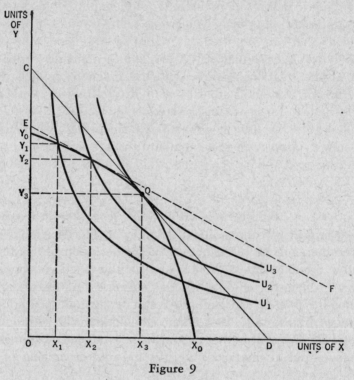

Figure 9

Effects of Commodity Taxation Upon the Production Pattern and Consumer Welfare

Suppose that homogeneous units of a resource, A, are being used to produce homogeneous units of products X and Y. The combinations of X and Y which can be produced from a given amount of A (say A_0) are represented by the points lying on the line X_0Y_0 (Figure 9). Assume that we wish to maximize the welfare of a single consumer. A plane section of the preference system of this consumer is represented by the indifference curves U_1, U_2, and U_3.

---

[2] An exception to this general case may be that in which the taxed commodity is produced under conditions of increasing costs (diminishing marginal productivity) while other commodities are produced under conditions of decreasing costs (increasing marginal productivity). Refer to Alfred Marshall, *Principles of Economics*, Book V, Chapter XIII, New York: The Macmillan Company, 1920.

If A_0 is allocated so that the combination X_1Y_1 is produced, the consumer can attain the welfare level U_1. Other welfare levels can be achieved if other combinations of X and Y are produced. The maximum welfare level will be reached when the combination X_3Y_3 is produced. At this combination the transformation curve (X_0Y_0) is tangent to the indifference curve U_3 at the point Q; the consumer's marginal rate of substitution of X for Y (the slope of U_3 at Q) is equal to the marginal rate of transformation between X and Y (the slope of X_0Y_0 at Q). Under perfect competition, the ratio of the prices of Y and X—the price of $Y(P_y)$ divided by the price of $X(P_x)$—will be equal to the consumer's marginal rate of substitution between X and Y and to the marginal rate of substitution between X and Y in production. The price ratio, $\dfrac{P_y}{P_x}$, is the slope of the iso-revenue line CD.

If a tax is imposed upon X, increasing the relative returns from producing Y, a new iso-revenue line, EF, will represent various combinations of X and Y yielding the same revenue. A combination containing less X and more Y will be produced. Assume this new combination is X_2Y_2. The welfare of the consumer obviously has been diminished by the reallocation of the resource.

This conclusion is not altered if the welfare of additional consumers is also considered—maximum welfare being defined as that condition in which the welfare of any consumer cannot be increased without diminishing the welfare of other consumers.[3]

Effects Upon Income Distribution

Since savings—cash balances and securities—are not taxed by levies upon commodities, it is obvious that persons spending the largest percentages of their incomes upon taxed goods and services are taxed proportionately most. For example, suppose that two individuals, Smith and Jones, each earn $2,500 per year. A general sales tax of 11.1111. . . . . per cent is invoked and shifted forward to buyers. Smith spends $1,000 upon commodities, $100 of this being tax, while Jones spends $2,000 upon commodities, $200 of this being tax. The tax takes 4 per cent of Smith's income and 8 per cent of Jones'.

In general, low-income receivers save relatively less of their

---

[3] Refer to Oscar Lange, "The Foundations of Welfare Economics," *Econometrica*, 10 (July–October, 1942), pages 215-228.

incomes than do high-income receivers. For example, the 1935-36 study of consumer purchases[4] indicated that families in the income group $1,250-1,500 saved, on the average, $14, or about 1 per cent of their income. Families in the income group $20,000 and over had average annual incomes of nearly $42,000 and saved more than 50 per cent of this. A general sales tax of 10 per cent, if shifted entirely forward, would take 10 per cent of the income of the low-income family and only 5 per cent of the income of the high-income family.

Thus general sales taxes, when they are shifted forward, probably tend to be regressive—to take a larger percentage of smaller incomes than of larger incomes and to increase income inequality.

This regressivity of general sales taxation is fairly widely recognized. In attempts to minimize it, selected excises upon goods purchased primarily by the higher-income groups but not by the lower-income groups have been suggested. For example, so-called "luxury" taxes upon jewelry, furs, cosmetics, and the like were levied by the Federal government during the war (and have been extended through 1948). These taxes, however, have been levied upon inexpensive jewelry, furs, and cosmetics as well as expensive items of these commodities. Their effect upon income distribution probably has been little different from that of a general sales tax.

Although items purchased primarily by the higher-income groups could be identified and taxed, such taxes are likely to yield relatively little revenue as compared with more general commodity taxation. Consequently, confining commodity taxes to such items appears unlikely to be practiced.

Effects Upon Expenditures for Goods and Services

Commodity taxation is generally considered to be one of the most deflationary forms of taxation. Other things—the level of government expenditure, the volume of bank credit and liquidity preference schedules, for example—being unchanged, *a given amount* of tax revenue collected from the taxation of commodities is likely to reduce people's expenditures for goods and services by more than would the *same amount* of taxes collected by a personal-income tax. This would be the case if the personal-income tax were a flat percentage tax upon income. The differences

---

[4] *Family Expenditures in the U. S., Statistical Tables and Appendixes,* National Resources Planning Board, June, 1941. Table 1, page 1.

would be even greater if the personal-income tax had personal exemptions and if the rate structure were progressive—characteristics of our Federal income tax and of most state income taxes.

This relatively greater deflationary impact of commodity taxation follows from (1) the encouragement to hold cash balances or securities that are not taxed, and (2) the heavier proportionate taxation of low-income receivers. People in the lower-income groups spend a larger proportion of their incomes upon goods and services that would be taxed than do people in the higher-income groups. Low-income consumers have less opportunity to maintain their purchases of commodities for they have little savings.

For example, a family with an annual income of $2,000 may spend all of this for goods and services. If commodity taxes are introduced and take $200 of this, the net expenditure upon commodities is reduced to $1,800. A family with an annual income of $10,000 may spend $8,000 on goods and services. If commodity taxes are introduced and take $800 of this, net expenditure on goods and services is unlikely to fall to $7,200, even though it may not be maintained at $8,000. The family with $10,000 is likely to increase its gross expenditures by reducing its savings. In the first case, net expenditure for goods and services has fallen by 10 per cent. In the second case the decrease is likely to be less than 10 per cent.

This effect of commodity taxes has been used as an argument against this form of taxation, and as long as *a given amount of taxes* is to be collected, it has some force. State governments would be wise to take it into consideration. At the Federal level, however, this argument has less relevancy if the Federal government is determining tax collections in view of their effects upon employment. If commodity taxes are being collected the total tax bill should be smaller than if income taxes are being collected. The anti-inflationary impact of *a given amount* of taxes collected from personal-income taxation can also be accomplished by *a smaller amount* of taxes collected from commodity taxation. The effects on *total money expenditure* for goods and services as a whole can be made equivalent.

Effects Upon Consumer Welfare

In addition to the undesirable effects upon consumer welfare which result from the resource misallocations encouraged by commodity taxes, there are still other undesirable features. It can be demonstrated that *a given amount* of tax collected from *a given individual* by a commodity tax will leave him in a welfare position inferior to that in which he would be left if the same amount of tax were collected from him by an income tax.

Suppose that a given consumer has an income of $3,000, all of which is spent upon two commodities, X and Y. The price for X is $1 per unit and the price for Y is $2 per unit. A section of his preference system for X and Y is illustrated in Figure 10. Under the conditions postulated, he will have achieved his maximum position when he purchases 700 units of X (an expenditure of $700 on X) and 1,150 units of Y (an expenditure of $2,300 on Y). This position is represented by the point P on the indifference map.

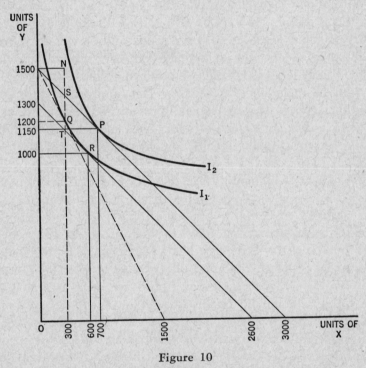

Figure 10

Comparative Welfare Effects of Excise and Income Taxes

Assume that a tax of $1 per unit is levied upon X and that this tax is all shifted forward so that the consumer must now pay $2 per pound for X. The price of Y remains unchanged. He will then purchase 300 units of X, paying $300 (the equivalent of QS in terms of Y) indirectly to the government in the form of a tax and $300 ($SN$ in terms of Y) directly to the seller of the commodity. This position is represented by the point Q on the indifference map.

One way by which we might compare the effects (upon the consumer) of an income tax and the tax upon X is by answering the question, "How much could he pay for the opportunity to purchase at the old prices of $1 per unit for X and $2 per unit for Y and still be no worse off than he is when he has an income of $3,000 and has to pay a price of $2 per unit for X and $2 per unit for Y?"

In order to be neither better nor worse off than at Q, he may rearrange his purchases in any fashion in which he wishes as long as the rearrangement leaves him with combinations on indifference curve I_1. At the pretax prices, the rearrangement will lead him to R, where he will be purchasing 600 units of X and 1,000 units of Y. This arrangement is worth as much to him as the arrangement at Q, where he was paying $2 per unit for X, $300 ($SQ$ in terms of Y) going to the government as tax. At the point R, however, he could pay $400 ($ST$ in terms of Y) to the government if he were able to buy X at $1 per pound, and he would be as well off as when he paid $2 per unit for X and had a money income of $3,000. He would thus be equally willing to pay $400 (the equivalent of 200 units of Y) in the form of income tax or $300 in the form of a tax on X.[5] Government would be as well off, and the taxpayer would be better off, to have the $300 collected in the form of an income tax rather than an excise levied upon X.

Sumptuary Taxation

Taxation of some commodities has been rationalized by supporters of commodity taxation as a means of discouraging the consumption of such commodities. A good deal of support for tobacco and liquor taxation undoubtedly could be mustered because of the belief that consumption of such commodities is undesirable and that taxation will help to discourage such consumption.

The argument that taxes should be levied on harmful commodities is beset with many difficulties. First of all, what

[5] See M. F. W. Joseph, "The Excess Burden of Indirect Taxation," *Review of Economic Studies*, VI, 3:226-31. There are, of course, alternative ways of measuring the differences in welfare.

commodities can be generally voted as harmful? Once the list has been compiled why should any consumption of such goods be permitted, that is, why not legally prohibit the sale of such commodities? If the tax rates are not prohibitive, consumption by high-income receivers can be accomplished without relatively great sacrifice, while consumption by low-income receivers may be reduced, but the consumption that is maintained by the low-income groups will be at the expense of other more (socially) desirable commodities.

For example, high liquor taxes are unlikely to discourage liquor consumption among high-income receivers significantly, since their expenditures upon liquor are unlikely to constitute a very large percentage of their total expenditures, almost regardless of liquor prices. Among low-income receivers, there will be some individuals whose "tastes" for alcohol are such that either consumption will be approximately maintained at the higher prices or more physically harmful products such as canned heat, wood alcohol, and shaving lotion will be consumed in larger amounts. If the former occurs, expenditures for other items in the budget—perhaps food, clothing and shelter—will be cut. The health of other members of the family will be impaired. If the latter occurs, another kind of health impairment will result.

Of course, among the lower-income groups there will be some persons whose demands for liquor are fairly elastic and whose consumption will be cut as the price of liquor is raised. But one can hardly argue that the opportunity to drink low cost products should be granted or denied on the basis of income, unless one believes that a highball is more harmful to a low-income consumer than it is to a consumer whose income is high.

Thus sumptuary taxation, as an instrument for directing consumption, is not likely to produce reasonable results. Perhaps the most important reason for levying such taxes has not been the expected decline in consumption, but the estimated inelasticity of demands for such commodities. Taxes on liquor and tobacco have been excellent revenue raisers. This, in itself, is reasonable evidence that such taxes have not much influence in eliminating tobacco and liquor purchases.

A case might be made for taxation of some commodities on the grounds that the prices of such commodities represent less than their true costs. For example, consumption of cigars and cigarettes may be responsible for considerable losses through fires, or increased liquor consumption may require increased facilities to care for alcoholics and their dependents. Just as the proceeds of gasoline taxes are usually used to construct and maintain highways, the proceeds of taxes on cigarettes and cigars might be used to reduce fire insurance rates to the levels which would prevail if people did not consume cigars and cigarettes. Taxes on alcoholic beverages might be levied to defray the costs of maintaining wards for alcoholics and providing relief for their dependents.

Taxation on such grounds would assume, however, that *all* cigar and cigarette consumption increased fire losses and that *any* alcohol consumption made the consumer an alcoholic in some degree. Such an assumption does not appear very realistic. Nevertheless, taxation on these grounds would represent a decidedly superior basis for sumptuary taxation than the bases now being used.

Some Commodity Taxes Are Easy to Collect

Such taxes as the general retail sales tax have contained one good feature—they have been relatively simple to administer. Both the taxpayer and the tax collector can easily compute the tax. Compliance with the tax provisions is generally relatively inexpensive, as long as sellers of taxed goods keep records of the money volume of their sales. Few resources need to be employed by government or the taxpayer in collecting or paying the tax.

This simplicity tends to disappear, however, as the taxes become confined to fewer commodities unless the number of producers is relatively small. A tax upon corn would be rather difficult to collect because of the large number of producers and sellers. Many interfarm sales would escape taxation. Cigarette and liquor taxes have been less difficult to collect because of the relatively small number of manufacturers.[6]

Problems in Removing Commodity Taxes

Some opposition to the removal of taxes on a few commodities —liquor, cigarettes, and margarine, for example—has grown out

---

[6] However, the shots which some small-scale liquor manufacturers, otherwise known as "moonshiners," have taken at "revenooers" are legend.

of a belief that production in such industries is highly concentrated and that removing the taxes will not result in lower prices
to consumers. This is equivalent to saying that changes in producers' marginal costs (the demand for their product remaining
unchanged) will not result in a change in their output.

If there were only one producer in the industry, such a conclusion would be inconsistent with the assumption that the monopolist prefers a higher to a lower profit, other things being
unchanged. In oligopoly situations, however, it is possible that
reductions in costs will not result in an expansion in output and
reduced prices to consumers. As has been suggested by Sweezy[7]
and others, oligopoly may lead to discontinuities in the firm's
marginal revenue schedule. A range over which marginal costs
may be altered without changing output is thus introduced.

It is possible that production of some commodities on which
taxes are levied does conform to this pattern of oligopolistic behavior. There are, however, many possible behavior patterns for
oligopolists,[8] and analysis of the outcome of each is far from complete. To assure that commodity-tax elimination did not result
only in higher profits, removal of the taxes could be made conditional upon price reductions, or excess-profits taxes could be invoked as a temporary transition measure.

Summary

Although commodity taxation is rather firmly entrenched in
our tax system, such taxation has few advantages and many disadvantages when compared with some other taxes, particularly
the personal income tax. Commodity taxes interfere with achieving the best allocation of resources in that they tend to push
resources out of producing taxed commodities and into producing
other commodities. Because of their impact upon relative prices,
a given amount of tax revenue collected from a tax upon a commodity will diminish consumer welfare more than would the same
amount of tax revenue collected from a personal-income levy.

Ease of administration and potential flexibility are virtues of a
general sales tax. However, these advantages do not—in our
estimation—offset the disadvantages posed by such levies. The

---

[7] Refer to Paul M. Sweezy, "Demand Under Conditions of Oligopoly," *Journal
of Political Economy*, Vol. 47 (August, 1939), pages 568-73.

[8] Refer to John Von Neumann and Oskar Morgenstern, *Theory of Games and
Economic Behavior*, Princeton, New Jersey: Princeton University Press, 1944.

regressivity of commodity taxation is an important factor in limiting the usefulness of such general commodity taxes as the sales tax. Problems of removing commodity taxes from the tax structure are both economic and political; solution of neither problem is impossible.

SELECTED READINGS

1. Duke University, *Law and Contemporary Problems, Consumption Taxes*, Durham, North Carolina: School of Law, Summer, 1941. See particularly contribution by Albert Gailord Hart, "Consumption Taxation as an Instrument of Control."
2. Joseph, M. F. W., "The Excess Burden of Indirect Taxation," *The Review of Economic Studies*, 63:226-31, London.
3. Lange, Oscar, "The Foundations of Welfare Economics," *Econometrica*, 10: (July–October, 1942).
4. National Resources Planning Board, *Family Expenditures in the United States*, Washington, D. C.: United States Government Printing Office, June, 1941.
5. Sweezy, Paul M., "Demand Under Conditions of Oligopoly," *Journal of Political Economy*, 47:4 (August, 1939), pages 568-73.
6. United States Treasury Department, *Treasury Bulletin*, November, 1946, and the *Revenue Acts of 1943 and 1946*, Washington, D. C.: United States Government Printing Office.

CHAPTER XVII

DEATH AND GIFT TAXATION[1]

LIMITATION upon the amount of property which a person might obtain through inheritance has long received the endorsement of prominent economists. As far back as 1848, John Stuart Mill held that it was desirable to permit inequalities in individuals' incomes in a private enterprise system, but that society should place a rather low limit on the amount of property which an individual should be permitted to inherit. Such limitation, he implied, would discourage the development of an undesired rentier class—living on the income from previously accumulated property—and would encourage those in each new generation to work actively for their living.[2]

Taxes on the transfer of property at death have proved to be a useful social instrument in the limitation of inheritance. Such taxes usually have been of two types: the estate tax and the inheritance tax. Either or both may be buttressed by a gift tax. The estate tax, such as that used by our Federal government, falls on the entire estate, after a specific exemption from tax and deduction of the costs of settling the estate. The inheritance tax, used by most of our states, falls upon distributive shares of an estate received by various heirs. In our state tax structures, inheritance taxes generally have a double progression: rates in-

[1] For technical discussion of problems involved in death and gift taxes, the writers wish to acknowledge substantial reliance on the recent investigations of Professor Harold M. Groves, *Postwar Taxation and Economic Progress*, Chapter IX. For aid in their brief outline of problems in Federal-state relationships in death taxation, the writers have been assisted by the recent Federal study, "Federal, State and Local Government Fiscal Relations," pages 469-496.

[2] Mill said: "The inequalities of property which arise from unequal industry, frugality, perseverance, talents, and to a certain extent even opportunities, are inseparable from the principle of private property, and if we accept the principle, we must bear with these consequences of it; but I see nothing objectionable in fixing a limit to what anyone may acquire by the mere favor of others, without any exercise of his faculties, and in requiring that if he desires any further accession of fortune he shall work for it." See John Stuart Mill, *Political Economy* (Ashley edition), Book II, Chapter II, page 228, 1929. Reprinted by permission of Longmans, Green & Co., Inc.

crease with the size of the inheritance and with the distance of relationship of the heirs to the deceased. (An illustration of this double progression is given in Table 24, page 354.) Because of its greater adaptability to varying distance of relationship of heirs to deceased, the inheritance tax is generally considered superior on social grounds to the estate tax.

Fiscal Importance and Development in the United States

In 1941, just before our entrance into World War II, the national government and 47 of the states collected taxes on the transfer of property at death, supplemented by a Federal gift tax and 11 state gift taxes. Such taxes raised about 4.27 per cent (524.7 million dollars) of total tax collections. These taxes had some effect on the limitation of inequality in wealth (and income). The Federal estate tax (death tax) alone rose to 77 per cent on the marginal portion of net taxable estates in excess of $10,000,000. But despite our steeply progressive death taxes, their relative prewar importance in our tax systems was still far below their prewar importance in the British tax structure, where they supplied about 10 per cent of total tax revenues.

John Stuart Mill wrote his comments on death taxation at a time when, and in a society in which, death taxes were already partially established. The earliest British death tax was imposed in 1694. After additional experiments with death taxes in the eighteenth and nineteenth centuries, England established the structure of its present death tax in 1894. In the United States, death taxation was just then getting under way. The first successfully administered state death tax was passed by New York in 1885, and a permanent Federal death (estate) tax did not come until 1916. We will briefly review Federal and state developments in this tax field.

Development of Federal death and gift taxation. The Federal government experimented briefly with death taxation from 1798-1802, from 1861-1870, and from 1898-1902, but present Federal taxation of the transfer of property at death began with the Federal estate tax in 1916. This tax exempted all estates of $50,000 or less and imposed rates rising from 1 to 10 per cent. Although tax rates were increased—principally in the decade before World War II—the tax carried an exemption of $60,000 in 1946. Rates now begin at 3 per cent on the first $5,000 of taxable estate and rise to 77 per cent on the portion of taxable estates of $10,000,000 and above. (See Table 23.) Recognizing that the estate tax was being avoided, the Federal government imposed a gift tax from 1924-1926 and again beginning in 1932. The latter tax, which was still in effect in 1946, is levied at rates three-fourths as large as those which apply to the estate tax. Gifts for charitable, educational, and religious purposes are exempt from the tax.

In developing its death tax system, the Federal government sought to induce some uniformity in death-tax practices by the states, and thus to reduce interstate competition for residence of persons of wealth. Under the 1924 Revenue Act, a credit up to 25 per cent against Federal taxes was established for states having death taxes large enough to absorb the credit. The credit was raised to 80 per cent in 1926. It still applies only to Federal taxes due under the exemption and rate schedule of the 1926 act. Federal tax rates have been raised so greatly since 1926 that, in 1941, the effective tax credit had fallen to an average of about 11 per cent of Federal estate taxes collected. Nevertheless, the tax credit in 1924-1926 induced all of the states (except Nevada) to adopt or maintain state death taxes with rates which would at least absorb the Federal tax credit. A few states, notably Florida,

TABLE 23

Federal Estate Tax Liability and Tax Credits, 1946
(All Citizens and Resident Aliens)

Size of Net Estate[a]	Federal Tax Liability	Maximum Credit for State Taxes[b]	Final Federal Tax Liability[c]	Highest Tax Rate
$ 60,000				
65,000	150		150	3%
75,000	$ 1,075		$ 1,075	11
100,000	4,800		4,800	28
150,000	5,600	500	5,100	30
250,000	47,700	$ 2,400	45,300	30
500,000	126,500	10,000	116,500	32
1,000,000	304,500	33,200	271,300	37
5,000,000	2,430,400	391,600	2,038,800	63
20,000,000	13,742,000	2,666,800	11,075,200	77

[a] The net estate given above is before a specific exemption of $60,000, applicable to all residents, citizens, and aliens.
[b] Credits for state taxes are based upon the 1926 exemptions and tax rates.
[c] Under 1946 laws nonresident aliens have an exemption of $2,000.

abandoned the practice of levying no death taxes. Thus, the credit reduced interstate differences in the taxation of the estates of wealthy individuals. But the credit is out of date in terms of current Federal estate taxation, and needs to be revised and brought in line with present levels of such taxation. Estate taxes imposed by 1946 Federal laws, together with the effect of the tax credit on Federal tax liability, are given in Table 23 for estates of selected sizes.

Because of the large exemptions which the Federal estate tax has always permitted ($60,000 in 1946) and the many loopholes which have been available for avoidance of the tax, a relatively small number of estates have been filed for Federal taxation. Such estates (for citizens and resident aliens) reached a peak of 17,642 for the (calendar) year 1938, and totaled 16,030 in 1943 when tax liability, before tax credits, was 363.4 million dollars.

Development of state death and gift taxation. While state inheritance taxes date back to a Pennsylvania law of 1826, early laws were poorly drawn and administered. The foundation for present state death taxes was laid by New York in 1885 and by Wisconsin in 1903. Carefully drawn and effectively administered, the New York tax first applied only to collateral heirs— those not closely related to the deceased—and was imposed at a flat rate. Although the law was extended in 1891 to direct heirs, the Wisconsin law of 1903 was a further step applying *progressive* rates to inherited shares of an estate. The New York law of 1885 was followed by 20 new state inheritance taxes between 1885 and 1900. A further stimulus to state death taxes was given by the Wisconsin law. In 1916, when the present Federal estate tax was adopted, 43 states had some form of inheritance or estate taxation. By 1927, after the adoption of the Federal credit already explained, 47 states (all except Nevada) were using some form of death taxation. From 1933-1942, 12 states enacted gift taxes, the primary objective being to check avoidance of death taxes imposed by the states. Death and gift taxes reached their maximum importance in state tax structures in 1931, when they produced 9.2 per cent (187.1 million dollars) of state tax revenue. Even though the most common form of state death tax is the inheritance tax, a recent summary indicated that the states employed several combinations of death taxes (as of 1941). The following groups stand out: (1) 7 states had an inheritance tax

TABLE 24[3]

Connecticut Inheritance Tax

Relationship of Heir to Decedent	Exemption	Rates Which Apply to Portion of Inheritance (above Exemption) From:							
		0 to 25,000	25,000 to 75,000	75,000 to 150,000	150,000 to 250,000	250,000 to 400,000	400,000 to 600,000	600,000 to 1,000,000	1,000,000 up
A. Class A[a].........	$10,000	2	3	4	5	6	7	8	9
B. Class B[a].........	3,000	3	4	5	6	7	8	9	10
C. Class C[a].........	500	6	7	8	9	10	11	12	13

[a] Class A: Includes parents, grandparents, husband, wife, lineal descendant, adopted child, adopted parent, and lineal descendant of an adopted child.

Class B: Includes husband or wife of any child in the direct line, any stepchild, brother or sister of full or half blood, and any descendant of such brother or sister.

Class C: Any heirs not included in either Class A or Class B.

[3] Source: Tax Systems, 1942, page 301.

Other information contained in communication from Connecticut Tax Commissioner, December 11, 1946.

only; (2) 29 states had an inheritance tax, plus an estate tax; (3) 7 states had only an estate tax designed to obtain only the maximum credit for Federal taxation established by the 1926 law; (4) 4 states had special types of inheritance taxes, estate taxes, or both.[4]

Incidence and Annual Burden of Death and Gift Taxes

The incidence of taxation has received general discussion in Chapter XII and will only receive special application to the case of death and gift taxes here. Death taxes fall on the (estate of) the deceased under an estate tax to the extent that an individual has anticipated such taxes and has provided for them in advance by taking out insurance to cover their payment. Under an inheritance tax, they fall on the various recipients of the distributive shares in an estate. Gift taxes clearly fall on the donor. In none of these cases, all of which involve transfer of property without directly involving price transactions, does the opportunity for tax-shifting arise.[5] The incidence may be partly with the donor and partly with receivers but not with outsiders.

We noted in Chapter XIII, however, that inheritances and gifts could reasonably be included in a definition of taxable income. Nicholas Kaldor has suggested procedures by which death taxes, payable under a separate schedule of tax rates, might be stated in terms of the annual income burden of such tax payments.[6] These procedures essentially involve an estimate of *maximum* annual burden and *minimum* annual burden of future estate taxes. The estimate of maximum annual burden assumes efforts to maintain the net value of the estate constant over successive generations, through the use of insurance to cover probable estate taxes. The estimate of minimum annual burden assumes no net saving during successive generations, so that the amount of the estate decreases with successive transfers.

Kaldor's estimates of present annual burdens assume an interest rate equivalent to the actual annual yield of estates subject to tax returns. A method similar to Kaldor's has been applied in esti-

---

[4] See Fiscal Relations Report, page 473.

[5] An opportunity for partial shifting of the tax may be present where insurance is taken out, since state jurisdictions typically impose a 2 per cent tax on gross premiums of insurance companies.

[6] See N. Kaldor, "The Income Burden of Capital Taxes," *Review of Economic Studies*, Vol. IX, No. 2 (Summer, 1942), pages 138-157.

mating the present annual burden of Federal estate taxation in this country. (See Table 25.) The calculations in Table 25 have been based on 1946 tax rates and assume that sufficient annual savings are made to maintain the value of the estate transferred to the next generation.

Tax rates might be such that for large estates annual savings to maintain the value of the estate would not make economic sense. Additional saving would reduce the annual net income of the estate (after taxes). At this "critical" point (Kaldor's terminology), annual savings for the benefit of the succeeding generation would not be further increased.[7]

Main Issues in Death Taxation

Apart from questions of incidence, and of tax avoidance, death taxation has been the subject of much controversy in public finance. Those favoring a prominent role for death taxes in the tax structure contend that: (1) most of the factors which are favorable to the accumulation of capital operate in spite of death taxes; (2) relatively high death taxes tend to increase equality of opportunity among members of a new generation; (3) inheritance taxes fall on unearned income, which should be heavily taxed; (4) limitation in the inequality of wealth (and of income) is itself a desired end. Most of the arguments against effective death taxation center around counterattacks on the arguments which have just been enumerated.

In examining these major arguments for effective death taxation, we may first note that there are several factors which contribute to accumulation of a fortune. One is the economic desire itself to build up a substantial fortune. Incentives to accumulate personal capital are probably less disturbed under death taxes than under income taxes. While the latter reduce the net product of current economic activity, death taxes are typically regarded as a much more remote event. Except for provision for one's family in the future, which can be handled under death tax exemptions or by techniques such as insurance, most people are relatively indifferent as to what happens after death, and their current economic efforts will not be much affected by the prospect of a heavy death tax at some remote time in the future. While it is clear that death taxes do cut into savings, there is no

[7] Refer to N. Kaldor, "The Income Burden of Capital Taxes," pages 138-157.

TABLE 25

Net Burden of Federal Estate Taxes, Assuming Given Net Incomes (after Personal Income Taxes) to Be Provided by Estate

(1)	(2)	(3)	(4)	(5)	(6)	(7)	(8)
Annual net income provided by estate (after deduction of income taxes)	Annual gross income necessary to yield net income in col. 1 (1946 personal income tax rates)	Net estate necessary to yield gross income in col. 2 (3% yield)	Gross estate necessary to yield net estate (col. 3) and pay estate taxes	Estate taxes	Effective estate tax rates	Annual net savings (after income tax) necessary to pay estate taxes & leave estate in col. 3[a]	Annual net burden of estate taxes (col. 7 ÷ col. 1) per cent
$ 300	$ 300	$ 10,000	$ 10,000	$		$	
900	900	30,000	30,000				
1,500	1,500	50,000	50,000				
2,250	2,308.64	76,954	78,375	1,421	1.8 %	22.82	1.0 %
3,000	3,234.57	107,819	116,425	8,606	7.4	138.19	4.6
4,500	5,112.51	170,417	204,453	34,036	16.6	546.54	12.1
6,000	7,059.75	235,325	297,178	61,853	20.8	993.22	16.6
7,500	9,107.70	303,590	397,206	93,616	23.6	1,503.25	20.0
15,000	21,792.54	726,418	1,047,489	321,071	30.7	5,155.65	34.4
22,500	39,848.37	1,328,280	2,099,055	770,775	36.7	12,376.86	55.0
30,000	64,332.07	2,144,402	3,871,224	1,726,822	44.6	27,728.75	92.4
42,000	127,592.24	4,253,075	11,282,935	7,029,860	62.3	112,883.24	275.3

[a] It is assumed that saving is spread at the same rate over a 35 year period and invested at 3 per cent interest compounded annually. Calculations are based on 1946 tax rates.

evidence that such taxes have produced a scarcity of capital for new investment.   Much saving by higher-income groups is done quite automatically, after desired consumption purchases have been made.   Further, our attention in the United States since 1930—except for the years of World War II—has been directed increasingly to the probability that current savings may be excessive compared to investment opportunities which are considered profitable by new borrowers.

In the appraisal of the factors affecting capital accumulation, too little emphasis has been placed on such noneconomic factors as the desire for power and position which accompany command over large fortunes.

Effective death taxes, imposed at steeply progressive rates on fortunes of large size, would greatly increase relative equality of opportunity among new contestants for economic prizes in a new generation.   There seems no good social reason why one person, because he has been fortunate enough to inherit ownership or control over a large capital fund, should be given a substantial "running head-start" over another person with equal ability in business operation and management.   Of course, to implement successfully something like an equal basis for equal talent would also require similar opportunity under our educational system for advanced training in business and professional techniques for any two persons of equal potential talent and skill.   (Refer to Chapter X.)

Effective death taxes would penalize mere status in society, arising from windfall inheritance of wealth.   Granting social desirability of a reasonable degree of provision for the immediate family of a deceased, heavy death taxes above such permitted exemptions would recognize that recipients of inherited wealth have done nothing to deserve a substantial share of the total economic product of society.   It would also recognize that, simply as inheritors of wealth accumulated by members of a previous generation, the recipients have demonstrated no special ability to administer and conserve the assets which they have received. They have not demonstrated that their management of the property would be more productive than other managements. Studies which have been made, in fact, indicate that special talents of business leadership and administration have not often been passed on within the family.

A strong reason for effective death taxation at steeply progressive rates is to limit the concentration of wealth and income in society. Limitation of economic inequality has been accepted as a major economic objective of policy throughout this book. Most of the problems in connection with it have been taken up in Chapter X, and our only effort here is to apply the criterion to progressive death taxation. The problem of application is less simple than it may sound. It is true that payment of a stiff estate or inheritance tax may require receivers to liquidate part of their inherited assets in order to pay the tax. But it is also true that sale of such assets will probably be made to other wealthy individuals or corporations which have liquid assets which they may wish to invest. Hence, payment of death taxes may simply involve the transfer of assets to other wealthy individuals or to a corporation where the amount of assets held is substantial.

To the extent, however, that death taxes are really effective in dispersing a particular concentration of wealth with the transfer of property from one generation to the next, available funds for investment will come partly from the capital accumulated by the current generation rather than more largely from capital passed on from the past generation. The fact that present inequality in the ownership of property may not be reduced by death taxes does not necessarily reflect the failure of death taxes to limit the amount of property which one individual may pass on to his heirs.

Those who are critical of death taxes direct their attention principally to the arguments for death taxes which have already been presented. The charge that death taxes consume capital has been made, but probably the only point that will stand test here is that such taxes do tend to reduce funds available for new investment more than taxes mainly on lower-income groups who necessarily cannot save much. It has already been pointed out that death taxes probably interfere less with motives for current saving than do income taxes.

It has been contended that, by breaking up large accumulations, death taxes tend to make other savings sterile. The funds of large-capital owners complement the funds of small-capital owners. It is from the large accumulations that risky investments may be made. These accumulations may be supplemented by funds of small-capital owners. But, if it were not for the large accumulations, small-capital owners would not be able to invest their savings as effectively as when they are combined with those of large-capital owners. The writers, however, do not believe that this possibility is important enough to warrant abandoning substantial death taxes.

It has been contended that death taxes operate to break up effective productive units, but our death-tax laws provide techniques whereby the effect of death taxes on a particular productive unit may be "cushioned." One technique is for the taxpayer to take out life insurance payable to his estate at death: this provides an opportunity for the special accumulation of liquid assets available for death taxes. Another is the paying of death taxes on the installment plan over a period of years: up to ten years in the case of the Federal estate tax. In addition, many business units today are owned through capital shares of a corporation, which may be widely held. A change in the ownership of these shares need not affect corporate management. Finally, past studies indicate that business talent and initiative are often not handed down with the bequest of property, and that some pressure on members of a new generation to undertake new business enterprises may be socially desirable.

There is a miscellany of arguments against death and gift taxation. It is contended that heavy death and gift taxes which fell on philanthropic gifts or bequests for charitable, educational, or religious purposes would lessen private philanthropy. This would probably be true, since such gifts and bequests are now exempt from gift and death taxation. The attitude on extension of gift and death taxes to cover these bequests and gifts will depend largely on political attitudes toward the relative roles which the public and private sectors of the economy should play in making assets available for educational and charitable purposes. It is also contended that death taxes work against the maintenance of family welfare, but this is not necessarily so if such taxes provide substantial exemptions for family members closely related to the deceased, and especially for a surviving wife.

Finally, it is argued that death taxes encourage individuals to avoid risk-assumption in new enterprises by bringing about the holding of large estates in liquid form for the purpose of meeting expected taxes. To the extent that there is widespread preparation for death and gift taxes, through insurance policies and gifts not subject to death taxes, funds available for new investment will be reduced. Observed trends in the composition of estates in preparation for Federal taxation bear out this contention, but the practice probably follows in part from the faulty procedures which have been followed in the valuation of assets by administrators of estates after death. These procedures have failed to give adequate recognition to losses incurred in the liquidation of part of an estate for tax purposes.

Principal Deficiencies in Death and Gift Taxation

The main deficiencies of death and gift taxation as they operate in the United States are: (1) Avoidance of taxes through existing loopholes; (2) problems of multiple, interstate taxation.

Effects on tax avoidance of incomplete integration of death and gift taxes. The very substantial avoidance of our Federal estate tax is due primarily to a combination of two factors: (1) a Federal gift tax which, with a higher effective exemption and with lower rates, is not fully integrated with the estate tax, and (2) the development of legal devices, such as the life-estate-remainder combination which makes it possible to avoid at least one payment of the estate tax every other generation. Until these loopholes are removed, Federal death taxes will continue to be much less efficient as a method for accomplishing the basic objectives of death taxation than would otherwise be the case.

While the purpose of the Federal gift tax, enacted in 1932, was to check avoidance of the Federal estate tax, the actual effect of the tax has been to encourage taxpayers to combine the use of the gift tax and the estate tax in such a way as to reduce sharply the total taxes which they pay on the transfer of property by gift or at death. Thus, the nominal rates of the gift tax are set at three-fourths those of the estate tax, but the effective rates are much lower for any given estate, due to the liberal exemptions which the gift tax permits. Not only is the taxpayer permitted a $30,000 exemption, plus $3,000 in any one year, but in determining the gift tax, the tax which would be due on a certain gift base is first computed, and then deducted from this base in determination of the actual gift-tax base. It is on this base that the gift-tax liability is computed. Such procedure is not permitted in determination of the estate tax. These procedures operated, together with the rate structure, to make gift-tax liability in 1946 on a base of $1,000,000 only about 51.5 per cent of the maximum estate tax liability on the same base.

An example will illustrate. Let us assume that an individual in 1942 had $1,000,000 which he could give away or make subject to an estate tax later. Let us assume no changes in the provisions of the estate and gift taxes in the following ten years, and that he dies in 1954 with enough additional assets to provide for the settlement of the estate at that time though still leaving the net estate at $1,000,000. We will also assume that his bequests or gifts are not for philanthropic purposes which, rather broadly interpreted, are exempt from either gift or death taxes.

Under the Federal estate tax, his estate will have a specific exemption of $60,000. On the remaining $940,000, a total estate tax of $303,500 will be imposed, at a top marginal rate of 37 per cent. If, on the other hand, he gives away his $1,000,000 during his lifetime, he is entitled to an outright exemption of $30,000 plus $3,000 a year for gifts made to any one individual. If he makes ten such annual *inter-vivos* (among the living) gifts before he dies, his total cumulative gift-tax exemption will be $60,-000. If, before he dies, he then gives away the remaining $940,-000, his gift tax, calculated after deduction of the original tax of $27\frac{3}{4}$ per cent on the highest marginal portion of the $940,000 will be $156,302 or only 51.5 per cent of what his estate tax would have been.

This is only a hypothetical example. If the individual wishes to combine taxable gifts and bequests and philanthropic gifts or bequests, he can reduce the tax on his $1,000,000 of assets to a much lower total than his gift tax itself, as given above, would be. There may be only one possible limitation in his plans. The Federal estate law provides that gifts "in contemplation of death" are to be included in taxable estates, and the Bureau of Internal Revenue may try to show that some of his gifts made shortly before death fall in this category. But government units have never been very successful in proving "presumptive" contemplation in the courts, and the Supreme Court has held unconstitutional any attempts to define gifts within some definite period before death as constituting conclusive "presumption." The only answer to this particular problem of tax avoidance is to use fully integrated death and gift taxes, with the same base (using all transfers by death or gift), one set of exemptions (which should be cumulative with gifts given before death), and one rate schedule.

Effects of Available Legal Devices on Tax Avoidance

A second major loophole to avoid estate taxes is found in a whole series of legal devices, especially the so-called "life-estate-remainder" combination, powers of appointment by an estate owner for subsequent disposition of his property, and revocable trust funds. These loopholes have recently been subjected to careful, critical analysis by Professor Groves.[8] He found in the life-estate-remainder sequence the legal possibility of avoiding death taxes on transfers of property every other generation, since A can leave property to B for life, with remainder after B's life to go to C, with only an initial death tax on the transfer of property of A to B. He also found in powers of appointment, rapidly developed in recent years, the possibility of avoiding death taxes every other generation. For example, A can leave property to B, with the power to appoint control over disposition of the property to B's children, whom we will call C. Federal estate tax would apply to the transfer of property to B, but not to C.

The only thorough solution to the loopholes which Professor Groves found is the use of a fully integrated death and gift tax, applied to all successive transfers of property, except to the extent that such transfers are specifically exempt from taxes under income-tax, gift-tax, or estate-tax exemptions. There is precedent for a more rigorous application of death-gift taxes than we have applied under property laws in this country. All successive property transfers as a result of death are subject to death taxes[9] under English laws.

This brings us to a brief discussion of the trust fund and its use to create legal loopholes for the avoidance of estate and gift taxation. Many of our legal loopholes have been provided through the trust-fund device, especially the revocable trust fund and uses of powers of appointment in trust funds in recent years. A trust

---

[8] See his *Postwar Taxation and Economic Progress*, Chapter IX.

[9] Stricter application of an integrated death-gift tax should allow for possible inequities which may arise due to successive transfers of property within unexpectedly short periods of time, such as an accident which may kill members of three or more generations at the same time. Present Federal laws exempt from estate tax a second transfer of property which is made within five years of a preceding transfer. This principle might be retained, although refined.

fund itself is a device under which one person (the creator) transfers title to another individual, individuals, or institutions (the trustees) for the benefit of a third individual or group of individuals (beneficiaries). Such arrangements have been established in about as many ways as legal ingenuity has been able to devise. Some trust funds are irrevocable; others may be revoked within the lifetime of the creator, if he so desires. Some trust funds may be set up so that the benefit, or income, goes to the beneficiary immediately. In others, the trust fund creator may retain a life interest in the property, with income going to the beneficiary only after death of the creator.

In an effort to keep up with those lawyers who devise trust-fund arrangements, Congress has made irrevocable trust funds with benefits reserved to the creator subject to estate taxation. In general, revocable trust funds are also taxable, but the issue as to whether or not a given trust fund is revocable is unsettled. There are still ways in which such trust funds can be established so as to avoid estate taxes or to take advantage of much lower gift taxes which exist. Furthermore, if a trust fund is established for some philanthropic purpose within the meaning of the law, it is entirely exempt from estate or gift taxes.

As in the case of the life-estate-remainder combination and the use of powers of appointment, application of a fully integrated death-gift tax to successive transfers of property is probably the only solution to the problem of tax avoidance through trust funds. Use of an integrated death-gift tax, it has been pointed out, would permit the creators of trust funds to accomplish desired objectives in the disposition of property, without special attention to possible tax liability, although they would still have to decide the time at which death or gift taxes would be paid. One problem of public policy in the use of trust funds is to decide whether gifts and bequests for philanthropic (charitable, religious, and educational) purposes should continue to be exempt from death-gift taxation.

This brief outline of present deficiencies in the use of Federal death and gift taxes, together with the high exemptions which are permitted under both taxes indicates the principal factors which have made these levies produce relatively low yields. In 1926, when estate-tax exemptions were $100,000 and tax rates were much lower than in 1946, Professor Shultz estimated that at least a quarter of the property of decedents was being transferred through the use of life-estates with remainders.[10] This legal device has permitted the avoidance of death taxes every other generation. With the availability of this and other legal devices in 1946, when estate-tax exemption was $60,000, it is probable that most estates of decedents over $60,000 which are subject to full estate taxes are those where death has come unexpectedly so that potential taxpayers have not had time to put their legal houses in order.

Problems of Multiple, Interstate Taxation

It was pointed out earlier that state death (or death and gift) taxes are found in 47 states and that, historically, the development of state death taxes preceded the permanent development of Federal death taxation. Moreover, apart from state estate taxes to take advantage of the Federal credit established under the 1926 law, the states have primarily developed inheritance taxes, as contrasted with estate taxes. We earlier found inheritance taxation to be a tax instrument which was more adaptable to the taxation of shares in an estate received by heirs of varying distance of relationship to a decedent. Partly because of priority in time of development, partly because property is actually transferred under the property laws of the states, and partly because the states have concentrated on inheritance taxation as a type of death tax, there have been proposals from time to time that the Federal government should leave the field of death taxation to the states.[11]

Despite these proposals, death (and gift) taxation has become, to an increasing degree, more important as a source of revenue to the Federal than to state governments. In 1946, death and gift taxes supplied more than 4.7 per cent more revenue to the Federal than to all state governments. The Federal government, indeed, seems to have important advantages over state governments in the use of these taxes. It does not have the problems of determining jurisdiction for tax purposes which the states have. It has the possibility of administrative economy and efficiency. By

---

[10] William J. Shultz, *The Taxation of Inheritance*, Chapter XIV, page 231, Boston: Houghton Mifflin Co., 1926.

[11] See the stand taken by the National Tax Association in 1925 and by former Secretary of the Treasury Andrew Mellon, in *Hearings, Revenue Revision, 1927-28*, House Ways and Means Committee, 69th and 70th Congress, page 13. This same attitude has been taken recently by a committee in which R. Magill and H. Lutz have been prominent.

modernizing the out-of-date 1926 state tax credit against Federal tax liability, it could greatly increase the uniformity in state death-tax rates, and reduce remaining tendencies of individuals to migrate from one state to another in order to reduce tax liability.

Jurisdictional problems center largely about the taxation of intangible personal property such as securities. It is quite well established that transfers of real estate are taxable by the state in which the property is located, and that tangible personal property is taxable where it is situated or is customarily kept by one who dies. Intangible property, however, may be subject to death taxes by two or more states. For instance, it is taxable by the state where the deceased taxpayer was making his home at time of death, and also by other states under the protection of whose laws such property has come. The securities of a person who has been residing in New York state, but has been keeping these securities in a safety deposit box in Pennsylvania are subject to state death taxes by both states. If Delaware incorporated the company which issued these securities, it can also tax the transfer of such securities by the nonresident who lived in New York state. This situation is not only inequitable among individuals, but could be solved if Congress would prescribe a few jurisdictional rules as to the taxable situs of intangible property for purposes of death taxation.

To the extent that Federal administration of death taxes could be substituted for the 47 state administrative agencies in this field, a real economy of resources as well as an improvement in efficiency would be achieved. Several years ago, Heller and Harriss found that "among major State taxes none is more poorly administered than the death tax, whether judged by principles of organization, by equity of application, or by available quantitative measures." [12] Substitution of Federal for state administration, of course, would be considered as interference with the sovereignty of states, and so is subject to political limitations. But such limitations might be partially overcome, and a closer coordination between Federal and state death-tax administrations might be secured if the now out-of-date Federal credit

[12] See Walter W. Heller and C. Lowell Harriss, "The Administration of State Death Taxes," *Iowa Law Review*, Vol. 26, No. 3 (March, 1941), pages 628-673.

for state death taxes were brought in line with current rates of Federal taxation.

A recent study of Federal, state, and local fiscal relations indicated that the Federal estate-tax credit for estates of all sizes had dropped from 80 per cent of the tax levied by the Federal government at 1926 rates to about an 11 per cent average of the estate taxes collected in 1939 (calculated at 1941 rates).[13] The same study recommended that the credit should be revised as a consequence of additional Federal estate taxes imposed after 1926, and in general, that such credit in the future should represent some proportion of *current* Federal tax liability. The objective of upward revision of the tax credit was to increase state revenues from the use of such revised credit to the point where nearly all the states would find such revenues more than adequate compensation for state death-tax revenues separately imposed. On the basis of 1941 rates, the study proposed a Federal credit for state taxes of 50 per cent of Federal tax liability on net estates not over $100,000 and 25 per cent on the amount of net estate exceeding $100,000, with a reduction in specific exemption and insurance exemption to $20,000 each.[14] Variations in state death taxes have continued to be great, in spite of previous tendencies toward uniformity brought about by the first Federal tax credits in 1924 and 1926. An unpublished Treasury study of 1937, quoted in the Fiscal Relations Report, indicates that in that year effective state death-tax rates on an estate of $1,000,000 for a group of selected states, varied from 3.24 per cent in Pennsylvania to 11.05 per cent in North Dakota.[15]

It is to be hoped that modernization of the death-tax credit will induce the states to withdraw from separate death taxes and administration of such taxes. However, additional Federal tax credit should be accompanied by a requirement that the states accept Federal determination of domicile and distribution for estates which are interstate in nature, for purposes of determining

[13] See "Federal, State and Local Government Fiscal Relations," page 487. 1941 Federal rates were still in effect in 1946, although the specific Federal exemption was raised from $40,000 in 1941 to $60,000 in 1942.

[14] See Fiscal Relations Report, page 489. The insurance exemption was abolished in 1942.

[15] State death-tax rates and exemptions on property transferred at death have not changed in many of the states since this study was made.

the distribution of Federal credit on any given estate which may be due the states involved.

Other Problems of Death Taxation

One of the problems of equitable death taxation is the valuation of assets of the decedent. In the early provisions of Federal estate-tax laws, after 1916, assets were valued at time of death, but this sometimes placed an excessive burden on the estate, when large blocks of securities had to be sold at one time, and could temporarily "break" current market values. In the early years of the thirties, security values were falling so rapidly that realized value from their sale was sometimes insufficient to meet estate taxes which were levied. One observed result was a tendency, particularly for larger estates, to shift from stocks to bonds. This development was definitely against the broad social interest of having substantial savings invested in the development of newer, if riskier, enterprises.

Federal laws and regulations in effect in 1946 attempted to remove tax considerations which led to increased liquidity of estates by giving executors of estates up to a year after death of the former estate owner in which to dispose of assets for tax purposes, including the option of choosing the time when assets should be liquidated for purposes of meeting tax liability. Such liquidated assets (as of 1946) could be valued, in the option of the executor, as of time of death or actual disposition. In the opinion of some tax experts, however, the period of time permitted for liquidation and valuation of assets after death of an estate owner should be extended to cover several years in order to reduce the practice of getting estates into liquid condition in anticipation of death.

Recent critical analyses of Federal estate and gift taxation suggest, among other things, that: (1) the present specific exemption of $60,000 should be replaced by varying exemptions for widows and dependent children, available only at time of death of the estate owner. The writers do not anticipate that the Federal government will, after more than 30 years, abandon the use of estate taxation for the use of inheritance taxation, even though the latter is probably socially superior as a form of death tax. (2) Total exemption should be greatly reduced, to make subject to taxation at relatively low rates estates which are worth less than $60,000. The recommendation for a reduction to $20,000 in specific exemption for purposes of Federal-state coordination of death taxation has already been noted. (3) The prevailing exemption of bequests or gifts designated as charitable should be carefully supervised to minimize abuses in such bequests or gifts when some control over such estates may remain in the hands of the descendants. (4) More attention should be given to the possibility of taxing death transfers of property according to the length of time which has elapsed since the previous transfer. One suggestion is that the present exemption from estate tax where additional transfers (beyond the first) are made within five years might be refined to weight the age differentials between the donor and the heirs. For instance, the proportion of estate exempt from transfer tax might vary inversely with the age differences between the deceased and the heir (or heirs) of the estate, or the proportion of the estate exempt from taxation might vary inversely with the age of the heir (or heirs).

Summary

1. Death taxes and fully integrated gift taxes may be used to achieve several desired social ends. They can be used to improve equality in opportunity for individuals of similar talents. Death and gift taxes probably do not interfere with incentives to accumulate capital as much as do income taxes. They can be used to limit inequalities in wealth and income when imposed at progressive rates.

2. Death taxes are either (a) *estate taxes*, levied on the entire estate, after specified expenses connected with its transfer from decedent to heir(s), and some specified exemption(s) from taxes; or (b) *inheritance taxes*, levied upon distributive shares of an estate. The Federal government uses the former type of death tax, supplemented by a gift tax, while the states use primarily the latter type.

3. The incidence of death taxes is either on the estate of the decedent, if he has made advance savings to pay such taxes, or upon the recipients of inherited shares in an estate. It is possible to state the ratio of potential death taxes in terms of an annual income burden on income from the estate upon which such taxes may be imposed.

4. Our death and gift taxes (1946) are relatively inefficient in accomplishing desired social objectives. This is due to the incomplete integration of the estate and gift tax and to various legal

devices which make it possible to avoid death and gift taxes every other generation. In addition, Federal estate and gift taxes have such high exemptions that most estates transferred do not become subject to Federal taxation at all. Just prior to our entrance in World War II, such taxes provided only 4.27 per cent of total tax revenue.

5. Despite certain claims of the states to the field of death taxation, the superiority of Federal taxation of the transfer of property by death or gift is widely accepted. Such superiority is due to a number of factors: (*a*) the problems of interstate jurisdiction of property for taxation are not present in Federal taxation; (*b*) state death-tax administration is relatively inefficient and overlapping; (*c*) the revision of the Federal tax credit against state death and gift taxes, established in 1924, but unchanged since 1926, would induce greater uniformity in state death taxes, and reduce still-existing incentives to migrate from one state to another to avoid state death taxes.

6. Modernization of the existing Federal tax credit to the states should not only increase it substantially, but the credit should be kept uniform by restatement under each successive Federal revision of estate and gift taxes. One effect might be to cause many states to cease efforts to apply and administer separately their own death taxes.

7. Critical attention should be given to various other problems in Federal death taxation. Among them, consideration should be given to extension of the time at which the executor of an estate must value the assets of the estate.

SELECTED READINGS

1. Barna, Tibor, "The Burden of Death Duties in Terms of an Annual Tax," *Review of Economic Studies,* Vol. 9, No. 1 (November, 1941), pages 28-29.
2. "Federal, State, and Local Government Fiscal Relations," Senate Document No. 69, 78th Congress, 1st Session. Washington, D. C.: United States Government Printing Office, 1943.
3. Groves, Harold M., *Postwar Taxation and Economic Progress,* Chapter IX, New York: McGraw-Hill Book Co., Inc., 1946.
4. Heller, Walter W. and Harriss, C. Lowell, "The Administration of State Death Taxes," *The Iowa Law Review,* Vol. 26, No. 3 (March, 1941).

5. Kaldor, Nicholas, "The Income Burden of Capital Taxes," *Review of Economic Studies*, Vol. 9, No. 2 (Summer, 1942), London.

6. Mellon, Andrew, *Hearings, Revenue Revision, 1927-1928*. House Ways and Means Committee, 69th and 70th Congress, Washington, D. C.: United States Government Printing Office, 1928.

7. Mill, John Stuart, *Political Economy*, Book 2, Chapter 2 (Ashley edition), New York: Longmans, Green & Co., 1929.

8. *Proceedings of a Special Session of the National Tax Association*, at New Orleans, Louisiana, 1925. New York: 1926.

9. Shultz, William J., *The Taxation of Inheritance*, Boston: Houghton Mifflin Co., Inc., 1926.

CHAPTER XVIII

SPECIAL-BENEFIT REVENUES

S PECIAL-BENEFIT revenues presumably represent revenues received by government from the dispensation of public services where the benefits go largely to the users of these services. Such revenues include (1) receipts from the sale of public services (that is, the gross revenues of public enterprises), (2) taxes collected to finance highways, (3) taxes levied to finance public social-security programs, and (4) such nontax revenues as special assessments, fines, licenses, and fees.

The concept of a tax as a special-benefit levy is one that is relatively new and has only gradually been incorporated into public thinking about taxes. Acceptance of the special-benefit levy in the tax system has been speeded by the imposition of highway and social security taxes. The long-accepted concept of it as a tax confined it to a compulsory levy to finance general government functions, without reference to special benefits received.

Special-benefits revenues are a much larger part of the public economy in the United States than is generally believed. In 1941, when the Bureau of the Census made a thorough investigation of how Federal, state, and local governments are financed in the United States,[1] about 58 per cent of state-raised government revenue and 25.5 per cent of locally raised government revenue had a special-benefit character. In 1945, when total tax and nontax revenue receipts of the Federal government were 46.8 billion dollars, about 9 per cent of Federal revenue was derived from special-benefit sources. For any given recent year, the United States post-office has been among the 12 largest business enterprises in the United States as measured by volume of sales. Its receipts in (fiscal) 1945 exceeded $1.1 billion. A summary of special-benefit in relation to general government revenue is given in Table 26.

---

[1] See *Financing Federal, State and Local Governments, 1941,* Bureau of the Census, Washington, D. C., 1942.

TABLE 26

Special-Benefit Revenues in the Public Economy of the United States[a]

(in millions of dollars)

Type of Revenue	Unit of Government		
	Federal (1945)	State (1941)	Local (1941)
1. Social Security Taxes........	$1,780,000	$ 901,363	$ 4,992
2. Levies on Highway Vehicles and Users................	(b)	1,452,011[c]	30,800
3. Revenue from public Enterprises (Gross)..............	1,347,309[d]	283,015	873,577[e]
4. Service Charges for Current Services..................	118,696	207,004	330,382
5. Revenues from Use of Public money and property[f]....	682,856	149,907	106,818
6. Licenses Offsetting Services.		33,926	50,020
7. Special Assessments........			102,121
8. Penalties and Other[g].......	153,054	40,183	51,177
9. Total Special-Benefit Revenue.....................	4,081,915	3,067,409	1,549,887
10. Total Revenue from Own Sources	45,317,655	5,299,164	6,069,831
11. Per Cent of Total Revenue Made Up by Special-Benefit Revenue.................	9.0%	57.9%	25.5%

[a] Unless otherwise indicated, state and local data for 1941 are derived from *Financing Federal, State and Local Governments, 1941*, Bureau of the Census, 1942 and the *Annual Report* of the Secretary of the Treasury 1945. Repayment of loans and reimbursements are excluded. Federal and most state and local data are on a cash basis.

[b] Federal tax collections of $755,171,000 on gasoline, motor vehicles and accessories, and auto use are excluded from special-benefit revenues for reasons noted in the discussion.

[c] Data on state motor-vehicle levies are for calendar year 1941, and were taken from *Public Roads*, Vol. 73, No. 5 (July–September, 1942), pages 100-102, and No. 6 (October–December, 1942), pages 137-140.

[d] This was the gross revenue of United States Post Offices in 1945, as given in the annual statement of the Postal Department, 1945, page 100, plus $152,-611,000 in public-power revenues and $81,821,000 in interest and charges for loan services of agencies of the Farm Credit Administration.

[e] These are the amounts of the gross revenues of state and local enterprises.

[f] Includes profits and seigniorage from operation of mints, interest, rents, royalties, dividends, and sale of Federal government products and property.

[g] Includes fines, forfeits, escheats, and donations in the case of state and local governments, plus miscellaneous revenues in the case of the Federal government.

Highway Revenues

State taxation of highway users developed with the coming of the motor vehicle era. These taxes grew from relatively little in

1915 to the largest source of state revenue in the years preceding our entry into World War II. Their growth was facilitated not only by the demand for better roads for motor vehicles, but by general agreement that the motorist should pay his share of the expense of road improvement. As they existed in 1941, state highway taxes consisted of three main taxes: (1) taxes on the use of motor fuel which varied from 2¢ to 7¢ per gallon (averaging about 4¢) among the 48 states (and the District of Columbia); (2) taxes on vehicle registrations which were progressively heavier for passenger cars, trucks and tractor-trucks, and busses; (3) special taxes on vehicles used in commercial highway transportation.

85.5 per cent of state highway revenues were devoted to highway purposes. A few states, especially New York, devoted substantial amounts of highway taxes to other purposes. Without counting the highway revenues diverted [2] to other purposes by New York in 1941, 89 per cent of state highway revenues was used for highway purposes. By 1941, a relatively few local government units had applied special motor vehicle taxes, as Table 26 indicates. A summary of state motor vehicle levies and their disposition is given in Table 27.

The Federal government began a system of grants-in-aid for state highways (and subsequently for secondary farm-to-market roads) in 1916 and has continued these aids to the present time. During the period 1917-1945, the Federal government provided about 3.1 billion dollars to the states, principally for state highway construction (in addition to several billion dollars expended on roads by Federal work relief agencies from 1933-1941). For most of these grants, prerequisites for Federal aid were (1) that the states must supply funds to equal Federal grants and (2) that construction standards for projects receiving Federal aid must be maintained at a Federally defined level. Over that period (1933-1941), the Federal government levied and collected sufficient taxes on vehicles, vehicle parts, and vehicle use to more than cover these grants, but there is no clear evidence that such taxes were imposed for the purpose of providing Federal aid, and they have not been included in special-benefit revenues.[3] Fed-

[2] Refer to pages 380-81 for a discussion of diversion of highway revenues.

[3] Certain World War I taxes were imposed on vehicles and accessories, effective in 1918, and were continued through 1928. There were no new taxes on

Table 27[4]

State Vehicle Levies and Their Disposition
(Calendar) 1941

(in millions of dollars)

	Amount of Disposable Funds	Per Cent of Total
I. Type of Levy:		
a. Taxes on motor fuels...............	$948,038	65.2
b. Vehicle registration fees.............	482,834	33.3
c. Special taxes on motor carriers.........	21,139	1.5
d. Total state vehicle levies.............	$1,452,011	100.0
II. Disposition of state vehicle levies:		
a. State highway purposes..............	$833,289	57.4
b. Secondary rural roads...............	295,567	20.4
c. City streets........................	58,537	4.0
d. Administration.....................	54,282	3.7
e. Non-highway purposes..............	210,336	14.5
	$1,452,011	100.0

[a] Federal taxes on vehicles and their use in fiscal 1941, amounting to $537,-530,000 have been excluded as not constituting special-benefit revenues.

[b] Sums for city streets include only specific allocations in 23 out of 49 tax jurisdictions. Where reported separately, funds for urban extensions of state trunk roads have been included under state highway purposes.

eral-state fiscal cooperation in the highway field has developed into one of the most satisfactory patterns of intergovernmental fiscal relations. But there are some valid objections to the states and the Federal government providing equal funds for Federal-aid highway projects. These objections will be examined in the last chapter of this book.

Just before the beginning of the last war, a number of issues had grown out of the expansion of highway and street expenditures to more than 2 billion dollars a year. Disagreement was largely between highway-user groups (who favored a rapid development

vehicles and their use until the Revenue Act of 1932, and these taxes have been continued to the present time (1946). They were increased somewhat by the Revenue Act of 1942. But there has never been any consistent relationship between the size of the Federal Aid highway program and internal revenue collections on vehicles, accessories, and vehicle use.

[4] Based on data given in *Public Roads*, Vol. 23, No. 5 (July–September, 1942), pages 100-102, and No. 6 (October–December, 1942), pages 137-140.

of highways and relatively low tax levies on highway users) and representatives of the railroads. The railroads, suffering from the expansion of highway transportation, favored a more inclusive definition of annual highway costs and the covering of most of these costs by taxes on highway users.

The main fiscal issues which have grown out of the expansion of highway expenditures are these: (1) What is the nature of highway costs? (2) How should such costs be allocated between vehicle users as a group and general taxpayers? (3) How should highway costs borne by highway-vehicle users be allocated among various classes of vehicle users, such as private passenger cars, auto trucks, and busses? (4) What principles should determine the distribution of highway revenues among different classes of rural-road and urban-street systems? (5) Should highway revenues be diverted from highway use, and if so, under what circumstances? [5]

Defining highway costs. The definition of highway costs is somewhat arbitrary. There are four interpretations of what constitutes "highway costs." Popularly, highway costs are identified with all expenditures for highway purposes in a given time period (such as a year) and would include capital outlays, payment of interest and principal on debt, as well as expenditures for maintenance, engineering, administration, and traffic control. Highway-user groups are inclined to confine highway costs to that portion of the total annual expenditures necessary to maintain the present plant, finance replacements, meet interest and principal on the outstanding debt, and cover costs of traffic control. A national committee of the Highway Research Board in 1929, however, concluded that annual highway costs should be considered the annual sums necessary to provide full payment for the use of resources devoted to existing highways as against alternative forms of investment. [6] Under this concept of highway costs, there are included the annual sums necessary to maintain the present plant in a usable condition, to provide for its future replacement to the extent that it is depreciated currently, and to

---

[5] For a more detailed discussion of some of these issues, see Edward D. Allen, "Highway Costs and Their Allocation," *Journal of Land and Public Utility Economics,* Vol. XV (August and November, 1939), pages 269-276 and 404-415 respectively.

[6] See "Report of the Committee on Highway Transportation Costs," *Proceedings,* Highway Research Board, 1929, Vol. 9, Washington, D. C., 1930, pages 360-368.

cover interest on the entire unamortized investment (an estimate of the "opportunity costs" of these resources). Railroad
interests have accepted this definition, but insist that cost should
be further increased by an amount equal to taxes which otherwise
would have been levied on this property if it had not been
publicly owned.

The definition of highway costs adopted by the Highway Research Board is most acceptable from an economic standpoint.
It includes not only cash outlays for maintenance, supervision,
and administration, but also a charge for annual depreciation and
interest on the investment.

Whether taxes foregone on public investment in highways
should be included as an element of annual highway cost is
definitely arbitrary. One of the writers has concluded else-
where that such a tax equivalent should not be regarded as one
of the basic highway costs.[7]

Allocating highway costs between vehicle users and taxpayers.
Taking the Highway Research Board concept of annual costs,
how should such costs be allocated between vehicle users and
general taxpayers? This was a central issue in at least seven
widely publicized studies during the thirties. There was general
agreement that most of the costs of intercity trunk highways
should be charged to vehicle users as representing special-benefit
costs and that a much smaller portion of the costs of streets (excluding city extensions of rural trunk highways) could reasonably
be charged to vehicle users.[8] The many benefits derived by
urban residents from the presence of a street system, apart from
the use of private motor vehicles, has generally been recognized.
There was wide disagreement, however, as to the proportion of
costs of non-trunk rural highways which should be charged
against users of motor vehicles.

Such disagreement is to be expected from the different relative
emphases which it is possible to place on social or on special
benefits derived from the use of a highway and street system.

---

[7] See E. D. Allen, *Analysis of Highway Costs and Highway Taxation with an
Application to Story County, Iowa*, Bulletin 152, Iowa Engineering Experiment
Station, Ames, Iowa, 1941, pages 27-28.

[8] The highest proposed cost allocation to vehicle users for the use of city streets
was 51 per cent—in a study for railroad interests. See William D. Ennis, "Motor
Vehicle Taxation in New Jersey," Hoboken, N. J.: Associated Railroads of New
Jersey, 1935, page 35.

An added source of disagreement has arisen from the number of separate investigations of the allocation of highway costs, and the presence (in most of them) of the influence of highway-user or railroad groups, interested in obtaining results favorable to their own special interest.   One independent Federal study made the judgment that vehicle users have paid more than their share of annual highway costs.[9]   This does not mean that vehicle-user charges are necessarily excessive as long as such revenues in excess of costs are in the future devoted to further improvement of widely used roads.   The Federal study to which reference has been made indicates that about 46 per cent of total costs may equitably be charged to vehicle users.   A study of highway and street costs in an Iowa county, conducted by one of the authors, indicated that about 54 per cent of total costs could be charged as special benefits to vehicle users.[10]

Allocating user costs among different classes of vehicles.   If annual cost data were available for highways on a state-wide basis (which at present is not the case) and if the special-benefit proportion were charged against vehicle users, the problem of allocating special-benefit costs of motor vehicle users among classes of motor vehicles would still remain.

Two methods of cost allocation among vehicles have been favored in discussions of highway taxation.   One, the increment method, would charge to all vehicles an equal share in the cost of a basic highway adequate for such basic vehicles as private passenger cars.   But additional costs necessary to provide an adequate highway for heavier and larger vehicles would be charged to these vehicles.   The other, the use method, would differentiate total charges for highway use (through gasoline and vehicle registration charges) on the basis of relative use—the relative number of ton-miles transported in an annual period, for example.

Both methods are roughly represented in the types of vehicle registration taxes which have been evolved in the various states.

[9] See Federal Coordinator of Transportation, *Public Aids to Motor Vehicle Transportation*, Washington, D. C., 1940, page 159.   A subsequent Federal study (yet unpublished) has been reported to have reached an opposite conclusion, although the analysis has been challenged.

[10] See report of the Federal Coordinator of Transportation previously mentioned and Bulletin 152 of the Iowa Engineering Experiment Station.   See also E. D. Allen, "Highway Costs and Their Allocation."

Thus, in 1941, state motor-vehicle fees averaged $9.42 for passenger automobiles, exclusive of busses; $23.34 for trucks and tractor-trucks; and $50.52 for busses.[11] Fees on trucks and tractor-trucks varied from a relatively small amount to several hundred dollars for larger, heavier units in most states.

Neither method establishes a "scientific" basis of automotive fees in terms of current operating data on various classes of vehicles. The increment method is deficient because highway engineers have not been able to agree to what extent highways have been constructed differently than they otherwise would have been in the absence of such heavier vehicles as trucks and tractor-trucks. The use method is deficient, not only because it assumes that relative use is necessarily a measure of relative benefit, but because its application would unavoidably lump into various classes vehicles which travel, on the average, with widely varying ratios of actual capacity.

Nevertheless, the use method, as it has been employed, has been administratively superior to the other methods. The nation-wide Highway Planning Surveys of 1935-1936 computed the distribution of vehicle weights and indicated that the average loaded weight of a given class of vehicle was an important indication of its relative use of the highway. Such data, if kept up to date, could provide a reasonably satisfactory basis for imposing vehicle-registration taxes. In constructing (or reconstructing) a schedule of vehicle-registration taxes based on the use method, mileage traveled and gasoline taxes paid must also be considered, as the number of ton-miles per gallon of gas tends to drop sharply with the increasing gross weight of the vehicle.[12]

In addition, third-structure taxes—those imposed in addition to regular registration fees and gas taxes—may be required. These were imposed on commercial users of highways by 44 states in 1941. Such taxes generally take the form of additional registration fees, or taxes based on the number of ton-miles traveled.

[11] Derived from data published in *Public Roads*, Vol. 23, No. 6 (October–December, 1942), pages 137-140.

[12] An application of the work of the State-wide Highway Planning Survey was made in Iowa in 1939. Registration fees for trucks and tractor-trucks were changed from a licensed capacity to a maximum gross-weight basis. These changes were based on data on average loads and mileage traveled by such vehicles, gathered by the Highway Planning Survey. Such a registration schedule needs to be revised from time to time, with the aid of new field data gathered by state highway planning authorities.

Political factors rather than equity, explain the customary exclusion from such additional taxes of the private vehicles of many businessmen (such as farmers) which are often used for business purposes, although not on a for-hire basis. To the extent that we retain separate business taxes, third-structure taxes on common-carriers having an exclusive franchise between certain points, have an added justification. Such taxes might reasonably be based on the net profits of such trucking or bus concerns and represent a partial recapture of monopoly profits which they earn.

Disposition of highway revenues among street and road systems. A fourth issue in highway economics relates to the disposition of highway-tax revenues among the various road and street systems. Historically, emphasis during the motor-vehicle era has been on the development of an efficient intercity system of trunk highways, and most state and Federal highway funds have gone to this purpose. State highways make up a comparatively small portion (about 11 per cent) of our total rural mileage, however. Since about 1930, increasing attention has been devoted to the improvement of secondary, farm-to-market roads. Beginning in 1933, Federal funds have been invested in the improvement of these roads, and since 1938 the Federal aid program has formally recognized farm-to-market roads.

Using additional resources to improve highways further may be justified on economic grounds alone, as long as the annual costs of these improvements do not exceed the annual reduction in motor-vehicle operating costs. Detailed research has shown that improved highways do, in fact, reduce vehicle operating costs sharply.[13] In the case of many low-traffic rural roads and city streets, of course, general benefits—the value of constant access to one's residence—must also be included in order to merit road or street improvement. Expenditures for such highways frequently have been paid for out of general taxation, rather than out of special-benefit motor-vehicle revenue.

Urban streets, on which more than 50 per cent of all motor vehicle travel is made, have been especially neglected in the allocation of state highway funds.[14] As Table 27 indicates, in 1941 only about 4 per cent of state highway revenues were specifically

---

[13] See, for example, R. A. Moyer, "Economic Selection of Projects and Self-Liquidating Facilities." Short Course in Highway Economics, Iowa State College, January, 1940. Mimeographed.

[14] See Public Roads Administration Release, October, 1941, Table G.

allocated for city streets. Only 23 out of 49 taxing jurisdictions (the 48 states and the District of Columbia) distributed funds for city streets. An additional unstated amount was spent by state highway authorities on urban extensions of rural trunk highways. City street systems are composed of a variety of streets, all the way from busy thoroughfares to little side streets providing largely land-access for a few residents. But it seems clear that a larger portion of special-benefit state highway-tax funds should be made available for use on urban streets.

Actually, the problem of an unsatisfactory allocation of state highway funds to various road and street systems arises out of the lack of cooperation between the various political jurisdictions—state, county, and municipal—under which most of our roads and streets are administered. If the varied activities of the State-wide Highway Planning Surveys of a few years ago were to be continuously carried on, and if we were willing to give to state highway authorities powers to determine the allocation of state highway funds among the various road and street systems with the object of developing optimum (economic) highway and street systems, we would probably get a more economic allocation of state and Federal highway funds than is now the case. Since it is unlikely that we will be willing to grant even this much centralization in the allocation of highway funds, it is unlikely that we will obtain the optimum use of these funds in the near-run future. In the meantime, urban street authorities should continue to press for a larger share of state highway funds than has been allocated to cities and towns in the past.

Diverting highway taxes to other uses. A final major issue in highway economics is the so-called "diversion" of highway tax funds to non-highway purposes. Such diversion amounted to 210.4 million dollars in 1941, about 14.5 per cent of total state highway levies. Of this amount, however, New York state alone diverted 64.4 million dollars. (Without New York state, "diversion" was 11 per cent.)

Such fiscal action converts special-benefit highway levies into excise taxes for general governmental purposes. The financing of general government through sales taxation has already been found undesirable, compared to other means of financing general benefit activities of government.

Diversion itself, however, can not be said to exist unless expenditures on highways financed from other sources of funds are less than the amount of highway-user taxes spent for purposes other than highways. From this point of view, there was no net diversion in New York in 1941, where local (county-city-town-village) real estate taxes for highway purposes were 76.5 million dollars.

Where highway tax funds are used to finance general government, diversion is not the fiscal issue at stake. The issue is fundamentally what types of taxes should be used for general government, such as property taxes, consumption taxes—for instance, general sales and highway taxes—and income taxes. The writers find little merit in the anti-diversion amendments to state constitutions which have been enacted in 19 states in recent years. The optimum development of a highway-street system may logically require the reduction in highway-user taxes imposed by a state. It does not render desirable the permanent freezing of the largest single source of state tax revenues for some particular purpose.

Taxes and Social Security

Beginning with the Social Security Act of 1935 [15] the Federal government undertook an extensive system of government benefit payments for old-age retirement and unemployment compensation, as well as a variety of annual grants to the states for old-age assistance, aid to dependent children, aid to the blind, aid for maternal and child health services, and for other similar social security functions. [16]

Before 1946, most grants to the states were accompanied by the same fiscal condition attached to Federal aid for highways: the states were required to match Federal funds. [17] Amendments in the Social Security Act passed in 1946 have made possible Federal grants without equal matching by the states. Both Federal and

[15] Amended in 1939 and in 1946 and supplemented by the Carriers' Tax Act of 1937 applying to railroad employees.

[16] Including grants to the states to cover costs of unemployment compensation administration, public health work, services for crippled children, and child welfare service.

[17] An exception to dollar-for-dollar matching through July, 1946, was found in Federal aid for needy children. The state was required to put up $2 for each $1 of Federal funds. No matching is required for reimbursement of state costs of unemployment administration. The Federal government collects its own special tax which is more than sufficient to cover costs of state administration.

state governments secured funds for these grants chiefly from general tax revenue. From 1936-1946, the Federal government made grants to the states totaling 3.96 billion dollars (including 482.6 million to state unemployment-insurance units for administrative expenses). The grants were principally for old-age assistance and aid to dependent children (if the administrative expenses of state units for unemployment compensation administration are excluded). Monthly payments for old-age assistance among the 48 states (plus the District of Columbia) in September, 1946, varied from $12.02 in Kentucky to $53.93 in the state of Washington, which made more than the maximum monthly payments ($40) in which the Federal government was willing to share. (This amount was increased to $45 in August, 1946.)

In addition to the provision for financing social security grants just outlined, the Federal government imposed three new taxes to finance the old-age retirement and unemployment compensation (insurance) systems which it established. To finance the old-age retirement system, it imposed a 1 per cent tax on employers and a 1 per cent tax on employees on the first $3,000 of employee's annual wage. Collection of these taxes began in 1937. The employer turns over to the Federal government his own "contribution" as well as that of the employee. Taxes were originally scheduled automatically to increase by one-half per cent every three years until they reached 3 per cent cash donation for the employer and employee by 1949. However, Congress has several times legislatively delayed these automatic increases, and contributions remain frozen at their beginning 1 per cent rate. Subsequent amendments to the original act liberalized benefit payments. They were inaugurated in 1940 instead of in 1942 and have been extended to cover widows and children of the insured. By a separate tax act, the railroads have joined the Federal plan of old-age pensions.

The Federal government also imposed a 3 per cent tax on employers (covering individual wages-salaries up to $3,000) of 8 or more persons to finance unemployment-compensation payments. In this case, however, the Federal government made use of the tax-credit device, already established in the field of death taxation, to secure state-wide adoption and state administration of unemployment compensation (insurance) systems. An employer was permitted to pay 90 per cent of his Federal tax liability to any state which had in operation a system of unemployment compensation satisfactory to the Federal Social Security Board. All of the remaining 10 per cent goes to the Federal government partly to reimburse approved state administrations for costs of administering their unemployment-compensation systems. However, to the extent that the states do not need all of this 10 per cent, the balance is used for Federal administrative expenses in connection with its Social Security Program and to help meet the costs of its social security grants to the states. As in the case of old-age retirement, the railroads have chosen to make their unemployment tax contributions directly to the Federal government. One general effect of the tax-credit approach to the financing of unemployment compensation was the creation of separate state administrations for unemployment insurance in all the states and the District of Columbia.

Changes in social security provisions. In 1946, also, neither old-age nor unemployment compensation covered certain groups of workers. Public employees, domestic servants, and agricultural laborers are the principal groups not included in the established system.[18] In addition, several hundred thousand workers are excluded from unemployment compensation because they are employed by concerns hiring less than 8 employees. Such firms are not subject to payroll taxes nor are their employees entitled to unemployment compensation. A number of states, however, had extended their unemployment payroll taxes to cover firms hiring even 1 person by 1946. This development is to be desired on a national scale.

As amended, the old-age insurance plan provides qualified workers monthly pensions when they retire at the age of 65 or later. The pensions range from $10 to $85 a month, and vary with the average monthly earnings of the insured, the number of working years during which employer and employee have contributed, and with the number of dependents. In August, 1946, there were important amendments to the Social Security Act, under which the Federal government increased its matching basis for old-age assistance payments from $40 to $45 and increased its

[18] By 1946, several states had established independent systems for retirement of public employees. Some of these systems are being administered by the Social Security Board.

matching for dependent children.[19]   It also took a step in the
direction of the Connally proposal of 1940 under which the Federal government would provide more than 50 per cent of the
funds required.   In old-age assistance, for example, the Federal
government may now provide two-thirds of the first $15 of
average monthly payment for old-age assistance and aid to
the blind.   It will continue to provide one-half of additional
funds up to the legal maxima, $45 in the case of old-age assistance.   It has been estimated that the total annual cost to the
Federal government under the extended assistance programs will
be 560 million dollars a year.   For the same basic assistance
programs, the Federal cost in 1946 was 430.8 million dollars.

Operating under Federal matching of 50-50 in recent years, the
various states (plus Hawaii, Alaska, and the District of Columbia)
have developed varied programs of their own.   As of April, 1946,
old-age assistance monthly payments varied from a maximum of
$20 a month in South Carolina to actual average payments of
$47.72 in California.   In twelve of the 51 state or territorial
jurisdictions, no maxima were imposed, but discretion was left
entirely to administrative authorities.   As of the time of writing,
(early 1947) most state or territorial jurisdictions had not had
sufficient time in which to amend their own laws to take advantage of Federal liberalization amendments of August, 1946.

Unemployment compensation payments vary widely among
states.   While the range in waiting period before obtaining compensation was not great in 1946, varying from no waiting period
to two weeks, with one week commonest, the range in weekly
payments was from $28 in Connecticut and Michigan[20] to $15 a
week in 10 states, of which Virginia, Montana, and Arizona may
be cited as examples.

"Experience rating" as a factor in determining the annual tax
levied upon a given employer has been a widespread development in unemployment compensation methods.   Briefly, this
factor imposes a lower tax on those employers who have a record
of providing relatively continuous employment.   As of 1946, 44
out of 51 state and territorial jurisdictions were using this factor

[19] All the information about characteristics of, and recent changes in, the social
security system was obtained from a series of releases and publications, through
courtesy of the Social Security Administration, Federal Security Agency, Washington, D. C.

[20] Texas also provided for $36 per week for the first two weeks.

in determining their payroll tax rates.   Partly because of the use of this factor plus the accumulation of large state balances for unemployment compensation, the tax rate actually imposed on individual employers varied in 1946 from 4.5 per cent to zero. Experience rating has been estimated as having saved employers 793 million dollars in 1946, and is an important factor, together with widespread opportunities for employment from 1940 through 1946, in the drop of the national average payroll-tax rate in 1946 to 1.4 per cent (a record low) from 1.6 per cent in 1945.   With a rise in unemployment, of course, this rate might be increased sharply after a lag of a few months.   Only a few states retain the original 2.7 per cent state tax as provided under the original Social Security Act.   Yet, in 1946, as Mr. Altmeyer, chairman of the Social Security Board, has pointed out, "no state yet provides for both a maximum weekly benefit of $25 and uniform duration of 26 weeks."   The provision of such minimum national uniformity was urged by the late President Roosevelt.

Benefits under unemployment insurance are related to contributions.   Thus, unemployed persons who have not contributed because they have been excluded from the program receive no benefits.   Persons who contributed, but whose incomes and contributions were small, receive less in benefits than do higher-income contributors.   The procedure of maintaining in periods of unemployment the same relative distribution of incomes as in periods of full employment can be questioned, particularly in view of a widespread belief that there are certain minimum income standards which should be met at all times.   This belief also provides a further basis for bringing into the social security system groups which are now excluded, such as farm laborers.

On the basis of expected higher costs of living in the future than prevailed at the time when the Social Security Act was passed, a strong case can be made for increasing the amount of income covered under the Act.   The present law provides for coverage of the first $3,000 of income.   This maximum probably should be raised to $4,000 or $4,500.   For individuals with average annual incomes in excess of this maximum, a case can be made for their complete exclusion from social security provisions.   Such individuals might reasonably be expected to make financial arrangements for the future with private agencies.

One aspect of providing for public assistance of all types,

which is found in a study of data supplied by the Social Security Administration, is the great variation among the states in the provision for public assistance. For 1946, per capita public assistance varied from $25.75 in the state of Washington to $1.77 in Virginia. Low per capita assistance tends to center in the southeastern United States.

Incidence and effects of social security taxes. The incidence of the Social Security taxes is complex, but its main outlines have been indicated in Chapter XII. In the period before a worker reaches "old age" and during periods of regular employment, these taxes provide funds which are accumulated for the subsequent special benefit of the worker. Social security taxes operate to impose a measure of forced savings (among some workers) for the purpose of anticipated future benefits. It seems likely that the contributions made by employees for old-age retirement are a direct reduction in the wages-salaries of workers.[21] It also seems likely that the 4 per cent contributions required of many employers for old-age retirement and unemployment compensation tend to fall on workers. Unit costs of production are increased, but the marginal productivity of workers is unchanged. The taxes may be shifted forward to fall on the purchasers of business products, but as business products enter into final consumer products, higher prices will tend to reduce the purchasing power of the disposable incomes of the general body of consumers—largely the same people for whose special benefit the taxes on employers have been imposed. The widespread coverage of the taxes on employers makes it unlikely that in the short run the taxes will be shifted backward through the movement of labor resources to the relatively few untaxed employments.

The incidence of payroll taxes on employers is being constantly revised as new labor contracts are made. Where unions are strong in the particular industry, resistance to reduction in workers' wages may, in a short run, prevent these contributions from being deducted. There is no question, however, that any rise in costs resulting from these taxes on employers does give a continuing incentive for employers to substitute the use of capital equipment for labor. In the short run, unemployment may be created

---

[21] This conclusion implies that the presence of contributions (and expected benefits) will not increase wages either through raising workers' productivity or cutting into profits, although either of these might happen.

by the taxes on employers. In the long run, the factors which make it difficult to shift part or all of such taxes to employees will be weakened.

Size and use of social security reserve funds. A second question of economic interest relates to the size and use of reserve funds which have been built up under the systems of old-age retirement and unemployment compensation. Accumulated funds under these provisions of the Social Security Act become available to the Federal government, although it holds unemployment compensation deposits by the states in a special fund for repayment when requested. As such funds accumulate, they have been invested in special interest-bearing government bonds, and the funds have been used for general government purposes. This means that when the rate of withdrawal from the funds exceeds the current additions to the funds, the Federal government will have to draw on general government funds (secured through such fiscal devices as borrowing and taxation).

Available data indicate that the time when general government funds will be needed to meet social security commitments is nearer in the field of unemployment compensation than in old-age insurance. During the war years, invested funds in the Unemployment Trust Fund rose rapidly. Employment was high, unemployment was low, and the invested balance (exclusive of interest on "investments") was 6.8 billion dollars at the end of 1945, as compared with 2.6 billions at the end of 1941. During 1945, total contributions to the Unemployment Trust Fund were 1,375 million dollars, whereas withdrawals and administration expenses were only 109 millions. During 1946, contributions of 1,193 million dollars did not quite meet total withdrawals and administrative expenses of 1,205 millions.

Prospects for such withdrawals in excess of receipts (in the absence of further changes in legislation) are probably ten years away in the case of old-age payments. At the end of 1946, invested funds (excluding interest on investments) were about 7.4 billion dollars compared with 2.3 billions at the end of 1941. Despite Congressional action in freezing contributory tax rates, liberalizing benefits, and advancing the time of first benefit payments from 1942 to 1940, tax contributions to the old-age funds in 1946 were about 1,521 million dollars as compared with benefit payments and administrative costs of about 512 millions.

An over-all picture of the general financial benefits of the Social Security program to the Federal government through 1946 indicates that the program had made about 11.7 billion dollars available to it for general governmental purposes for varying periods of time. A summary is given in Table 28.

TABLE 28[22]

Social Security Collections and Payments (1936-1946)

(in millions of dollars)

1. Tax Receipts
   a. Old-age retirement insurance......................... $8,935.8
   b. Railroad retirement insurance........................ 1,780.1
   c. Unemployment trust fund, including state deposits and railroad deposits.. 10,257.7
   d. Federal unemployment tax............................ 1,145.3

   e. Total tax receipts.................................... $22,118.9

2. Social Security payments
   a. Old-age benefit payments............................ 1,104.0
   b. Railroad retirement benefit payments................. 1,108.0
   c. Unemployment benefit payments...................... 3,412.6
   d. Grants to the states for various purposes
      (excluding unemployment administration)............. 3,483.2
   e. Administrative costs................................. 1,012.2
   f. Tax refunds... 72.1

   g. Total social security expenses....................... $10,192.27

3. Net funds available for investment in special government securities, 1936-1946:............................... 11,926.5[a]
   a. Amount not yet invested as of 6/30/46 was $76.1

[a] This represents the amount of social security funds available for general governmental purposes. 1936-1946.

Financing social security. It is a moot question as to how social security benefit payments should be financed. Payments for old-age retirement (under the old-age retirement system) and for unemployment compensation yield special benefits to their recipients. From this point of view it is probably not unsatisfactory to impose some of the costs of providing such payments on those who will receive the benefits.

However, individuals who do not receive payments may also benefit from such social security programs as old-age assistance

[22] Source: *Treasury Bulletin,* August, 1946, pages 12-14, and June, 1941, pages 12-13.

and unemployment insurance. For example, the burden of caring for relatives in old age and in unemployment may be reduced, and such programs may add considerably to the stability of the social order in which we live. From this point of view, there is some justice in financing a part of social security by general taxation.[23]

As we have already indicated, our present social security taxes probably are largely borne by those who receive the direct benefits. However, to the extent that the workers' disposable incomes are reduced, the market for consumption goods may be weakened and certain (unnecessary) costs upon the rest of society may be imposed as a result of unemployment.

This deflationary aspect of social security taxation has been severely criticized.[24] One proposal is that all social security expenditures should be financed out of general governmental funds and that payroll taxes should be abolished.

Many labor groups are in opposition to financing social security from general taxation. They fear that an antilabor Congress might refuse to make appropriations to cover such payments. They argue that as long as the program is self-financing the probability of its being abolished is small. There may also be a belief among organized labor that income differentials between organized and unorganized labor should prevail even during periods of unemployment. Discarding the contributory principle in favor of financing from general funds probably would level benefits. While it is true that payroll taxes are more deflationary than the personal income tax or death-gift taxes, this alone does not constitute sufficient basis for discarding them. Offsets to these deflationary impacts can be provided by securing funds to finance the rest of government expenditures. However, the payroll tax system should provide that: (1) the timing of large benefit payments for old-age retirement should be further advanced, at existing tax rates, so that present old-age retirement reserve funds of the Federal government do not increase further. (2) Unemployment compensation tax rates, while not permitted to go above the present 3 per cent rate, should be made more flexible below the 3 per cent rate. (Favorable results from ex-

[23] The Canadian national system of unemployment compensation, which began in 1941, is financed 80 per cent by payroll taxes, 20 per cent by general revenues.
[24] See, for example, Beardsley Ruml and H. Christian Sonne, *Fiscal-Monetary Policy*, National Planning Association, Pamphlet No. 35.

perience rating led several states to impose no unemployment taxes in 1946.) (3) Differential benefits in unemployment compensation and in old-age insurance should not be principally dependent upon previous earnings.

Socially, it is desirable that social security benefits should be extended to cover public employees, domestic workers, agricultural workers, and (for unemployment compensation) workers in establishments which employ as few as 1 or 2 persons.

Government Enterprises

With certain important exceptions, government enterprise in the United States has been largely directed toward activities designed to make the private economy perform more satisfactorily in the interest of the general welfare.

The principal exceptions are the postal system, certain state liquor monopolies, and municipally operated public utilities. Some government enterprises have provided services—for example, absorbed certain business risks which were not assumed by private agencies. The Reconstruction Finance Corporation (in its early activities), Farm Credit Administration, Defense Plants Corporation (during the war), and Federal Deposit Insurance Corporation were enterprises of this nature. The TVA and several other Federal projects have become an important source of electric power. The TVA has also served as a yardstick for private power producers in the Tennessee Valley. TVA's price policy has been credited for the marked increase in electricity consumption in this area. In addition, the TVA and other public enterprises of a similar nature have also been designed to facilitate operation of the private economy by providing flood-control, irrigation, and improved navigation of some of our rivers.

At the Federal level, it has previously been indicated that the postal system with a revenue of over 1.1 billion dollars in 1945 is one of the largest single business enterprises in the country. Outside the postal field, the largest investment of the Federal government is in those facilities for producing and distributing power, irrigating land, controlling flood waters, and rendering some rivers more navigable than before. These four purposes have been combined in the development of the Tennessee river valley since 1933 (under the direction of a new administrative agency, the Tennessee Valley Authority). One or more of these objectives has been sought by the Federal government in developing other production facilities which it operates.

At the end of 1945, the indicated Federal investment in facilities under the Bureau of Reclamation (such as the Grand Coulee and Boulder dams), TVA, and the Rural Electrification Administration (REA) exceeded 2.2 billion dollars. Of these, only the REA represented a *loan* of Federal funds in anticipation of repayment by the nearly 1,300,000 farmers using its facilities. Receipts from the sale of electric power in 1945 by the Federal agencies enumerated above was slightly over 152.6 million dollars. The experiments of TVA in expanding the sale of electricity by reducing power rates have indicated a relatively high elasticity in the demand for electric power.

Since 1916, the Federal government has been interested in providing credit for farmers at lower borrowing charges than were generally offered by private lenders. In 1916, the present Federal Land Banks were established to extend long-term mortgage credit for the purchase of farms. After various alterations in mechanisms for the extension of farm credit, the present Farm Credit Administration was established in 1933, principally to administer the various Federal agencies for provision of long- and short-term credit.

The oldest of these agencies were the Federal Land Banks, which had long-term mortgage loans outstanding at the end of 1945 of about 1,061 million dollars. Another was the Federal Farm Mortgage Corporation, created in 1934 to extend long-term credit where Federal Land Banks did not consider loans completely sound business investments. Most of the approximately 1,500 million dollar loans which it made in the first two years of its life have turned out to be good economic risks. Repayment of loans was rapid and at the end of 1945, the Federal Farm Mortgage Corporation had only 308.9 million dollars of mortgage loans outstanding. Another major lending unit in the Farm Credit Administration consists of the Banks for Cooperatives, which were providing cooperatives with loans of about 137.7 million dollars in June, 1945. Intermediate- and short-term credit was also being advanced by local production credit associations, production credit banks, and Federal intermediate credit banks, amounting to 738.8 million dollars at the end of

1945.[25] For the services of these agencies, farmers paid, (in 1945) about 81.8 million dollars in interest and loan-service fees. From 1933-1945, the Federal government subsidized farm credit agencies to the extent of 626.1 million dollars, thus making it possible for these agencies to provide funds at lower interest rates.[26]

Many major enterprise activities of the Federal government have operated through the Reconstruction Finance Corporation, first created in 1932 to save railroads, banks, and insurance companies by underwriting them with credits from the Federal government. In its early operations through 1937, it extended over 2 billion dollars in loans to banks and trust companies. It also subscribed to, and purchased, bank stocks and notes of 1.1 billion dollars and loaned 537.1 million dollars to railroads. During recent years, it has been used to extend credits to various government-created corporations and agencies, among which are the Commodity Credit Corporation (to extend loans on farm-produced commodities) and many wartime subsidiaries. Its book assets at the end of 1944 were 10,225 million dollars of which 8,365 millions represented advances to other government corporations.

Among other Federal enterprises designed to facilitate the operation of private enterprise may be mentioned (1) Federal Deposit Insurance Corporation, which will guarantee the deposits of an individual (up to $5,000) in a particular bank; (2) the Federal Housing Administration, which guarantees private loans for private housing (under specified conditions) up to 90 per cent of the value of the construction outlay; (3) the Home-Owners' Loan Corporation. From its creation (in 1933) to June 1936, this agency loaned 3.09 billion dollars, mostly to refinance private mortgage loans. It was an important depression-time Federal agency which enabled over a million owners of homes to retain their properties until the return of a degree of business prosperity.

Enterprise revenue of the states in 1941, as shown in Table 26,

---

[25] There were several other Federal farm lending agencies in existence in 1945.
[26] Based on an unpublished research study of Fenton Shephard, Bureau of the Budget (formerly of the Bureau of Agricultural Economics), on the costs of Federal governmental agricultural programs, 1930-1944. Losses of several hundred million dollars by the Federal Farm Board and Commodity Credit Corporation have been excluded.

was 283 million dollars, almost all of it from the operation of state liquor monopolies in 16 of the states. Enterprise revenue of local government units in 1941, as indicated in Table 26, was 873.6 million dollars. The bulk of this came from the operation of municipally owned utilities—especially water-plants—but between 1932 and 1941, the local government units also expanded considerably in the field of housing.

Nontax Revenues

Considerable importance for such nontax revenues as licenses offsetting services, service charges for current services, revenues from use of public money and property, and such miscellaneous revenues as penalties, fines, forfeitures of property, and donations was indicated in Table 26. In addition, it was indicated that, in 1941, local governments raised over 102 million dollars in special assessments. It is the purpose of this section to summarize these nontax revenues briefly.

All of these sources of revenue available to the Federal government gained considerably in size during the war.[27] Service charges for current services were 118.7 million dollars.[28] Revenues from the use of public money and property were 682.9 millions.[29] Penalties and other—fines, fees, forfeits, donations, spe-

---

[27] Source: *Annual Report of the Secretary of the Treasury, 1945,* Washington, D. C., pages 731-732, 735-737. Excluded from the Federal summary (1945) are repayments of loans amounting to 60.8 million dollars, of which the repayment of rural rehabilitation loans of 37.7 millions, made by the Farm Security Administration was the largest single item. Also excluded are reimbursements totaling 2.36 billion dollars. The largest reimbursement item so excluded was 2.04 billions due to renegotiation of war contracts. But the 188.1 millions of surplus postal revenue has been included in the statement of postal revenue already given in Table 26. That portion of Federal power revenues (27.8 million dollars) included in the *Treasury Report* is also incorporated in Table 26. The total miscellaneous items reported at 3.6 billions are based on collection reports and are not adjusted to actual receipts as given in the Treasury *Daily Statement,* which reduces the gross total by 127.1 million dollars.

[28] Of which receipts for "laundry and dry-cleaning services" were 40.9 million dollars and services of prisoners of war and of civilian internees were 34.3 millions. *Treasury Report, ibid.*

[29] Including mint receipts and siegniorage of $124 million; interest, dividends and exchange receipts of $140.5 million; sale of government property and products of $326.4 million; rents and royalties of $92 million. Source: *Treasury Report, op. cit.,* pages 732-734, 737. The classification "revenues from the use of public money and property" probably grows out of a period in history during which interest on public funds deposited in banks was a relatively important source of revenue.

cial deposits for defense aid, and minor "special taxes"—were
153.1 million dollars. Some of these sources of funds to the
Treasury, such as sale of surplus property and products, will
cease, or become relatively unimportant. This is also true of reimbursements due to renegotiation of wartime contracts.

State-local nontax revenues. "Licenses offsetting services"—
business inspection, regulation of business to ensure adequate
purity and quality of production, and various charges for the
privilege of engaging in a particular profession or occupation
(such as annual fees for engaging in the practice of medicine, or
operating public eating places)—are a fairly important source of
state-local revenues. To some extent, these fees are part of the
occupational tax structure which was described in Chapter XV.
There has also been some tendency for such license fees to become part of state business-tax structures. This is evidenced in
the area of state insurance taxes (generally on gross premiums),
which have been retained at levels bringing collections far in
excess of the costs of state inspection and administration of insurance companies. The expenses of state insurance departments
in 1938 were about 5 million dollars, although collections from
state insurance taxes were about 107 millions.[30] Except in the
provision of some additional revenue, it is difficult to find economic objectives served by the excess revenue provided by many
state and local license fees (and taxes). Some service charges
such as state charges for the cost of examination of state-char-
tered banks, and occasional municipal charges for garbage collection and sewage disposal are explainable on special-benefit
grounds.

For state and local governments, "revenues from the use of
public money and property" simply means that these governmental units own certain properties which they lease to private
individuals or businesses. Revenues are also obtainable from the
sale of public property, such as school lands.

Local governmental units have long relied on special assessments on property to cover the cost of improvements which are
contemplated, such as the costs of a street improvement or the installation of a sewage system. It is generally anticipated that

---

[30] Source: *Insurance Bulletin,* Insurance Department, Chamber of Commerce of
the United States, Washington, D. C., February 8, 1940.

such improvements will increase the value of the land sufficiently to more than cover the cost of the improvements, although this result does not always follow.[31]

Special assessment problems have centered about the definition of the area that could be expected to benefit, and the financing of special assessment costs. These problems are analyzed in detail in many standard public-finance texts,[32] and the analysis will not be repeated. But two things may be pointed out. Special assessments are being used much less frequently to finance urban improvements. Local special assessments in 1941 were 34.6 per cent of their 1932 level (they fell from 295.1 to 102.1 million dollars).[33] Means of paying for costs of improvements under special assessments have been devised which permit the issue ·of special assessment bonds, typically payable by property-owners benefited in annual installments over a ten-year period. The sale of these bonds also provides funds with which to pay immediately for the costs of improvement incurred by a contractor.

SELECTED READINGS

1. Allen, Edward D., *Analysis of Highway Costs and Highway Taxation with an Application to Story County, Iowa*, Ames, Iowa: Iowa Engineering Experiment Station, Bulletin 152, 1941.
2. ———, "Highway Costs and Their Allocation," *Journal of Land and Public Utility Economics*, Vol. XV (August and November, 1939).
3. *Annual Report of the Secretary of the Treasury, 1945*, Washington, D. C.: United States Government Printing Office.
4. *Annual Reports of the Social Security Board, 1936-46*, Washington, D. C.: United States Government Printing Office.
5. Federal Coordinator of Transportation, *Public Aids to Motor Vehicle Transportation*, Washington, D. C.: United States Government Printing Office, 1940.

[31] Note the early financing of the costs of improving some trunk highways, whose benefits went principally to intercity motor vehicle users of these highways, and the financing of the costs of improving some urban subdivisions during the twenties, when these subdivisions did not subsequently attract residents.

[32] Such as W. J. Schultz, *American Public Finance*, 3rd edition, Prentice-Hall, Inc., 1942, pages 612-619.

[33] See *Financing Federal, State and Local Government, 1941*, page 35.

6. Highway Research Board, "Report of the Committee on Highway Transportation Costs," *Proceedings, 1929,* Washington, D. C., published in 1930.
7. *Insurance Bulletin,* No. 50, Washington, D. C.: Insurance Department, Chamber of Commerce of the United States, 1940.
8. Public Roads Administration, *Public Roads,* Vol. 23, No. 3 (October-December, 1942), Washington, D. C., 1943.
9. Shultz, W. J., *American Public Finance,* 3rd edition, New York: Prentice-Hall, Inc., 1942.
10. United States Department of Commerce, Bureau of the Census, *Financing Federal, State and Local Governments, 1941,* Washington, D. C., 1942.
11. United States Treasury Department, *Treasury Bulletins,* June, 1941, and August, 1946, Washington, D. C.

CHAPTER XIX

PROPERTY TAXATION: OPERATION
AND INEQUALITIES

IN COLONIAL times, property taxes on land and often on improvements were the most important part of our tax structure. Such property taxes (largely on land) were broadened during the first half of the nineteenth century to include most improvements on land, tangible personal property, and even intangible property claims to wealth—such as the stocks and bonds of corporations. By the middle of the nineteenth century, the property tax had become a general property tax. It is the purpose of this chapter and the next to analyze the role of these taxes in our fiscal system.

While all taxes eventually fall on individuals, property taxes are imposed on *things* and therefore are what fiscal students call *ad rem* taxes. General and selective property taxes remain an important part of our tax system, despite increasing exemptions and the relatively small amount of success in applying the tax to certain forms of property (especially intangible property claims to wealth).

In 1941, just as we were beginning to experience the great increases in taxes which accompanied our participation in World War II, property taxes were the largest single source of public revenue, making up 24.1 per cent of the total.[1] Today they remain the chief tax levied by local government units (see Table 29, which indicates that they made up 92.5 per cent of local tax revenue in 1942). They are the principal source of all government revenue for these units, despite the rapid growth of intergovernmental aids for them which increased from only 76 million dollars in 1902 to 1,760 millions in 1942. Other sources of local revenue included enterprise earnings and receipts from miscellaneous sources (see Table 30).

In contrast to their dominant role in local tax structures, prop-

[1] Source: *Financing Federal, State and Local Governments, 1941*, page 27.

TABLE 29[2]

Tax Revenues of State and Local Government Units in the United States, 1942

(in millions of dollars)

Government Unit	Property Taxes	All Other Taxes	Total Taxes	Property Taxes as a Per Cent of Total Taxes
State governments.......	$270,939	$4,703,826	$4,974,765	5.4%
Counties	896,972	36,848	933,820	96.1
Townships and towns	257,498	20,986	278,484	92.5
Urban Places	2,026,272	299,098	2,325,370	87.1
School Districts.........	1,077,470	1,361	1,078,831	99.9
Special Districts........	89,687	——	89,687	100.0
Total[a]	$4,592,678	$5,062,119	$9,654,797	47.6%
Total, except for state governments........	4,321,739	358,273	4,680,012	92.3

[a] Detail does not add to total.

erty taxes have declined almost steadily in relative importance in state tax structures since 1902, when they represented about 51 per cent of taxes collected by state governments. In 1946 only 3.8 per cent of state tax revenues came from property taxes. This change has been due largely to the development of new sources of tax revenue by the states, such as motor vehicle taxes, sales and gross-receipt taxes, special business taxes, payroll (social security) taxes, and taxes on personal- and business-net income.

A number of states now levy no state property taxes. In 1946, state property taxation was fiscally most important in New Jersey, California, Texas, Wisconsin, Michigan, and Ohio respectively. In each of these states the property tax provided the state with more than 12 million dollars in tax revenue. A property tax levy yielding over 4 million dollars was part of the state fiscal system of 7 out of 10 of the states in southeastern United States (Alabama, Arkansas, Georgia, Kentucky, Louisiana, North Carolina, Virginia). On the other hand, it provided to state tax revenue, less than $100,000 in Delaware, Iowa, Oregon, and Rhode Island.[3]

[2] Source: *Governmental Finances in the United States, 1942*, Bureau of the Census, Washington, D. C., 1945, page 27.

[3] Source: Bureau of the Census, *State Tax Collections in 1946*, Washington, D. C., August, 1946.

TABLE 30[4]

Relative Importance of Selected Sources of Government Revenues in the United States, 1942

| Government Unit | Total Revenues | Taxes | Percentages of All Government Revenues From: | | | |
			Property Taxes	Intergovernmental Aid	Charges for Current Services	Miscellaneous
State governments	100.0%	81.4%	4.4%	13.2%	3.6%	1.8%
Counties	100.0	57.1	54.9	33.7	6.6	2.5
Townships and towns	100.0	75.1	69.4	20.2	2.7	2.0
Urban areas	100.0	74.5	64.9	16.3	3.3	6.0
School Districts	100.0	60.0	59.9	35.9	2.3	1.8
Special Districts	100.0	60.7	60.7	3.1	21.3	14.9
Total	100.0%	73.5%	35.0%	19.6%	3.9%	3.1%

[4] Source: *Governmental Finances in the United States, 1942*, Bureau of the Census, Washington, D. C., 1945, page 27.

Property taxes have played almost no part in Federal taxation, probably due to a Constitutional provision that has made such taxation impracticable.[5]   Municipalities have found themselves especially restricted by the conditions under which they may impose taxes.   Such units typically operate under property-tax and debt-rate limitations of varying degrees of severity imposed by their state governments.   Yet municipalities find it difficult to impose taxes, other than property taxes, which yield substantial revenue.   Meanwhile, they have experienced a rising demand for public services.   The mobility of resources is sufficiently great so that a municipality cannot successfully apply substantial income, sales, or business taxes unless other local units also levy such taxes at similar rates.[6]

For example, there is greater possibility of tax avoidance or evasion with a local sales tax than with a tax on certain forms of property.   It is possible to go outside a local taxed area to buy consumption goods free of a local sales tax, but it is impossible to move a piece of land or a large business structure outside a certain taxing district for the purpose of evading property taxes.[7] On the other hand, certain forms of personal property, such as household goods and clothing, and personal holdings of stocks and bonds, may be very difficult to assess for taxation.   One result of this difference is that property taxes have increasingly tended to become taxes on real property (real estate) rather than on personal property.   A special Census bulletin of 1939, while indicating a downward trend in the assessed value of all classes of property since 1932, showed that the assessed value of personal property was only 15.7 per cent of the assessed value of all prop-

[5] See Article 1, Section 9 of the Constitution, which requires that all direct taxes (property taxes have been held to be "direct" taxes by the courts) must be apportioned among the states on the basis of relative population.   There are only three cases of Federal use of property taxation, once in 1798, again during the War of 1812, and once during the Civil War.

[6] A few municipalities, nevertheless, use some taxes to supplement property-tax revenues.   The best examples are the 2 per cent sales tax used by New York City and the 1½ per cent tax on gross income earned within Philadelphia imposed by that city.   A few municipalities impose supplemental taxes on motor fuel and vehicle uses, and most of them impose a variety of business-license fees.   For all local units of government in 1942, however, all taxes other than property taxes yielded less than 8 per cent of total tax revenue.

[7] While differences in property taxes between areas will not move a fixed asset, such as a factory, out of one taxing area and into another, differences in property taxes may have some effect upon the location of new businesses.   This has been recognized in the exemption from municipal property taxation offered to new business by some cities, particularly in the South.

erty.[8] This represents a reversal of the tendency previously noted for the property tax to become more inclusive during the nineteenth century.

Nature of the General Property Tax

In usual economic terminology, property represents ownership rights to real wealth, but in taxation "property" has been identified with both wealth and property rights against wealth. An undesirable consequence of this definition is the possibility of inequitable double taxation for certain forms of property. The types of property which may be subject to taxation are, broadly, these:

1. Real property (real estate): land, buildings, and permanent improvements. Generally such property is attached to a certain location and is not movable.
2. Personal property (such property is generally movable).
   a. Tangible personal property:
      1) That which, directly or indirectly, yields a money income: inventories of all types; farm crops; machinery; farm animals.
      2) That which is used in final consumption: household goods and personal effects.
   b. Intangible personal property: claims against tangible wealth, such as stocks, bonds, mortgages, promissory notes, bank deposits, money and so forth.

While this is a broad property classification which includes the various types of property, we find in practice that over 85 per cent of the property taxes levied in 1946 in the states with the largest local government budgets were levied against real estate. In most states, liberal exemptions of tangible personal property from taxation have been granted, or assessors have not usually chosen to seek out tangible personalty and place it on the tax assessment rolls. Two states, New York and Delaware, had given up trying to assess personal property before 1946. Intangible personal property is so easily hidden from the assessor and may so obviously become the object of a second tax falling on an article of wealth—such as a mortgage on land—already assessed

---

[8] See Census bulletin of June, 1939, *Assessed Valuation of Property Subject to General and Selective Property Taxes by States: 1937*, Bureau of the Census, Washington, D. C., 1939.

for taxation that the majority of states, in 1946, had either ceased attempts to assess intangibles (preferring to reach taxable ability under an income tax) or had classified intangibles separately and imposed a low flat-rate millage tax on their capital value.

A true general property tax would tax all property (as defined above), valued uniformly at its market, or exchange, value. Under the uniformity provision written into many state constitutions, the tax rate per dollar of value is necessarily uniform within any given taxing district. This does not preclude different tax rates in different tax districts. Thus, in District A, a tax levy of 5 mills per dollar of assessed valuation may be levied by the state government, one of 20 mills may be imposed by the county, one of 30 mills may be levied by a school district, and one of 20 mills may be levied for municipal purposes. In District B, a rural district near by, within a different school district, state and county tax levies per dollar of assessed valuation would be the same, but the school tax might be 15 mills. The total relative levies in the two districts might be 75 and 40 mills, respectively. But under a strict uniformity clause which does not permit classification of property for taxation, each unit of property *within* each of the two districts would be taxed at the same total rate per dollar of assessed value.[9]

Common assumptions underlying the general property tax are (1) that ownership of property is a satisfactory measure of ability to pay or benefits received as a basis for taxation, (2) that all types of property will be listed and assessed uniformly for taxation, and (3) that the tax will be collected. Before we examine these assumptions, none of which is completely realistic, let us look briefly at the process by which property taxes are levied and collected.

The property tax process.

The property tax process consists essentially of four steps:
1. Assessment of the value of property for taxation, which involves (a) discovery, (b) listing, (c) valuing the listed property for tax purposes, (d) review and equalization of assessed values.

[9] Because of common tendencies of assessors not to value units of property at their full value, and varying opportunities to shift or capitalize those property taxes which are imposed, this does not mean that the taxes which finally fall on the value of property so assessed are likely to be as great as 75 and 40 mills, respectively. These possibilities of avoiding taxes on property values will be analyzed in more detail later.

2. The tax levy: determination of the amount of money to be raised through property taxes in various taxing jurisdictions (state, county, township, school district, municipality, and perhaps a special district). Such taxes are typically certified to a designated official, often the county treasurer.

3. Determination of the tax rate per dollar of equalized assessed value in any given tax district by dividing the tax levy for property in that district by the assessed valuation.

4. Collection and distribution of the tax levies, together with provisions for the collection and distribution of delinquent taxes.

(1) *Assessment.* Assessors are typically employed on a part-time basis, except in larger cities, are popularly elected, and are not required to have special qualifications for their positions. This usually results in low operating efficiency. Assessors have the legal obligation to place property subject to taxation on the tax rolls and to place a value on such properties for purposes of taxation, however.

Taxpayers have the legal right to ask some constituted authority—either a local municipal body, a county board of supervisors, and ultimately the courts[10]—for a review of the assessments which have been imposed on their property. That this right of review is not used very frequently is primarily a reflection on the quality of our property assessments. Property is often assessed below its true value or is not assessed at all, as is frequently true of personal property. The result is that a protesting taxpayer is more likely to have the assessed value of his property increased rather than decreased. A useful function in some states (such as Wisconsin) is performed by state bodies, which may undertake to equalize assessed valuations among various taxing districts or even within a given taxing district. The function of state equalization or "central assessment" will be discussed in more detail in the next chapter.

(2) *Determining the tax levy and tax rates.* Once a year, tax-levying bodies in various tax jurisdictions (see Table 31) determine how much they must levy in the form of property taxes, after taking into account total probable expenditures and receipts from such other sources as state aids in the case of school dis-

---

[10] In a few states—such as Indiana and Iowa—taxpayers have the right to appeal tax levies themselves, usually to a state board of certain state officers acting *ex officio.*

tricts or net earnings of enterprises in the case of municipalities. They then levy the amount of property taxes which are required to make up the difference between probable expenditures and receipts from other sources. Requirements may exceed some maximum permissible collections often established by state laws. In this case, special permission must be obtained from state authorities to impose the additional tax levies. In recent years, the rising costs of public services and the improved economic position of property owners has brought about pressure for removal of maximum tax levies which have been established, most of them during the depression of the thirties.

TABLE 31[11]

Governmental Units in the United States: 1942

Type of Governmental Unit[a]	Number of Units	Number of States in Which Found	Per Cent of All Units	Per Cent of All Units (Except School Districts)
Total................	155,148	49[b]	100.0	100.0
U. S. Government......	1		(c)	(c)
States...............	48	48	(c)	(c)
Counties.............	3,050	47	2.0	6.6
Townships (or towns)..	18,884	22	12.2	40.6
Municipalities........	16,189	49[b]	10.4	34.6
School Districts.......	108,644	43	70.0	
Special Districts.......	8,322	49[b]	5.4	18.0

[a] All these units, with the probable exception of the Federal government, are potential property-tax-levying units.
[b] Includes the District of Columbia, which has one municipality and one special district.
[c] Less than .05 of 1 per cent.

The determination of tax rates to be imposed on assessed property in any given tax district is simply a matter of dividing combined tax levies by equalized assessed values of property.

Many states have applied both tax-rate and debt-rate limitations to local units of government. Such limitations were especially common in the twenties. As a double control device, these limitations have not been very successful. If a given community has received its maximum tax rate and the amount of debt permitted, it has always been possible to increase assessed valuations. By such action, not only additional taxes, but also addi-

[11] Source: *Governmental Units in the United States: 1942;* U. S. Department of Commerce, Bureau of the Census, Preliminary Summary, January, 1944.

tional debt, have been made possible since debt limitations are often imposed as some percentage of assessed valuation.

In those states which impose a maximum to over-all tax rates against property,[12] there is a problem of determining how the total rate and proceeds shall be allocated among the various governmental units. One of the results of such maxima has been an expansion in state aid for local services—as in the growth of state aid for public schools in Michigan after 1933—or a reduction in the amount and quality of local services. The same economic factors which have produced pressure for the removal of maximum tax levies in recent years have produced increased pressure for removal of these state-imposed maxima in property-tax rates.

(3) *Payment of property taxes.* Tax levies are paid, frequently semiannually, to a designated central official—often the county treasurer. This official distributes the tax funds to the various levying agencies, including the state government, if it has made a property-tax levy. Typically, the various states permit an additional payment period for delinquent taxes, plus interest and penalties, with a tax sale if overdue taxes are not paid within a specified period. If the property owner does not redeem his property by full payment of back taxes, interest, and penalties within some period after taxes become due (most commonly two years) the property sold for taxes becomes the property of the purchaser, and he (the purchaser) acquires title to it.[13]

Principal deficiencies of the property tax. The main charge which has been brought against the general property tax is that the tax has proven inequitable as a means of distributing the tax burden. In examining this charge, we shall see that there are two main reasons which support it: (1) On the whole, the administration of property taxation has been unsatisfactory. This is due both to actions of state legislatures in exempting property from taxation and to inequalities in assessment. Both lead to inequitable distribution of the property tax burden. (2) Even if property were equitably assessed, the value of property held is not

---

[12] Examples are Ohio, West Virginia, Michigan, Indiana, Washington, and Oklahoma.

[13] Not all states have tax sales, however. In some, the government may purchase property for the amount of taxes, penalties, and interest due against it (tax lien) and then sell the property after a further period of time has passed, if deficient taxes, interest charges, and penalties are not paid.

an adequate index of an individual's ability to pay or the benefits
which he receives—accepted criteria for distribution of the tax
load. In spite of these limitations, there are bases for the continuance of property taxation. Some of the attempts which have
been made to improve its operation will be examined in the next
chapter.[14]

Inequalities and Inequities of the Assessment Process

A major criticism of the general property tax on the grounds of
inequity lies in the inequalities in the assessment of property, principally real property. It is really a criticism of the whole assessment process. The major types of inequality in the levying of
property taxes upon potential taxpayers are: (1) failure to assess
some property; (2) a general tendency toward undervaluation;
(3) a tendency toward a competitive undervaluation by different
assessors of types of properties located in different taxing districts; (4) a tendency for assessors to value different properties
of *the same type and value* at widely varying ratios to true or
exchange value; (5) a tendency for a given assessor to assess low-
valued properties at a higher ratio to true value than properties of
relatively high value.

Some of these inequalities can be substantially reduced: state
tax bodies with full-time personnel could (and generally do)
assess some large value-unit properties, such as railroads, which
extend through various districts. Such bodies provide varying
degrees of supervision over local assessments, and may equalize
tax valuations by districts or even reassess individual property
holdings within tax districts. Some of the inadequacies in local
assessment, however, are a product of the method for selecting
assessors. This method is almost universally one of popular election, without special qualifications, for a limited period of time—
usually 1 to 4 years. Except in larger cities, assessors are chosen
for a part-time job in the various townships and municipalities,
and depend on re-election for continuance of their positions.
This places them under heavy pressure for favorable assessments
from economically powerful groups and individuals.[15]

[14] In examining the principal limitations of the general property tax, we are
simultaneously examining the limitations in the basic assumptions underlying the
tax.

[15] The rather obvious remedy for this defect is appointment on a merit basis and
removal only "for due cause" by the courts. This remedy, however, is not one

Failure to assess property. Failure to assess tangible property at all has centered in the failure to assess some real estate in larger cities and in the widespread variations in assessment of tangible personal property where such has been attempted. A considerable percentage of real property in a city like Chicago was not assessed at all during the thirties. The development of tax maps for a given block or rural area (partly through the process of aerial mapping) has sharply reduced this type of tax evasion in recent years. The amount of tangible personal property which is assessed in a given district varies considerably with the activity of different assessors, who are typically poorly paid even for part-time work, and usually are not anxious to pry into the personal holdings of tangible wealth which an individual may have. An over-all effect of failure to assess a relatively large amount of tangible personal property has been approximate conversion of the property tax into a tax on real estate, as we pointed out earlier.

Underassessment of property. The tendency of assessors to value property below its true market value is very general. In a special study in 1945, one of the writers found that, in five midwestern states, the average ratios of assessed to actual values of farm real estate for nine selected years from 1920 through 1944 followed the pattern indicated in Table 32. It will be noted that these ratios tended to rise during the depression years of the thirties when, typically, assessors did not reduce assessed values as rapidly as the sales value of farm real estate fell. The averages also conceal wide fluctuations in ratios of assessed to actual values *among* the taxing districts of the various states.

The average ratio of assessed to actual value *within* any given taxing jurisdiction is of only limited economic significance. Assuming, for instance, that the tax levy for a municipality and a conterminous school district is $10,000, it makes little difference to taxpayers within that district whether the prevailing ratio of assessed to true value is 60 per cent or some other ratio, as long as all individual assessments are made at the prevailing ratio.[16]

which has appealed to the electorate in the United States, except in the rare instances where supervisors of local assessors are so appointed. The inequalities growing out of assessment have apparently been preferred to a presumably superior method which would take direct control over choice of assessors out of the hands of the people.

[16] Actually, use of the same ratio for different individuals is not a realistic assumption, as will be indicated below.

TABLE 32[17]

Ratios of Assessed to Actual Values of Farm Real Estate in Five
Midwestern States, Selected Years, 1920-1944

Year	Ratio	National Income (in billions of dollars)
1920	48%	
1929	64	$83.3
1935	74	55.7
1939	76	70.8
1940	81	77.6
1941	77	96.9
1942	72	122.6
1943	67	149.4
1944	57	160.7

But there is some economic significance of varying average
ratios among taxing districts. Property owners in a taxing district where the ratio of assessed to true value is high will be paying inequitably high taxes to higher governmental units (such as
the county) which impose the same levy upon property in all
districts. For example, a property in assessment district A may
be assessed at 50 per cent of its true value, whereas an equivalent
property in district B may be assessed at only 20 per cent of its
true value. The county levy may be 10 mills. The taxpayer in
district A will be paying $2\frac{1}{2}$ times as much taxes to the county as
will the taxpayer in district B.[18] The difference in ratios may
prove sufficient to shift investments to other taxing districts where
the tax ratios are more favorable.

Inflexibility in assessment. As has been mentioned, it is characteristic for adjustment in assessed values to be "sticky": to lag
considerably behind actual values of various items of property.
This has several effects: One is to cause ratios of assessed to actual
value automatically to rise during depression years and to fall
sharply during periods of business prosperity and increases in
property values. This, in turn, causes the property tax to bear
down with special severity on property owners during periods of
depression, when liquid funds for tax payments may be scarce.

[17] Refer to Edward D. Allen, "Postwar Prospects for Agricultural Land Values
and Property Tax Assessments," Proceedings of the Thirty-Eighth Annual Conference on Taxation, pages 217-226, Washington, D. C.: National Tax Association,
1946.

[18] In Iowa, the prevailing ratio of assessed to actual value had sunk so low that,
from 1897-1933, the ratio was legally established at 25 per cent. In 1933, assessed values were legally established at 100 per cent of actual value. Since
assessed values did not increase by anything like four times, the 1939 session of
the General Assembly established a legal ratio of 60 per cent. An effort has been
made to keep assessed values in relation to actual values at this level since then.

Such scarcity of liquid funds may, as the depression of the thirties indicated, greatly increase the rate of property-tax delinquency and may undermine the long-accepted fiscal belief that the property tax has a very high degree of fiscal dependability, despite other defects which it may have.[19]

Competitive underassessment. Often, the general tendency to assess property below its full value has been accompanied by incentives for competitive underassessment. Competitive underassessment has arisen where property owners in two or more different taxing districts have shared in a joint tax liability; that is, when properties located in two or more assessment areas—such as a city and rural area in the same county—also pay taxes imposed by some higher unit of government. Thus, if a county has levied $5,000,000 in property taxes, it is to the advantage of taxpayers in any given local tax area (city or rural) within the county to pay as small a share of the $5,000,000 as possible. An obvious means has been to keep down total assessed value of property within the local unit. If the rural area reduces its assessment, the city taxpayers will pay a larger share of the $5,-000,000.

In the early years of the century, when state property taxes were a large share of total state taxes, it was urged by some writers that a complete separation of tax sources (and state relinquishment of property taxation) would remove local incentives for competitive underassessment. But the decline of state property-tax levies to small amounts in most states (no levies in some) has not removed the incentive. It is still necessary for property-owners assessed by township or municipal assessors to pay their share of county taxes, which were 19.5 per cent of all property tax collections in 1942.

Some of the inequity of competitive underassessment can be removed where there is county-wide assessment by county assessors, with small or nonexistent state property-tax levies, or where there is state equalization (sometimes called "central assessment") among counties. The possibility of competitive underassessment will exist as long as small tax districts, locally assessed, must pay taxes to some higher level of government.

[19] Such a situation tends to produce competitive underassessment, which is discussed later. It may be noted, however, that it is common in Europe to keep assessments constant over a period of several years. Property taxes are relatively less important in European tax systems than in ours.

Other inequities in the assessment of property. Two other deficiencies in the assessment process, both of which result in inequities among individuals, have not been discussed. It is frequently the case that a given assessor will assess properties which have identical values at widely varying amounts. This may be because of several factors. Perhaps a particular individual is politically powerful (a consideration which an elected assessor is not likely to overlook). Ordinarily, an assessor has neither the trained judgment nor the time to appraise "scientifically" two residential structures, one of which may be constructed of brick, the other of wood. The former may simply appear to represent a greater investment, and receive a higher assessed value. Perhaps too, assessors are not always required to make a complete reassessment except at intervals of several years, and may rely primarily on the assessment book of a predecessor, who has not had time, energy, or facilities for making a careful appraisal and assessment.

Again, a given assessor may often assess properties of lower value at a higher ratio to actual value than is the case for properties of higher value. This may be largely due to the fact that the typical assessor is better acquainted with properties of small than of larger value. In one study, Joseph D. Silverherz found that, in Maryland, rural properties worth less than $1,000 were assessed at 92.1 per cent of actual value. The assessment ratio for properties worth from $1,000 to $5,000 was 76.4 per cent, while rural property worth over $5,000 was assessed at 56.7 per cent of its value. The same tendency showed up in urban properties where, for the same three value-classes of property, the assessment ratios were 76.2 per cent, 61.2 per cent and 54.5 per cent, respectively.[20] In an extensive study of the sales of nearly 72,000 pieces of real estate from 1910 to 1925, the New York Tax Commission found that the ratios of assessed to sales value varied from 92.7 per cent for property worth less than $1,000 to 58.4 per cent for property worth more than $100,000.[21] The same tendency showed up in a study by Dr. W. G. Murray of Iowa farm real estate sold in 1936-1937. Dr. Murray found that the ratio of assessed to sales value for 37 Iowa counties fell steadily

[20] See Joseph D. Silverherz, *The Assessment of Real Property in the United States,* Albany, New York: J. B. Lyon Company, 1936, page 69.
[21] See the New York Tax Commission, *Annual Report,* 1925, page 449.

from the lowest to the highest one-fourth of rural properties, classified according to their sales value. The average ratios which he found were: 85.4; 71.1; 58.3 and 47.7 per cent, with an over-all average at 65.6 per cent. These changing ratios of assessed to sales value also held true within the counties studied, and for some counties where the quality of land was relatively poor, the ratio of assessed to sales value for the lowest one-fourth of valued properties rose above 100 per cent.[22]

Part of the tendency for assessors to value larger-valued properties at relatively low ratios to actual value can be minimized by transferring the assessment of properties which cross the territory of more than one assessor to the state for state assessment. Part of the tendency to value properties of the same type, but of varying size, at different ratios to actual value can be minimized by strong central supervision and cooperation in the assessment process, such as exists in Wisconsin. However, part of the faulty assessments among properties comparable in type or in value is probably inherent in the traditional popular choice of assessors— usually on a part-time basis, and without requirements of previous training for the appraisal and assessment process.

Deficiencies in Property Taxation

Property-tax exemption. The general property tax fails to reach all parts of a property-tax base because: (1) there has been almost continuous increase in tax-exempt properties in most states because of legislative action. This defect in the use of property taxes arises not from improper assessment but from tax policy at the state legislative level. (2) There is large-scale evasion of taxation of intangible and tangible property.[23] On the basis of a recent study of tax exemption in Iowa by one of the writers, it was found that about 35.5 per cent of all privately held tangible property in that state in 1944 in addition to more than a billion dollars of publicly owned property most of which it

---

[22] See W. G. Murray, *Corporate Land, Foreclosures, Mortgage Debt and Land Values,* Research Bulletin 266, Iowa Agricultural Experiment Station, 1939, page 329.

[23] In view of inequity in the taxation at similar rates of tangible property which has no intangible claims (like a mortgage) against it and of both tangible property and claims which may exist against it, it is undesirable that all taxable property should be taxed at the same rate, anyway. For this and other reasons, many states have attempted to tax intangible property on a low-rate millage basis or through state income taxes.

was not reasonable to place on tax-rolls, was exempt from taxation. In addition, the study found that, in 1944, only about 32 per cent of intangible claims against real wealth were subject to taxation. The Tax Commission data indicate that little more than one-fifth of the taxable amount was reached under a low-rate tax on intangibles limited to 5 mills per dollar of assessed value.[24]

These exemptions have been increasing. During the depression years of the thirties, political pressure increased for the relief of home owners from at least some part of property taxation. By 1944, about one-fourth of the states had responded in varying degrees to this pressure, generally providing partial, though not complete, freedom from property taxes.[25] Most states were already providing partial freedom from property taxes for veterans of past wars when the United States entered World War II. Now a new group of veterans is receiving some exemption from taxation in most states, and the exemptions for veterans of previous wars is often being increased.

The net effects of these increasing exemptions are, of course, to restrict the property tax base further and to make tax levies for a given amount of public expenditures greater for those who do have to pay taxes, or to place a larger portion of the costs of local services on the state, or to increase further the need for Federal grants to help finance local and state services.

To the extent that exemption has not been granted and special rates have not been provided, property taxation does not differentiate between money income and nonincome earning property (money)—merchants' inventories and household goods, respectively. Furthermore, inequitable double taxation is involved in taxing at full rate both wealth and rights to wealth, such as a mortgage. Thus, A may own a piece of land worth $5,000 against which there are no property claims except his own. B (across the road) also owns $5,000 worth of land, against which C may hold a mortgage for $2,000. If B is assessed on his prop-

[24] The study on "Tax Exemptions in Iowa" was made by Edward D. Allen for a special tax group, the Iowa Postwar Tax Study Committee. So small a portion of taxable intangible claims to wealth was actually taxed that the final report of the Tax Study Group (1946) recommended the repeal of the so-called "monies and credits" tax.

[25] Brief discussion of these homestead tax relief measures will be given in the following chapter.

erty-holding of $5,000 and C is also assessed on his mortgage, the same amount of real wealth has greater taxes imposed against it in one case than in the other. It may well be that C will evade the tax by concealing his mortgage or it may be that B and C may come to some agreement on the terms of lending which will shift the tax to B through a rise in interest rate. In case C is taxed at all on his intangible wealth, inequitable double taxation will arise. This example is an indication of the lack of homogeneity in taxable property under modern conditions. This sort of situation complicates the application of a general property tax which is inherently not equitable among individuals.

Property tax evasion. The avoidance and evasion which has accompanied the general property tax has been due to a number of factors, only part of which are explained by the exemptions which have been granted. They can be traced partly to faulty assessment, under which property may not be assessed at all or at only a fraction of its true value. They may also be traced to the ease with which intangible property rights—such as stocks, bonds, promissory notes, and bank deposits—may be "moved" or "hidden" from the assessor. This makes relative taxation of those intangible property rights which assessors do reach and assess all the more inequitable among individuals.

Inequities and capitalization in the property tax. Property taxation has proved inequitable as a means of apportioning the tax burden among individuals in several ways. For one thing, some types of property taxes tend to be shifted forward (or backward) and to increase inequality in the distribution of income. This is probably true of taxes on improvements and on tangible personal property intended for later sale to consumers—such as merchants' inventories—of some taxes on intangibles—such as on mortgages against real property—and even of taxes on land, in so far as they fall on reproducible elements of fertility contributing to land value and not upon the location value of land. Such shifting may take place principally in longer-run periods.

For some types of property, the burden of an additional tax may fall on the previous owner through the process of capitalization (refer to Chapter XII). This is certainly true of property taxes which fall on location elements in land value, of taxes on long-term bonds and stocks, and (for some period of time) of taxes which fall on reproducible improvements on land. To the (unmeasurable) extent that property taxes are capitalized, of course, the purchaser of real wealth or property rights against the wealth is able to take taxes into consideration; the purchase price of the property is reduced, and the existing burden of property taxes on their new owners is reduced. Under specified conditions this means that the purchaser of property may buy it "free" from the burden of differentially heavy taxes which may have been imposed on it. This does not mean that the new owner will not pay taxes due, but that his anticipated net income after taxes, at time of purchase, will be as great as in the absence of such differentially heavy taxes. The correct generalization relative to capitalization and shifting which has often been made is that if a tax is capitalized, it cannot be shifted and *vice versa*.

Benefits received and ability to pay in property taxation. In colonial days, when ownership of real estate was an individual's main index of ability to pay, property may have provided a fairly equitable basis for taxation. But the same argument can scarcely be given much weight today. Sources of income which were less important in colonial days have grown with the development of our highly industrialized economy. For example, in (calendar) 1944, wages-salaries represented 72 per cent of the national income. This makes wages-salaries an important element in the personal income-tax base. Net income to proprietors was not split into income from the use of property and of services in 1944, but even so was but 15 per cent of national income. Interest, net rents, and net corporate profits represented the remaining 13 per cent.[26] Ability to pay (as we have used the term) may provide a slight basis for property taxation in the case of owners of farm real estate. Despite the sharp rise in personal income taxes in recent years, it is generally conceded that income from farming has not been very successfully reached by the income tax. To some (unmeasurable) extent, therefore, it is possible that property taxes which fall on farm real estate do tap elements of ability to pay that are not reached under the income tax. This is particularly true where capitalization of part or all of existing property taxes by present owners has occurred, together with some evasion of income-tax liability.[27]

[26] Source: Derived from data in *The Survey of Current Business*, February, 1945, page 5.

[27] It is not possible to develop a quantitative statement on capitalization or income-tax evasion. Capitalization is impossible to measure satisfactorily, unless all property taxes were removed—a tax policy which is not advocated here. The

General taxation according to benefits received cannot provide much of a basis for property taxation. As a society, for instance, we have accepted the idea that an owner of property shall pay taxes for the support of his own school district, whether or not he has children to educate or even lives in the school district. We have also accepted the idea that local police- and fire-protection should be extended to all, whether or not they pay a portion of the property taxes which are imposed. Undoubtedly, some property taxes can be reasonably explained on a special-benefits basis.[28] This does not justify their continued use as the principal tax of local governments. Some of the expansion in state and Federal aids to local governments can be explained by a desire to keep down the expansion in property taxation. Furthermore, property taxes which are imposed on improvements increase the cost of shelter, and impinge with severity on renters when such taxes are shifted forward.

Basic Reasons for Deficiencies in Property Taxation

Property is no longer easy to assess. One fundamental reason for deficiencies in property taxation is that property no longer has the high degree of homogeneity which it had in colonial times when the major index of individual wealth and income was the ownership of property, principally real property. "Property" for tax purposes today is a complex bundle of wealth and rights to wealth, of movable personal property (intangible and tangible), of small and large business units, of property which may earn money income—such as the sale of farm crops and livestock and of merchants' inventories—and of real personal property which is used primarily in consumption. A large share of our intangible property rights have developed with the growth of corporations which issue shares of stock, and sometimes bonds, to acquire the real wealth which they employ.

Important consequences follow from this breakdown in homogeneity of property. Today, there is a great difference in the

---

Bureau of Internal Revenue does not distinguish the tax returns of farmers and those of other individuals. In a few states—such as Iowa—the distinction in tax liabilities is made, but this gives an insufficient clue to the amount of tax evasion which may have occurred.

[28] See Edwin H. Spengler, "Is the Real Estate Tax a Benefit Tax?" Memorandum No. 5, *Report of the New York State Commission for the Revision of the Tax Laws*, Albany, N. Y., 1932.

relative ease with which taxes may be levied and collected on property. For one thing, there are more complex industrial units whose assessment by a relatively untrained local assessor is difficult, particularly when the business of these units extends over a large area which involves many taxing districts. To some extent, the development of state assessment of railroad and public utility properties has relieved local assessors of this particular problem, but there are still many manufacturing and mercantile units with plants in a particular taxing district whose assessment is very difficult for the typical local assessor. Again, the great growth in intangible and tangible personal property has presented problems which the typical local assessor either cannot, or is unwilling to, attack vigorously.

Furthermore, property under present-day conditions differs greatly in its ability to pay. Some kinds of property—such as urban land—may earn income when it is difficult to shift the tax and tax capitalization has occurred. Logically, owners of such property might be expected to pay some taxes as part of a general plan for greater equality in income distribution. But other types of property (as enumerated earlier) may be used to earn money income when possibilities of tax-shifting definitely exist. Further, some types of property, such as household goods, private motor vehicles, and other personal effects may not be used to earn money income at all. Taxes imposed on these types of property are not likely to be shifted and may intensify inequality in the distribution of incomes.[29]

Deficiencies in property tax administration. A second major reason for deficiencies in property taxation is that *administration* has not been satisfactory. This deficiency is due in part to inherent difficulties. The increasing complexity of property for taxation has made assessment at uniform rates of various types of property more and more difficult.[30]

There is certain to be some variation in the relative abilities of different assessors no matter how they are selected or supervised. However, deficiencies in property-tax administration are largely

[29] As we shall see in the following chapter, the various states have sought to limit in four main ways those deficiencies of present-day property taxation due to the complexity of property.

[30] See National Association of Assessing Officers, *Assessment Organization and Personnel*, Chicago, 1941, for a very complete discussion of assessment organization in the United States.

due to factors which are not necessarily inherent in the administrative process. One is the general method of popular election by which assessors are chosen. Another factor is the smallness of the area within which local assessors operate. Each township and municipality selects assessors, and except in the case of larger cities, the task of assessment is only a part-time position which is usually carried on as a side-line. Therefore, assessors are often inexperienced and untrained in the field of appraisal and assessment. Even for the few weeks out of any given year that a typical assessor works, he is poorly paid and lacks both the resources and incentives to make the best possible assessment. Except in a few states (such as Wisconsin), central supervision of local assessment is not very significant.

Why Do We Retain General Property Taxation?

In the following chapter we will attempt to survey briefly some of the attempts to improve property taxation, but, on the basis of the analysis so far, it is relevant to inquire: *In view of all its deficiencies why is the general property tax continued?* The main economic reason for its continuance is that much capitalization of property now held has already occurred, and to abandon property taxation would cause a rise in these property values which would place an unearned subsidy in the pockets of those who have benefited from such capitalization.

Fiscally, property taxation provides revenues to local units of government which are large, quite dependable, and relatively predictable (except when a deep depression like that of the early thirties sharply increases the percentage of property tax delinquency). Furthermore, in the absence of state and Federal grants of a size which people in most localities are not yet ready to accept, the property tax is the principal tax tool which can be employed with some degree of efficiency by most local units of government.

Nevertheless, our experience has demonstrated that, even with high quality administration, it is not desirable to treat the complex bundle of items which we call "property" for taxation as a homogeneous mass. Personal property should probably be entirely omitted from taxation; certain other exemptions of privately held property can be justified.

SELECTED READINGS

1. Allen, Edward D., "Postwar Prospects for Agricultural Land Values and Property Tax Assessments," *Proceedings of the Thirty Eighth Annual Conference on Taxation,* pages 217-226, Washington, D. C.: National Tax Association, 1946.

2. Murray, W. G., *Corporate Land, Foreclosures, Mortgage Debt and Land Values,* Ames, Iowa: Agriculture Experiment Station, Research Bulletin 266, 1939.

3. National Association of Assessing Officers, *Assessment Organization and Personnel,* Chicago, 1941.

4. New York Tax Commission, *Annual Report, 1925,* Albany, New York, 1926.

5. Silverherz, Joseph D., *The Assessment of Real Property in the United States,* Albany, New York: J. B. Lyon Company, 1936.

6. Spengler, Edwin H., "Is the Real Estate Tax Benefit Tax?" Memorandum Number 5, *Report of the New York State Commission for the Revision of the Tax Laws,* Albany, New York, 1932.

7. United States Department of Commerce, Bureau of the Census, *State Tax Collections in 1946,* Washington, D. C.: United States Government Printing Office.

8. United States Department of Commerce, Bureau of the Census, *Assessed Valuation of Property Subject to General and Selective Property Taxes by States: 1937,* Washington, D. C.: United States Government Printing Office, 1939.

9. United States Department of Commerce, Bureau of the Census, *Governmental Finances in the United States, 1942,* Washington, D. C.: United States Government Printing Office, 1945.

10. United States Department of Commerce, Bureau of the Census, *Governmental Units in the United States: 1942,* Preliminary Summary, Washington, D. C.: United States Government Printing Office, 1944.

11. United States Department of Commerce, *The Survey of Current Business,* February, 1945, Washington, D. C.: United States Government Printing Office.

CHAPTER XX

PROPOSALS FOR IMPROVEMENT
IN PROPERTY TAXATION

MANY of the criticisms of general property taxation noted have received attention, both by legislators and by students of taxation. Among the types of improvements in the operation of property taxation which have been suggested—many of which have been tried—are these: (1) classification of property for tax purposes, (2) improved administration of property taxation, and (3) limitation of the property-tax base to real property (real estate).

Among the most widely known of property tax reformers was Henry George. A small group of advocates and economists still follow his views, a few of which we will mention. George advocated that all taxes except those upon land be abolished. The basis for this argument was that the land was "God given," that its supply was fixed, and that its value was constantly rising as population increased. These factors provided windfalls to property owners which could be taxed away without affecting the supply of land.

The slackening of population growth, improvement in agricultural technology, and arrest of increases in site values make the single tax inapplicable as a needed reform measure. Rents and royalties constitute only a small fraction of the national income. In addition, government functions have been so greatly increased that the single tax would be completely inadequate as the source of government revenue.

Property Classification for Tax Purposes

In the previous chapter, we noted that there has been a considerable amount of property tax evasion. We also noted that taxation of some kinds of property—intangibles, for example—represented double taxation, and that the tax load on some other kinds—such as household goods—was out of line with the earning capacity of the property. One attempt to reduce these inequities and to increase revenue from property taxes is the classification of property for tax purposes.

As Professor Leland has remarked, the "essence of classification is the differentiation in the effective rates of taxation applied to the various classes of property." [1] Classification may consist principally of separate, low-rate taxation of intangibles or principally of a comprehensive classification of various types of property for taxation. The common practice in comprehensive classification is to assess different types of property at different ratios to their true value.

As of 1944, about one-third of the states had separately classified intangibles for taxation at low millage rates (a levy of 2 to 5 mills was common). Six states (Minnesota, Montana, Kentucky, Virginia, West Virginia, and Ohio) had adopted a comprehensive system of classification for all types of property, following the precedent set by Minnesota by a 1906 state constitutional amendment permitting broad classification.

Because the Minnesota classification is basic in the Minnesota tax system, we will describe it briefly, although, as Professor Leland has pointed out, it is not clear that broad classifications which have been set up by legislators have always distinguished classes of property which are economically different.[2] Much has depended on such other considerations as the relative political strength of property-owning groups likely to be affected and the expected relative ease in the assessment of various types of property.

Minnesota has developed an elaborate system of classification, which largely operates by applying varying ratios of assessed to true value for different classes of property. Iron ore, whether mined or unmined, is assessed at 50 per cent of true value; platted urban real estate is assessed at 40 per cent; rural real estate and a considerable percentage of personal property is assessed at 33⅓ per cent; household goods are assessed at 25 per

[1] See Simeon E. Leland, "Some Observations Concerning the Classified Property Tax," *Symposium of the Tax Policy League: Property Taxation*, Tax Institute, 1939, pages 83-116. For a more complete statement on classified property taxation, see Simeon E. Leland, *The Classified Property Tax in the United States*, Boston: Houghton Mifflin Company, 1928.

[2] See Simeon E. Leland, "Some Observations Concerning the Classified Property Tax," pages 85-86.

cent (when they are assessed at all); rural personal property is assessed at only 10 per cent. Up to the first $4,000 in value, urban homes are assessed at only 25 per cent and the ratio for rural homesteads is 20 per cent. The first $4,000 of the true value of homesteads is exempt from such property taxes as the state government may impose.[3] Minnesota has minimized property tax exemption by requiring that exemptions can be granted only by constitutional amendment. Its decision to tax exhaustible resources (iron) with relative severity and household goods (difficult to assess) quite lightly is represented in the property classification which it has adopted.

Several results of low-rate taxation of intangibles should be noted. Professor Leland may be correct in his contention that such taxation has resulted in a larger amount of taxable property being listed for taxation,[4] but evidence is less clear that such classification has resulted in greater tax revenue. Also, there would appear to be no strong reason why owners of intangibles should be expected to pay a property tax in addition to those taxes which have been imposed on the real wealth against which such intangibles are merely claims.

Recognizing the difficulties of tax assessment, a few states— such as Minnesota—have recently repealed their low-rate taxes on intangibles; many are reaching intangibles through state income taxes. Income from intangibles is included among various items of taxable income. In Iowa, where experience with a low-rate tax on intangibles has been quite unsatisfactory, a 1946 tax study recommended the repeal of most of such taxes. A few other states—such as Ohio, Tennessee, and New Hampshire—did not have a general state income tax as of 1946, but did apply income taxes to intangibles as the preferred method of taxing this type of property.

Professor Leland has pointed out that the movement for classification probably reached a peak about fifteen years ago. He has stated that:

The principal service of classification has not been as a fiscal measure to fill public treasuries, but to provide greater justice and flexibility

[3] Minnesota repealed its 3-mill tax on the full value of intangibles, effective in 1946. Minnesota collected only a 2-mill state property tax in the same year.

[4] See Simeon E. Leland, *The Classified Property Tax in the United States*, page 403.

in the operation of the property tax. . . . It has given legislatures greater freedom in the taxation of property and has demonstrated that, by and large, these assemblies can be trusted in adopting tax measures not to abuse seriously the privileges conferred upon them. . . . Property classification may well find a place under a system of taxes *in personam* [as well as in the traditional *ad rem* function of property taxes] . . . . The differentiation of unlike things is the essence of classification. Such differentiations are vastly broader than property taxation. They underlie the whole field of government support. If, however, the property tax should be converted into a net fortunes tax, some use of the classification principle would seem to be in order.[5]

Improved Administration of the Property Tax

Efforts to improve the administration of the property tax have centered largely in two fields: (1) Increased control of state tax commissions or other state authorities over local assessors; (2) transference to state tax authorities of assessment of certain properties, especially railroads and other public utilities, which generally cover more than one local taxing district.

While some states, notably Wisconsin, have made outstanding advances in state supervision and control over local assessment, the quality of property-tax administration is far from that which most fiscal students would like to see. Thus, while all states have some type of central tax authority, the members of this body are rarely appointed on a merit basis, free from politics, for long terms, and eligible for reappointment on the basis of competency of service. Those in control of the majority party have been able to appoint a majority of the members of the state tax commission.

Further, a strong politically free tax commission should assess all property or business of interstate or state-wide (rather than of a localized) character, types of properties which raise special problems of assessment. They should also assess local properties which raise special problems—such as mineral and timber resources—and local industrial enterprises of considerable size. The common practice is to have state assessment of only specific and limited types of business enterprises—most commonly railroads and other public utilities.

[5] See Simeon E. Leland, "Some Observations Concerning the Classified Property Tax," pages 115-116. The comment in brackets is by the writers.

A strong state tax commission should have and exercise the power not only to supervise, but also to remove "for cause" locally selected assessors, subject only to court restraint. In the few cases where power of removal has been granted, it has seldom been used, due to general opposition to centralized methods of supervising assessment, which might become arbitrary. Some of the central tax groups equalize and reassess property among various taxing districts. This is especially important where there is a state property-tax levy. Typically acting as the final board of review for local assessments, such state bodies should have the power to reassess local individual properties in order to have the most equitable tax base.

At the local level, prevailing assessment districts should be enlarged to provide full-time employment at attractive salaries for local assessors, who should be appointed on a merit basis—possibly by the county boards of supervisors—rather than popularly elected, as at present.

Many of these rather obvious improvements in the system of property-tax administration have not occurred, and will not take place, as long as the local electorate prefers election of (or influence over the appointment of) tax administrators to removal of the inequities of property tax administration.

Wisconsin has had one of the most successful and equitable systems of property-tax administration, especially during the period 1901-1940.[6] The choice and use of tax administrative bodies during this period was not different from the process in most states except for one exception which exception was important. Forty supervisors of local assessments were appointed, on a merit basis, and free from political interference.[7] They cooperated primarily with locally elected assessors in improving property assessment, but also with the state tax commission (now "department") in providing the best possible data for central assessment or equalization of assessed values among tax districts. Although Wisconsin has county boards of assessment (and

[6] See Harold M. Groves and A. Bristol Goodman, "A Pattern of Successful Property Tax Administration: The Wisconsin Experience," *Journal of Land and Public Utility Economics,* Vol. XIX (May, August, and November, 1943), pages 141-152, 300-315, and 418-435, respectively.

[7] From 1911 to 1934, the assessors divided their time between assessment of the state income tax and supervision of local assessment of property. Their number was reduced to 4 by legislation in 1940.

equalization), it has not chosen to try taking the selection of local assessors "out of politics." The supervisors of assessment have worked diligently with these local assessors to obtain the fairest possible local assessment of various properties. They also have worked with county boards of assessment to determine "final" equalized property values for taxation. County boards came to rely on the assessed valuations of property submitted by the supervisors. In the years just before 1940, this had made the assessments by county officials and the subsequent assessments by state supervisors (for equalization purposes) much the same.

State assessment (or equalization) of locally assessed property is important in Wisconsin for several reasons: (1) it provides a more equitable distribution of state property-tax levies among local taxing districts by classes of property, especially where industrial properties are important, for such properties are characteristically given a relatively favorable assessment, (2) it provides a fairer basis for the determination of such local tax-rate and debt-rate limitations as are imposed, (3) it reduces competitive undervaluation, (4) it establishes a fairer basis for the distribution of state school-aid, which is distributed on the basis of local assessed value, (5) it establishes a reasonably equitable basis for the central assessment and subsequent taxation of railroads and utilities.[8]

There are three main techniques available for assessment of property. One is the use of sales data on property. However, the infrequency and erratic nature of such sales in certain tax districts led to the use of appraisals (guided by the supervisor of assessments) as a supplement to sales data in Wisconsin. Finally, there is the possibility of a rather rapid "mass" assessment —assessment without full use of detailed current information— or central reassessment of property in a given district. Local assessors in Wisconsin have tended to use sales data or appraisals more frequently than "mass" assessment, although it has been pointed out that "the more detailed it (mass assessment) becomes, the more like appraisal it appears to be. In fact, there is a constant shading from 'mass estimate' through 'mass assessment' to

---

[8] Other reasons are also given by Groves and Goodman in their discussion previously mentioned. Actually, the tax rate applicable to railroads and utilities is determined by dividing the total property-tax levies of the state and its subdivisions by the equalized assessed value of all other taxable property (exclusive of railroads and utilities).

appraisals." [9]   The Wisconsin Tax Department has been increasingly inclined to accept property valuations certified to it by supervisors and does not reassess individual properties within particular taxing districts.

On the basis on which Wisconsin operated until 1940, Groves and Goodman have concluded that "the unique contribution of the state lies in a vigorous and workable program of state assessment supervision and equalization. The result has been much improvement in the quality of the product . . . The (property) tax is so well adapted to supply local revenues without reliance on central units of government that its future retention in some form is assured." [10]

They do not mean, however, that further improvements cannot be made in the tax.   Both writers point out that they have simply attempted to summarize certain administrative aspects of the tax. They see no reason why the pattern of administration which has been developed in Wisconsin could not be applied in other states as well, but they emphasize that supervisors of taxation must be selected on a nonpolitical basis if locally elected assessors are to gain the benefits of continued experience and to regard the supervisors as individuals set apart from the ordinary political process.   Special problems involved in assessment of such properties as railroads and other public utilities, exhaustible resources, timber, and other types of property will be examined later. [11]

Making the Property Tax a Tax on Real Estate

A third type of development in property taxation which has improved its operation has been the growing tendency to center such taxation on real estate. [12]   This tendency is partly evidenced by the increasing exemptions granted to personal property. Two states, New York and Delaware, had abandoned the taxation of personal property before 1946. Household goods are often specifically exempt from property taxes; where they are not, they are seldom assessed for taxation to a (relatively) large extent.

[9] Groves and Goodman, "Successful Property Tax Administration," *op. cit.*, page 313.

[10] See Groves and Goodman, *ibid.*, pages 433-434.

[11] Property assessment has been facilitated in Wisconsin by the fact that certain classes of personal property have been exempt from taxation. These include intangibles, household goods, and motor vehicles.

[12] See Census Bulletin of June, 1939, *Assessed Value of Property Subject to General and Selective Property Taxes by States: 1937,* Bureau of the Census, Washington, D. C., 1939.

Motor vehicles are often exempt because they are taxed under special motor-vehicle taxes.   Experiments with low-rate taxation of intangible claims to wealth have been widespread, but often have not increased tax revenues, even though the total listing of such articles of property probably had been increased by the low-rate tax measures.   One state (Minnesota) recently abandoned the taxation of intangibles; others, like Iowa, were proposing their abandonment in 1947.   The principal types of personal property typically assessed are merchants' inventories, farm livestock, and farm machinery.

The development of the property tax as a tax on real estate is an improvement for several reasons.   Under the so-called "general" property tax, there were various types of inequities.   Some individuals evaded taxation.   Taxes on inventories, livestock, and machinery are elements of business cost which, in the long run, are shifted and tend to increase inequality in the distribution of incomes.   Low-rate taxes on intangible claims to wealth already taxed were one variety of inequitable double taxation. This does not mean that even a high-quality assessment of all real estate constitutes a measurably good base for the property tax. Some of the taxes imposed on land are capitalized, rather than shifted.   To avoid the discouragement of improvements on land, a strong case can be made out for relatively lower rates of taxation (or a period of exemption) on new improvements.[13]

Elements of a "Good" Property Tax

Although the writers recognize that the property tax is not the best of various possible taxes, it is very unlikely that property taxation will be discontinued.   Furthermore, there is merit in the continuance of some locally imposed taxation, even though the growth of extra-local aspects of local government brings about a continued increase in intergovernmental fiscal aids to local governments.

As has been indicated previously, property taxation may make it possible to reach elements of ability to pay, especially among owners of farm property, who may otherwise evade personal income taxation.   It is probable that there will be a continued expansion of intergovernmental aids, particularly Federal aids,

[13] See Harold S. Buttenheim, "The Case for Low-Rate Taxation of Improvements," *Symposium of the Tax Policy League*, Tax Institute, 1940, pages 135-152.

to local governments. This is partly because these units are (in most cases) not able to apply successfully forms of taxation other than the property tax, while at the same time, they are expected to provide an increasing range of government services. Those who are interested in retaining local interest in government expenditures contend that local property taxes are one effective means to stimulate and maintain interest in the efficiency of public services.

Tax capitalization often occurs in the transfer of real property. To reduce existing property taxes substantially probably would increase sale values of existing properties and give present owners substantial windfalls.[14] It is possible that these windfall gains could be recaptured through a system of capital-gains taxation, although it would be extremely difficult to recapture all of them.

From the standpoint of revenue only, property taxes have provided relatively stable and predictable revenues, when swings in real estate values or incomes of property owners have not been great. The revenue argument was somewhat weakened by the wave of property-tax delinquency which swept the country in the early years of the thirties. This meant that assessors did not pay much attention to changes in actual property values when they made their assessments.

Assuming the retention of the property tax in our local-state fiscal system, the desirable characteristics of such a tax would be: (1) it would be confined to real estate, with especially favorable treatment of new improvements, (2) it would be administered with a high degree of equity in assessment. These characteristics have already been discussed.

The part that property taxes should have in the total tax base depends on the extent of intergovernmental fiscal aid to local units of government. Such aids grew from 76 million dollars in 1902 to 1,760 million dollars in 1942.

The continued fear of centralized governmental administration in the United States probably means that sufficient extension of intergovernmental (particularly Federal) aid will not come for some time. If the amount of intergovernmental (especially Federal) aid which these proposals imply were accepted, the local property tax would be much less important fiscally than it is at the present time. The logic and problems involved in inter-

[14] See Henry Simons, *Personal Income Taxation*, pages 32-33.

governmental aids are part of the subject matter of the final two chapters of this book.

The components of "good" property tax administration have already been discussed at some length, and will not be repeated. It is sufficient to say that the movement toward substantial improvements in property tax administration of the type which has been outlined is very slow.

Special Problems of Property Taxation

Even good property taxation presents problems in practice. The continued use, and accompanying modification, of the property tax, however, has given rise to certain special problems. Among these are: (1) tax exemptions; (2) tax-rate and debt-rate limitations; (3) the assessment of certain types of property, such as railroads, other public utilities, exhaustible natural resources, and certain types of land; (4) the assessment of merchants' inventories.

Tax exemptions. It has been indicated that tax exemptions have been increasing. They present special problems partly because, as exemptions increase, the property-tax levies on that part of the property remaining in the tax base are either increased, or an increased amount of intergovernmental aid is required. This amount may exceed that which those interested in maintaining home-rule and home-finance are willing to accept.

A special type of tax exemption which has received attention since the early years of the thirties is the partial exemption from taxation of "homesteads," generally defined to include some (or all) property which is occupied by a property owner. As of 1944, about one-fourth of the states had responded to political pressure for specially favorable treatment of homesteads. A few—such as Iowa and Louisiana—replaced the loss in local revenue by grants to local governments made from state tax sources. Minnesota and Montana give homesteads especially favorable classification under their comprehensive property-tax-classification laws.

Homestead tax exemption may be evaluated in a number of ways. It may be regarded partly as expression of a social desire to stimulate home ownership.[15] Promotion of home ownership

[15] In Iowa, for example, the number of homesteads qualifying for special treatment increased steadily from 304,000 in 1936, when the law first became effective, to 395,000 in 1944. Since Iowa has replaced exempted local taxes with

is also found in personal income taxation where owners are permitted to deduct property taxes but renters are not permitted to deduct rents. Partial homestead tax exemption unquestionably reduces the fixed charges attached to home ownership. On the other hand, such special treatment of homesteads offers nothing to renters. In fact, they may have to bear increased state taxes when replacement for the loss of local tax revenue is provided. Part of the existing taxes on homeowners may already have been capitalized, and to this extent, homestead tax exemption gives to existing homeowners a windfall.

Another important factor in the development of partial homestead tax exemption was the severe depression of the early thirties. Only a portion of the effects of homestead tax exemption can be analyzed in economic terms. One serious effect in most states where such exemptions are offered is that the sources of local government's tax revenue, already restricted in large part to the property tax, have been further restricted by the exemption of additional property from the tax base.

A number of states, like Wisconsin, have used a system of tax offsets, whereby taxes on personal property could be offset against taxes on incomes. The system of tax offsets has been severely criticized by some prominent students of taxation, among them Professor Herbert Simpson, who has contended that

> the offset operates not only in a capricious way, dependent on arbitrary ratios of income and property, but introduces a positively vicious element in the redistribution of burdens which it brings about.[16]

Professor Simpson has probably overstated his point. For one thing, taxes on personalty are themselves capricious and should be abolished. What is saved under the income tax is paid under the property tax. The offset combination does operate to establish some floor for property-tax revenue, and operates to lessen the variability in income-tax revenue. Such variability is important to state and local governments, which are forced to live within their current revenue resources. It is true that the

state funds, the annual drain on the state treasury has increased from $11,000,000 to over $15,000,000. The basic law providing for such credits has itself not been changed.

[16] See Herbert D. Simpson, *The Effects of a Property Tax Offset Under an Income Tax*, Institute for Economic Research, Chicago, 1932.

offset combination implies the retention of greater resources for purpose of tax administration than if state and local taxes were based primarily either on property or on income taxes.

Tax-rate and debt-rate limitations. A few comments have already been made on tax- and debt-rate limitations, especially in the few states which imposed over-all limitations during the lowest-income years of the thirties. Most states have given their subdivisions comparative freedom in establishing tax rates for particular purposes, although maximum tax rates to be imposed in any one year have often been specified. Pressure against the various maxima have become quite intense during the forties, although permission to impose levies in excess of established maxima has been granted largely on an emergency basis to date. In the past, it has been common to circumvent tax-rate limitations by increasing funds through borrowing, although some states have imposed an over-all limit to borrowing of a specified maximum ratio (such as 5 per cent) of borrowed funds to assessed value of property within the local unit.

In general, tax-rate and debt-rate limitations create more problems than they solve. Such limitations reflect lack of trust in local officials by state legislators. They sometimes cause a falling off of important public services.[17] They almost inevitably result in an increase in state aid, although the new sources of tax revenue which the states have secured since 1930 consist largely of general sales taxes or gross-receipts taxes.[18] Our previous analysis of such taxes makes it difficult to give them a much higher priority in the tax structure than may be given to property taxes. On the whole, the net merit of local tax- and debt-rate limitations has yet to be demonstrated.

Assessment of special types of properties. Certain types of property assessments create technical and economic problems which the typical local assessor is not able to solve. Among these are the assessment of railroad and other public utility properties (which typically are already assessed by the state), forest,

---

[17] A famous case occurred in West Virginia. There, faced with an over-all tax- and debt-rate limitation, Morgantown vacated all offices and positions and ordered the discontinuance of street lighting and fire protection. The state was forced to come to the aid of its localities.

[18] Apart from the collection of payroll taxes for unemployment insurance beginning in 1936. As was indicated in Chapter XVIII, payroll tax revenues may become the basis for payment of unemployment benefits, but they do not become part of state general revenue available for desired purposes.

mineral, and petroleum resources, and certain types of land—such as cut-over timber land.   High quality in assessment can only be obtained for such properties by having state assessment, after which the assessed values which fall within various tax districts can be certified back to these districts and local taxes can be imposed on these valuations.

(1) *Assessment of railroads and public utilities.*   State assessment (and certification of value) is typical for railroads and other public utilities.   It has been seen for many years that no local assessor can survey a short stretch of railroad property which happens to be in his district and from that survey get any idea as to the taxable value of a portion of what may be a transcontinental railroad line.   This does not mean that even state assessment of a complex railroad or other utility property will be simple.   Such factors as capitalized net earnings and gross earnings (both allocated to a particular state), value of outstanding securities, and even the tangible property within the particular state should be considered in order to arrive at a state-determined assessed value for a particular year.[19]

A few states—especially Minnesota, Connecticut, and Maine—levy gross- (allocated) earnings taxes on railroads in lieu of other property taxes.   It is claimed for such taxes (the Minnesota tax of 5 per cent is a good illustration) that they reduce the amount of work in property valuation, as compared with the more common *ad valorem* method of assessing railroad properties.   This may be questioned, however, since the specific basis on which such gross-earnings taxes have been held constitutional was the statement that these taxes would not exceed those levied on a property-value basis.   It is difficult to see how a state can make such a comparison legally without also making an *ad valorem* assessment for the entire railroad property allocated to that state.

Problems of state assessment are less difficult in the case of many domestic utilities, where an interstate allocation of earnings and of property may not be required.   It is probably that state assessment, however, should also extend to all industrial properties of any considerable size.   A local assessor is likely to be be-

---

[19] For a quite complete discussion of the problems of railroad assessment, see Harley L. Lutz, *The Taxation of Railroads in New Jersey*, Princeton, New Jersey: Princeton University Press, 1940.

wildered by the complexity of a large factory, with its various types of personal and real property.

(2) *Assessment of forests, minerals, and other natural resources.* Forest, mineral, and other natural resources offer special problems in assessment which will not be discussed in detail here.[20] It is clearly undesirable to levy an annual *ad valorem* property tax on growing forests. Such taxation may encourage the early cutting of forests not yet fully developed in order to pay taxes. It is preferable to make the bulk of the tax coincide with the time when the forest product is cut, and probably to make such a tax fall on gross value product, rather than on value of property. It is not inequitable to impose *some* annual taxes on forest property. In Minnesota, Michigan, and Wisconsin a flat acreage tax is levied. As of 1944, more than half the states applied special provisions in the taxation of forests, and most of them replaced the loss in local tax revenues with state funds.

The problem of taxing mineral resources has not been satisfactorily solved in all of the states where such resources are found. However, there is general agreement that taxes on mines do discourage mining. This is not necessarily undesirable if the people of a given state wish to preserve exhaustible natural resources located in the state, especially where the bulk of minerals extracted are sold (or used in products sold) primarily to people living outside the state, as in the case of iron mined in Minnesota. We observed in Chapter XV that, as of 1946, 23 states had imposed special "severance" taxes on the extraction or sale of natural resources.

In addition to such severance taxes, however, there may be the question of the application to mineral resources of regular property taxation. In some states such property-value taxes are levied, sometimes at relatively high rates, as in Minnesota where mineral resources receive the highest percentage classification for property taxation. Some other states impose taxes on such resources on a basis of the value of tonnage produced. Other states apply taxes on the basis of some (arbitrary) multiple of the net proceeds resulting from extraction as indicated by tonnage,

[20] For more detailed treatment see, for instance, Harold M. Groves, *Financing Government,* revised edition, pages 365-383, New York: Henry Holt & Co., Inc., 1945.

gross production, or net production; or they employ ordinary *ad valorem* property taxes. It is reasonably clear that ordinary *ad valorem* property taxes are an unsatisfactory method by which to assess property used for the purpose of extracting petroleum and its products.

(3) *Classification of land for purposes of assessment.* It has been widely recognized for some years that certain types of land —such as cut-over forest areas—should be classified for taxation and assessed at a very low rate, or made entirely exempt from property taxes. Some, although not enough, progress has been made in the direction of land-use classification for purposes of taxation.[21] In areas like northern Minnesota, the problem is not only one of land-use classification for taxation, but also one of persuading a relatively small number of people to move. Their continued presence causes a drain on public treasuries in order to provide a minimum of public services. Application of the classic Henry George idea of a "single tax" on land value to such land-use areas would yield little revenue. It would also be highly inequitable although it might shorten the time when such areas would revert to the state. It is clear that such lands should be devoted to land-uses different and more highly simplified than lands used for typical farming enterprises.

(4) *Assessment of Inventories.* A further problem in equity which arises from present property assessment methods is the assessment of merchants' inventories. The writers have already urged that taxation of personal property should be abandoned. A sharp reduction in taxation of personal property may still leave the typical problems of assessing inventories for taxation, however. As in most cases, the essential problem here is one of relative equity among individuals. For two individuals expecting to do the same volume of business, one—like a retail merchant—may have to carry a much larger inventory than another—like the operator of an electric light plant. Even though such taxes are business unit costs which ultimately may be shifted, the immediate impact of the property tax is much more severe on the seller who has a relatively large inventory on hand.

One way for a particular individual seller to minimize this tax

[21] Some of the fundamental work was done by O. B. Jesness, Reynolds I. Dowell, *et al.* in *A Program for Land Use in Northern Minnesota,* Minneapolis, Minnesota: The University of Minnesota Press, 1935.

is to have a relatively low inventory on assessment day. Circulation in the economic system of a given amount of goods to satisfy an expected demand is necessary, and it is quite likely that a tax on inventories will fall with relative severity on someone, perhaps a wholesaler. As between two merchants in the same line of business, it is quite probable that a tax on inventories will fall with greater severity on an independent merchant than on the owners of a particular chain store. Chain-store organizations have learned how to make inventories move with relative speed, which is another way of saying that they keep on hand a relatively small inventory for a given volume of sales in any particular period. Some students of taxation suggest that this differential advantage provides one of the most equitable claims for relative penalization of chain-store enterprises. The writers prefer to say that it exhibits just one more reason why efforts to tax personal property probably should be abolished.

Recasting the General Property Tax

Since about 1920, general property taxation has been relatively unpopular and opposition to its extension has become more effectively organized. Despite this unpopularity and opposition, property taxes are the principal local taxes which can be levied and collected, for reasons already indicated. One consequence of the growing unpopularity of property taxation, together with increased demands for public services on localities, has been the increased extension of state and Federal fiscal aids. For municipalities, in fact, one expert has said that "the real financial hope of the cities . . . lies in the further extension of grants-in-aid and city-sharing in centrally collected taxes." [22]

Meanwhile, the fiscal problems of municipalities and other local units of government have continued to increase. Some of these problems are due to inequitable, inefficient assessments. Some remedies for poor assessments, involving a large measure of state supervision and cooperation, have been suggested earlier. It is common, however, even with relatively good assessment, for local units of government to find it difficult to raise sufficient money from local property taxes. In addition, local units have been subject to varying degrees of restrictions in amounts of tax

[22] See A. M. Hillhouse, *New Sources of Municipal Revenue*, Municipal Finance Officers Association, 1935, page 3.

levies and outstanding debt imposed by their state governments. Moreover, some of our larger cities have found an increasing portion of their populations moving out to suburbs. One result of this has been to restrict further the property-tax base for the municipality. At the same time, the presence of a large portion of this suburban population as a working group, plus continued growth in resident city populations, have required an increasing range of public services from municipalities, whether they are affected by strong suburban movements or not.

A few cities have found it possible to levy and administer new types of local taxes—the New York City sales tax and Philadelphia earned-income tax are illustrations. Most localities have found themselves tied to the use of property taxation as a source of large tax revenues, and with property taxation they have often operated under severe state-imposed restrictions. The Fiscal Relations Report has indicated that apparently what is needed is:

> . . . Some new source of local revenue which will (1) not overlap existing federal and state taxes, (2) enable the localities to tap their own resources without running hat in hand to central governments, (3) cover all or a vast majority of the interested citizenry, and (4) not be regressive.[23]

Since localities must depend on property taxes in large part, arriving at some of these objectives means a thorough recasting of the property tax, including a relatively large amount of freedom in the application of the tax by localities. One way of recasting would be to break the property tax down and (1) collect a tax from landlords (including owner-occupants) in the nature of a service charge for local benefits to property plus (2) impose a tax on occupants according to the rental value of their property. These taxes could be adjusted to allow for size of family, and, given such an adjustment, a progressive rate might even be used. Business rental taxes would be imposed at flat rates. Unused properties could still be subject to tax in hopes of encouraging their development for productive purposes.[24]

The Fiscal Relations Report suggests certain other things about local tax revenues. In the property-tax field, it points out the

[23] See Fiscal Relations Report, page 409.
[24] In Fiscal Relations Report, page 410, it is recommended that unused properties be exempt from tax.

possibilities of using unearned-increment taxes and suggests the further refinement and use of special assessments, admitting that their use has not been highly satisfactory in the past. It wisely urges that past tendencies to grant tax exemptions rather freely be abandoned (since a growth in tax exemptions in any particular taxing jurisdiction means higher tax rates to finance a given volume of public expenditures for the benefit of other property owners within the taxing jurisdiction).

It is suggested that many municipal services yield special benefits and that the cost might reasonably be covered by special charges—charges for sewage disposal and garbage collection, for instance. While some municipalities operate certain public utilities to gain profits for transfer to general city funds, others do not. The operation of local municipal utilities on a profit basis (1) provides funds for operation of municipal governments, and (2) keeps down property tax levies. As we have indicated in the final chapter of the book, Federal payments in lieu of property taxes on Federal-owned property, such as housing, should be more generous and dependable. If everything else proves inadequate as a source of local revenues, local experimentation with income taxes or even sales taxes might be tried. But the over-all impression of local taxation and service charges which one gets is that localities are certain to depend more and more on shares in state or Federal-collected taxes and on grants-in-aid from larger units of government.

The Future of Property Taxation

It is difficult to predict future developments accurately; nevertheless, we will make a few general predictions about the future of property taxation in the United States in the next decade.

1. The relative importance of property taxes as sources of tax revenue will diminish.
2. Property taxes will, for some time, remain the principal taxes levied and imposed by local units of government, partly because there will be a widespread desire to retain some local tax powers and partly because no other tax than the property tax can be used efficiently by most local units of government.
3. Property taxes will be recast to establish the use of several kinds of real estate taxation. More freedom will be allowed in the use of the property tax than the states have permitted since 1933.

4. The property tax will continue to be increasingly based on real estate, rather than on personal property.

5. The administration of property taxes which are retained will improve. This improvement will come about through a further extension of state supervision and assessment and through the growing desire for better-trained local assessors. Better-trained local assessors will be secured partly through increased supervision of assessment and partly through an extension of the area in which a typical assessor works—permitting assessment to become a full-time job. A widespread development of country-wide assessment systems will take place.

6. Property taxes will continue to decline as sources of revenue for state governments.

7. Revenues of local units of government will come increasingly from Federal and state governments. Grants will be made to help underwrite some minimum standards of public education, roads, public welfare, and recreation.

SELECTED READINGS

1. Buttenheim, Harold S., "The Case for Low-Rate Taxation of Improvements," *Symposium of the Tax Policy League, 1939*, published in 1940.

2. "Federal, State, and Local Fiscal Relations," 78th Congress, 1st Session, Senate Document 69, Washington, D. C.: United States Government Printing Office, 1943.

3. Groves, Harold M., *Financing Government*, Chapters 3, 4 and 5, revised edition, New York: Henry Holt & Co., Inc., 1945.

4. ———— and Goodman, A. Bristol, "A Pattern of Successful Property Tax Administration: The Wisconsin Experience," *Journal of Land and Public Utility Economics*, Vol. XIX (May, August, and November, 1943).

5. Hillhouse, A. M., *New Sources of Municipal Revenue*, Chicago: Municipal Finance Officers Association, 1935.

6. Jesness, O. B., Dowell, Reynolds I., *et al.*, *A Program for Land Use in Northern Minnesota*, Minneapolis: The University of Minnesota Press, 1935.

7. Leland, Simeon E., *The Classified Property Tax in the United States*, Boston: Houghton-Mifflin Co., Inc., 1928.

8. ———, "Some Observations Concerning the Classified Property Tax," *Symposium of the Tax Policy League, 1939, 1940*.

9. Lutz, Harley L., *The Taxation of Railroads in New Jersey*, Princeton, New Jersey: The Princeton University Press, 1940.

10. Simons, Henry C., *Personal Income Taxation*, Chicago: The University of Chicago Press, 1938.

11. Simpson, Herbert D., "The Effects of a Property Tax Offset Under an Income Tax," Chicago: Institute for Economic Research, 1932.

CHAPTER XXI

ECONOMICS OF PUBLIC BORROWING

ONE set of fiscal problems in which nearly everyone currently expresses considerable interest consists of those problems associated with public borrowing. The United States net Federal debt on January 1, 1947, was approximately 260 billion dollars—more than ten times the level reached at the end of World War I and approximately five times the level at the end of the fiscal year 1940-41. At the end of the calendar year 1945, state and local net debt totaled 13.7 billion dollars while private debt totaled around 140 billions.[1] The Federal debt was thus almost twenty times as large as state and local debt and nearly double the total of private debt.

There is considerable confusion in popular thinking about the problem of public borrowing. A part of the confusion stems from viewing public borrowing as one views private borrowing. For some kinds of borrowing, particularly international loans and borrowing at state and local levels, this approach yields reasonable approximations. For other kinds of borrowing, particularly domestic loans at the Federal level, this view gives rise to important errors. Some of the similarities between public and private borrowing are discussed later in this chapter. The fact that the Federal government has utilized borrowing in connection with efforts to increase total money expenditures for goods and services as well as to drain off excess purchasing power has added further to the confusion in popular conceptions of the effects of public borrowing. The borrowing of the thirties was designed to expand money expenditures for goods and services. Sales of bonds to individuals during and immediately after World War II were designed to help drain off excess purchasing power.

In this chapter, some of the important economic considerations in determining the role of public borrowing will be analyzed.

---

[1] Data are from Elwyn T. Bonnell, "Public and Private Debt in the United States," *The Survey of Current Business*, Vol. 26, No. 9:10-17 (September, 1946).

These will focus upon problems at all levels of government—state and local as well as Federal.

It is generally conceded that in the past public borrowing has been somewhat misused.   Most fiscal experts agree that the present Federal debt, incurred largely since 1940, need not have been as large as it is.   Some analysts, however, believe that the debt was not expanded enough during the thirties.   Others believe that the debt at the beginning of the war was too large.   There is little merit in concentrating on debate over past policies.   "The egg cannot be unscrambled."   Our most reasonable course is to do the best we can toward solving the problems which will arise rather than to bemoan the fact that such problems would not have arisen if another course had been pursued.   In the hope that our analysis can help to solve these problems, we are devoting the next chapter to a brief discussion of managing the existing debt.

Situations Accounting for the Increase in Public Debt

Public borrowing is but one of the ways by which government may secure funds.   Taxation is more frequently employed, although the Federal government may also issue money with which to pay its bills.   As we have pointed out before, Federal borrowing from the banking system has approximated money issue in so far as such government borrowing did not restrict the extension of private loans.

In the past, two major kinds of situations have prompted an expansion in public borrowing in the United States:

(1) *Government has desired to use resources that otherwise would have been used in the private domestic economy.* State and local governments used such resources largely to construct highways, streets, facilities for sewage disposal, transport facilities, public school buildings, and other items of public wealth.   The Federal government, during two recent wars—1917-1919 and 1941-1945—has used such resources to build and operate tanks, planes, guns, battleships, atomic bombs, and other weapons.   Borrowing from private individuals living in the United States— as has been the nature of nearly all state and local borrowing—was selected in preference to taxation as a means for

government to secure claims to the resources needed for constructing much of this public plant.[2] In so far as private citizens were induced to cut their expenditures for goods and services by turning money over to government and receiving in exchange certain interest-bearing claims on future income (securities), resources were released for public purposes.

(2) *Government has desired to get into production resources that were unemployed.* In using borrowing as a part of an employment expansion program, the expenditures of the private sector of the economy did not need to be reduced. Consequently, borrowing from banks with the resultant creation of additional claims to goods and services (money) was the procedure utilized during the depression of the thirties. Such a procedure is more effective than borrowing from private individuals who would substitute securities for goods and services and thus cut their expenditures for goods and services.

In addition to these two general situations which have accounted for the bulk of planned borrowing, governmental units have borrowed to meet unplanned (emergency) situations. For example, funds to provide relief from such disasters as major fires or floods cannot be immediately secured by taxation. Short-term borrowing in anticipation of tax collections in subsequent years has been used in such instances. Similarly, in a given fiscal year, governmental receipts may have fallen short of expectations, and short-term borrowing has been employed to carry the unit until additional tax receipts were secured in the next fiscal year.

Some Government Borrowing Resembles Private Borrowing

With the exception of borrowing to increase total expenditure for goods and services, government borrowing is conducted to achieve objectives not unlike those of private borrowing. A unit of government plans to use resources. It must secure money in order to purchase these resources. If these funds are to be secured from within the country and the resources of the country are already fully employed, these resources must be diverted to

[2] For the five years, 1941-45, Federal expenditures totaled 312.6 billion dollars. Federal tax collections during the same period amounted to 127.7 billions, or 40.8 per cent of Federal expenditures.

government from other uses. If policy-makers (legislators or administrators) believe that the money needed to purchase these resources cannot (or should not) be secured by next year's taxation, they may try to induce people to part with money in exchange for government securities. Total private expenditure for privately produced goods and services is diminished by the same amount in the period during which government is using the resources, whether the government secures the money by taxation or borrowing. The public project is paid for while it is being constructed in the sense that other alternative uses for these resources must be sacrificed during this period.[3] However, taxpayers who do not buy bonds will be able to purchase relatively more than they would have been able to purchase if all of the money had been secured by taxation. A greater percentage of the sacrifice is voluntary.

A private business constructing additional plant also may divert resources from other alternative uses. Its plant is being paid for currently in that there is reduced production of other goods and services which could have been produced with the resources used in building the plant. If the business has borrowed from other businesses or from individuals to finance this plant construction, and these lenders have cut their expenditures, they have made the sacrifices of current expenditure and have paid for the plant. In the future, they expect to be able to increase their purchases as a result of the interest on the loan which they made.

Government and Private Borrowing Are Not Totally Similar

The similarities in some features of private and government borrowing have led many people to believe that the two kinds of loans are similar in all aspects. The argument is something like this: "Both government and private businesses borrow to secure the use of goods and services. A private business cannot, in the long run, repay the loan unless the investment is productive. Consequently, government loans must be for productive purposes or government, like a business, will bankrupt itself."

It is true that the total product of the economy may be reduced

---

[3] These alternative uses for resources consist of production of both consumption and investment goods. The statement that the workers on the public projects are "supported from the product of the private economy" is merely another way of saying that these workers could have been producing consumption goods if they had not been employed on the public project.

if government uses the proceeds of its borrowings for projects which yield lower returns than could have been secured if the resources had been used in other ways. The total product may be equally reduced, however, if the proceeds of *tax collections* are spent inefficiently. The losses *are not* a result of the particular way in which government has secured the money. There is danger of inefficient use of resources when the funds are secured by taxation as well as when the funds are secured by borrowing.

The analogies which have been drawn regarding the effects of government and private borrowing may have grown out of analyses of government borrowing from foreign lenders. National governments have borrowed, and are continuing to borrow, from other national governments or from private lenders residing in foreign countries. The proceeds of such loans have been utilized to help in procuring outside resources to carry on wars, build up capital plant, or provide relief from wars, floods, famines, earthquakes, and other disasters. For example, the United States borrowed from France, Spain, and Holland during the Revolutionary War. The loan of 3.75 billion dollars made by the United States to the United Kingdom in 1946 was for a variety of purposes including relief and reconstruction from the ravages of the recent war. Some governments have guaranteed the obligations of private borrowers who have borrowed from foreign lenders, although such guarantees have not always been kept.

The carrying charges on foreign-held debts may go outside of the borrowing country. Consequently, foreign loans that are *unproductive*—that is, do not add to the total product by as much as the carrying charges—reduce the amount of product available for domestic use. Such loans can be a burden upon all of the citizens of the borrowing country.[4] The burdens imposed by reparations after World War I are evidence of the kinds of problems which may arise.

Internally held debts, however, need not impose such burdens on the nation as a whole. There may be losses in that more relatively productive uses of the resources could have been found, but interest payments are made to economic units within the country. The problems associated with internally held debts are frequently problems associated with taxation for any purpose.

---

[4] If the loan is not repaid, a burden is imposed upon the citizens of the lending country.

(1) *"Government Bankruptcy"*

The phrase "government bankruptcy" recurs in discussions about government borrowing. Exactly what is meant by this phrase, however, has not been made clear. Bankruptcy is a term referring to the procedure whereby an individual may declare himself unable to meet his obligations, arrange for a voluntary settlement with his creditors, and start over again with a clean slate. When a private business is said to be bankrupt, one usually implies that it is insolvent—that its assets are exceeded by its liabilities. The relationship between assets and liabilities can be ascertained for a private individual. Applying this test to government may be very difficult; although one may be able to determine government's liabilities, the asset side of the ledger cannot be filled in. The assets of government are largely "accounts receivable," and these can be changed by levying larger or smaller taxes (or by direct money issue).

One way in which the term "bankrupt," as applied to government, might be given some meaning is with reference to the terms at which government is able to borrow. One might specify the terms—the rate of interest on bonds of a given character—and say that if government had to offer terms more favorable than these in order to get money, it was bankrupt. For example, one might say that government was bankrupt if it could not borrow at the same (or more favorable) terms than those offered to other borrowers.

For present day central governments, default in the redemption of bonds is highly improbable, since such governments can usually issue money to repay debt. The fear that this procedure might be used may underlie some fears of government bankruptcy. In such cases, the level of prices during repayment rather than the rate of interest is the important criterion of bankruptcy.

(2) *Differences between government and private borrowing may arise because of differences in sources of funds for debt repayment.* Although government and private businesses or individuals may borrow for the same purposes—to secure the use of resources—the means avail-

able to secure funds for repayment are not the same for both units. Both may make unsound investments, but government does not have to rely solely upon the returns from such investments for funds to repay the debt. It may levy taxes (or issue money, if it is the Federal government) to meet its commitments. A private business cannot collect such compulsory contributions from outside the business

Consequently, even though uneconomic use of the proceeds of borrowing by either government or private business affects adversely the total product of the economy, the financial impacts upon government are not the same as those upon a private business. In fact, little public borrowing is conducted with the expectation that the project will be profitable, for relatively little of the goods and services of government are sold.

Economic Effects of Government Borrowing from Banks

During World War I, the depression of the thirties, and World War II, banks have been by far the most important class of purchasers of Federal securities. About 45.5 per cent of all the (Federal) public marketable interest-bearing debt outstanding on September 30, 1946, was held by banks (see Table 36, Chapter XXII.)[5]

For the most part, Federal borrowing from banks has increased the quantity of money (currency and bank deposits subject to check). The expansion has been by about the same amount as if the Federal government had merely printed the money and banks' reserve requirements had been increased to prevent this money from being used as a basis for expansion in bank loans. A bank buys a Federal security—a short-term bond, for example. It credits the Federal government with a deposit against which checks may be drawn. If it wishes, the bank may utilize the bond as collateral for a loan from its Federal Reserve Bank, the proceeds of the loan being credited as additional reserve for the bank. A bank may also sell the bond to the Federal Reserve Bank.

Assume that the government completely withdraws its deposits, transferring them to other banks. Since the banks which have

---

[5] Banks include commercial banks, stock savings banks, and mutual savings banks, commercial banks being by far the most important category.

purchased the securities can exchange them for reserve with the Federal Reserve Banks, they have potentially the same reserve and can lend as much to other economic units as before they bought the bonds. Moreover the amount of money outside the banking system has been increased by approximately the amount of the purchase price of the bonds.

The economic units to which government transferred its deposits may not choose to withdraw these deposits from the banks. (They may make transfers among themselves but this merely changes the distribution of individual claims upon the banks.) The banks—by selling the bonds or using them as collateral for additional reserves—are in a potentially stronger reserve position than before purchasing the government securities. They can further expand their loans.

The expansionary monetary effects of government borrowing from banks has grown out of the fact that loans to government have not been substituted for loans to private economic units. As long as Federal Reserve Banks have been willing to buy government securities, or loan to members with government securities as collateral, the member banks' reserve positions have not been weakened by purchasing government securities. In fact, borrowing from banks under conditions which effectively made bank holdings of government securities redeemable nullified possibilities for restricting credit through reserve requirements. Monetary authorities have not been certain that they could restrict credit. If banks could not use government securities as a basis for borrowing from Federal Reserve Banks, the purchase of government securities would be made at the expense of potential loans to private economic units. Banks, therefore, probably would have been more reluctant to buy government securities since each purchase would weaken their liquidity position.

One of the important effects of our large bank-held debt is that we cannot have large contractions of bank investments or wholesale bank failures such as we had during the depression of the thirties. The large proportion of bank assets (about 55 per cent) made up of government bonds gives us virtually undeflatable bank money, and bank money is by far the most important element of our money supply.

Borrowing from banks may create problems in debt management. The procedure which the Federal government has been following in borrowing from banks has already brought problems.

First of all, the extent of such borrowing has had an important influence upon the size of liquid holdings. Between December, 1941, and June, 1946, total liquid asset holdings (currency, bank deposits, and United States government securities) increased from 81.2 billion dollars to 222.5 billions. Holdings of individuals and trust funds grew from 55.5 billion dollars to 152 billions.[6]

The relatively large expansion in liquidity has been an important factor in bringing a considerable rise in the general level of prices. This condition, however, can result from any technique which expands liquidity. Money-expanding measures, including government borrowing from banks, should not have been used as extensively as they were.

Secondly, the banks probably have been paid excessively for the function which they have performed. They have had to sacrifice little. The cost of getting the money from other expansionary sources (printing money or borrowing from the Federal Reserve Banks) would have been small. These sizable income transfers to banks may make more complex some of the problems of income redistribution in the future.

The problems arising in connection with the impacts upon interest rates of certain techniques in debt management have already been mentioned. These will be discussed again in the next chapter.

Economic Effects of Borrowing from Nonbanking Sources

Unlike borrowing from banks, which has usually had inflationary effects, borrowing from nonbanking sources—individuals and businesses—within the country usually has a deflationary impact.[7] The cash balances of those from whom the government borrows are reduced. Government securities are substituted for other assets in the balance sheet.

If securities are substituted directly for goods and services, the deflationary impact is obvious. However, when the effect is a substitution of securities for cash, the effect is indirect and may be spread over a longer time period. Even though the immediate impact is always only a substitution of securities for cash, an

---

[6] Data are from "Estimated Liquid Asset Holdings of Individuals and Businesses," *Federal Reserve Bulletin*, November, 1946, page 1237.

[7] The net effect of the transactions associated with the borrowing may be inflationary. However, this is the effect of government *borrowing and spending* rather than borrowing alone. Refer to Chapters III and IV.

economic unit's expenditures for goods and services may be some-what dependent upon its cash balance as well as upon the total value of its assets. Indirectly, securities may be substituted for goods and services as well as for cash.

In a case where the economic unit's cash balance is large, how-ever, the substitutions may be only between money and securities. Expenditures for goods and services may be relatively unaffected. Borrowing is less certain to be deflationary than taxation since taxation affects both the size and composition of privately held assets while borrowing affects only the composition. Conse-quently, if it is desired only to influence money expenditure for goods and services, taxation rather than borrowing should be employed. If, however, the terms of borrowing—the interest rate, for example—are also a factor to be controlled, government borrowing can be employed as a technique to make the securities market less favorable as a seller's market.

Interagency Borrowing

A sizable amount (about one-tenth) of the Federal debt out-standing on September 30, 1946, was held by United States gov-ernment agencies and trust funds—primarily social security and various retirement trust funds. Such borrowing represented a transfer of funds from one part of government to another. These funds are typically transferred and used for general governmental purposes.

If such funds otherwise would not have been spent, these transfers had approximately the same short-run effects as if the one agency of government had printed the same amount of money as was borrowed from the other. Under such conditions the money available for the private economy would have been in-creased by an amount equal to the size of the borrowings. The cash balance of government as a whole would have been dimin-ished.

On the other hand, if such funds would have been spent by the lending agency, such transfers may have no important expansion-ary effects. Total money expenditures by government would be unchanged. The effects would depend not upon which agency of government spent the funds but upon the private economic units which received them.

Between the end of 1941 and September, 1946, the holdings of

United States government securities by United States government agencies and trust funds increased by about 22 billion dollars—from 8.2 billions to 30.4 billions. Although the holdings of these agencies grew substantially during the war, these agencies had been purchasing government securities before the war.

Some concern has been expressed about the ability of the trust funds to meet their obligations since "their money has already been spent." If there were dangers from the procedures which have been followed, similar concern should be expressed about the ability of banks to meet the obligations which they owe to their depositors. The banks are also heavy holders of government securities—55.8 per cent of bank assets being in such securities at the end of 1946. Money can be transferred back to these agencies and trust funds as their obligations fall due. The important effects of such intergovernmental borrowing have been the inflationary impacts rather than inability of the agencies and trusts to meet their obligations.

Economic Effects of a Public Debt

The economic effects of a public debt depend to some extent upon the practices which are followed in managing the debt—in repaying the debt and meeting interest payments. They also depend upon the broader fiscal policies which are being pursued. For example, a large public debt may help to bring about an occasional serious weakening of markets if there must always be a balanced budget. On the other hand, because certain ways of repaying it may expand the level of public expenditure, a large debt may be a vehicle by which markets can be strengthened, if a balanced budget is not required. However, there are many other devices which could encourage such an improvement in demand.

If fiscal policies were framed to aid in maintaining full employment with a minimum increase in the general level of prices, it is likely that a variety of situations would arise. Some of these would call for budget surpluses while others would call for deficits. Consequently, some of the economic effects of a public debt may be discussed independently of specific management practices.

Earlier in this chapter, we examined the notion that a large public debt may lead to national bankruptcy. We concluded that the term "national bankruptcy" cannot be given specific meaning. However, the size of the debt may have important effects upon the terms of borrowing—the interest rate, for example. A large debt may make it necessary for government to offer better terms to lenders if it wishes to expand its borrowings.

The opposite of this contention that national bankruptcy may result from a large debt is that the debt has no adverse economic effects. This belief is perhaps as unfounded as that of national bankruptcy. Some of the relationships between the size of the debt and the level of interest rates have already been mentioned. The effects of the present debt-ownership pattern upon the distribution of personal income were examined in Chapter X. In addition to these impacts upon resource allocation and income distribution, the transactions involved in servicing the debt may have effects upon incentives—supplies of resources which are used—and hence upon the size of the total national product. This point has been well illustrated by Meade.[8]

Assume that general market conditions warrant a balanced budget, that government is taxing and spending only to make transfer payments and that the amount it is transferring is equal to one-sixth of income payments including transfer payments. The amount of income payments including transfer payments will be assumed to be 120 billion dollars. Ignoring the differential effects of the ways in which taxes will affect various individual income earners in the economy, taxation will take one-sixth of each dollar of disposable income. A typical income receiver will lose the enjoyment of one-sixth of any income he decides to earn.

Let us imagine that, overnight, in this economy a large public debt is incurred and that its pattern of ownership is such that every income receiver holds the same amount of government securities. Assume that the carrying charge on the debt amounts to 80 billion dollars annually. Income payments will still be 100 billion dollars; government transfers will be 100 billions; taxable income will be 200 billions; tax collections (assuming still a balanced budget) will be 100 billions; and net disposable income will be 100 billions. Although net national income is unchanged, tax collections now take one-half of each dollar of taxable income.

---

[8] Refer to J. E. Meade, "Mr. Lerner on 'The Economics of Control,'" *The Economic Journal*, LV, 217:47-70 (April, 1945). The authors draw heavily upon Meade's analysis in this presentation of the effects of debt upon incentives.

A typical income receiver will lose one-half of any additional income he decides to earn.

TABLE 33

Effects of Public Debt upon National Income, Transfer Payments, Taxable Income, Disposable Income, and Ratio of Tax Collections to Taxable Income[a]

	Day before Debt Growth (in billions of dollars)	Day after Debt Growth (in billions of dollars)
Net National Income........	100	100
Government Transfer Payments..	20	100
Non-debt transfers........... 20		20
Debt transfers.............. 0		80
Taxable Income..............	120	200
Tax Collections.............	20	100
Disposable Income...........	100	100
Ratio of Tax Collection to Taxable Income...............	0.166...	0.50

 [a] This table is modeled after one presented by Meade. J. E. Meade, op. cit., page 62.

Thus, unless taxation discriminates between sources of income —taxing at 100 per cent the interest received from debt holdings— the expansion in the level of transfer payments brought about by the increase in the debt may result in a reduction of incentives. This effect recedes as economic conditions warrant servicing more of the debt from new money issue. If all the debt is serviced in this fashion, additional tax collections resulting from the debt become zero.

These effects, although interesting from a theoretical viewpoint, are of secondary importance compared with the losses in national income which have resulted from depressions such as that of the thirties. Interest payments on our present Federal debt made up less than 5 per cent of our national income in 1946 and are unlikely to reduce incentives seriously. Nevertheless, even though the losses resulting from the transactions involved in servicing the debt are small, they might be avoided through using alternative methods of securing funds—such as direct money issue. As we have already suggested, a Federal debt as large as that we now have has not been warranted by economic conditions. A more thorough understanding of the effects of public debt may result in less frequent resort to public borrowing in the future.

Economic Appraisal of Borrowing as a Fiscal Device

In the previous discussion we have distinguished between public borrowing from banks and from nonbanking sources. A distinction between borrowing at the Federal and at state and local levels is also useful. The Federal government has a wider range of fund sources than have state and local governments and may not have to resort to borrowing for the same uses as state and local governments.

Federal borrowing. As an anti-inflationary device, Federal borrowing from banks has certain limitations. If government borrowed from banks and withdrew the proceeds but did not spend them in the private economy, banks could make fewer loans to other borrowers. However, government borrowing from banks under these conditions has been negligible. Since government has spent the proceeds in the private economy, banks have been able to substitute loans to government for loans to other economic units. There has been no contraction in the money supply due to government borrowing and spending transactions. There may be (and usually has been) a net expansion in the total money supply in the hands of nonbanking units, since banks have made loans to government *in addition* to their loans to other economic units.

Borrowing from nonbanking sources may check money expenditures for goods and services, provided that the terms of borrowing induce economic units to substitute government securities for purchases of goods and services rather than for money holdings alone. Such inducement can be provided through relatively high interest rates on government securities sold to individuals.

As an antideflationary technique, Federal borrowing from banks can be roughly equivalent to money issue, the differences arising from factors connected with debt growth. Unless banks substitute loans to government for loans to other economic units, the quantity of circulating media is expanded by an amount equal to the size of the loans to government.

There are other fund sources—money issue, if deflation is to be combated, and taxation, if inflation is being fought—available to the Federal government. Borrowing and the resultant growth of public debt influence not only the general market situation, but also the structure of the economy (through the effect upon interest rates), the distribution of income, and the supplies of resources available for use. Consequently, public borrowing should be compared with these other techniques in determining when it should be employed.

Although any technique which alters the money supply may affect interest rates, borrowing is likely to have more adverse effects upon incentives than would money issue and taxation. Consequently, if changes in markets are the primary considerations, techniques other than borrowing should be relied upon. If the interest rate is a policy variable, both purchases and sales of securities should be available for government to utilize.

For example, if encouragement to markets is to be provided through government action, government might cut taxes and fill the gap between expenditures and tax collections through direct money issue. This action may, however, increase securities prices and reduce interest rates. If this reduction in interest rates is considered too great, securities can be sold by government. The amount of borrowing should be dictated by the desired level of interest rates.

Similarly, if markets are too strong, government might increase taxes, thereby drawing money out of the private sector of the economy. If this action reduced securities prices and increased interest rates by too much, government might buy securities. Again, the amount of securities purchased should be determined in the light of impacts upon interest rates.[9]

State and local borrowing. Since state and local governments do not have available all of the fund sources upon which the Federal government may draw, they are not in a position to employ borrowing in the same way as it should be employed by the Federal government. State and local governmental finance could be more closely integrated with Federal finance through expanded intergovernmental fiscal relationships. However, until this is done, state and local borrowing will resemble private borrowing in many respects.

[9] This thesis has been mode adequately developed by Lerner. Refer to A. P. Lerner, *The Economics of Control*, Chapters 21-25, New York: The Macmillan Company, 1944.

At the state and local levels, borrowing has been useful in financing long-term projects. In fact, on welfare grounds it might be argued that many states have not borrowed enough. They have either neglected to provide public services adequately or have financed too many projects currently through taxation. Uneconomic resource allocation—too few resources used by government, or too much squeezing of the consumption of taxpayers during a short time—may be the result.

In the absence of other compensatory fiscal techniques, it would be desirable for state and local governments to borrow more extensively during periods when markets are weak. The result might be to strengthen markets since the lenders are unlikely to cut consumption as much in order to purchase securities as the receivers of the government expenditure are likely to expand consumption. In any event, the effect would be much less deflationary than was the expansion in commodity taxation which took place during the thirties.

Legal limitations on state and local borrowing. Abuse, and the fear of abuse, of the borrowing privilege has prompted enactment of limitations upon the amount of borrowing which could be done by some state legislatures and by local governments. Limitations upon municipal borrowing are sometimes incorporated into state constitutions. The upper limit of the debt as a percentage of the taxable valuation of the municipality is often specified.

Limitations upon the powers of state legislatures to incur debt from time to time have been inserted into state constitutions.[10] Some states, for all practical purposes, prohibit their legislatures from incurring debt. Such states can borrow effectively only by constitutional amendment. Other states require that borrowing proposals be submitted to the voters. Still others have constitutionally specified the maxima of their states' debts. In only a handful of states are the legislators free to borrow as they see fit.

While debt limitations have curbed borrowing abuses, they have also curbed the benefits from borrowing. Some state and local governments have found it impossible to undertake enough worth-while projects. Resort to inferior kinds of taxes, particularly during the depression of the thirties, has been another result which we have already mentioned.

[10] For an extensive analysis of state debt, refer to B. U. Ratchford, *American State Debts*, Durham, North Carolina: Duke University Press, 1941.

These borrowing limitations need to be reconsidered and revised. There are reasons for limitations, particularly those designed to prevent states from borrowing to establish loan funds
and to promote certain private industries. The objectives sought
in such limitations, however, might be achieved through restricting the purposes for which borrowed funds might be used rather
than limiting all borrowing.

SELECTED READINGS

1. Bonnell, Elwyn T., "Public and Private Debt in the United
   States," *The Survey of Current Business,* September, 1946,
   Washington, D. C.: United States Department of Commerce.
2. Federal Reserve Board, "Estimated Liquid Asset Holdings of
   Individuals and Businesses," *Federal Reserve Bulletin,* November, 1946.
3. Lerner, A. P., *The Economics of Control,* New York: The Macmillan Company, 1944.
4. Meade, J. E., "Mr. Lerner on 'The Economics of Control,'" *The
   Economic Journal,* LV, 217:47-70 (April, 1945).
5. Ratchford, B. U., *American State Debts,* Durham, North Carolina: Duke University Press, 1941.

CHAPTER XXII

DEBT MANAGEMENT[1]

NEARLY everyone is aware that the Federal debt has grown tremendously during the war years and that it now stands only a little short of its all-time high—a peak of about 279 billion dollars reached during February, 1946. A proportionately large increase in the Federal debt also occurred during the first World War. However, the interest-bearing Federal debt was only slightly in excess of 25 billion dollars at the end of 1919 and was gradually reduced during the twenties. A brief examination of Table 34 indicates that total net public debt (Federal, state, and local) showed only a small decrease in the period 1919-1930 because of the considerable expansion in state and local debt during this period. The recent upturn in outstanding Federal debt began in 1941 and continued until 1946.

During the war period, outstanding state and local debt was reduced. State and local debt expanded somewhat during the thirties and began diminishing during the year 1941. The Federal debt, however, far overshadows state and local debt as can be noted in Table 34.

The existence of public debt—like that of the United States government—commits government to a definite time schedule of

---

[1] The studies of various aspects of the Federal debt as it stood at the end of the war are very extensive. Further additions to this fund of information are to be expected for many years to come. Consequently, we are not endeavoring to give a detailed analysis of all of the complexities of debt management. Instead we have sketched briefly a general analysis of publicly held Federal debt management.

For further discussion, refer to such works as: Evsey D. Domar, "Public Debt and National Income"; Roland I. Robinson, "Monetary Aspects of National Debt Policy"; and Henry C. Wallich, "Public Debt and Income Flow," all included in Board of Governors of the Federal Reserve System, *Public Finance and Full Employment*, postwar Economic Studies No. 3 (December, 1945); Evsey D. Domar, "The Burden of the Debt and the National Income," *American Economic Review*, 36:4 (December, 1946), pages 833-842; Henry C. Wallich, "Debt Management as an Instrument of Economic Policy," *American Economic Review*, 36:2 (June, 1946), pages 292-311; Henry C. Simons, "On Debt Policy," *The Journal of Political Economy*, 52:4 (December, 1944), pages 356-361.

Table 34[2]

Net Public Debt at End of Calendar Years, 1916-1945

Year	Total (in billions of dollars)	Federal Government and Federal Agency (in billions of dollars)	State and Local Government (in billions of dollars)
1916	$ 5.6	$ 1.2	$ 4.4
1917	12.0	7.3	4.7
1918	25.9	20.9	5.0
1919	30.7	25.5	5.2
1920	29.4	23.5	5.9
1921	29.4	22.9	6.5
1922	30.1	22.4	7.7
1923	29.6	21.4	8.2
1924	29.4	20.4	9.0
1925	29.5	19.5	10.0
1926	28.9	18.2	10.7
1927	28.6	17.1	11.5
1928	28.6	16.3	12.3
1929	28.3	15.1	13.2
1930	28.9	14.8	14.1
1931	32.0	16.5	15.5
1932	35.0	18.2	16.8
1933	37.4	20.5	16.9
1934	39.0	23.0	16.1
1935	42.1	26.0	16.1
1936	45.8	29.5	16.3
1937	47.5	31.4	16.1
1938	48.6	32.7	16.0
1939	51.2	34.9	16.3
1940	53.3	36.9	16.5
1941	64.1	47.8	16.3
1942	109.4	93.6	15.8
1943	161.9	147.0	14.9
1944	219.1	205.0	14.1
1945	260.8	247.0	13.7

money payments to debt holders. All of our public debt has maturity dates. Consequently, government is committed to redeem its securities at specified times in the future. No one has suggested that redemption at maturity should not be made. However, funds for redemption can come from refinancing, from

[2] Data for 1916-1945 are from Elwyn T. Bonnell, "Public and Private Debt in the United States, *The Survey of Current Business,* September, 1946, Table 5, page 13. Net public debt excludes holdings of Federal debt by Federal agencies and holdings of state and local debt by state and local agencies.

new or accumulated cash, or from tax collections. Management of the debt thus provides government with additional sources of influence upon interest rates, markets for goods and services, the distribution of income, and incentives.

This chapter will be devoted to discussing management of public debt in the light of impacts upon these factors. Primary emphasis will be placed upon managing the Federal debt, although reference will be made to state and local debt management.

Objectives of Debt Management

Since management of debt may influence interest rates, markets for goods and services, and the distribution of income, various management procedures cannot be appraised adequately without reference to the general direction which changes in interest rates, markets, and income distribution should take.

We indicated in Chapter X that there is not complete agreement as to what constitutes desirable income distribution. There is, however, fairly general agreement that further redistribution of income should not reduce the incomes of the low-income groups. Consequently, debt-management procedures which provide for sizable transfers from low-income to high-income receivers are to be considered inferior.

Neither desirable changes in interest rates nor in market conditions for any time can be specified very far in advance. For example, at some times it may be desirable to raise interest rates in order to check private investment, while at other times it may be advantageous to encourage private investment through reducing interest rates. Similarly, economic conditions may call for a strengthening of markets or a draining off of excess purchasing power.

A decrease in the net debt may be inflationary or deflationary depending upon the source of funds and to whom they are paid. If government secures these funds from money issue, or from funds on hand, and pays them to nonbank holders of debt the net effect is likely to be inflationary. Funds secured in this fashion and paid to banks in exchange for debt which they hold, strengthen the banks' reserve position and may also be inflationary. Securing funds from tax collections and paying these to banks, however, is likely to be deflationary unless the banks replace the bonds with loans. As we indicated in Chapter III, collecting taxes and holding these tax revenues on deposit with a bank is deflationary since the spending power of the depositor is reduced. Even more deflationary is the collection of taxes by government and the holding of these revenues on deposit at Federal Reserve Banks, since the reserves of banks are reduced.

Thus, if it is desirable to raise interest rates and check private investment or to siphon off excess liquidity, good debt management *might* imply an increase in the net debt in times of prosperity. It might call also for earmarking surpluses collected by taxes for subsequent debt repayment at times of threatening deflation. This is in contrast to the traditional position that debts always should be reduced in times of prosperity.

Conversely, if it is advantageous to reduce interest rates or to encourage additional private expenditures for goods and services, good debt management might call for the reduction of the debt more rapidly than it is maturing. This reduction should be accomplished by the spending of accumulated surpluses or the creation of money rather than by the collection of additional taxes. Limits to the issue of money could be established in terms of the level of employment or the level of prices.

Maturity Distribution and Kinds of Federal Debt Holders

Types of issues and maturity dates. The Federal debt outstanding on September 30, 1946, is classified according to types of issues and maturity dates in Table 35. Nearly 70 per cent of the debt consists of marketable securities, 21 per cent being non-marketable, and 9 per cent being held by government agencies and trust funds.

Of the total marketable debt, more than one-half (56 per cent) matures within five years. Short-term securities—treasury bills, certificates of indebtedness, and treasury notes—maturing within one year or less and held largely by banks and governmental or quasi-governmental agencies make up nearly one-third of the marketable issues.

Types of holders of Federal debt. As can be noted from Table 36, more than half of the public marketable debt outstanding on September, 1946, was held by banks and by governmental or quasi-governmental agencies. Banks were particularly important holders of certificates of indebtedness, treasury notes, and short-term treasury bonds. Most treasury bills were held by United States government agencies and trust funds and Federal Reserve Banks.

At the end of 1946, 55 per cent of the total assets of all insured commercial banks were in United States securities. Insurance

TABLE 35[3]

Composition of Total Outstanding Federal Debt by Types of Issues and Maturity Dates, September 30, 1946

Type of Issue	Maturity Date	Amount (in millions of dollars)	Per Cent of Total Debt	Per Cent of Marketable Issues
I. INTEREST BEARING SECURITIES				
A. Nonmarketable				
U. S. Savings Bonds (Current redemption value)[a].		$ 49,545	18.67	
Treasury savings notes.		6,096	2.30	
Depository Bonds.		385	0.14	
Total nonmarketable.		56,025	21.11	
B. Special Issues to Government Agencies and Trust Funds.		23,854	8.99	
C. Marketable Issues				
Treasury Bills.		17,008	6.41	9.23
Certificates of Indebtedness.	Sept. 1, 1947 or before	34,478	12.99	18.70
Treasury Notes.	Sept. 15, 1947 or before	9,603	3.62	5.21
Treasury Bonds[b].	Before Jan. 1, 1948	1,460	0.55	0.79
	Jan. 1 to Dec. 31, 1948	9,971	3.76	5.41
	Jan. 1 to Dec. 31, 1949	6,682	2.52	3.62
	Jan. 1 to Dec. 31, 1950	10,723	4.04	5.82
	Jan. 1 to Dec. 31, 1951	11,996	4.52	6.51
	Jan. 1, 1952 to Dec. 31, 1956	27,282	10.28	14.80
	Jan. 1, 1957 to Dec. 31, 1961	11,158	4.20	6.05
	Jan. 1, 1962 or later	43,959	16.57	23.85
	All bonds	123,231	46.44	66.85
Other Marketable Issues.		18	—	—
Total Marketable.		184,338	69.46	100.00
Total Interest-Bearing Securities. .		264,217	99.57	
II. OTHER NONINTEREST-BEARING SECURITIES OR SECURITIES ON WHICH INTEREST HAS CEASED				
Total Debt.		1,152	0.43	
		265,369	100.00	

[a] Although United States Savings Bonds are nonmarketable. they are quickly redeemable. Hence they constitute a large item of immediate potential spending power.
[b] Date of first call on callable issues.

[3] Summarized from the United States Treasury Department, *Treasury Bulletin*, November, 1946. Discrepancies are due to rounding.

companies' holdings of Federal securities constituted almost one-half of their total assets. About one-half of Treasury borrowing from government agencies was accomplished through sales of treasury bills, and nearly two-thirds of the borrowing from banks was achieved through sales of short-term treasury bonds.

Outstanding United States savings bonds (nonmarketable although readily redeemable) held by investors other than banks or insurance companies, totaled about 46.7 billion dollars. Of the approximately 55 billion dollars of government bonds (marketable issues) maturing after January 1, 1957, it was estimated that about 18.5 billions were held by investors other than banks, insurance companies, United States government agencies, trust funds, and Federal Reserve Banks.[4]

Significance of these characteristics for debt management. Management of our large Federal debt is significant as an instrument of economic policy because a sizable amount of debt is maturing each year for the next two decades. An additional and continuous opportunity may be provided to use debt repayment as an antideflationary device. However, the existence of a large debt may make a fight against inflation by fiscal policy more difficult. Additional debt may be resisted politically. Moreover the liquid nature of the debt makes for a sizable potential expansion in bank credit. In spite of these possible difficulties, the existence of a large debt may make it politically easier to increase taxes in times of threatening inflation.

If the Federal debt were widely dispersed among our population so that its ownership was not concentrated in particular types of financial institutions, debt repayment could be handled as any other type of Federal expenditure. The transactions involved in debt repayment would effect markets, incentives, and income distribution in a manner similar to that of other government expenditures. However, much of the debt is short term and is held by banks. Conversion of bank's securities into cash could pave the way for a marked expansion in bank loans and deposits.

Of course, banks might not expand their loans and deposits at the time when their government securities are converted into

---

[4] These data are based on monthly Treasury surveys of the ownership of securities issued or guaranteed by the United States. The banks and insurance companies covered in the survey owned about 95 per cent of the total United States securities owned by banks and insurance companies in the United States. See *Treasury Bulletin,* November, 1946.

TABLE 36[5]

Estimated Ownership Pattern of Outstanding (Federal) Public Marketable Interest-Bearing Securities; September 30, 1946

| | | Percentage of Each Issue Held by Groups of Investors[a] | | | | | | |
Type of Security	Total Amount Outstanding	Commercial Banks	Stock Savings Banks	Mutual Savings Banks	Life Insurance Companies	Fire, Casualty, and Marine Insurance Companies	All U. S. Gov't Agencies, Trust Funds, and Fed. Res. Banks	Other Investors
Securities issued by United States								
Treasury bills..........	100.0	5.5					86.5	7.9
Certificates of Indebtedness.....	100.0	42.1	0.1	0.8	1.2	0.5	23.1	32.2
Treasury Notes...........	100.0	65.0	0.2	1.9	3.4	1.3	5.1	23.1
Treasury Bonds—bank restricted[b].........	100.0	2.7	0.4	15.7	33.3	2.2	10.0	35.6
Treasury Bonds—bank eligible.	100.0	66.6	0.3	4.5	5.9	2.0	3.1	17.6
Postal Savings and Other Bonds.	100.0	8.1		0.2	0.2	0.3	20.0	71.2
Guaranteed by United States......	100.0	26.9	2.3	7.8	29.1	1.8	21.2	11.0
Total..............	100.0	39.0	0.3	6.2	11.7	1.6	16.6	24.7

[a] Discrepancies are due to rounding.
[b] Issues which commercial banks are not permitted to acquire prior to a specified date.
[5] Data are from U. S. Treasury Department, Treasury Bulletin, December, 1946, page 50.

cash. They might prefer to strengthen their reserve positions. However, these large reserves could later be used as a basis for credit expansion. The existence of the debt in a form in which it may be very readily converted into cash makes it desirable to take special steps to prevent inflation from accompanying net debt reduction.

One such step might be to increase banks' reserve requirements as banks' holdings of securities are reduced—through conversion into cash, for example. This would be a step in the direction of a 100 per cent reserve plan for banks. However, all banks are unlikely to reduce their securities holdings in the same way. Some banks held proportionately more of their total assets in the form of government securities than others, and not all banks are members of the Federal Reserve System and hence are not subject to the reserve requirements of the system. Consequently, all banks would not be affected in the same manner as a result of changes in reserve requirements.

It has been suggested that debt management might be utilized as a means for a relatively smooth transition from a fractional reserve to a 100 per cent reserve banking structure.[6] Banks would be given a choice between converting their governmental securities into cash or into nonnegotiable securities. Those banks preferring to exchange their government securities for money would find their reserve requirements as well as their reserves increased. Those banks preferring to hold securities would become largely investment trusts.[7]

Another proposal is to create a special security, continuously redeemable and callable, which could be held only by banks. This security would be required as reserve against bank deposits.[8] The effect of incorporating this proposal into policy would be essentially the same as that of increasing banks' reserve requirements as their securities were converted into cash

[6] See Chapter V for a brief discussion of the proposed 100 per cent plan for banks.

[7] Refer to Henry C. Simons, "On Debt Policy," *The Journal of Political Economy*, LII, No. 4 (December, 1944), pages 356-361.

[8] This proposal was advanced by Henry C. Simons, *Debt Policy and Banking Policy*, unpublished mimeographed note, July 1, 1945. See Lawrence H. Seltzer "Is a Rise in Interest Rates Desirable or Inevitable?" *American Economic Review*, XXXV: 831-50 (December, 1945). Also refer to the alternative proposals advanced in *Public Finance and Full Employment*, Postwar Economics Studies No. 3, 1945, a publication of the Federal Reserve System.

Alternative Management Procedures

Many procedures have been suggested to manage the Federal debt. Although many have been called to our attention, it is unlikely that we have been exposed to all of them. Many of the techniques, however, are likely to fit one of the general categories which we will discuss.

Make no attempt to reduce the debt. The suggestion has been made that there should be no attempt to reduce the size of the debt. Interest payments should be met from taxation or from money issue, but when a security has matured, funds to meet repayment should be secured by selling other new securities. The experience of the British, whose net debt has grown steadily since early in the seventeenth century, is pointed to as evidence of the success of this procedure.

The British, however, issued consols (fixed-interest securities without specific maturity dates) and have at various times refunded in order to reduce interest charges. In issuing consols rather than securities with definite maturity dates, the British indicated at the outset an intention to avoid a definite time pattern in debt repayment. Buyers of United States securities probably have a different expectation regarding the pattern of debt repayment than British security holders, and look forward to redemption of their securities at stated future dates.

Although economic conditions might by chance warrant following this procedure, it appears unlikely that this course would be best suited to all circumstances. Pursuing such a policy would not take advantage of potential opportunities to strengthen markets through debt repayment. Of greater importance, it would disregard opportunities to keep interest rates from rising if such was considered a desirable policy. Nongovernmental debt, which has been markedly diminished during the past decade, might warrant growth during future years, or the demand for securities might fall off. Private businesses might not be able to secure borrowing terms sufficiently favorable to induce the desired amount of private investment. A procedure which would permit a reduction in the debt would make it possible to prevent the interest rate from advancing beyond any given level.

Conversion of debt into consols and money as the debt matures. Another procedure which has been suggested for managing the debt is to convert all of the Federal debt, which now has definite maturity dates, into consols and money.[9] Banks' reserve requirements would be increased to prevent the increased money from becoming the basis for bank credit expansion.

This procedure is not unlike some of those which have been suggested for managing bank-held Federal debt, except that it would apply to all debt. It has the merit in that it would reduce the potential variations in the money supply which have grown out of the "near-moneyness" of much of our existing debt. However, the advantages offered by this proposal are not as great as they might appear. Private short-term debt would still exist and would continue to complicate monetary management. Furthermore, monetary management is certainly not impossible even though much "near money" does exist.

Treat interest and principal payments like other Federal expenditures. As we have already pointed out, the present United States Federal debt with its 5 billion dollars of annual interest charges and its definite maturity schedule will constitute a large annual item of Federal money payments for some time to come. Some debt repayment could be lumped together with other Federal expenditures for the purpose of considering the combination of taxing, reborrowing, and money issue which should be utilized by the Federal government to obtain funds. Such short-term issues as treasury notes and certificates of indebtedness probably would be managed separately. These issues are held largely by banks and other financial institutions. Special considerations such as banks' demands for such securities are important in determining the amount of such securities outstanding.

For example, by the calendar year 1951, Federal expenditures, exclusive of debt repayment, might be about 30 billion dollars. During this year about 12 billion dollars of United States government bonds (public marketable issues) will mature. Assume that budget deficits and surpluses constituted the only way by which the quantity of money could be changed and that markets did not need strengthening nor did excess purchasing power need to be drained off (that is, there was full employment and no tendency toward increases in the general level of prices). Under such conditions, somewhat less than 42 billion dollars in taxes

---

[9] Refer to Henry C. Simons, "On Debt Policy," *Journal of Political Economy*, 52:4 (December, 1944), pages 356-361.

probably should be collected—the bulk of the 1½ billions of debt repayment would increase money expenditures for goods and service by less than 12 billions of tax collections would diminish such expenditures. Moreover, expected improvements in technology would warrant some increase in the quantity of money. The deficit—the difference between expenditures and tax collections—could be filled by money issue or by reborrowing. The proportion of funds to be secured from each source would be determined solely by interest-rate considerations. If markets were weakening (or getting too strong) the deficit would be larger (or smaller) than in the situation just discussed. However, the combination of money issue and borrowing which should be employed to make up the deficit would still be determined in the same fashion.

A special debt budget. A procedure similar to that just discussed for debt management is the establishment of a special debt budget. The expenditure side of this budget ledger during a given year would consist of payments on debt that was maturing during the year. The receipts side would consist of surpluses (excesses of tax collections over expenditures) transferred from the regular budget, money issue, and the proceeds from reborrowing. The payments side would, of course, be inflexible. But the receipts side could be made up according to the desired effects upon markets for commodities and securities. When both markets were weak, some payments could be made from money issue. If both were excessively strong, the net debt might be desirably increased.

Handling debt repayment through a debt budget has advantages in a political setting which requires the regular budget to be balanced always. However, as we indicated in Chapter V, influencing the commodities market through operations in securities is not likely to prove very effective. If the restriction of a balanced regular budget is not present, this procedure is not superior to that of considering debt repayment along with the items of money payments in the regular Federal budget.

Further Need for Monetary-Fiscal Coordination in Debt Management

The proposals we have examined for managing the Federal debt are not exhaustive and do not consider the many detailed problems of debt management. Examination of these proposals, however, reveals that management of the Federal debt should be coordinated with other fiscal activities and with such direction of the banking system as can be achieved.

Following any plan for debt repayment could have disastrous effects upon markets if it were pursued independently of other fiscal and credit policies. Appropriate steps would have to be taken to prevent overexpansion of bank credit. Changes in banks' reserve requirements would need to be coordinated with redemption of bank-held debt. Such weakening of markets as might come about through taxing to secure funds for debt repayment would need to be offset by expansionary financing of regular government expenditures.

Management of State and Local Debt

As is shown in Table 34, state and local debt is small compared with Federal debt. Management of such debt, consequently, probably is of less importance than management of Federal debt. Furthermore, management of local and state debt more nearly approximates private debt management than does Federal debt management.

State and local debts differ from private debt in that the former are often incurred in order to provide facilities for such services as highways and education. Borrowing has taken place to permit highway improvement and construction of school plants. Such improvements are expected to provide the basis for repayment of loans—either from tax revenues or from the sale of services—within their period of usefulness. Unlike the Federal government, state and local units must rely primarily upon tax receipts for revenue. They cannot issue money.

An expansion in Federal aid for such purposes as highways and education could sharply reduce the amount of state and local debt required for these purposes, although it would not alter the character of the remaining debt nor the nature of its management. It is recognized that an expansion in Federal aids imply a substantial degree of Federal control over state and local expenditures. However, there is precedent for such controls in some present Federal aids. Further discussion of intergovernmental aids will be made in the two final chapters of the book (which follow this chapter).

SELECTED READINGS

1. Federal Reserve Board, Postwar Economic Study Number 3, various authors, *Public Finance and Full Employment,* Washington, D. C., 1945.
2. Seltzer, Lawrence H., "Is a Rise in Interest Rates Desirable or Inevitable?" *American Economic Review,* 35:4 (December, 1945), pages 831-850.
3. Simons, Henry C., "On Debt Policy," *Journal of Political Economy,* 52:4 (December, 1944), pages 356-361.
4. United States Treasury, *Treasury Bulletins,* November, and December, 1946, Washington, D. C.
5. Wallich, Henry C., "Debt Management as an Instrument of Economic Policy," *American Economic Review,* 36:2 (June, 1946), pages 292-311.

PART FIVE

INTERGOVERNMENTAL FISCAL COORDINATION

CHAPTER XXIII

INTERGOVERNMENTAL FISCAL RELATIONS: DESCRIPTION OF PROBLEMS[1]

Objectives and Development of Intergovernmental Aids

SINCE we have chosen a Federal system rather than centralized government, problems of intergovernmental fiscal relations inevitably arise. In 1942, there were 155,000 separate governmental units in this country. Local governments are expected to provide public services, many of which have an extralocal character. Services provided by one local unit may have important effects upon the residents of other units. If local units of government were forced to rely upon their own sources of tax revenue, these would be confined almost entirely to property taxation.

A larger governmental unit, especially the Federal government, may be most efficient in collecting many taxes, while smaller units most effectively carry on many governmental functions. Such a division of functions is noted in Federal highway aids to the states.[2] Further intergovernmental fiscal cooperation is needed so that this specialization of functions can be carried out in connection with other services.

Efficiency in the use of resources may also be encouraged if each unit of government is not forced to rely exclusively on local sources of revenue. Intergovernmental fiscal aids can help to eliminate the use of taxes which reduce consumer welfare more than would other tax sources yielding the same revenue.

[1] This is the first of two chapters on this topic. This chapter is designed to be primarily a description of various devices of intergovernmental fiscal coordination, while the next chapter will try to appraise the usefulness of these devices. In both chapters, the principal source of reference is "Federal, State, and Local Fiscal Relations," Senate Document 69, 78th Congress, 1st Session, Washington, D. C., 1943.

[2] A qualification to the notion that local units can best administer such highway funds is contained in the requirement that the Public Roads Administration (formerly the Bureau of Public Roads) should approve plans for expenditure of Federal funds on state highways before Federal aid can be granted.

Since governmental tax and spending policies affect the level of employment in the private economy, coordination of the fiscal activities of the many units is desirable. It has been recognized earlier that fiscal actions of state and local governments may counter fiscal action of the Federal government to influence markets. Counter-cyclical arrangements for Federal aids for highways and education would permit full-employment fiscal policy to be followed by the smaller units of government as well as by the Federal government.

The writers also believe that an important objective of state or Federal aids should be to raise, through equalization of costs and opportunities, the level of the services performed by the smaller units of government. Intergovernmental transfers of income represent a way by which the richer areas may invest in the poorer ones with benefits to both. Federal and state grants should require some minimum local participation in the financing of particular local functions—such as public education. One reason for some continued local, financial participation is to discourage extravagance in the expenditure of public funds which otherwise might have been received from government units entirely outside the local taxing district. State or Federal units of government may wish to establish certain minimum standards for particular functions as a prerequisite of granting aids. Such minimum standards of local expenditure (or service) are frequent in state aids to public education.

State-Local Fiscal Relations

Federal and state aids to local government units grew from 76 million dollars in 1902 to 1,760 millions in 1942. In the early part of this century, it became apparent that proper performance of local functions often required revenue in excess of the amounts which local governments were receiving. In some instances, the state governments took over some of the functions that had been performed locally. Many students of taxation, however, thought that the local problem could be solved by separating the sources of revenue from which the state government and the local governments drew. Several states withdrew from the field of property taxation completely, while others levied only token property taxes. In 1900 the states in the aggregate obtained slightly over one-half of their tax revenue from property taxes. In 1946 they obtained just under 4 per cent of their tax revenues from property taxes. Taxation of business and individual income, and sales and excise taxes (particularly taxes on motor vehicles) became the primary sources of state revenues, the property tax being left largely to local units. (Refer to Chapter XIX.)

This compartmentalization of sources of revenue has continued to be important, particularly between state and local governments. It has, however, broken down between the states and the Federal government and resulted in the development of multiple taxation of many types. For some units of government, particularly the larger municipalities, almost exclusive reliance on property taxes has impaired their proper functioning. They have been left without sufficient revenue or have been forced (and able) to resort to taxation which is inferior on welfare grounds. Poor administration of the property tax together with the general unpopularity of the tax—an unpopularity related to the poor administration—has "starved" some local units.

Two principal techniques have been devised or reintroduced in order to alleviate the local situation. One of these is the sharing of tax sources by states and local governments. The other is state grants-in-aid to local governments. In addition, a few local government units, such as New York City, have applied new, special, local taxes with relative fiscal success.

Shared taxes. Sharing with the local governments revenues from taxes collected by the state government is a relatively frequent procedure. Although revenues from shared taxes made up a rather small percentage of total local revenues in 1940, states most commonly shared gasoline, liquor, general sales, and public utility taxes. Income and inheritance taxes were also shared, but less frequently.

Under the sharing procedure, the state collects the tax and divides some of the receipts among the local governments according to an agreed rule for distribution. The gasoline tax is the principal tax which is shared with the local units by the states. About one-fifth of state gasoline-tax collections were prorated among local governments in 1940. The local governments' share of gasoline taxes made up nearly two-fifths (about

37 per cent) of their total of shared taxes in 1940. A summary
of tax sharing between state and local governments is presented
in Table 37.

Sharing of taxes has the advantage of permitting taxes to be
collected by a single unit of government. Some saving in re-

TABLE 37[3]

State-Local Shared Taxes, 1928 and 1940

Tax	1928 (in millions of dollars)	1940 (in millions of dollars)
Personal Income	57.5	37.6[a]
Corporation	62.0	45.4[a]
Death	4.6	3.2
Motor Vehicle	67.0	80.2
Motor Fuel	64.2	179.8
General Sales		30.4
Liquor		52.7
Other	11.8	43.9
Total	267.2	484.6
Proportion of local revenue	5.4%	3.4%

[a] Plus 11.4 million dollars from income taxes not separable into personal and corporation.

sources is thus effected. However, tax sharing does not appear
to offer a major contribution to the solution of the fiscal problems
of local governmental units. Distribution of most shared taxes
among the local governments has been largely in line with contributions—relative collections of the shared taxes within the
various local units. If this principle of sharing were abandoned
and "distribution according to need" could be the rule, tax sharing
would closely resemble equalization grants-in-aid.

State grants-in-aid to local governments. At many places in
this book we have pointed to the "extra-buyer" benefits attached
to some of the services provided by government. The benefits
from public education, for example, do not accrue entirely to the
persons attending the public schools. Similarly, public health
programs, public highways, public facilities for youth recreation,
and other kinds of public services may provide benefits which are
widely disseminated among the population.

Many of these public services can best be produced at the local

[3] Data are from W. J. Shultz, *American Public Finance*, 3rd edition, Table 40,
page 727, New York: Prentice-Hall, Inc., 1942.

level, under local supervision and administration.   The resources of a given locality, however, may be severely taxed if each locality must provide adequate public services and finance such services from its own revenues.   Unless outside aids are provided, the level of public services in a relatively low-income (per capita) area is likely to be low; and citizens of other areas, as well as the relatively low-income one, will reap the results of these low levels of services.

The disadvantages of ignoring the interdependence of local units of government in the provision of highway services were obvious to the motorists of the twenties and early thirties.   Highways in one county might be well paved, while those in an adjoining county would be at times impassable.   Cross-country transport was impeded by the poor highways of some local areas. The highway system has been markedly improved through partially shifting revenues from one area to another.   Federal and state funds secured from outside a locality have been used to finance highways within the local area.

A fiscal device which has been useful in this shifting of tax revenues from one area to another is the grant-in-aid.   A state grant-in-aid to a local governmental unit is a definite sum appropriated by the state to be spent by the local unit for *a specified purpose*.   The grant may also include a specification of standards which must be met by the receiving unit.   Both the size of the grant and the manner in which it is to be used are known by local officials.

To the local unit the grant-in-aid differs from the shared tax in two principal aspects: (1) the receipts from the grant-in-aid are known in advance and are relatively stable from one time period to another, whereas the receipts from the shared tax are uncertain and variable over time, and (2) the way in which the grant-in-aid is to be used by the local unit is well defined, whereas the receipts from the shared tax frequently may be used as the local unit sees fit.   Shared taxes, however, have been earmarked for specific purposes—for example, shared gasoline taxes are frequently to be devoted to highway purposes.

(1) *Desirable basis for distribution of grants-in-aid*.   The degree of tax relief provided to local governments by grants-in-aid depends upon the rules followed by the states in distributing grants-in-aid.   If these grants are distributed in accordance with

the relative need for the services to which they are to be devoted, they represent genuine relief to some local governments. For example, if grants-in-aid for education were distributed inversely to the ability (as indicated by per capita income) of local school districts to provide adequate educational facilities, the level of education in these districts where per capita incomes are relatively low could be raised. Similarly, if grants for highway purposes were distributed according to the need for highway development, highways probably would be improved in the areas where they are poorest.

(2) *Importance of state grants-in-aid to local governments.* States have been making grants to local governments, particularly for the use of schools, since the days of colonial government.[4] State aid for schools has been expanding almost continuously. With the rapid development of the motor car, state aids to counties for improving highways became of some importance during the twenties. The expansion of welfare aids—poor relief, old-age assistance, and care of the blind, for example—was very rapid after the inception of the New Deal. The relative importance of state grants to local units for various purposes is summarized in Table 38.

(3) *State fiscal aid to local education.* State fiscal aid to local governments for education may be taken as an illustration of state grants to local governments. State governments have made continuously increasing grants for the purpose of helping to pay the costs of public elementary and secondary education. These

TABLE 38[5]

State-Local Grants-in-Aid, 1945

Purpose	Amount (in millions of dollars)
Education	$ 831.3
Highways	302.0
Welfare	349.0
Other	371.8
Total	1,854.1
Proportion of local revenue	7.5%

[4] William J. Shultz, *American Public Finance,* 3rd edition, page 735, New York: Prentice-Hall, Inc., 1942.
[5] Source: United States Bureau of the Census, *State Finances: 1945,* Vol. 3, Statistical Compendium, Table 5, page 7.

grants, which were very small at the beginning of the present century, had grown to represent from 35 to 40 per cent of the costs of local education by the early forties. A variety of methods has been used to distribute these funds. Some states, like New York, have concentrated on the equalization of educational costs and opportunity among local school districts. Others, like California, have given primary attention to providing general aid to all school districts.

Some states, again, have gone much further in assuming financial responsibility for local schools than have others. Delaware, New York, and California are examples of states providing substantial aids for education. At the other extreme, such states as Oregon, Kansas, and Iowa have lagged far behind the general development. Fundamentally, the basis for extensive education aid from larger to smaller units of government is the high degree of mobility in our population. For example, New York City cannot be assured that a person trained in upstate communities having less adequate school systems will not become a permanent resident of the city. Consequently, New York City should be concerned with the schools in the rest of the state. In addition, since migration takes place among states, inadequate education in other states should be a concern to residents of New York City, as well as to other communities in New York state where workers may come in from states having less adequate school systems. The extra-local nature of the benefits from public services in the field of education is especially clear.

Federal-State Fiscal Relations

A Federal system almost inherently involves some overlapping of functions and of taxation between the Federal government and the states. Although this leads to some waste of resources, it is considered to be part of the price we pay for the advantages of a Federal system—the virtues of some centralization combined with considerable freedom of action at the local level. This area of overlapping, however, can be considerably reduced through further specialization of functions and through various fiscal devices. In the fiscal area, such specialization might take the form of greater centralization of taxation in the Federal government and decentralization of a greater proportion of governmental expenditure functions in the state and local governments.

Fiscal cooperation between the Federal and state governments has recognized the need for this specialization. The techniques to effect such cooperation are not unlike those employed in state-local relations. Thus, Federal grants-in-aid to the states are the most important device by which both specialization and cooperation are effected. In addition, coordination devices such as state credits against Federal taxes, deductibility (often reciprocal) of taxes due one jurisdiction by individuals of another, and joint administration of taxes employed by both have been used. The use of state supplementary rates on certain Federal taxes (like the personal income tax) and the sharing of certain taxes have also been suggested.

In Federal-state relations some separation of tax sources was provided by the Constitution itself. Only the Federal government was given authority to levy taxes on imports, and through the nineteenth century, receipts from customs duties represented the principal source of Federal revenues. As we shall mention later in this chapter, however, an important fiscal development of the thirties was the manner in which most states circumvented this restriction by imposing special state restrictions (often in the form of special state taxes) for the privilege of doing business in a particular state.[6]

Another provision of the Constitution made it impracticable for the Federal government to rely on the use of the property tax, as indicated in Chapter XIX. Such taxes can only be apportioned among the states on the basis of population, and except on three occasions,[7] the Federal government has not found such allocation practicable for purposes of taxation. The result has been the concentration of property taxes with local units of government.

Current proposals for separation of sources and tax-sharing. Apart from constitutional separations of tax power, the states and the Federal government have imposed multiple taxes which overlap at many places, and repeated suggestions for a separation of sources between Federal and state governments have not been accepted. More recently, the Fiscal Relations Report of 1943[8]

---

[6] The 21st Amendment to the Constitution, repealing prohibition, directly aided the growth of state restrictions by placing control over the liquor industry in the hands of the states.

[7] See Chapter XIX, page 401, for a summary of these uses of the property tax.

[8] This name is used for the report on "Federal, State, and Local Fiscal Relations," Washington, D. C., 1943.

has urged that the Federal government should retire from the field of motor-vehicle taxation, largely on the ground that such taxes as motor-vehicle licenses and gasoline taxes have been developed and applied by the states as special-benefit taxes. The same report, however, proposed that the Federal government retain the sole taxation of aviation fuel, since aviation is largely interstate in character.

The Report suggests other changes in taxation which would have the effect of separation of sources. Being able to collect taxes on tobacco from relatively few sources of manufacture, the Federal government has a substantial administrative advantage over the states, which collect the tax from distributors. The Fiscal Relations Report recommended that the collection of excise taxes on tobacco be confined to the Federal government, with the proceeds being partially shared with the states. (A total tax of $8\frac{1}{2}$ cents per package of cigarettes with payment of 2 cents per package to the states on some agreed basis of consumption was suggested, together with the use of some sharing formula which would favor relatively urban states.)

The Report suggests that, if taxes on business continue to be levied, their collection should be largely centralized with the Federal government. The proceeds would be partially shared with the states. But the Report recommends that a prerequisite for such sharing should be the withdrawal by the states from the varied fields of business taxation. Some of these forms, often arbitrary and capricious, were noted in Chapter XV. As indicated in Chapter XVII, the Report also urges the modernization of the existing system of Federal death-tax credits, together with a sharp reduction in exemptions for existing Federal estate taxation, and the distribution of sufficient death-tax revenue to the states to more than cover existing state death-tax revenue. The proposal contemplates gradual abandonment of separate state death-tax administrations, in which case an additional separation of revenue sources would be obtained. In the analysis of death taxes, the Report indicates that state administration has been relatively incompetent and also urges that death and gift taxes should be completely integrated. The advantages of such integration have already been indicated.

From this brief survey, however, it is clear that too much cannot be expected of separation of revenue sources as a device of intergovernmental coordination.[9]   To the extent that such separation is achieved, economy in the use of resources for tax administration is secured.   But it is also clear that separation of sources is likely to be accompanied by sharing-of-taxes or grants-in-aid from larger to smaller units of government.   The bases for such tax-sharing or grants-in-aid involve added problems in intergovernmental fiscal relations which cannot be avoided.[10]

State credits against Federal taxes.   Although the states and the Federal government share no taxes, arrangements have been made whereby the Federal government permits state taxes to be credited against Federal death taxes up to 80 per cent of the total Federal levy based on 1926 rates.   Federal death-tax rates have since been increased on five occasions.   These made the average state credit in 1941 only 11 per cent.   A 90 per cent credit for state payroll taxes to finance unemployment insurance is permitted against Federal payroll taxes collected for this purpose.

In a sense, this crediting of state taxes against Federal taxes is not unlike tax-sharing.   If the states take advantage of the credits, they split the tax with the Federal government, a definite percentage going to each of the units involved.   Of course, if a state does not levy death taxes, no such division of the tax between the state and the Federal government is made.   The large proportionate credit given to the states for payroll taxes to finance unemployment insurance has been a major factor in encouraging all the states to set up unemployment insurance.   A degree of uniformity in state death taxes resulted from enactment of Federal credits which began in 1924 at 25 per cent—Florida, for instance, repealed a state constitutional amendment forbidding death taxes.

[9] In addition to the proposals made in the Fiscal Relations Report, there have been other plans for separation of tax sources.   Some of these appear to aim toward eliminating taxes rather than merely separating sources.   Elimination would (in fact) be brought about by reserving for the states some taxes which they might not choose to impose.   For example, if death taxes were allocated to the states, tax competition and costly administration would discourage their use at the state level.   In cases where death taxes were not employed by the states, allocation to the states would debar these taxes from the tax system.

[10] While the Federal government shares no taxes with the states or local governments, many proposals for Federal tax-sharing have been made in the past twenty-five years.   One of the most widely publicized was the Graves-Edmonds Plan of 1934.   This plan proposed that the Federal government collect and share with the states the proceeds of certain liquor taxes, a gasoline tax, and a manufacturers' excise tax.   See the *Proceedings of the Twenty-seventh National Tax Association,* 1934.

Federal grants-in-aid to the states and local governments. The grant-in-aid has been rather extensively employed by the Federal government in encouraging states to expand performance of certain functions. Grants have been made for such purposes as education, highways, forest conservation, and unemployment relief.

Educational aids provided by the Federal government to the states have not been relatively large. Federal funds have been allotted to the states for expanding vocational education, particularly vocational training in agriculture. The agricultural experiment stations, which are an integral part of many state colleges or universities, are supported partly by Federal funds.

Federal grants and loans to localities in order to construct public works and provide employment were substantial during the period from 1933-1939. During part of this period, 1933-1936, the Federal government administered unemployment-relief expenditures totaling around 3 billion dollars through grants to the states. This method was scrapped for direct Federal administration under the Works Projects (Progress) Administration in 1936, which expended 11.3 billion dollars in the fiscal years 1936-1943.

Uses of Federal grants-in-aid. Federal aid began with grants of parts of public lands to the states as provided in the Ordinance of 1785 for sale of the public domain (plus several Federal distributions of surplus funds in the first half of the nineteenth century). Under this type of aid, the states have received around 250,000,000 acres of land, much of the proceeds from the sale being set aside for educational purposes. But mismanagement, graft, and fraud accompanied the use of these lands. As of 1944 there were few states that had much to show in state funds for the large amounts of lands received.

Federal aid for specific purposes really got started in 1887, when small grants were made to states for purposes of supporting agricultural experiment stations. Federal grants for education—chiefly to promote research in higher education—have continued to grow, but slowly. The grants were expanded in 1914 to include agricultural extension work and to cover vocational education in 1917, and vocational rehabilitation in 1920. Federal grants for unemployment relief were made to the states from

1933 to 1936. A variety of public welfare grants under the Social Security Act began in 1936. A summary of Federal aids for specific purposes as of 1945 is given in Table 39.

TABLE 39[11]

Federal Grants-in-Aid to States, 1945

Type of Aid	Amount (in millions of dollars)
Public Assistance	508.2
Highways	95.2
Education	119.9[a]
Agriculture	38.5
All Other	87.3
Total	849.1

[a] Includes 48.1 million dollars for training of defense workers.

Prior to 1935, Federal aid was largely in the field of highway construction. In the late twenties, the proportion represented by all other grants was low. Provision for such aid for the purposes of stimulating highway construction was first made in 1916, and has been the largest continuous Federal aid program in operation since that time. Federal aid expenditures for highways increased from only $34,000 in 1917 to an average of over 80 million dollars a year in the years 1925-1930. These aids rose to a peak of 338 millions in 1937, and were in part designed to stimulate employment during the early years after the deep depression of the early thirties. Such aids totaled 89 million dollars in the last year of World War II.

Plans have been highly developed for the use of Federal funds on highways in the postwar years, particularly for the purpose of modernizing major interstate trunk highways to serve anticipated postwar traffic requirements. The matching basis required of states in order to obtain Federal funds has been severely criticized. However, Federal highway aid has developed some of the best control devices for intergovernmental fiscal relations.

Under the Social Security Act of 1935, Federal grants to the states (exclusive of compensation for administration of unemployment compensation laws) had grown from nothing in 1935 to about 437 million dollars in 1946. The principal grants are

[11] Source: *Facts and Figures on Government Finance, 1946-1947*, page 25, New York: The Tax Foundation, 1946.

for old-age assistance and for aid to dependent children. Here, also, the matching bases which have been used has been criticized. These grants will probably continue to grow, and some *immediate* growth is to be anticipated under amendments to the Social Security Act in 1946 (see Chapter XVIII).

Despite a Federal interest in public education, Federal grants have never grown to more than 2 per cent of the revenues of the public schools. The Federal government has never made any general grants for local education. Here is a gap in the system of Federal grants (see Chapter XXIV).[12]

Experience with Federal grants-in-aid has not been universally favorable. Criticism has been made of the lack of autonomy of the states and local governments in administering these aids. It has been claimed that these units have not been free to spend in the most effective manner the funds granted to them. The common state matching basis of 50 per cent has also been criticized. (In the field of social security grants, the matching basis was modified in August, 1946, along lines proposed by Senator Connally in 1941. See Chapter XVIII.) Such criticisms may be warranted. In spite of them, however, Federal grants-in-aid (in the judgment of the authors) do not appear to have been extended as far as is commensurate with the advantages of such aids. Some of the problems arising in expanding such aids will be discussed in the following chapter.

Tax deductibility as a coordination device. One of the operating devices of fiscal coordination which has received least attention is that of *tax deductibility*. Such deductibility (for most taxes) is permitted in the determination of the tax base—such as taxable net income, in the case of state taxes and in the case of Federal income taxes—except in some state tax jurisdictions (such as New York and California).[13] The operation of such deductibility, particularly reciprocal deductibility, has important

[12] This excludes several billions of dollars which the Federal government will eventually spend for the education of veterans under the "G.I. Act." Nor does it include the large amounts currently being spent for military research—such as expenditures for investigation of the possibilities of atomic energy. It does not include possible appropriations under the Hope-Flannagan Act of 1946. Appropriations had not yet been made to carry out the provisions of this act at time of writing (early 1947). If appropriations are made in 1947, it is probable that around 60 million dollars will be allotted to agricultural research in 1950 for marketing and related fields.

[13] As of 1942, 22 of the 33 states imposing individual income taxes permitted full Federal deduction. Two others limited it and 9 denied it completely.

effects. Not only does it reduce the total amount of two taxes of the same type which may be due, but in the case of net income taxes, it reduces the differentials between tax liability in a non-income-tax state and in an income-tax state. Furthermore, it avoids the possibility that the two taxes together will represent confiscation of income. An illustration of the effects of deductibility upon effective tax rates is given in Table 40. It may be observed from the table that mutual deductibility makes the effect of the combined taxes of the two units approximate the effect of one unit levying a heavier tax.

TABLE 40[14]

Percentages of Taxable Income Taken by Hypothetical Federal and State Income Taxes (Each Assumed to Be a Flat Percentage of the Amount Taxable Under It) Under Various Assumptions as to Deductibility.[a]

| Assumption | Percentage of taxable income (*i.e.*, excess of income over exemptions and "deductions" other than income taxes) taken by: | | | | | |
	Federal Tax at 80%	State Tax at 15%	Combination	Federal Tax at 40%	State Tax at 10%	Combination
1. Neither tax deductible in calculating the other..	80.0%	15.0%	95.0%	40.0%	10.0%	50.0%
2. State tax deductible in calculating Federal tax but not *vice versa*	68.0	15.0	83.0	36.0	10.0	46.0
3. Federal tax deductible in calculating state tax but not *vice versa*	80.0	3.0	83.0	40.0	6.0	46.0
4. Each tax deductible in calculating the other........	77.27	3.41	80.68	37.50	6.25	43.75
5. State tax credited on Federal tax...	65.0	15.0	80.0	30.0	10.0	40.0

[a] Since the Federal tax law permits deduction of state income taxes, assumptions 2 and 4 reflect actual situations in the majority of states, while 1 and 3 are unrealistic except in so far as taxpayers' total deductions including state taxes fall short of the 10 per cent of adjusted gross income (or $500 maximum) allowed as "presumptive deduction" under Federal tax.

[14] Based on "Federal, State, and Local Fiscal Relations," pages 438-39.

Use of supplementary tax rates as a coordination device.   Another proposal for intergovernmental fiscal coordination is that smaller units—such as local and state governments—be permitted to apply supplementary rates to taxes levied by larger units—such as the Federal government and state governments.   Such a method of coordination—like that of separation of resources— would reduce administrative costs and resources involved in tax collection.   To the extent that it is used, this method of coordination would eliminate diversity in the definition of tax bases.[15] Moreover, it would provide increased flexibility for the taxing unit which applied its supplementary rates to a tax administered and collected by larger units of government, as in the case of state income-tax rates appended to the Federal tax.   Even indirect coercion of smaller units would not be involved, contrary to the case of Federal tax credits for unemployment compensation.   Supplementary local rates to taxes of central governments are used considerably in some other countries.

Use of joint tax administration as a coordination device.   Still another device of coordination which has proved valuable and may develop more in the future is *joint administration* of the same kind of tax at the Federal-state level and among the states. Federal-state cooperation has been increasingly useful in the field of income taxation.   While Congress did not specifically provide for the inspection of Federal income-tax returns by the states until 1926, the Commissioner of Taxation in Massachusetts was using such inspection as early as 1920.   More recently, the Bureau of Internal Revenue has been willing to supply the states with an automatic transcript of Federal audit and delinquency action at a very low cost.   Under this service, in one year, Kentucky received the equivalent of 20 auditors' work at a total cost representing the salary of one investigator for less than one month.

In general, the income-tax states have built their systems of auditing returns around the availability of Federal information. Yet a few of the states do not yet avail themselves of what is a very low administrative cost for this particular tax.   Techniques of cooperation have been more highly developed and applied in the field of liquor taxation than anywhere else.   The Fiscal Relations Report indicates that informal cooperation between state

[15] Past experience, however, has not made it possible to produce a uniform Federal-state income tax return.

and Federal officials in this field has been developing, to the mutual satisfaction of both Federal and state administrators. Future possibilities of joint administration are probably best in the field of death taxation. Here, as we have seen, the present crediting device might be so altered that separate state administration of death taxes might gradually disappear.

Instances in which the Federal government makes use of state tax data are not as important, but as of 1942, they included: (1) in connection with excises on dealers, Federal agents were supplied with lists of licensed dealers, (2) lists of corporations were supplied by some states, especially New York and Delaware, (3) the states were providing credit slips on every taxpayer contributing to state unemployment taxes. These were matched with Federal returns to uncover any delinquencies.[16]

Interstate Fiscal Relations

In the earlier chapters devoted to discussion of business taxation and to taxation of personal income and commodities, some aspects of interstate fiscal relations were raised. Particularly important are the trade barriers raised by state excise taxes and the discrimination in taxing which results from overlapping taxation—two or more states taxing one individual's income while the incomes of other individuals are taxed by only one state.

Interstate trade barriers result from such taxes as state taxes and license fees on interstate motor carriers, the excises on oleomargarine, liquor taxes, use taxes, and possible multiple state taxes on certain kinds of personal property. These devices tend to reduce the flow of trade between the states.

Overlapping taxation of business enterprises. Overlapping taxation occurs in the taxation of enterprises that do business in more than one state (see Chapters XI and XXIV). Such enterprises are subject to business taxes of all the states in which they operate. Such taxation must recognize that not all of interstate corporate business is done in one state and must allocate some reasonable portion of corporate income or capital stock to a particular state, as determined by the courts.

A variety of allocation formulas are used by taxing states, although corporate managements generally have an opportunity to work out some reasonable allocation with state tax officials,

[16] See "Federal, State, and Local Fiscal Relations," page 144.

if they consider that the tax results given by a particular formula are unfair. For an interstate corporation, all such formulas are certain to be arbitrary to some extent. It is quite possible that a particular interstate corporation will find that it is subject to taxes by all taxing states on a base of more than 100 per cent of its total net income or capital stock in a given year.

Use of interstate taxes to favor home industry. Liquor taxation is a good illustration of attempts by various states to encourage intra-state industry. States were given a free hand in liquor regulation and taxation by the 21st Amendment. As of 1941, 43 states made use of liquor-tax legislation not only for the purpose of regulation, but also to protect intra-state industry, to retaliate against discrimination by other states and to favor the products of some states against the products of others.[17]

Another illustration of state taxation to encourage home industry is the special taxes falling on oleomargarine. Just before the last war, about half the states imposed margarine taxes: taxes included licenses on manufacturers, dealers, and "importers," and specific, state excise taxes of 5 to 15 cents a pound. There was considerable variance between states in this type of special taxation. Some southern states impose excise taxes only on margarines which use oils produced outside the state. Nebraska, Minnesota, and Wyoming levy an excise tax only on margarine not having a minimum of fats derived from animal sources. Testimony before the Temporary National Investigating Committee a few years ago indicated that some of these taxes have been designed to destroy consumption of margarine. A consequence of the protective legislation has been that the taxes yield relatively little tax revenue—a characteristic of an effective protective tariff.

Interstate taxation and regulation of motor vehicles. Special state taxes on motor vehicles doing business in more than one state are common. They are so diverse as to almost defy description. Sometimes they take the form of an extra license fee; sometimes they are levied on the basis of ton-miles of travel within the state during a certain period, generally a year. Extra taxation has been rationalized on the ground that a motor vehicle from outside the state increases costs of highway maintenance

[17] See Thomas S. Green, Jr., "The Liquor Tax as an Interstate Tax Barrier," *Journal of Commerce and Commercial*, Vol. 187, No. 14 (January 24, 1941).

within the state. The extra taxes, however, are frequently more than enough to cover such extra costs. In addition, some states have specifications as to such factors as maximum over-all length and gross weight of various vehicles. A result of such specifications is that it has been legally impossible for certain types of trucks to pass through some states.[18] To implement their restrictions, many of the states during the thirties developed what have been called "ports of entry." At these points any given commercial vehicle could be checked for required taxes, load, length, width, and other factors before being allowed to enter the state.

To facilitate war traffic, the Federal government called a conference of state officials in 1942 and obtained a wartime agreement that an effort would be made to obtain state-wide uniformity in restrictions on length, load carried, and so forth. This agreement was ratified by all the states in June, 1942. However, it did not cover the field of interstate taxation. Some of the states had, in 1946, returned to their own heterogeneous controls over length, extent of load, and other operating factors, but most of the states were continuing the arrangements for standardization agreed upon in 1942.

A special problem of inequitable multiple taxation in the field of motor-vehicle taxation has arisen from changes in operator's state of residence during the course of a given year. Even if such a change occurred only once, an individual may be required to buy two sets of license plates and two driver's licenses during one year.

Interstate taxation of insurance companies. State insurance taxes are imposed by all 48 states. Such taxes are usually levied as a fixed percentage (most commonly 2 per cent) of gross premiums received in a given state in a given year. Provisions are often made for the greater taxation of companies chartered outside the state in case another state imposes higher rates on companies chartered in the given state. Such potential retaliation or provisions for reciprocity in treatment were used (as of 1942) by all except six states.

Interstate problems in personal-income taxation. Problems of overlapping personal income taxes are numerous. They arise

---

[18] Thus, in 1941, the maximum length of trucks permitted varied from 30 feet in Kentucky to 85 feet in four states, and the maximum gross weight permitted varied from 18,000 pounds in Kentucky to 120,000 pounds in Rhode Island.

partly from the judicial acceptance of the income-tax base as being both in the state of residence and in the state where the income is received. Thus, a state income-tax payer in Wisconsin is subject to Wisconsin tax only on income received within the state, but in Delaware (and many other states) he is subject not only to a tax on income earned within Delaware, but also on income earned in any other state (including Wisconsin). The result is inequitable double taxation. There are problems of interstate tax competition, which result in an undetermined amount of migration. There are also legal problems resulting from the fact that some states—such as Illinois—have found it impossible to levy personal income taxes, under the common uniformity rule in state constitutions.

Interlocal Fiscal Relations

The relationships between fiscal units at levels below the state level have not been extensively analyzed, partly because of the multiplicity of such units and the variability of relationships between local units, and partly because there has not been a great deal of such cooperation. However, some of the techniques which have been worked out appear to be fairly satisfactory and might be utilized with advantage at the higher levels of government.

County governments, municipalities, and school districts rely essentially upon the same tax for revenue—the property tax. Although the property tax is not the best of all possible taxes, the principle of several units, using the same source with some success could be extended to other kinds of taxes—the personal income tax, for example.

When pupils from one school district are taught in another district—an event which occurs frequently where a school has been closed and the pupils are sent to another school—the one district transfers funds to the other district for the services rendered. Similar cooperation between counties in the performance of other functions—road maintenance, recording, tax assessment, and protection of life and property, for example—could result in certain savings without county consolidation. Although consolidation perhaps could bring more marked improvements, the political difficulties in effecting consolidation may delay it for many years.

CHAPTER XXIV

APPRAISAL OF TECHNIQUES TO IMPROVE INTERGOVERNMENTAL FISCAL RELATIONS

IN THE previous chapter, we outlined the problems of intergovernmental fiscal relations, and concluded that some problems inevitably arise in a Federal system with many taxing and spending units. We also indicated some of the devices which have been proposed, and sometimes used, in order to minimize the problems. It is the purpose of this chapter to appraise the various devices of intergovernmental fiscal relations and to consider the future of these techniques. The criteria which we shall use to appraise these devices are: (1) Their expected effectiveness in achieving improved allocation of resources *within* the public economy. This can come about through reducing costs of collecting a given amount of taxes and administering funds for their collection. (2) Their effect upon resource allocation *between* the public and private economy. Improved allocation implies increasing the relative level of public services in the relatively lower (per capita) income areas through aids from other areas. (3) Their contribution to the maintenance of full employment.

Logically, any form of fiscal aid from larger to smaller units of government recognizes the fiscal limitations of smaller units in the performance of one or more government functions which are of more than local interest. Desirable emphasis on *extra-local* benefits may be subordinated in the case of tax-sharing, where supplementation of total local tax revenue may be the ostensible purpose. Although the principle of equalization of costs and opportunities among smaller units of government may not be specifically recognized, the collection of tax revenue and its distribution over a state or over the nation does involve some equalization. The tax revenue of larger units of government comes in considerable part from those people (and areas) where financial ability to pay taxes is relatively great, even though distribution of tax funds is on a per capita basis.

Separation of Revenue Sources

Historically, the oldest device of intergovernmental fiscal coordination which has been proposed is separation of revenue sources. In practice, separation of revenue sources by itself has not been found very useful. As has been indicated, something like a separation of sources in state-local taxation has been accomplished since 1900, with the withdrawal of most states from a significant amount of property taxation. Local units of government, left primarily to the unpopular general property tax (imposed subject to various restrictions in the various states), have found an increasing discrepancy between their tax resources and the growing volume of public services which they have been expected to perform.

This coordination device is often used with others. The increased fiscal aid to local units of government since 1900 suggests one significant aspect of separation of sources: such separation has generally been connected with one or more of the other devices for fiscal coordination. The increasing dependence of localities on state and Federal governments for fiscal assistance further emphasizes a point made in Chapter XX: that local units of government need to recast the property tax and to seek additional sources of tax revenue.

Separation of revenue sources offers little to recommend it as a major fiscal device. Units of government would have to rely upon their own sources of revenue. Consequently, the level of public services in the relatively lower (per capita) income areas is unlikely to be raised. In addition, leaving state and local governments dependent upon their own sources is likely to cause them to act perversely so far as stabilizing markets is concerned.

Tax-Sharing

Sharing-of-taxes presents a special set of problems. The basis of distribution of shared taxes among various government units must necessarily be presumptive, but must also be relatively simple and understandable. Sometimes tax receipts can be shared on the basis of local expenditures for taxed goods and services. For example, in the sharing of motor-vehicle taxes, relative purchases of motor fuel and registrations of motor vehicles could be used as a basis for distribution. Sometimes source allocation is relatively difficult, however—as in the case of net income taxes. The simplest type of tax-sharing occurs when part of the proceeds of a centrally collected tax are turned back to localities without specific provision as to the ways in which the funds shall be used.

At times, states have shared taxes for particular reasons or purposes—such as replacing local funds lost through systems of property-tax credits or exemptions, assuming financial responsibility for the servicing of highway debts (payment of interest and principal), or providing funds to cover part of the cost of welfare programs (payment of old-age assistance from state (and Federal) funds). Where shared-taxes are tied up with payments designed to cover part, or all, of the cost of a given governmental function, they shade into grants-in-aid.

Shared-taxes may improve the revenue position of local governments. Even though a tax is shared proportionately to estimated collections in various localities, some taxes that are collected by higher units and shared with lower ones could not have been levied by the local units. Sharing-of-taxes has the advantage of permitting taxes to be collected by a single unit of government. Some saving in resources is thus effected.

However, tax-sharing does not appear to offer a major contribution to the solution of the fiscal problems of local government units. One weakness of shared-taxes lies in their lack of equalization between local units. Some local units of government will be provided with more tax revenue than they can spend efficiently, while others still will not have enough to maintain local services at a high standard.[1]

The rule which has been followed in distributing most shared-taxes among the local governments might be called "distribution according to contribution." For example, if a state is sharing a tax with the counties, and if the tax receipts from County A are twice the receipts from County B, County A's share in tax revenue is usually twice that of County B. The local governments with the small tax bases are thus required, in practice, to continue to

[1] See Harold M. Groves, *Financing Government*, revised edition, page 458, for a compact statement of the various conditions which need to be fulfilled in order to make tax-sharing reasonably satisfactory as a fiscal device.

rely largely upon tax collections from their constituents. If this principle of sharing were abandoned and "distribution according to need" could be the rule, tax-sharing would closely resemble equalization grants-in-aid.

In addition, sharing taxes by states (the Federal government shares no taxes) will not in itself reduce the fiscal perversity of state governments—a tendency already noted.

Grants-in-Aid

Grants-in-aid, both state and Federal, have undergone a rapid development. These developments have centered around (1) Federal grants to states for purposes of stimulating highway development, (2) Federal grants to the states under the Social Security Act of 1935, (3) state grants to local units of government to help pay the cost of public elementary and secondary education, and (4) Federal grants and loans to localities to aid in the construction of public works, especially during the period 1933-1939.[2] The types of recent Federal and state grants-in-aid were indicated in the preceding chapter.

Grants-in-aid have generally had one or both of two purposes: (1) to stimulate some specified public activity by a smaller unit of government (a good example is Federal highway grants), (2) to equalize the financial ability of smaller units of government to carry on a specified public activity. Grants for this purpose are called *equalization* grants. Grants-in-aid have been distinguished from shared-taxes in that they represent an appropriation for a specific function of government, rather than funds to supplement locally raised funds for all functions of government. The two devices of intergovernmental coordination shade into each other. Certain common bases for distinction of shared-taxes and grants-in-aid were indicated in Chapter XXIII.

Grants-in-aid, in our estimation, constitute the most useful single device for intergovernmental fiscal coordination. They do not confine the services of a local unit to those that can be financed from the unit's own sources of funds. To the extent that they are made by the Federal government, they can be counter-cyclical in their effect. They do not need to be secured always

---

[2] In addition, during the years 1936-1943, the Federal government directly administered the expenditure of 11.2 billion dollars, under the Works Projects (Progress) Administration, to assist localities in coping with problems of unemployment.

from tax sources.   During periods of deflation, a part of the funds
for such grants can come from nontax sources—direct money
issue, for example.

Desired characteristics of future expansion of grants-in-aid.
Certain characteristics are desirable for the future development
of the most satisfactory system of intergovernmental aids.   (1)
Such aids should come increasingly from the Federal government and should not necessarily be dependent upon tax revenue.
Rather, the amount of tax revenue which the Federal government
raises should be a function of such general fiscal ends as maintaining full employment.

(2) There should be some, but relatively little (Federal),
control over the expenditure of funds which are granted.   It
is desirable that certain standards be set up and enforced as
a basis for making grants-in-aid, however.   There are working illustrations in public grants for highways and for education.
In the highway field, the Public Roads Administration (formerly
the Bureau of Public Roads) has required since 1921 that plans
and designs for the expenditure of its funds should be approved
before the funds are granted.   In many state educational grants,
it is required that certain local levies shall be made to meet part
or all of the cost of some standard program if state aid is to be
obtained.   The establishment of such standards of performance,
rather than direct interference in the expenditure of the funds,
constitutes adequate control.[3]

(3) There is further need for the recognition of the equalization factor in the granting of Federal or state funds.   Such a
factor has not been specifically included in Federal grants and
has been recognized only to a limited extent in state grants.

In the past, grants-in-aid have been distributed largely in
relation to fiscal ability to finance local functions from local
sources of revenue.   Thus, school districts with highest per pupil
taxable valuations may be given the largest grants, or grants for
highways may be made directly in accordance with the existing
development of the highway system in the locality.

The result of such a distribution pattern is the return to each
local unit funds that were collected from the constituents of that
unit.   Little over-all improvement in the level of public services

---

[3] Very detailed standards, however, are frequently considered (by the units of
government receiving Federal grants) as interference.

is likely to follow from such a pattern—except in so far as the kinds of taxes employed by the state cannot be used by local units and an increase in the total of state and local tax collections is the result. The units which have the largest tax bases are likely to substitute grants-in-aid for locally collected revenues The units which have the lowest tax bases receive relatively small grants and cannot expand the level of their services very markedly.

Opposition to distribution of grants in accordance with some principle other than the ability of local units to finance their own functions grows out of opposition to redistributing income from the richer to the poorer areas. Income redistribution, however, need not be the only issue in determining the bases for grants. Because of the interdependence between localities, the taxpayers of the richer areas have a stake in improving the level of public services in the poorer areas. The amount of income transferred from the richer to the poorer localities could be made equal to the amount which the taxpayers of the higher-income areas were willing to pay to increase the quality of public services in the poorer areas. If there is no such willingness on the part of the citizens of one area to pay for higher standards in other areas, the grant-in-aid has little place in the fiscal system.

When funds are paid on an equalization basis, the object is to underwrite some minimum opportunity for the residents of the receiving unit—the guarantee of some minimum opportunity for public education or for nutrition, for instance. A good example is found in some state equalization grants for public education, which require some standard (defined) participation by local units of government. Under such grants, not all local school districts need or can qualify for state aid.

The Fiscal Relations Report has pointed out that annual Federal equalization grants for public education of at least 200-300 million dollars could have been justified in 1940. A larger sum probably is justifiable now (1947). Such grants might reasonably be distributed inversely to per capita incomes in the various states, which varied in 1945 from $445 in Mississippi to $1,595 in New York.[4] Low-income states, centering largely in the south-

---

[4] Source: *The Survey of Current Business*, August, 1946, page 16. The amounts reported excluded Federal civilian compensation, and that of military personnel stationed outside the country.

east, also have a proportionately large share of the school population. Their relatively large school-tax burden might also be taken into consideration in allocation of Federal aid.

The Report also suggested that distribution of a Federal equalization grant might be conditional on reasonably efficient (in terms of district organization of) local school districts.[5] It recommended that, in the field of higher education, the Federal government should restore grants to individuals, based on their degree of competence and financial ability. The nearly 100 million dollar budgetary appropriation for the National Youth Administration in 1940 was largely for grants to individuals.

(4) The matching basis for Federal funds should give some consideration to variations in per capita incomes within the various states. In the past, Federal highway grants—the longest continuing grants of substantial size—have been based on three matching elements as a prerequisite for obtaining Federal aid. These three factors are included in the matching formula: area, population, and miles of post roads. The formula, which was not exclusively used during a few years of the middle thirties, has tended to favor large, sparsely populated areas. It has penalized the people living in relatively small states with low per capita incomes. It has been much harder for these states to raise funds which are required for matching. In the future, distribution of Federal highway funds should be partially weighted inversely to per capita income. This does not mean that users of the highways from other states should not pay additional amounts which bear some relationship to their use of highways within the state.

An alternative basis of matching in the field of public welfare which has received some attention, and was partially adopted in 1946, was a plan for variable Federal grants, proposed by Senator Connally in 1940.[6] Under this proposal, matching requirements under various categories of the Social Security Act would be as follows: the Federal government would provide $10 of the first $15 a month for eligible recipients; 50 per cent from $15 to $25; and $33\frac{1}{3}$ per cent from $25 to $40. Such a proposal has a num-

---

[5] It also favored elimination of existing discrepancies between expenditures for education of Negroes and whites and the use of Federal grants to aid in new school construction.

[6] See the "Connally Amendment" proposal, Senate Bill 3030, 76th Congress, January 4, 1940. Refer to Chapter XVIII.

ber of advantages: (a) A strong Federal interest in minimum standards can be indicated by high matching proportions, which can be reduced as Federal interest may decline. (b) More state money would be raised for matching at the higher over-all proportions. (c) More state money would be matched by the Federal government at the higher over-all proportions in the poor than in the rich states, thus securing a degree of interstate equalization. (d) A considerable degree of intra-state equalization would be secured, since the maximum Federal aid, relative to state expenditures, could be obtained by paying equal grants to all recipients within each category.[7]

(5) The Federal government should assume further responsibility for public welfare expenditures by aiding states and localities with grants for direct relief. This is partly an equalization problem. The Fiscal Relations Report indicates that the great majority of low (per capita) income states show relatively low figures for state and local relief as a percentage of total state and local funds applied for welfare expenditures. This situation in turn is attributed in part to the fact that Federal matching grants for social security purposes have tended to distort the budgets of these states away from general relief, in order to meet matching requirements.[8]

(6) Grants-in-aid should be devoted primarily to helping to finance expenditures where the extra-local element of benefit is especially clear; such as education, highways, and public welfare. It should be recognized, however, that, as our economy becomes more and more interdependent, the idea of local benefit will come to be less and less important and the logical role of grants-in-aid will continue to expand. This may be illustrated in the field of police protection. Not only have Federal and state governments undertaken direct activities in this traditionally local field, but varying percentages of local property are owned by persons residing outside the community or even outside the state.

The principal limitation of grants-in-aid (and of shared-taxes) is that such fiscal aid may tend to undermine local sense of financial responsibility and promote wasteful spending locally. With a continued growth in intergovernmental fiscal aids, such devel-

[7] See "Federal, State, and Local Fiscal Relations," page 551, for a more complete statement of possible advantages under this proposed plan.
[8] See "Federal, State, and Local Fiscal Relations," pages 548-549.

opments are indeed possible. These developments do not need
to occur, if some minimum local rate of tax contribution is required as a prerequisite for state or Federal aids. Furthermore,
grants-in-aid should carry with them some degree of control
over the local expenditure of funds, as we have suggested. Intergovernmental fiscal aid, preferably in the form of grants-in-aid,
will continue to grow, as an increasing range of public activities
is interpreted as having more than just local significance.

Use of Tax Credits as a Coordination Device

State tax credits against Federal taxes have been employed for
death taxes and unemployment payroll taxes. In the field of
death taxes, however, many states have continued to have their
own supplementary death-tax systems, largely inheritance taxes
rather than independent estate taxes. Furthermore, it was
pointed out in Chapter XVII that the tax credit, still based on
1926 rates, is relatively obsolete. Changes to modernize the
death-tax credit and to keep it current in relation to changing
Federal estate taxes were proposed in that chapter. The other
use of the tax credit which has been made was part of 1935
Federal legislation in the field of social security. This act provided that states providing for unemployment compensation satisfactory to the Social Security Board should be entitled to a 90
per cent credit on the payroll taxes provided under the act. A
result was the prompt enactment of unemployment compensation
acts by all the 48 states. Costs of state unemployment-compensa-
tion administration are paid for by the Federal government out
of the 10 per cent of the tax revenue which it gets. Grants for
such costs, however, have never exceeded 64.7 per cent of
Federal tax receipts under this portion of the Social Security
Act.[9] There are those who contend that the credit should be
increased to 100 per cent of Federal tax receipts with the states
bearing part of the costs of unemployment administration.

Appraisal of the use of tax credits. It has been proposed on
various occasions that the tax-credit system should be extended
further to include corporate and personal income taxes levied
by the states, and to the stock-transfer tax (at present limited to
the Federal government and to New York state). In considering
extension of the tax-credit system for income taxes, it must be

[9] See *Treasury Bulletin*, August, 1946, page 12.

considered that several of the states having the largest incomes—such as Texas—are without state income taxes. Furthermore, some of them—Illinois is a good example—have found it impossible to levy state income taxes under their state constitutions. Such a state could, of course, amend its constitution to permit income taxation.[10]

The Fiscal Relations Report concludes that a tax credit for stock-transfer taxes would be undesirable.[11] Not only is the tax fiscally unimportant to the Federal government, but New York is the only state which levies it. A tax credit might induce a number of other states to complicate our tax system further by enacting stock-transfer taxes applicable to transfers made within those particular states. Such taxes logically belong to the Federal government, as stock-transfers involve individuals all over the country. It is recognized that New York state developed such taxes, and an attitude of forbearance on the part of both New York and the Federal government is probably the best fiscal policy which can be followed in the application of this particular tax. The interest of New York in preserving a flourishing stock exchange will probably prevent that taxing jurisdiction from enacting laws which will have a repressive effect on stock transfers, in the event that combined tax laws of New York, other states, and the Federal government appear to be exerting such an effect.

Supplementary Tax Rates as a Coordination Device

Tax students are divided on their appraisal of this particular fiscal device of coordination. The late E. R. A. Seligman was one of its strong advocates.[12] Professor Groves has indicated that further use of this device can be approached gradually and finds it desirable in such areas as income and death taxation.[13] On the other hand, W. J. Shultz has found several objections to the use of tax supplements. In the field of state-local taxation, he has argued that only a few communities would find substantial

[10] Just as the Federal death-tax credits (established in 1924 and 1926) encouraged states to levy death taxes, an income-tax credit might induce Illinois to amend its constitution to enable it to levy an income tax.

[11] See the Report, page 537.

[12] See E. R. A. Seligman, "The Fiscal Outlook and the Coordination of Public Revenues," New York University Symposium, *Current Problems in Public Finance*, Chicago: Commerce Clearing House, 1933.

[13] See Harold M. Groves, *Financing Government*, revised edition, page 458.

benefits from such tax supplements: those communities in which the supplements for income-tax and death-tax purposes did not induce residents to change their domiciles, or in which a sales-tax supplement did not encourage residents to go outside the specially taxed area to make purchases. He has doubted the feasibility of using the device in the field of Federal-state taxation also. Income-tax supplements, he feels, would have to be levied on a residence rather than a source basis to make tax supplements administratively feasible, and he argues that any system of state supplements would have to be moderate, in order not to intensify the whole field of interstate tax competition.[14]

Further local or state supplements to state or Federal taxes might be usable in a few fields of taxation—such as personal-income and excise taxation. Like the other devices for fiscal coordination, tax supplements can probably serve only a limited role in intergovernmental fiscal coordination.

Tax Deductibility

Tax deductibility (often reciprocal between state and Federal governments) as a coordination device has not been sufficiently emphasized. Deductibility acts as a tax credit, although not explicitly. One result of deductibility is that the total amount of two taxes of a given type levied by two taxing units is reduced and cannot confiscate an individual's entire income even though both tax rates may be high. This result was noted in Table 40 in the preceding chapter.

Two aspects of tax deductibility have seldom been pointed out. It reduces sharply the difference in tax rates for taxpayers as between states which have and which do not have income taxes. This acts to check tendencies to migrate in order to reduce taxes. Further, Federal tax deductibility for state tax purposes operates as an indirect subsidy to the states. In effect, by leaving funds with the states which otherwise might have been collected, the Federal government provides part of the funds for the public and private economies in the states. Mutual deductibility is not characteristic of all state income-tax systems—those of New York and California being among the exceptions. The effect of not permitting deductibility of Federal income taxes for state income-

[14] See W. J. Shultz, *American Public Finance*, 3rd edition, pages 732-33 and 758-59.

tax purposes is to make the combined tax slightly higher (with given state rates) than where mutual deductibility is permitted (refer to Table 40, Chapter XXIII). The indirect Federal subsidy to the states is also relatively higher than where mutual deductibility is permitted.

Joint Administration as a Coordination Device

We noted in the preceding chapter that Federal-state coordination in the joint administration of particular taxes has been successful and might be further extended. Interstate administrative cooperation also has possibilities, not yet fully exploited. This is particularly true in the field of income taxation. State administrators need to exchange information on tax returns submitted by corporations operating in more than one state and to check the relative weight given by interstate corporations to different items—such as tangible property and sales—in formulas of interstate allocation of corporate income. Such checking might serve the purpose of seeing that the various formulas submitted have not been deliberately weighted in such a way as to minimize corporate-tax liabilities in the various states. In addition, the various income-tax states need to move in the direction of uniform allocation formulas for corporation incomes earned in more than one state. Individuals earning income in more than one income-tax state should have the opportunity to deduct taxes paid to states of nonresidence from total taxes paid to the state of residence. This is particularly true if the state of residence makes its income base all income earned in all states, as it may legally do. There must be interstate cooperation in order to have such checks made. Perhaps one of the most desirable developments would be the growth of an interstate clearing house for information. To provide such a clearing house is one of the functions which could be performed by a Federal-State Fiscal Authority. Some analysis of the way in which this authority might be set up and of the functions which it might perform will be examined shortly.

Joint administration reaches its peak in the exercise of authority which might be delegated by the Federal government to the states. Given some assurance that Federal standards will be maintained, the Bureau of Internal Revenue might be willing to delegate some of its tax functions to state tax administrations in the future. In this respect, several other countries have ad-

vanced far beyond our present stage of administrative cooperation. Thus, in Australia, where there is a simpler federal system,
and where both the states and Federal government have had an
income tax (though the states gave up theirs for the period of
World War II), the central government has administered both
its taxes and most of the state taxes in one of the states. In the
other states, the states' governments have administered both
national and state income taxes. Administrative duplication has
been greatly reduced. Professor Haig has reported that the arrangements have justified themselves on the basis of economy
and the stimulation given to uniformity of laws and practices.[15]

A Proposed Federal-State Fiscal Authority[16]

We have observed that none of the fiscal devices for intergovernmental coordination in this country can be labeled as the
"solution," though each may have certain contributions to make.
To administer the continuous operation of our overlapping fiscal
systems in this country really requires some public body, especially selected for the purpose. Through such a body, avenues
of interchange for information could be facilitated, and the results
of various operating devices for fiscal coordination could be appraised. Such a body might be found in a Federal-State Fiscal
Authority.

Continuous cooperation in the field of Federal-state fiscal relations could serve several useful purposes. The number of officials for this proposed authority could be initially limited to
three, and the group could operate under an initial budget of
$150,000 to $200,000, provided jointly by the Federal and state
governments. One member could be appointed by the President, another named by a council of delegates appointed by state
governors, and a third could be named by the two appointed officials. Legislation establishing such an authority could reasonably provide that one of its members should be familiar with the
fiscal affairs of local government units.

Such a group (whose membership might be later expanded)
could be expected to do the following things, among others:

[15] See Robert Murray Haig, "Amalgamated Federal-State Tax Administration in
Australia," *Proceedings of the National Tax Association, 1937*, 1938.
[16] The proposals summarized here are suggested in "Federal, State, and Local
Fiscal Relations," pages 149-51.

1. To promote close cooperation between state and Federal administrators toward securing joint administration of selected overlapping taxes. Joint administration of net-income taxes, business taxes, and death taxes appears to offer the greatest possibilities.

2. To promote interstate cooperation. Such cooperation might be speeded up in the case of interstate reciprocity of taxation for commercial vehicles doing business in more than one state; for the agreement on some relatively uniform method of allocating among the various states the income of corporations doing business in more than one state; for reciprocity in taxing individual income which arises in more than one income-tax state.

3. To act as a clearing house for Federal payments, in lieu of local and state property taxes, on Federally-owned property. Such payments have often been made in the past, but without the development of any consistent principles underlying such payments.

4. To act as a clearing house for complaints relative to Federal payments in lieu of local and state property taxes and for data and complaints regarding the use of state taxes and other instrumentalities as trade barriers.

5. To conduct research in such fields as (a) costs of tax administration, including costs of taxpayer compliance, (b) effects on interstate business firms of the various formulas for the allocation of taxable income among the states, (c) effects of state taxation on tendencies of business firms to migrate from one state to another in order to reduce the load of taxation. Relatively little is known about any of these important aspects of taxation.

6. To create public interest in intergovernmental fiscal relations.

7. To distribute among the states information on Federal taxes and economic trends as they affect the states.

8. To promote better governmental reporting, accounting, and statistics. Particularly in some local and state taxing jurisdictions, fiscal information is either unavailable, or is presented in a manner which is incomplete and unintelligible except to a few people interested in fiscal information.

The impression should not be given that agencies of informal cooperation do not exist at the present time. The considerable amount of cooperation among Federal and state tax administrators has already been indicated. The Constitution provides for the use of interstate compacts, upon approval by Congress, but in more than 150 years, relatively few of these have been made in the field of taxation. Something has been accomplished by reciprocal arrangements among the states whereby each agrees not to levy a certain tax (rate) if another state does not do so. Such agreements have been especially frequent in the fields of income taxation, motor-vehicle taxation, death taxation, and insurance taxation. Important voluntary associations interested in intergovernmental fiscal coordination have developed. The National Tax Association, the Council of State Governments, the Tax Administrators' Association, and the Municipal Finance Officers' Association are examples. The recommendations of existing organizations and arrangements might have a greater probability of receiving serious consideration if there were a Federal-State Fiscal Authority.

There are certain specific recommendations of the Fiscal Relations Report which would fall within the general framework of the proposed Federal-State Fiscal Authority already outlined. Among these are: (1) Promote high-quality governmental reporting by all units of government. (2) Initiate a thorough study of the costs of taxpayer compliance and of administration. (3) Renew efforts to develop a uniform income-tax return for purposes of Federal and state taxes. Such efforts have been made before, but have proved unsuccessful. They imply willingness of states to accept the allocation of income either on the basis of residence or of source.[17] (4) Encourage additional collaboration of state and local units of government with the Federal government relative to the further expansion of Federal aid. The operation of a Federal-State Fiscal Authority would provide a desired mechanism for cooperative collaboration rather than expansion through dictation from above, as is now likely to be the impression. (5) To direct specific, continuous attention to the problems of minimizing interstate barriers to trade. Here the Fiscal Authority could make effective use of studies already made[18] and further stimulate interest in a problem about which much was said and some things done in the years immediately preceding World War II.

[17] W. J. Shultz has held that only the latter method of income allocation would prove acceptable politically and administratively, but this has not yet been conclusively determined.

[18] Such as *Interstate Trade Barriers*, Council of State Governments, Chicago, Ill., 1941.

Solving Problems of Interstate Fiscal Relations

Relatively little progress has been made toward securing greater fiscal cooperation between the states. Each state must look largely to its own sources for tax revenue, and no state can force another state to abandon a tax unless that tax is unconstitutional (as would be a specific state tax on imports). One of the keys to solving some of the problems appears to lie in greater centralization of taxation with the Federal government and expansion of Federal grants-in-aid to the states.

The Council of State Governments is one of the organizations which have been attempting to reduce interstate trade barriers, secure greater uniformity in taxing, and improve in general the level of state cooperation in nonfiscal matters. The Council is only an advisory body, however. It can point out to the states the implications of policies which are being followed, but it cannot make policy itself.

Even achievement of a large measure of state cooperation with the proposed Federal-State Fiscal Authority probably is not sufficient to solve many important problems of interstate and local relations. Any fundamental solution to the problems of interstate tax barriers which result from special state taxes and restrictions may require an amendment to the Federal Constitution which would specifically prohibit the use of state taxes and regulations as barriers to trade (specifying the major taxes and regulations which would be regarded as barriers). In the absence of such an amendment, some steps can still be taken to minimize the complicated problem of interstate multiple taxation and regulation.

Reciprocal arrangements between states. An immediate attack can be launched to solve the problems posed by interstate taxation of motor vehicles, businesses (such as insurance companies), and personal and corporate income, through the working out of reciprocal agreements between states—agreements which would reduce the extent of multiple taxation.

There is full reciprocity among the states in the acceptance of the license plates of passenger cars from other states, although (as of 1942) 13 states required passenger cars from other states to obtain visitors' permits. As of 1942, six adjoining states in the far west had entered into liberal bilateral reciprocity agreements governing freedom from extra taxes on commercial vehicles from the states concerned. Michigan had worked out a reciprocal agreement with Indiana, Illinois, and Ohio. In addition to nation-wide uniformity in the regulation of sizes and loads secured by the Federal government during the war, the American Association of State Highway Officials had worked out and promoted a uniform regulatory statute which (as of 1942) had been accepted by 18 states.

In the taxation of insurance companies, some state laws already include provisions which automatically call for reciprocity and for retaliation. Several of the personal-income-tax states allow individuals credit for income taxes paid in other states. In most of the personal-income-tax states, there is also provision for exchange of secret information from income-tax returns.

Additional arrangements which need to be made between states in the taxation and regulation of motor vehicles include: (1) extension of reciprocity in the treatment of commercial vehicles (principally trucks and busses), and (2) institution of interstate credits under which taxes paid in the first state (of an individual changing residence during a given year) would be credited against taxes paid in another.[19]

It has already been indicated that for corporations doing business in more than one state, any given state is judicially required to make an allocation of the corporate tax base which will allocate to it no more than its reasonable share of the income of the corporation's capital stock for purposes of taxation. What is reasonable may be determined by conferences between tax administrators and corporate managements, but generally some type of allocation formula is provided for use. The National Tax Association has repeatedly proposed that such allocation be determined by a fractional formula made up of three factors: payrolls, tangible property, and gross sales, each of which would be given equal weight in the final result (the so-called "Massachusetts" formula). Despite this proposal, there were 16 diverse formulas of income allocation being used in 1942. Among

---

[19] A few states, such as Maryland, have a "title tax" in addition to a regular registration tax. Where transfer of residence to another state occurs from Maryland, the new state of residence could reasonably credit total taxes due with all taxes paid in Maryland.

these, the three-factor formula given above was most widely used, and it is proposed that this formula should be extended and made uniform for all the states. One suggested duty of the proposed Federal-State Fiscal Authority would be to facilitate uniformity in the use of state formulas.

Deductibility of income taxes—particularly deductibility of state taxes for purposes of determining Federal taxable income—has proved a useful device for reducing multiple taxation. Probably the most constructive possibilities in the reduction of overlapping state income taxes are the further expansion of reciprocal agreements among the states not to tax the income secured outside a given state, provided other states accord the same treatment to income received in those states, and the deduction of taxes paid in State *A* from total tax liability incurred by a resident of State *B* to State *B*. Since income taxes are one of the taxes affecting consumer welfare least adversely in an otherwise regressive state-local tax structure, states should remain in the income-tax field, while cooperating with the Federal government in the further refinement of Federal income taxes. Such developments should be accompanied by continued expansion of Federal grants-in-aid.

Minimize state protection of particular products. Without Federal action to reduce or eliminate the freedom of the states to regulate and tax the use of liquor under powers granted by the 21st Amendment, a limited amount of action can be anticipated toward greater uniformity among the states. It is true that such an agency as the Council of State Governments may provide current information on the effects of varied state taxing and regulatory practices, but the information provided through the Council becomes available to a limited group of state officials, not to consumers generally.

Assuming the provision of current information on the taxation of butter substitutes (mainly margarine), the prospects are brighter for greater uniformity in state laws. For one thing, most people making purchases of consumer goods are purchasers of butter or butter substitutes. In the case of both butter substitutes and of liquor, it is possible that rising consumer demand will result in market situations where private firms may consider it economically unprofitable to seek continuance of existing protective taxes against butter substitutes and liquor consumption. Pressure for the reduction of punitive taxation on these products will likely occur much later in the case of liquor products than in the case of butter substitutes, however.

Provision of information to the states. Although it is not difficult to say that there should be expanded cooperation between the states in handling fiscal problems, it is difficult to point out how such cooperation can be brought about. Perhaps expansion of work like that accomplished by the Council of State Governments is the most practicable way for key state officials to see the potential benefits of extended reciprocal agreements.

SELECTED READINGS

1. Council of State Governments, *Interstate Trade Barriers*, Chicago: Council of State Governments, 1941.
2. "Federal, State, and Local Fiscal Relations," Washington, D. C.: Senate Document 69, 78th Congress, 1st Session, 1943.
3. Graves, Mark and Edmonds, F. S., "Report of Committee on Fiscal Relationships of Federal and State Governments," pages 161-170, *Proceedings of the National Tax Association, 1934*, Washington, D. C., 1935.
4. Green, Thomas S., Jr., "The Liquor Tax as an Interstate Trade Barrier," *Journal of Commerce and Commercial*, January, 1941.
5. Groves, Harold M., *Financing Government*, Chapter 21, revised edition, New York: Henry Holt & Co., Inc., 1946.
6. Haig, Robert Murray, "Amalgamated Federal-State Tax Administration in Australia," *Proceedings of the National Tax Association, 1937*, Washington, D. C., 1938.
7. Seligman, E. R. A., "The Fiscal Outlook and the Coordination of Public Revenues," New York University Symposium, *Current Problems in Public Finance*, Chicago: Commerce Clearing House, Inc., 1933.
8. Shultz, W. J., *American Public Finance*, Chapters 19 and 20, 3rd edition, New York: Prentice-Hall, Inc., 1942.
9. United States Treasury Department, *Treasury Bulletin*, August, 1946, Washington, D. C.

10. United States Department of Commerce, *The Survey of Current Business*, August, 1946, Washington, D. C.: United States Government Printing Office.

11. United States Treasury Department, *Annual Report of the Secretary of the Treasury, 1945*, Washington, D. C.

APPENDIX

APPENDIX A

Fuller Explanation of Table I

The first series for government expenditures in the table is for fiscal years, ending June 30 in each year. National income data prior to 1919 are for fiscal years, while data for 1919 and subsequent years refer to calendar years. The series for national product (adjusted) and government expenditures (adjusted) are for calendar years. The adjustments in these two series are the addition of "transfer payments" to the series published in the *Survey of Current Business*.

Current dollars were converted into 1939 dollars by use of an index of changes in the cost of living used by the National Industrial Conference Board. (See its *Economic Almanac, 1944-1945*.) From 1940 on, however, the wartime index used in the income-product reports of the *Survey* was employed. See the *Survey*, April, 1944. An adjustment made in both series on government expenditures was to exclude expenditures for debt retirement. Expenditures for 1943 and subsequent years include "net social security costs," that is, gross payments by social security trust funds less interest paid by the government to these funds.

Changing ratios of public expenditures to national income are only of limited usefulness. For widely separated years, such as 1890, 1913, 1929, and 1940, however, the persistent increase in the ratio of public expenditures to national income may be accepted as indicating that the relative importance of the public economy has been growing. This is particularly true after 1913.

The main reason for introducing an additional series on income–product with which to compare government expenditures is that national product is a more inclusive concept than national income, and is a more adequate indication of our total economic effort. See *Survey*, March, 1942. To put both product and expenditure figures on a comparable basis is impossible for reasons explained in the *Survey*, April, 1943, "The Relation Between Government Expenditures and the Gross Flow of Commodities and Services." Reasonable comparability, however, is obtained by adding current estimates for the value of income simply transferred among the people, though not considered to be a part of national product or of government expenditures for goods and services, to estimates in the *Survey* on "government expenditures for goods and services" and to "national product." (Examples are social security payments, pensions, and direct relief.) These sums have been added back in estimates of adjusted national product and of adjusted government expenditures, for the series beginning in 1929.

In addition to sources not already mentioned, the writers have received help from Marvin Hoffenberg, "Estimates of National Output, Distributed Income, Consumer Spending, Saving and Capital Formation," *Review of Economic Statistics*, May, 1943, and from several other issues of *The Survey of Current Business.*

APPENDIX B

Derivation of Figures Used in Table 2

The bulk of these figures was obtained from *Financing Federal, State and Local Governments, 1941,* Department of Commerce, Bureau of the Census, 1942. A good summary is given on page 52. All figures given below are in millions of dollars.

1. *Protection*, $7,462
    This includes military forces, police, fire, inspection, and payments of military pensions.
2. *Public Assistance and Welfare*, $5,677
    This includes work relief, general relief, other public assistance, institutional expense, costs of benefits and administration under old-age and unemployment insurance, expenditures for health, hospitals, sanitation, and recreation, payments of pensions and of workmen's compensation. The net additions to social security reserves were excluded, contrary to the Census series. Pension payments rather than contributions to pension funds were included, contrary to Census practice also. Federal civil pensions were given in the *Combined Statement of Receipts and Expenditures, 1941,* page 668. Payments under state and local retirement systems, and under workmen's compensation systems were obtained from a study by the Federal Security Agency, Social Security Board for 1941, called *Payments under Selected Social Insurance and Retirement Programs.*
3. *Cost Payments of Government Enterprises and Corporations,* $4,100
    This figure was obtained from *Financing Federal, State, and Local Governments, 1941,* Department of Commerce, Bureau of the Census, 1942, page 84. It includes only net contributions to public service enterprises in the case of territories ($15.4), for lack of more complete information.
4. *Education*, $2,636
    This includes $2,579 for public schools and $57 for libraries.
5. *Transportation*, $2,023
    This includes $1,693 for highways and $330 for waterways and other public transportation.

6. *Interest on Public Debt,* $1,610

This is the closest approximation to cash interest which it was possible to derive. Federal cash interest of $896 for fiscal 1941 was derived from the *Treasury Bulletin* for August, 1941. State and local interest of $512 is an average of $514 for calendar 1940 and $511 for calendar 1941, as given by Commerce Department releases. To these amounts has been added $202 of enterprise interest, the difference between interest of $1,885 on public debt, including enterprise debt, as given on page 74 of the Census study, and of $1,683, as given in the summary excluding enterprises on page 52.

7. *Natural Resources,* $1,442

This includes $1,188 for agriculture and $254 for forests, reclamation, and other resource projects.

8. *General Administrative, Legislative and Judicial,* $1,236

See *Financing Federal, State, and Local Governments, 1941,* Department of Commerce, Bureau of the Census, 1942, page 52.

9. *Miscellaneous and Unspecified Aid,* $423

See *Financing Federal, State, and Local Governments, 1941,* Department of Commerce, Bureau of the Census, 1942, page 52. Includes "unspecified aid" of $203 to local governments not allocable by functions.

10. *Debt Retirement,* $1,843

For the Federal government, this is made up of $65 under established budgetary procedures plus $750 of debt retirement by enterprises and public corporations, exclusive of amounts repaid to the Treasury. For state and local governments, there is included $964 on regular government account, plus $164 on account of public enterprises. No data are available on territorial enterprise.

APPENDIX C

Federal Income-Tax Rate Schedule, 1914 and 1946

I. Normal Tax
  1. In 1914, this was a tax of 1%, levied on taxable net income, after deduction of corporate dividends received from taxable net income.
  2. In 1946, this was a tax of 3%, levied on taxable net income.

II. Surtax

Net Income Subject to Surtax		Rate Per Cent	
Exceeding	*Equaling*	*1914*	*1946*
$ 0	$ 2,000	0	17%
2,000	4,000	0	19
4,000	6,000	0	23
6,000	8,000	0	27
8,000	10,000	0	31
10,000	12,000	0	35
12,000	14,000	0	40
14,000	16,000	0	44
16,000	18,000	0	47
18,000	20,000	0	50
20,000	22,000	1%	53
22,000	26,000	1	56
26,000	32,000	1	59
32,000	38,000	1	62
38,000	44,000	1	66
44,000	50,000	1	69
50,000	60,000	2	72
60,000	70,000	2	75
70,000	80,000	2.5	78
80,000	90,000	3	81
90,000	100,000	3	84
100,000	150,000	4	86
150,000	200,000	4	87
200,000	up	4% increasing to 6%	88

III. Tax on basis of normal tax and surtax in 1946 was subject to a reduction of 5 per cent.

APPENDIX D

Percentage of Net Income Taken by Federal Income Taxes,
Selected Years, 1914-1946[a]

Calendar Year	Net Income Before Personal Exemption			
	$2,500	$5,000	$25,000	$100,000
1914	—	0.2%	1.0%	3.6%
1916	—	0.4	1.9	3.9
1917	0.4%	1.2	13.0	23.4
1918	1.2	3.6	14.9	35.0
1920	0.8	1.6	11.5	31.2
1924	—	0.8	6.1	22.5
1929	—	0.1	3.4	14.8
1932	—	2.0	9.8	30.0
1935	—	1.6	10.0	31.8
1940	0.5	2.2	15.4	43.5
1942	9.3	14.9	36.9	63.2
1945	14.4	19.5	45.9	69.4
1946	11.4	15.9	36.3	63.1

[a] Data are for a married couple, without dependents, filing a joint return. All income is assumed to come from personal compensation.

APPENDIX E

Summary of Federal and Net Income Taxes (1946)

I. Normal Tax on Corporations in General

Normal Tax Net Income	*Rate of Tax Which Is Applicable*
Up to $5,000	15%
$5,000 to $20,000...............	$750 plus 17% of amount over $5,000
$20,000 to $25,000..............	$3,300 plus 19% of amount over $20,000
$25,000 to $50,000..............	$4,250 plus 31% of amount over $25,000
Over $50,000..................	24% of entire normal tax net income

II. Surtax on Corporations in General

Surtax Net Income	*Rate of Tax Which is Applicable*
Up to $25,000	6%
Over $25,000 but not over $50,000.	$1,500 plus 22% of amount over $25,000
Over $50,000..................	14% of entire surtax net income

III. Special Corporation Surtaxes (one, but not both of the following additional taxes may be imposed)
   A. *Corporations Improperly Accumulating Surplus*
      1. Such a corporation is defined as one which was formed or has been used for the purpose of preventing the imposition of surtax upon its shareholders, or upon the shareholders of any corporation.
      2. On undistributed net income for a corporation so designated, an *added* tax is imposed of 27½ per cent of the amount not in excess of $100,000 plus 38½ per cent of the amount in excess of $100,000.
   B. *Personal Holding Companies*
      1. Such companies are defined as those where at least 80 per cent of gross income is from investment sources and where at least 50 per cent of outstanding stock is owned directly or indirectly by or for not over 5 individuals.
      2. On undistributed net income of such a corporation, an *added* tax is imposed of 75 per cent of amount not above $2,000 plus 85 per cent which is above $2,000.

IV. The following types of corporations receive special treatment:
   A. *Insurance Companies:* Most such companies are subject to the same tax rates as ordinary business corporations, but

income is defined somewhat differently, being confined primarily to investment income.

B. *Regulated Investment Companies:* Such companies are subject to a normal tax of 24 per cent and a surtax of 14 per cent. They are also subject to a tax of 25 per cent on any excess of net long-term capital gain over the sum of net short-term capital loss and the amount of capital gain dividends paid during the year.

C. *Foreign Corporations:* Such corporations are not subject to normal tax, and nonresident foreign corporations are not subject to surtax.

D. *Western Hemisphere Trade Corporations:* Such corporations are not subject to surtax.

E. *Exempt Corporations:* Such corporations are not subject to corporation income tax. Among these are farmers' cooperative marketing and shipping associations, if they comply with specific requirements to prove that they operate primarily for the interests of members and patrons.

INDEX

INDEX